One Hundred Years
of Hockey

One Hundred Years of Hockey

Brian McFarlane

SUMMERHILL PRESS

Toronto
1990

Published by:
Summerhill Press Ltd.
52 Shaftesbury Ave., Toronto, Ontario
M4T 1A2

© Brian McFarlane 1989, 1990

2nd edition, revised
1st edition published by Deneau Publishers

Printed and bound in Canada

Distributed by:
University of Toronto Press
5201 Dufferin Street
Downsview, Ontario M3H 5T8
Photograph of Brian McFarlane: Ian Chrysler

Canadian Cataloguing in Publication Data

McFarlane, Brian 1931 –
One hundred years of hockey

2nd ed., rev.
ISBN 0-929091-26-4

1. Hockey – Canada – History. 2. National Hockey
League – History. I. Title.

GV848.4.C2M34 1990   796.962'64'0971   C90-095513-9

CONTENTS

PREFACE

When two determined teams clash in a game of hockey on ice, the result is a rousing spectacle of speed and skill on skates. Players hurl themselves recklessly in pursuit of a small black puck which can be stickhandled cleverly around opposing players, passed swiftly to a charging teammate or shot with astonishing speed and accuracy at a padded goalie grimly protecting his cage. The crunch of body contact is common, spills and tumbles frequent and minor injuries inevitable. Hockey is for the adventurous, the daring, the thrill seeking. It has little appeal for the timid or the squeamish.

William Leggat, writing in *Sports Illustrated*, once described the violent skills of hockey this way:

> Hockey is fast, hockey is harsh, hockey is cruel and comical; a game of sticks and stitches, bruises and pratfalls. The best hockey is played in the NHL because the best skaters, the sharpest shooters, the quickest goalies and the toughest professionals that can be found, man the rosters.

One hundred years of hockey have produced scores of memorable team and individual accomplishments. It would be an easy task to produce thousands of words, complemented by dozens of photographs, about Gordie Howe, Bobby Orr, Wayne Gretzky, the Montreal Canadiens or Team Canada '72. All are names synonymous with excellence, the very best on ice. But this book's intent is to capture the changing face of hockey, touching on the deeds of hockey players, coaches and builders who played huge roles in shaping the fascinating history of the game. Ahead meet the movers and shakers, the builders and backers, the journeymen losers and jubilant winners, all of whom helped elevate hockey to the lofty pinnacle it enjoys today in the ever-changing realm of sport.

BRIAN MCFARLANE

I

OBSCURE BEGINNINGS

The Origins of the Game

Hockey, with its spills and speed, has been a rousing spectacle on ice for well over a hundred years. The game was immensely popular in many parts of North America long before the birth of the present century and decades before the National Hockey League, the premier showcase for the sport, was established in 1917. Pinpointing the exact origins of the game with any degree of accuracy is an impossibility. It is generally recognized as a Canadian game, although there is evidence that a form of hockey on ice was played in Europe before Canadians adopted the game and shaped it to their liking.

Perhaps hockey owes its birth to the British Royal Family, for included among the game's pioneers were members of the royal household. British journalist Ian Gordon, delving into the history of the game in 1937, concluded the idea for hockey originated at Windsor Castle.

> During the hard winter of 1853 [writes Gordon], Royal family members attending a house party at the country palace, looking for diversion on the frozen lake on the grounds, decided to play a form of field hockey on ice. Sides were chosen, sticks found and a wooden plug or stopper pried from a barrel was used as a puck. While Queen Victoria and her attendants stood by giving encouragement, officers of the Guards skated over the surface trying to score into a goal protected by the Prince Consort.

While the final score was not recorded, Gordon reports that all players were treated to a mug of well-spiced rum punch following their energetic play.

Journalist Gordon claims it was more than 20 years later that the game crossed the ocean to Canada when a student at McGill University came upon the game of field hockey while on a visit to England. When he returned to Montreal, he and his fellow collegians adapted the game to ice and were the first to play ice hockey in Canada. The natural playing resources of severe Canadian winters, with months of snow and ice, were ideal for the sport and the young pioneers promptly organized Canada's first hockey team at McGill.

Gordon's research into hockey's origins tells of a royal team being formed at Buckingham Palace in 1895. When a hard frost gave sufficient ice surface on the lake behind the palace, a challenge was issued to a rival squad. Buckingham Palace included in their lineup the Prince of Wales, later to become King Edward VII, and the Duke of York, later to become King George V. It is of historical importance that none of the royals was injured and of more practical significance that they lost in a one-sided affair. Until the end of the century, hockey games in England continued to receive considerable patronage from the royal family. When members of other European royal families came to visit they, too, were initiated into the intricacies of the daring game.

While Ian Gordon makes a convincing argument for Windsor Castle as hockey's birthplace, few North American researchers would agree with him. They would suggest he was unaware of hockey developments in Canada during the 1800s.

Homegrown historians and experts alike have squabbled for years over the birthplace of hockey. One theory takes an official Canadian report released in 1942 as its basis, stating that the first recorded hockey game anywhere was played at the British garrison in Kingston, Ontario, in 1855. The soldiers used field-hockey sticks, a lacrosse ball and a playing surface consisting of as much of the frozen Kingston harbor as the players were willing to clear of snow. But the suggestion is that there were many games played on the harbor ice long before this "official" event.

This theory, however, does not impress Nova Scotia historian Howard Dill, whose pumpkin farm borders Long Pond in Windsor, Nova Scotia. Dill claims that ice hockey was played in Windsor prior to 1810. In fact, Long Pond is credited by many as being the birthplace of hockey. Another historian, Dr. Sandy Young of Dalhousie University, supports Dill's theory. In his book, *Beyond Heroes: A Sport History of Nova Scotia*, Dr. Young points to a quote by Thomas Chandler Haliburton in an 1844 London, England, periodical called *Attaché*. Haliburton, born in 1796, was writing about his days at King's Collegiate, now Kings-Edgehill School in Windsor.

> The boys let out racin', yellin', hollerin' and whoopin' like mad with pleasure, and the playground, and the game at bass in the fields, or hurley on the long pond on the ice, or campin' out at night at Chester Lakes to fish...

Since Haliburton graduated in 1810, hockey, or "hurley" as it was known, must have been played prior to that time.

A third Nova Scotia researcher, Leslie Loomis, discovered another reference to hurley on Long Pond in an 1876 edition of the *Windsor Mail*. An anonymous writer, describing student life at King's Collegiate during his stay from 1816–1818 wrote:

> The Devil's Punch Bowl and the Long Pond, back of the College, were favorite resorts, and we used to skate in winter, on moonlight nights, on the ponds. I recollect John Cunard [the brother of Sir Samuel of steamship

fame] having his front teeth knocked out with a hurley by Pete Delancey of Annapolis.

Montreal historians take all this in stride. In 1941, John Knox, an 84-year-old Montrealer, spoke of evidence handed down from his father, Michael, that the first game of hockey was played in Montreal in 1837 when a Dorchester team met the Uptown Club. Others don't deny the earlier existence of a form of shinny or hurley in Halifax and Kingston. It's quite possible, they say, that the game goes back to the 1700s or even earlier. But that wasn't "pure" ice hockey. The origins of pure hockey are traced by some to a group of McGill students (one of whom may have been the traveling scholar referred to by Ian Gordon) who conceived the game in 1879. The students took the rules of several other sports—including field hockey, lacrosse and rugby—and produced a body-contact sport to be played on skates involving as many as 15 players per side. At first the puck was a lacrosse ball and then, to eliminate the bounce, the ball was sliced to create a flat piece of rubber that slid rather than bounced.

Regardless of its origins, early participants had a grand time playing the game. After the so-called "McGill Rules" were widely accepted and ice-hockey games became a popular addition to winter carnivals in many Canadian towns, improvements in the basic equipment followed. In the beginning, players seldom raised the puck off the ice, so goalies required no padding. Soon shooting skills improved and "hoisted" pucks sent goalies scurrying for protection. Gloves and chest protectors, borrowed from baseball, were donned and cricket pads strapped to goalies' shins. Early skates were the "spring-type" models, which were clamped on to a pair of heavy street shoes or boots. Even with the addition of straps, however, players' skates were often jarred loose and would send them crashing to the ice.

By 1880, several cities sported impressive new ice arenas; there were at least three in Montreal. During Winter Carnival week in that city there were hockey tournaments between teams representing McGill, the Montreal Amateur Athletic Association, the Crystals and the Victorias, which attracted hundreds of fans. By the early 1890s, the game had become so popular that the governor general of Canada was compelled to donate a small silver bowl to be presented annually to the hockey champions of Canada — the renowned Stanley Cup.

II

A TRADITION IS BORN

The Stanley Cup to 1917

The ultimate goal in professional ice hockey, the game's most prized award, is the Stanley Cup. Lord Stanley of Preston, the sixth governor general of Canada and a keen hockey fan, purchased the cup that bears his name for less than 50 dollars.

The year was 1893, the year of Lord Stanley's retirement. The trophy was to be held by the champion amateur hockey club in Canada and Lord Stanley directed that the first holders should be the Montreal Amateur Athletic Association team, winners of the Amateur Hockey Association title that season. The Stanley Cup is one of the oldest and most treasured trophies in sport. It came into being long before the Temple Cup, now long forgotten, but a trophy once awarded to the winners of baseball's World Series. It is seven years older than the Davis Cup, symbolic of preeminence in the world of tennis.

Originally, as set out in the terms of the donation, the Stanley Cup was to be a challenge trophy for which any team in any league was to be permitted to compete (subject to the discretion of the Cup trustees). Since 1910, when the National Hockey Association took control of the trophy, it has symbolized professional hockey supremacy, and since 1926 competition for the coveted trophy has been limited to teams in the National Hockey League.

Over the years champions of no less than 17 different leagues have challenged each other for it. Sometimes one challenge followed hard on the heels of another, and the successful contender in one playoff series could be called upon to defend the title again as soon as that series was over. Stanley Cup games have been played in December, January, February and March of the same season. Some series have been sudden-death affairs, two game matches or total goals to count and others have been best of three, of five and, as now, best of seven. The challengers have been pure amateurs, professionals and sometimes a mixture of both.

Lord Stanley, who began it all, never saw a Stanley Cup game. Having appointed two Cup trustees, Ottawa sportsmen Sheriff Sweetland and P.D. Ross, he returned to England in May of 1893 when his term of office expired. Although the Cup was first held by the hockey club of the Montreal Amateur Athletic Association, the first playoff for the prize was not played until 10 months after Lord Stanley had left Canada. On March 22, 1894, the first Stanley Cup match was played between the Montreal AAAs and the Ottawa Capitals.

A crowd of 5,000 spectators stood, some on a platform about 12 inches high surrounding the natural-ice surface of the rink, and some in balconies above. There were seven players on each team: goal, point, cover-point, rover and three forwards. (Point and cover-point are comparable to present-day defensemen except that one played in front of the other.) Lightly padded and without gloves, the players had to score into goals which were merely upright posts imbedded in the ice. There was no crossbar, no goal line from post to post and no net behind to stop the puck. The referee wore street clothes and a derby hat. A newspaper account of the game reported:

> Montreal—March 22, 1894—The hockey championship was decided here tonight, and never before in the history of the game was there such a crowd present at a match or such enthusiasm evinced. There were fully 5,000 persons at the match, and tin horns, strong lungs and a general rabble predominated. The ice was fairly good. The referee forgot to see many things. The match resulted in favor of Montreal by 3 goals to 1.

Both teams freely indulged in tripping and slashing, beginning a century-long tradition. When the game was over, Ottawa star Weldy Young fainted from exhaustion. Montreal fans ignored the prostrate Young as they raced onto the ice to hoist Billy Barlow, a two-goal man and the first Stanley Cup hero, onto their shoulders.

Referees had their critics in the early days just as they have now. After a game in Quebec in 1895 in which Ottawa defeated Quebec 3–2, two officials were seized by angry fans and dragged back into the rink with the aim of forcing them to declare the game a draw. The police had to rescue the shaken officials. A special meeting of the league executive was called and the Quebec team was suspended for the balance of the season.

In 1899 a referee named J. A. Findlay caused an uproar in a Cup game between the Montreal and Winnipeg Victorias. A Montreal player, Bob McDougall, hit Winnipeger Tony Gingras across the back of the leg with his stick and Gingras was carried off the ice. Findlay, after checking on Gingras' condition in the dressing room, announced a two-minute penalty to McDougall. The Winnipeg players, incensed at his leniency, left the ice and retired to their dressing room. When Findlay could not convince them to continue play, he left the rink and went home. After much debate he was persuaded to come back.

An hour and five minutes after play had been stopped, Findlay signaled for a resumption of the game. But since the Winnipeg team still refused to come out of their dressing room, Findlay awarded the game to the Montreal Victorias. Apparently some of the Winnipeg players weren't even in their dressing room. They had dressed right after the walkout and left hurriedly in order to sample the delights of Montreal night life.

In 1899 Fred Chittick, goaltender for Ottawa, refereed a Montreal–Quebec Stanley

Cup playoff game (it was customary in those days to use players as referees) and angry Montreal players insisted that he must have been celebrating prior to game time as he was in no condition to officiate. So incensed were the Montrealers that they skated off the ice with 12 minutes to play, and the game was never completed. A year before Chittick had refused to take part in a playoff game between Ottawa and the Victorias because he claimed that management had not allotted him a fair share of complimentary tickets.

Of the many challenges in Stanley Cup history, 1905 provided the most unusual. The famed Ottawa Silver Seven were challenged by a team from Dawson City in the Yukon. The Klondikers traveled 4,000 miles to Ottawa, part of the way by dogsled, where they were humiliated by one of the greatest teams ever assembled.

Ottawa's legendary scoring star, Frank McGee, scored just one goal in Ottawa's 9–2 triumph in game one. But in game two he set a record that stands to this day, beating Dawson City's 17-year-old goaltender Albert Forrest 14 times as the champions coasted to a 23–2 victory.

The Rat Portage (later Kenora) Westerners had first challenged Ottawa in 1903. The ice conditions were so atrocious that on one occasion the puck slipped through a hole in the ice and was never retrieved. As the gate receipts were minimal, Rat Portage lost $800 in their bid for the Cup, but two years later, following the outcome of the Ottawa–Dawson City playoff, they challenged the Silver Seven again.

Play was so rough when the teams met again in 1905 that the referee wore a hard hat and the fans roared each time it was knocked from his head. Rat Portage showed great team speed in game one and upset the Silver Seven 8–3. But the Ottawa ice-maker found a way to slow the visitors down in game two. He flooded the ice with an inch of water even though the temperature was well above freezing. Ignoring the screams of outrage from the challengers, the Ottawa boys plodded through the water and slush to a pair of wins. They won the Stanley Cup for the third year in a row.

The Westerners, now the Kenora Thistles, were back again in 1907. They had challenged the champion Montreal Wanderers for the 1906 Cup title, but no date could be found before January 1907. With Art Ross (borrowed from Brandon) teaming up with Tom Phillips on the attack, Kenora took the Cup. Two months later the same teams met again in Winnipeg for the 1907 title, amid much argument about "borrowed professionals." It is said that one official of the Thistles became so incensed at the attitude of the Cup trustees on the question of player eligibility, that he grabbed the trophy and threatened to throw it into the Lake of the Woods. When the dust settled, the Wanderers were victorious and took the Stanley Cup back to Montreal.

There were many highlights and sidelights to Stanley Cup play from the late 1890s to 1917, and the fans, though fewer than today, were just as vociferous and partisan.

In 1901, Russell Bowie of the Montreal Victorias led the scoring with a remarkable 24 goals in seven games, seven goals in a single game against the AAAs. A year later, Art Hooper of Montreal scored nine in a single game against the Shamrocks.

In 1904, Frank Patrick, Moose Johnson, Didier Pitre and Jack Laviolette all made their hockey debuts, and Russell Bowie was again the top sniper with 27 goals in eight games. The Federal Amateur Hockey League was organized that year and battled the Canadian Amateur Hockey League for playing talent.

The Winnipeg Rowing Club with Bad Joe Hall (one of the early "villains" of organized hockey) in the lineup, played Ottawa for the Stanley Cup. Hall had been accused of being a professional but the charges were never proved. Before the first game someone suggested that a goal line be painted on the ice from goalpost to goalpost. The move met with general approval. Ottawa took the series and went on to defeat the Toronto Marlboros and tie the Montreal Wanderers of the Federal League 5–5 in a game that saw the Wanderers' goaltender, Nicholson, race the length of the ice with the puck in an unsuccessful effort to score. As an argument developed over the site of a future game, that Cup series was never completed.

But Ottawa did not rest on their laurels. They accepted a challenge from the Brandon Wheat Kings where Lester Patrick, Frank's brother, was embarking on a hockey career that would cover 22 seasons. Ottawa won the two-game series with ease. In eight playoff games, Frank McGee had scored 21 goals.

In 1905 future Hall-of-Famers Art Ross and Ernie Russell became prominent, Russell with Montreal and Ross with a new team called Montreal Westmount, which included the Patrick brothers. The most bizarre event of the season occurred in a game with Quebec, when the Westmount goaltender, a fellow named Brophy, stole a page from Nicholson's book and raced down the ice with the puck. Brophy, unlike Nicholson, was successful. He scored against the famous Paddy Moran.

Newsy Lalonde, a sensational lacrosse player as well as an outstanding hockey prospect, broke in with Cornwall of the Federal League, but in his first game he severed an artery which put him on the sidelines for almost a full season. He came back in the last game, however, to restart a famous career.

In 1906, Ottawa inserted two of the famous Smith brothers into their lineup. Rookie Harry Smith had a sensational year, leading the scorers with 31 goals in eight games. His brother Tom, though less potent was very promising. Westmount's wandering goaltender, Brophy, now with the AAAS, scored another goal in 1906, this time against the Montreal Victorias.

Queen's University, the champions of the Ontario Hockey Association, challenged and played Ottawa for the Stanley Cup in 1906, during the regular season. They were swamped 16–7 and 12–7 by the powerful Ottawa team, but their top player, Marty Walsh, displayed some of the form he was to show playing for Ottawa two years later. McGee and Westwick notched four goals each in the first game, and Harry Smith scored five in both.

Ottawa then eliminated Smith's Falls, champions of the Federal League in two straight games, but lost no time in picking up the Falls' outstanding goalie, Percy LeSueur, before their series with the Wanderers. LeSueur did not play in the first game in which the Wanderers, paced by Lester Patrick, Pud Glass and Ernie Russell, upset the Silver Seven 9–1. He was in the nets, however, for the second game which was a 10–10 tie, until Lester Patrick beat him twice in the final minutes to give the Wanderers the trophy.

The year 1907 was a season of battle between amateurism and professionalism, with the Eastern Canada Amateur Hockey Association decreeing that while pros could play, all clubs must list which of their players were hired hands and which were "simon-pures." These lists were later published in the newspapers.

Hod Stuart, formerly with Pittsburgh in the International Pro League, signed on with the Wanderers and created a sensation by skating out apparently bare-kneed for the opening game; a teammate later revealed that he actually wore flesh-colored knee pads made of a stretchy material.

That same year, the Wanderers' Ernie Russell led all scorers with 42 goals in nine games.

A team from New Glasgow, Nova Scotia, challenged the Wanderers for the Cup in 1907, but proved no match for Russell, Patrick and company. In the space of two months the Wanderers lost and regained the Cup in their encounters with the Kenora Thistles.

In the Federal League that same season, a hockey star was killed in a game. Owen McCourt of Cornwall was hit over the head by a stick and died in hospital the next morning. Charles Masson of the Ottawa Vics was charged with murder, but at his trial several witnesses claimed that another player's stick had struck McCourt just prior to Masson's attack and he was acquitted.

Professionalism came into full bloom in 1908. Tom Phillips of Kenora was said to be asking $1,800 for the season and he signed with Ottawa, as did Marty Walsh of Queen's. Art Ross took over from the Wanderers' Lester Patrick, who went west. A few teams struggled along with amateur players but the winning teams were the teams that paid their players. There were many contract arguments that year.

The first completely professional league in Canada, the Ontario Professional League, was organized in Western Ontario in 1908. It consisted of Toronto, Berlin (now Kitchener), Brantford and Guelph. Newsy Lalonde of Toronto led the league in scoring with 29 goals in nine games. He scored eight goals in one game against Brantford.

The Wanderers defeated the Ottawa Vics and Winnipeg before accepting the Toronto challenge for the Stanley Cup. Although Bruce Ridpath was the best man on the ice and Newsy Lalonde was a constant threat, the Wanderers won the single game 6–4 and retained the trophy.

For the first time in the history of hockey in Eastern Canada, a referee presented a bill to the league for damages to his clothes. Referee William Nicholson, captain of the Shamrock team, was assaulted by fans in Quebec City after the Quebec–Wanderers game and the suit he was wearing was destroyed. Nicholson demanded $15, which the Quebec team was ordered to pay.

By 1909 the word *amateur* had been dropped from the name of the Eastern Canada Amateur Hockey Association because the withdrawal of Montreal and the Victorias had left the circuit with four teams, all of them professional. The Shamrocks introduced a new player, Harry Hyland, and Quebec unveiled a budding superstar, Joe Malone, who later was to score 44 goals in a 20-game schedule. In the ECHA Marty Walsh was tops with 38 goals in 12 games.

When Edmonton challenged the Wanderers for the Stanley Cup in 1909, they established a record of sorts by playing a "ringer" for every player on the Edmonton squad with one exception. The "ringers" included Lester Patrick, Didier Pitre, Tom Phillips and Harold McNamara, but the Wanderers still took the series 13–10.

A new league, the National Hockey Association, the forerunner of the NHL, was established in 1910 in Montreal. Franchises were awarded to the Wanderers, Renfrew, Cobalt, Haileybury and a team in Montreal to be called Les Canadiens. The mining boom was on in Northern Ontario, and the miners wanted the best hockey money could buy. Wealthy Ambrose O'Brien bought a great collection of stars for his Renfrew Creamery Kings, eventually known as the Renfrew Millionaires. He acquired Cyclone Taylor, the two Patrick brothers, goalkeeper Bert Lindsay (the father of Ted Lindsay, the NHL star of future years) and Sprague and Odie Cleghorn. The Patricks signed at $3,000 each, the highest salaries offered any players up to that time.

The ECHA had been replaced by a league called the Canadian Hockey Association, but midway through the season it became apparent that the two leagues, with five teams operating in Montreal alone, could not carry on. So, the NHA absorbed two of the CHA teams, Ottawa and the Shamrocks, and the CHA was soon disbanded.

This was the year, 1910, that the legendary Cyclone Taylor, playing for Renfrew, joked about being able to score a goal while skating backwards. Jesting or not, in the next-to-final game of the season against Ottawa, Taylor took a pass from Newsy Lalonde, another high-priced player picked up by Renfrew late in the season, and, whirling completely around, skated backwards for five yards and whipped the puck in for a goal. Lalonde, who had switched during the season from the Canadiens to Renfrew, was the top scorer in the NHA with 38 goals in 11 games. A player named Oren Frood was the leading goal-getter in the Ontario Professional Hockey League, with 34 goals in 17 games.

Ottawa, the Stanley Cup winners in the preceding year, had defeated Galt and Edmonton in Cup play early in the season, but had to turn the trophy over to the Wanderers, who were the champions of the NHA for the 1910 season. The Wanderers then accepted a challenge from Berlin of the OPHA and defeated them 7–3.

In 1911, Haileybury and Cobalt, small towns unable to pay the cost of major-league hockey, left the NHA, and the remaining club owners tried to cut down expenses by imposing a $5,000 total salary limit for any one club. This meant that stars who earned $1,500 to $1,800 in the previous year might now expect a salary of around $500 or $600. This prompted talk of a players' union. Eventually the clubs gave in and signed players for what they thought they were worth, much as they had done in the past.

In 1911, three periods of play were introduced to replace two periods of 30 minutes each. Also that year a youthful goaltender, Georges Vezina, attracted attention for his excellent work in the nets for the Canadiens. His coolness under pressure earned him the nickname "the Chicoutimi Cucumber."

In the west, Port Arthur, winners of the newly organized New Ontario League met Prince Albert, champions of the Saskatchewan League. When Port Arthur won both games, they set out after the Stanley Cup. But the Ottawa Senators who had just defeated Galt in a Cup contest proved more than a match for Port Arthur, swamping them 13–4, with Marty Walsh tallying 10 goals.

In 1912 franchises were awarded to two clubs in Toronto, the Torontos and the Tecumsehs. They were later dropped from the schedule when their arena was not ready for play.

A new rule went into force that, at first, drew much criticism. Each team was ordered to drop a player and play six-man hockey instead of seven. Large numerals were also ordered for the players' sweaters, and corresponding numbers with the players' names alongside were listed on a large board at rinkside. This identification system eventually led to printed programs with names and numbers included.

Moncton, New Brunswick, the champions of the Maritime Professional League, challenged the NHA champion Quebec Bulldogs for the Stanley Cup and were quickly defeated in the first Stanley Cup contest played under the new six-man rules. Meanwhile, out west, Lester and Frank Patrick, having left Renfrew, had organized the Pacific Coast Hockey League with teams in Vancouver, Victoria and New

Westminster. The new arena in Vancouver was the largest in the country and contained the first artificial ice in Canada. One of the league founders, Frank Patrick, was also one of its greatest stars. He scored six goals in one game while playing defense. Newsy Lalonde, playing for Vancouver, was the scoring champion. Players were recruited from Eastern Canada and many stars jumped to the Coast League where seven-man hockey was still in vogue. The league continued to raid the eastern clubs in 1913, and contracts often meant little more than the paper they were written on. The NHA, still unable to make up its mind on seven-man or six-man hockey, proposed to play six-man hockey for half the season and seven-man hockey for the other half. This arrangement was unpopular and, late in the season, a decision was made to play only six-man hockey.

The new teams in the NHA had some class players. Toronto had Happy Holmes, Harry Cameron, Frank Foyston, Frank Nighbor and Cully Wilson, among others. The Tecumsehs were weaker, but boasted the two McNamara boys, both solid defensemen. Harry "Punch" Broadbent cracked the Ottawa lineup and averaged a goal a game in his rookie season. Joe Malone of the Quebec Bulldogs scored nine goals in the first of a two-game Cup series with Sydney, Nova Scotia, which was won two straight by Quebec.

By 1914 the NHA was keeping a record of assists and the referees, tired of having their knuckles bruised by placing the puck between sticks on face-offs, were instructed to drop the puck to begin play. A goalkeeper caught lying down to stop a shot was subject to a $2.00 fine.

An agreement was worked out between the NHA and the PCHA for an annual Stanley Cup series between the respective league champions to be held alternately in the east and the west. Toronto won the NHA title and defeated Victoria in Toronto for the Stanley Cup in three straight games.

The PCHA found a top man to handle refereeing duties in Mickey Ion, who was to win fame as a hockey official. Ion also began selecting all-star teams in the PCHA, a practice that proved extremely popular.

The Pacific Coast League transferred the New Westminster franchise to Portland, Oregon, in 1915, and for the first time in hockey history an American city was eligible to compete for the Stanley Cup. But it was Vancouver, whose Mickey Mackay was the league's top scorer that year, which won the title and met Ottawa in the Stanley Cup finals. To the surprise of many easterners, Vancouver trounced Ottawa in two straight games with Frank Nighbor, Cyclone Taylor and Mickey Mackay showing the way, and the Stanley Cup went west for the first time.

The following year Seattle was added to the PCHA and their raiding of eastern teams resulted in a strong entry. The team, known as the Metropolitans, included Holmes, Carpenter, Foyston (the team captain), Wilson and Walker, who had all been with Toronto the previous year. The eastern teams retaliated by luring several western stars away from the PCHA. The Stanley Cup trustees officially confirmed that year that American cities were eligible to win the trophy as it was considered emblematic of world hockey supremacy. This policy departed from the original terms of the presentation by Lord Stanley, which had stated that the Cup was to be held by the championship team of Canada, but Lord Stanley had given absolute discretion to the trustees on Cup competition.

The Portland Rosebuds won the PCHA championship and challenged for the Stanley

Cup in 1916, the first American team to do so. Portland outplayed the Canadiens, the NHA champions, in the first game of the Stanley Cup finals and won 2–0. The score might have been higher but for the brilliant play of Georges Vezina. The Canadiens took the second game on goals by Poulin and Arbour and won the third by 6–1, with Didier Pitre scoring three times. Portland tied the series with a 6–5 victory, but the Canadiens wrapped it up in the fifth game with a score of 2–1.

The Americans had failed in their first bid for the Stanley Cup, but things were different in March 1917, when the NHA champion Canadiens went west to meet the Seattle Metropolitans, the champions of the PCHL. The Canadiens surprised most observers by defeating Seattle 8–4 in the first game, which was played under western rules, with seven men per side. But Seattle roared back to defeat their opponents 6–1 in the second game, played under eastern six-man rules, and went on to take the third and fourth games, 4–1 and 9–1. Bernie Morris of the Mets was the series star, scoring six goals in the final game for a series total of 14, the best record since the days of Frank McGee. For the first time in its history, the Stanley Cup had become an international trophy.

Over the years the Stanley Cup has received rude treatment at the hands of some of its holders, and many legends have sprung up around it. One story has it that the trophy was once kicked into the Rideau Canal in Ottawa by a drunken member of a Cup-winning team. The canal, fortunately, was frozen and when the punter sobered up hours later he was able to retrieve the silver cup. In another incident, in 1907, it nearly received a ducking in the Lake of the Woods at the hands of an enraged executive of the Kenora Thistles.

In Montreal many years ago, celebrating Cup-winners stopped their car on a street corner to change a flat tire and deposited the Stanley Cup on the sidewalk. Business done, they drove off without the trophy, but returned later to find the Cup still standing where they had left it.

As recently as 1962, a rabid Montreal fan, Ken Kilander, was suffering through a Canadiens' playoff loss to the Chicago Blackhawks. In the third period he could stand it no longer. Leaving his seat in the Chicago Stadium, he walked out into the lobby and jimmied open the glass case enclosing the Stanley Cup, which Kilander felt "rightly belongs in Montreal." He was staggering out the stadium exit with the huge trophy over his shoulder (it weights about 32 pounds), when he was spotted by two ushers. They struggled with the 25-year-old Montrealer until the police arrived.

Kilander, booked for disorderly conduct, later told reporters, "That Cup meant everything to me and here I was holding it. Guys who were great hockey players had held it—the greatest. The fate of the Cup was in my hands." The Blackhawks did not press charges against Kilander and the judge, obviously a fan, told him, "You're free to go back to the stadium tomorrow night and cheer for your almighty Canadiens. But the Cup will stay here in Chicago unless the Blackhawks lose, which I doubt."

Kilander's bid for the Stanley Cup, while illegal, was much simpler and less expensive than others. Hockey men with millions of dollars have spent fortunes buying franchises, purchasing players, building teams and battling other men with similar interests in an effort to win the right to challenge for the coveted trophy.

By 1917, with the importance of the Cup clearly established in the first 24 years of its history, the emerging National Hockey League had a trophy of international renown to shoot for from the day of its inception.

III

THE EXPANDING HOCKEY FRONTIER

One Trophy, One League—The NHL, 1917–1929

America's most colorful and exciting era of sports took place in the years after World War I and throughout the twenties. Sportswriters named it the Golden Age of Sport. Baseball had Babe Ruth, Jack Dempsey ruled boxing, Bobby Jones was the world's best golfer. Other stars like Bill Tilden (tennis), Paavo Nurmi (track), Nat Holman (basketball) and the four-legged wonder horse, Man O' War, captivated millions of sports fans.

Professional hockey had glittering heroes, too, but the National Hockey League was in its infancy, and professional players shared the spotlight with the top amateur players of the day. In Canada, 1917 was remembered more for the introduction of the income tax than for the birth of the NHL.

In the years from 1917 to 1929, the National Hockey League grew into a thriving 10-team international circuit. Many famous players made their professional debuts, notably Howie Morenz, Nels Stewart, King Clancy, Frank Boucher, Eddie Shore, the Cook brothers, Tiny Thompson and Aurel Joliat. Other great stars like Cyclone Taylor, Joe Malone, Newsy Lalonde, Bad Joe Hall and Georges Vezina had reached the end of the trail.

The old Pacific Coast Hockey League passed out of existence as did the Western Canada (later Western) Hockey League, the latter after only five years of life. Six-man hockey finally became universal, goalies became free to adopt any position to defend their goals and, by the end of the twenties, the forward pass was allowed in all three zones. Five of the six arenas which house the present day NHL teams were constructed during this period. Conn Smythe began his legendary career as a builder of champions, Foster Hewitt made his first hockey broadcast and, for the first time, the Stanley Cup came into the exclusive custody of the National Hockey League.

1917–1918

What a contrast in 50 years! When the National Hockey League doubled its size with its expansion draft in June 1967, hockey men from all over North America were in Montreal to watch as team owners from Los Angeles, San Francisco, Philadelphia, Pittsburgh, St. Louis and Minneapolis, having paid their $2-million entrance fees, gathered to select the 20 players allotted to them from the rosters of the six existing clubs. The event was front-page stuff. Hundreds of sportswriters and radio and television reporters kept all of Canada and much of the United States informed about the biggest shuffle of hockey talent ever witnessed.

One man in the crowd was veteran sports reporter Elmer Ferguson, the only sportswriter who was on the spot when the NHL was formed in 1917. In the early days of professional hockey not more than one or two reporters ever attended the hockey meetings to report on the goings-on. On November 22, 1917, Elmer Ferguson was the lone reporter dutifully waiting in the Windsor Hotel for news when the hockey sessions ended.

The first hockey man to emerge from behind the closed doors of the league meeting was red-haired Frank Calder, who had originally come to Canada from Britain to play soccer, but who had fallen in love with hockey. Ferguson, delighted to see the man he had succeeded as sports editor of the *Montreal Herald*, shouted across the corridor, "Hey, Frank, what happened in there?"

"Not too much, Fergie," replied Calder, stepping into the elevator. He was too modest to reveal that he had just been elected president of a new professional hockey league.

Out of the same room came George Kennedy, smiling. The jovial Kennedy, owner of the Montreal Canadiens, which he had purchased in 1910 for $7,500, took his friend Fergie by the arm and said, "We formed a new hockey league called the National Hockey League, and it's just like the National Hockey Association with one exception. We haven't invited Eddie Livingstone [owner of the Toronto team] to be part of the new set-up."

Sam Lichtenhein, owner of the Montreal Wanderers, joined the pair and hearing Kennedy's last remark, added, "Don't get us wrong, Elmer. We didn't throw Livingstone out. He's still got his franchise in the old National Hockey Association. He has his team, and we wish him well. The only problem is he's playing in a one-team league."

Tommy Gorman of the Ottawa club chortled over the maneuver. "Great day for hockey," he said. "Livingstone was always arguing. Without him we can get down to the business of making money."

The Quebec Bulldogs had been represented at the meeting by Mike Quinn, but as they were unable to attract enough fans to their games, even with the fabulous goal-getter Joe Malone in the lineup, the Bulldogs decided not to operate that year. To balance the league the Toronto Arenas were later admitted.

Then the Westmount Arena in Montreal, home ice of the Wanderers, burned to the ground, and the homeless Wanderers dropped out of the league. So, in its initial season, the NHL operated with only three teams—the Montreal Canadiens, the Ottawa Senators and the Toronto Arenas. A playoff system was devised whereby the season was divided into two halves, with the winners of each half (the Canadiens and the Arenas, as it turned out) meeting in the finals.

There was even a form of draft that first year. Since Quebec had withdrawn, its players were divided up among the other clubs. Quebec asked $200 per man but it is not recorded what amount, if any, was received. Before the arena fire had forced them out the league, the Wanderers had first choice and picked up four Quebec players but, incredibly, overlooked the great Joe Malone. The Canadiens grabbed Malone, as well as the rugged Joe Hall and, with Newsy Lalonde as player-manager and Georges Vezina in goal, they looked like the class of the league. Odie and Sprague Cleghorn lined up with the Wanderers, but Sprague broke a leg and was sidelined. Then brother Odie was exempted from military service, but only on condition he not play hockey. Jimmy Murphy was announced as manager of the Toronto Arenas, but he was hardly in the rink when he resigned in favor of Charlie Querrie.

The first games in the National Hockey League were played on December 19, 1917. Toronto was beaten 10–9 by the Wanderers in their first start, and only 700 fans attended, even though all soldiers in uniform were invited to be guests of the management. The Canadiens won their opener over Ottawa 7–4, with Joe Malone connecting for five goals.

During the season, a new rule was introduced allowing goaltenders to adopt any position on the ice. Previously they had had to maintain a stand-up position to defend the goal.

In February 1918, Ken Randall of Toronto was advised that a week-long suspension for quarreling with officials had been reduced to a $15 fine. If that amount, plus back fines adding up to a total of $35, was paid at once, he would be permitted to play in the game against Ottawa. The puckish Randall tendered $32 in bills plus 300 pennies to league officials. The bills were accepted, but the pennies refused. Randall placed the package of coins on the ice and an Ottawa player banged it with his stick, scattering pennies all over the surface. The players had to pick them up while Randall produced suitable folding money to make up his fine.

Joe Malone won the scoring title with 44 goals in 22 games. As Malone had missed two games, he actually scored 44 goals in 20 games. No NHL player has since come close to matching such a record.

In the second half of the season Toronto signed a forward, Jack Adams, who was to star as a player for many years and, later in his career, enjoy great success as manager of the Detroit Red Wings. Adams was the highest-paid Toronto player that year, receiving $900. He scored his first goal in professional hockey during the eastern finals between the Toronto Arenas and the Montreal Canadiens. Toronto won the opener 7–3 in a rough game that saw Bert Corbeau and Newsy Lalonde involved in most of the fighting. The second game in Montreal was even more brutal and although the Canadiens won it 4-3, Toronto took the round on total goals.

In the Stanley Cup playoffs between Toronto and the Vancouver Millionaires, the first game was played in Toronto under eastern rules. Cyclone Taylor, who had left Renfrew in 1911, got a big hand when he stepped on the ice for Vancouver. Taylor responded with two goals, but Toronto won 5–3. Vancouver, playing under western rules in the second game, evened the series with a 6–4 victory. Mickey Mackay and Cyclone Taylor displayed expert passing. Toronto won the third game 6–3, although Mickey Mackay was easily the best player on the ice. In the fourth game Mackay led Vancouver to an 8–1 triumph. Mackay was sensational in the final game, too, but it was won by Toronto 2–1. Corbett Denneny scored the winning goal and the Toronto Arenas became the first NHL team to capture the Stanley Cup.

1918–19

With the end of the World War I it was hoped that many great hockey players in military service would be back on skates, but few were demobilized in time to join their old teams and the NHL carried on with essentially the same players as in the preceding season.

Toronto was the favorite, but the champions lost six out of the first seven games, and the Canadiens clinched the first-half championship with Newsy Lalonde providing much of the punch. Odie Cleghorn, free of wartime restrictions, joined the Canadiens and, with a rash of goals in the second half of the schedule, beat out teammate Lalonde for goalscoring honors, 24–21. Punch Broadbent, who had won the Military Cross overseas, returned to Ottawa in time for the last game of the first half of the schedule. Ottawa were the champions of the second half, while Toronto became so inept that the Arenas withdrew before the full schedule was played.

The final series between the Canadiens and Ottawa was a best-of-seven affair. Ottawa, who lost ace Frank Nighbor before the series had started, because of a family bereavement, lost three straight. Lalonde scored five goals in the third game. With Nighbor back in harness, Ottawa won the fourth game on home ice 6–3, while the Ottawa fans pelted Bert Corbeau with lemons and vegetables because of an attack he had made on Jack Darragh.

Montreal took the championship with a 4–2 win in the fifth game and journeyed west to meet the Seattle Metropolitans of the Pacific Coast Hockey Association for the Stanley Cup. The Canadiens and Seattle were evenly matched and split four of the five games. In the second game Newsy Lalonde scored all four Canadiens' goals. The fourth game, which ended in a scoreless tie after one hour and 40 minutes of overtime, was described as the finest game ever seen on the coast.

It was in the fifth game that observers noticed how fatigued some of the players looked. Joe Hall retired early from the contest, complaining he was sick. Other players finished the game and then were confined to bed. The great influenza epidemic which had swept the continent that year had forced its way into the Stanley Cup finals. With Joe Hall in hospital and several others unable to get out of bed, the series was abandoned and no Stanley Cup winner was declared. Hall never recovered; he died in a Seattle hospital a few days later.

1919–20

In 1919 the Quebec franchise in the NHL was reactivated and players like Joe Malone, Harry Mummery and Dave Ritchie returned to the Bulldogs. The Toronto Arenas underwent a rebuilding job and changed their name to the St. Patricks. Old-timers say that Toronto wanted the luck of the Irish to descend upon them.

Ottawa won the first half of the schedule and Joe Malone stole the individual spotlight again when he counted seven goals against Toronto on the night of January 31. No one yet has surpassed or equaled that feat in the NHL. Malone almost equaled his record in the final game of the season when he scored six times against Ottawa. He was the league's top scorer with 39 goals in 24 games.

Large crowds turned out for games throughout the season, and Ottawa defeated the St. Pats in Toronto on February 21 in front of a record crowd of 8,500. Ottawa went on to clinch the second half of the schedule, and by winning both halves eliminated the need for an eastern playoff.

In the west, banner crowds attended the PCHA finals between Seattle and Vancouver. Seattle won on total goals, 7–3, and the Mets eagerly traveled east to meet Ottawa in the Stanley Cup finals. One minor problem had to be settled. Seattle's uniforms were striped in red, white and green and Ottawa sweaters were almost identical with red, white and black. Ottawa obligingly agreed to wear plain white jerseys.

The series got under way in late March but a warm spell made ice conditions intolerable. After skating through slush for three games, and with Ottawa holding a 2–1 lead, the rest of the series was transferred to the artificial-ice rink in Toronto, the only one at the time in eastern Canada. On Toronto ice the Mets, with Frank Foyston starring, easily took the fourth game to square the series. But Ottawa's veteran leader, Jack Darragh, scored three goals in what proved to be the final game and Ottawa won the Cup in a 6–1 decision over the western champions.

1920–21

Before the season began, the in-and-out Quebec Bulldogs finally dropped out of the NHL for good and the franchise and the players were transferred to Hamilton. With the exception of veteran Joe Malone, who had won individual scoring honors the year before, the Hamilton team was quite weak, and the other NHL members agreed to help out.

Toronto gave up Cecil "Babe" Dye, who promptly scored two goals in Hamilton's NHL debut, a 5–0 shutout over the Canadiens. Dye was immediately recalled to the Toronto club and the St. Pats sent Hamilton a player named Mickey Roach. Dye won the goal-scoring title that season, his sophomore year in the league, scoring 35 goals in 24 games. Cy Denneny of Ottawa was only one goal back.

Ottawa won the first half of the schedule and Toronto the second. Ottawa, which had shown poorly in the second half, was in top form in the playoffs, defeating Toronto 5–0 in the first game. George Boucher scored three goals while playing defense and Clint Benedict shut out Toronto again in the second game 2–0. Ottawa then went west to meet Vancouver for the Stanley Cup.

The Cup finals opened on March 21, and 11,000 fans, the largest crowd yet to see a hockey game in Canada, saw Vancouver squeak through 2–1. Ottawa took the next two games, only to have Vancouver tie the series in the fourth with Alf Skinner scoring twice. Over 2,000 fans were turned away for the final game which was won 2–1 by Ottawa, with Jack Darragh scoring both goals.

Cyclone Taylor was winding up his spectacular career playing for Vancouver; he scored his last three goals in the final game of the regular schedule. Used sparingly by Vancouver in the Stanley Cup series, he made his next-to-last professional appearance in the last game. Two years later Taylor came out of retirement to take one final whirl with Vancouver.

1921–22

What an eventful year this turned out to be! Before the season got under way, the split schedule was abandoned and a playoff was called between the first-place and second-place finishers. George Kennedy, one of the league's founders, sold his Canadiens Hockey Club to Joe Cattarinich and Leo Dandurand for $11,000 and a new league was formed in western Ontario.

Two youngsters, Frank Clancy and Frank Boucher, were added to the Ottawa roster, although they saw little action. Clancy did score a goal on his first NHL shot to defeat Hamilton in overtime, even though the puck failed to go in the net. He recalls it this way:

> I'm sittin' on the bench like a dummy, along with Frankie Boucher. We're in overtime against Hamilton and neither of us rookies have seen a lick of ice time. Then Petey Green sends us both out to play in the overtime. Well, the puck comes back to me like a watermelon right off the face-off and I get rid of it quick, sending it to a teammate. He throws it back to me and I don't have sense enough to stay back on defense. I go in on my wrong wing and take a wild shot at the net and, lo and behold, the goal judge [who stood on the ice behind the net] waves his handkerchief in the air signifying a goal. I had scored on my first shot. The Hamilton goaltender was so mad he was havin' a fit and I found out why a few days later. He told me the puck I shot didn't go in the front of the net but it went through the side of the net and it shouldn't have counted at all. But I was glad to count it no matter how it went in.

Punch Broadbent, with Ottawa, set an all-time record by scoring in 16 consecutive games, but although Ottawa won the NHL title they lost the two-game, total-point finals to Toronto.

A new league, the Western Canada Hockey League, had begun operations that season in Western Canada with teams in Calgary, Edmonton, Saskatoon and Regina. It boasted players like Dick Irvin, Bullet Joe Simpson, Duke Keats, Mervyn "Red" Dutton and Bill Cook. Keats led the goal scorers, and one night scored eight times in a game against Saskatoon.

It was agreed that the Western League champions would play the Pacific Coast champions with the winner moving east to challenge the NHL winners. Regina, paced by Dick Irvin and George Hay, represented the WCHL against Vancouver, champions of the PCHA. Irvin scored the winning goal in Regina's surprise 2–1 opening-game win, but Vancouver's Hugh Lehman shut out Regina 4–0 in the second game and Vancouver won the trip to Toronto.

In the Stanley Cup finals, Jack Adams scored three times against his old club as Vancouver took the opener 4–3. Babe Dye scored in overtime as Toronto evened the series with a 2–1 victory. Hugh Lehman then chalked up another playoff shutout in a

3–0 Vancouver triumph. But Babe Dye found the scoring range again, connecting for two goals in the fourth game and four more in game number five. Toronto won both games and walked off with the Stanley Cup.

It was in this series that Art Duncan of Vancouver tripped Toronto's Babe Dye, and Dye was awarded the first penalty shot in Stanley Cup play. Dye's shot from 36 feet away sailed high over the net. The next day the *Toronto Globe* reported that "the penalty shot was found to be somewhat of a joke."

The penalty-shot rule had been approved in the PCHA that season and one of the first players to stop one was Lester Patrick, the manager of the Victoria team. One night Patrick substituted on defense and when goalie Norm Fowler was sent off the ice for fighting, Lester took over Fowler's position in goal, where he played for 10 minutes. Observers said he handled the puck like a baseball player and earned a huge ovation when he stopped Jack Adams on a penalty shot. Two days later it happened again—Fowler was chased for fighting and Patrick took over in goal, standing off Vancouver for three minutes. Patrick even had the courage to try again in a Stanley Cup playoff game six years later in Montreal.

1922–23

Before the 1922–23 season opened, Leo Dandurand got rid of his temperamental star, Newsy Lalonde, by trading him to Saskatoon of the Western Canada Hockey League. Lalonde had been a great player for 18 years and he had three more good years before he played his final hockey game with Saskatoon. His lifetime scoring record was 441 goals in 365 games. In return for Lalonde, Dandurand obtained the services of a highly rated amateur, Aurel Joliat. Dandurand also traded Bert Corbeau and Bouchard to Hamilton for the veteran Joe Malone, while Toronto regained Jack Adams from Vancouver in return for Corbett Denneny. Ottawa lured Jack Darragh out of retirement and gave permission for Frank Boucher to go to the coast.

There is often talk about the endurance of modern-day hockey players. In today's game, a player is usually subbed every minute and a half. Compare this to the play of Ottawa's Frank Nighbor, who played six consecutive games at center ice during the 1922–23 season without a substitute and, what's more, averaged a goal a game.

Ottawa won the NHL title again and, late in the season, introduced a player named Lionel Hitchman who was to become an outstanding defenseman. Babe Dye of Toronto topped the goal scorers with 26, one more than Billy Boucher of the Canadiens.

Ottawa engaged Montreal in a rough playoff battle with Cleghorn and Couture of the Canadiens. Couture deliberately hit Ottawa's Cy Denneny over the head with a stick, knocking him senseless, and Cleghorn savagely cross-checked Hitchman. Leo Dandurand, a true sportsman, was so upset with his defensemen that he personally suspended them from the second game even after Ottawa took the opener.

Didier Pitre and Joe Malone filled in admirably as the Canadiens evened the series. Pitre, playing his last game after 19 years in hockey, was a bulwark on defense. Cy Denneny, recovered almost fully from a mild concussion, scored the winning goal as Ottawa won the round three goals to two.

Out west the PCHA decided in favor of six-man hockey, similar to the game played in the east, and an interlocking schedule with the Western Canada League was worked out and approved.

Lester Patrick announced his retirement from active play that season. Frank Fredrickson of Victoria scored 41 goals in 30 games to win the PCHA scoring race and Newsy Lalonde, playing manager at Saskatoon, led the WCHL scorers with 29 goals, one more than George Hay.

The Edmonton Eskimos won the WCHL championship, while Vancouver won on the coast. It was decided that Ottawa should journey west and play Vancouver, the PCHA champions, first, with the winner going on to engage Edmonton of the Western League for the Stanley Cup.

Over 9,000 fans saw Ottawa win the first game against Vancouver 1–0. Vancouver evened things up with a 4–1 victory, but Ottawa came back with 3–2 and 5–1 decisions to take the series. When it was over Frank Patrick called Ottawa the greatest team he had ever seen.

When Ottawa engaged Edmonton, the fans were wildly excited at the prospect of a man-against-man battle between Duke Keats and Frank Nighbor. Edmonton fans predicted that Keats would chase Nighbor right out of the rink. But Nighbor, one of the great players in hockey, played his usual superb game and Keats was hard pressed to handle the canny Ottawa player.

It was in one of this series' games that King Clancy played every position for the Ottawa Senators, including goal. Clancy played both defense spots and every forward position then, when goalie Clint Benedict was penalized and sent off, he handed his stick to Clancy and said, "Here kid. Take care of this place till I get back." Clancy did and was not scored on.

Ottawa took the best-of-three series in two straight games. Punch Broadbent scored the only goal of the second game and Eddie Gerard, the man who taught Clancy most of the tricks of play, played his last game as a professional. A growth in his throat had forced him into retirement.

In March 1923, a teenaged reporter and announcer with the *Toronto Star's* new radio station, CFCA, Foster Hewitt, was given an assignment to broadcast a hockey game between Kitchener and Parkdale at the Mutual Street Arena in Toronto. It was the beginning of a career that would make Hewitt's voice the most familiar one in Canada for the next 50 years.

1923–24

Ottawa had a new arena seating 10,000 ready for the 1923–24 season. The champion Senators had all their regulars back with the exception of Eddie Gerard. The Canadiens had just acquired Howie Morenz, who was beginning one of the greatest hockey careers.

In February 1924, a special meeting of the league was held to discuss plans for expanding into the United States and it was announced that a special trophy called the Dr. Hart Trophy would be awarded to the player judged most useful to his team during the season. The first winner of the Hart Trophy, which became the most coveted individual award in hockey, was Frank Nighbor who edged out Sprague Cleghorn by a single vote.

Cy Denneny, the league's leading scorer with 22 goals in 21 games, was lucky to escape with his life after a bizarre accident en route to Montreal for a game. The Ottawa star left the team train when it became snowbound and fell down a farmer's well. Fortunately, he was not seriously injured.

Ottawa went on to win the league championship and met Montreal in the playoffs. Rookie Howie Morenz, the darling of the Montreal fans, scored the only goal in a 1–0 Montreal victory. Eleven thousand fans turned out in Ottawa for the return match and Morenz, along with Aurel Joliat and Billy Boucher—a line that averaged 145 pounds in weight—stopped the Senators 4–2.

The Stanley Cup finals were held in Montreal and the Canadiens first took on Vancouver of the PCHA, beating them in two straight games, and then Calgary of the Western League. The Canadiens rolled to a 6–1 triumph in the opening game against Calgary, but the surface was so slushy that the second game was transferred to Ottawa, where the new arena there had artificial ice. The Canadiens won again, 3–0, to capture the Stanley Cup.

1924–25

The National Hockey League became an international league in November 1924 when, at the league's annual meeting in Montreal, a franchise was granted to the city of Boston. The purchaser of the franchise was Charles Adams. Applications from New York, Pittsburgh and Philadelphia were shelved, although a franchise was awarded to James Strachan and Donat Raymond who promised to ice another strong team, the Maroons, in Montreal.

Art Ross was named manager of the Boston Bruins and quickly signed an outstanding amateur player named Carson Cooper. Ottawa signed some new boys, too, including Alex Connell, a brilliant goaltender, Hooley Smith of the Canadien Olympic team and Ed Gorman. Bert McCaffrey and a good-looking youngster named Clarence "Hap" Day signed on with the Toronto St. Patricks. In Montreal a new arena, the Forum, was ready for play and 8,000 fans turned out for the opening game of the season.

The schedule had now been increased to 30 games and a new playoff system gave the first-place team a bye while the second- and third-place teams played off to determine who should meet the league champions. This system was partly responsible for sparking one of the most unusual happenings in hockey—a players' strike.

Hamilton had won the league title and drawn the bye. Now it was up to the Montreal Canadiens and the Toronto St. Pats to battle it out for the right to meet the Tigers. But Red Green, speaking for the Hamilton players, pointed out that his two-year contract called for 24 games a season. If the league and the Hamilton club would not come up with $200 more per player to play the additional games, he said the Hamilton players would not show up for the finals.

An angry league president, Frank Calder, ordered the players to suit up or else. When they remained adamant, he announced that the winner of the Canadiens–St. Pats series would be recognized as the league titleholder. But the Hamilton players remained on strike. Later, at a special league meeting on April 17, the Hamilton players were suspended and fined $200 each. This was the beginning of the end for hockey in Hamilton.

Babe Dye of Toronto won the NHL scoring race with 38 goals, eight more than Howie Morenz and nine up on Aurel Joliat. In the west, the PCHA had floundered, but two of its clubs, Vancouver and Victoria, joined the Western Canada Hockey League and Victoria emerged as the league champions. Regina, of the WCHL, introduced a new player, Eddie Shore, who soon made a great name for himself in hockey.

The Canadiens won the NHL title, defeating the St. Pats in two straight games, and journeyed west to meet the Victoria team in the finals. Victoria skated rings around the Montreal team in the first game, winning 5–2, and in the second, seen by 11,000 fans, they triumphed again. Howie Morenz was the spark plug of the Canadiens, banging in three goals as Montreal took the third game 4–1. But Victoria came back to win the fourth game and the Stanley Cup.

1925–26

Before the 1925–26 season got under way, the Hamilton franchise was sold to New York and the Hamilton players were transferred to the new NHL team, the New York Americans. A few weeks later, at another league meeting, the Pittsburgh Pirates were admitted to the league and Odie Cleghorn was named as the Pittsburgh representative.

Albert "Pit" Lepine, Albert Leduc and Hector Lepine were among the newcomers in the Montreal Canadiens' camp, and the Montreal Maroons added Nels Stewart and Babe Seibert. Stewart, playing both center and defense, was the scoring sensation of the season and went on to win the Hart Trophy. The New York Americans obtained Joe Simpson from Edmonton, and Pittsburgh landed Roy Worters, Lionel Conacher, Harold "Baldy" Cotton and Harold Darragh.

Alex Connell of the Ottawa Senators attained a sparkling goals-against average of 1.2 per game and made 15 shutouts in 32 games. But tragedy struck the Canadiens when their goaltender, the great Georges Vezina, was forced out of a game with the Pittsburgh Pirates early in the season and died of tuberculosis shortly after.

In the west, Eddie Shore was a big gun for Edmonton and Bill Cook and Dick Irvin were the top scorers in the western circuit, which was now known as the Western Hockey League.

Although he was 43 years old, Lester Patrick couldn't stay off the ice. When one of his Victoria players was injured, Patrick pulled on a uniform and scored a couple of key goals. Victoria won the Western League title and moved east to meet the Montreal Maroons for the Stanley Cup. In the NHL playoffs Montreal eliminated Pittsburgh and Ottawa. Nels Stewart was the star of the Cup finals, scoring six goals in four games as the Maroons took the series three games to one.

This series marked the last time that any team outside the NHL challenged for the Stanley Cup. The coveted trophy now came into the exclusive custody of the National Hockey League.

1926–27

Next to Canada's Centennial year, when new teams from six American cities gained admittance to the NHL, 1926 was the biggest single year in the expansion of the thriving hockey circuit. A second team, the Rangers, was admitted from New York. A team called the Blackhawks was installed in Chicago with Pete Muldoon at the reins, and the Cougars, coached by Art Duncan, were the new entry from Detroit.

The NHL, which had grown to 10 teams, was broken into two divisions. The Canadian Division consisted of the Toronto St. Patricks, the Ottawa Senators, the New York Americans, the Montreal Maroons and the Montreal Canadiens. The American Division was made up of the Boston Bruins, the New York Rangers, the Pittsburgh Pirates, the Chicago Blackhawks and the Detroit Cougars.

Colonel John Hammond had a franchise for his New York Rangers, but now he needed a man who could supply some players. A young man from Toronto, Conn Smythe, was recommended and hired. He pitched right in and picked up goaltender Lorne Chabot from Port Arthur, defensemen Ching Johnson and Taffy Abel from the Minneapolis team of the Central United States League and others like Bill and Bun Cook, Frank Boucher and Murray Murdoch. All turned out to be outstanding professional players, but the shrewd Smythe signed them, as well as 25 others, for a total of $32,000. It has been estimated that, even before today's inflated prices for hockey talent, the 31 men signed by Smythe were worth $300,000.

His reward? Before the first Ranger game in 1926 he was dismissed as manager-coach. It seems that someone had persuaded Hammond that while Smythe might recognize hockey talent, he lacked the experience to handle the new team. Hammond hired Lester Patrick and paid off Smythe.

Smythe, always a battler, vowed that he would some day organize another hockey team which would be even better than the club he had handed over to Lester Patrick. Smythe moved back to Toronto where the last place St. Pats were in trouble and up for sale. The asking price for the club was $200,000, which was exactly $190,000 more than he had to his name. But he turned over all the money he had to the St. Pats' owners, J. P. Bickell, Charlie Querrie, N. L. Nathanson and Paul Ciceri, in return for a 30-day option to purchase.

Smythe managed to raise $160,000 and then he convinced the owners that they would do well to sell out to a Torontonian who would guarantee that the team would not be transferred to another city. The idea appealed to the owners and the deal was made with $75,000 on the line and $85,000 payable within a month. Before a game was played under the new ownership, Smythe was offered $200,000 for his team—which he named the Maple Leafs—but he turned down the offer without a second thought.

The new 10-team NHL was strengthened by players streaming in from the Western Hockey League, which had folded at the end of the previous season and had sold all its talent for a bargain $258,000. Eddie Shore went to Boston, together with Duke Keats, Perk Galbraith, Harry Oliver and Harry Meeking. Detroit took Frank Fredrickson, Frank Foyston, Clem Loughlin, Art Duncan as coach, Jack Walker and Slim Halderson. The Cook brothers and Frank Boucher joined the Rangers. Leo Reise and Laurie Scott were signed by the Americans. Chicago snared Dick Irvin, Mickey Mackay, George Hay, Rabbit McVeigh, Percy Traub and Jim Riley, and the Montreal Canadiens grabbed Art Gagne, Herb Gardiner and Amby Moran. Jack Adams headed for Ottawa, Red Dutton went to the Montreal Maroons and Jack Arbour joined Pittsburgh. For the first time the best hockey players in the world were all playing under one roof.

The leading scorer in the Canadian Division in 1926–27 was Howie Morenz of the

Canadiens with 32 points, four more than Ace Bailey of Toronto. In the American Division Bill Cook of the Rangers edged Chicago's Dick Irvin by a single point, with 37.

Six teams were allowed to enter the playoffs for the Stanley Cup. In the Canadian Division, Ottawa finished on top and waited to meet the winner of a series between the second-place Canadiens and the third-place Maroons. The Canadiens won, but were eliminated by Ottawa, led by Cy Denneny, Frank Finnigan and King Clancy.

In the American Division, Boston met Chicago in the semi-final set, with the winner getting a chance at first-place New York. Boston ousted Chicago and, after a scoreless first game in the two-game series with New York, the Bruins won the series three goals to one in the second game.

The Ottawa–Boston clash was a memorable Stanley Cup series. The first game was a scoreless draw and Ottawa won the second 3–1. The third game went into overtime and was finally declared a 1–1 tie. When Ottawa won the fourth game 3–1, it also took the Stanley Cup because NHL president Frank Calder had ruled earlier that the series would be terminated after four games.

The final game almost ended the playing career of Billy Couture, then a Boston defenseman. He assaulted the game officials and was fined $100 and suspended for life, although he was later reinstated.

Ottawa had a fabulous team that year with players like Jack Adams, King Clancy, Alex Connell, Frank Nighbor, Cy Denneny, Frank Finnigan and Hec Kilrea. The Boston Bruins were sparked by Eddie Shore, who was to become a legendary figure in hockey.

1927–28

In 1927, Jack Adams, a member of the Stanley Cup champions of the preceding season, the Ottawa Senators, was asked to take over the Detroit Cougars as manager-coach. Art Duncan of Detroit moved on to play for the Toronto Maple Leafs, who were being reorganized by Conn Smythe.

Pete Muldoon was fired as coach of the Chicago Blackhawks, and in leaving, according to sports columnist Jim Coleman, put the "curse of the Muldoons" on the Chicago club. Strangely enough, this alleged curse stood up for 40 years. The Blackhawks finally shook Muldoon's magic by finishing first in the 1966–67 season.

In the Canadian Division the Ottawa Senators began to slip and finished third behind the first-place Montreal Canadiens and the second-place Montreal Maroons. Howie Morenz led all scorers. Boston was on top of the American Division, with New York and Pittsburgh not far behind.

The Rangers ousted Pittsburgh and then Boston to earn a Stanley Cup berth against the Maroons, who had defeated the Senators and the Canadiens in the Canadian Division. The finals got under way on April 5 in Montreal, with the Maroons taking the opener 2–0.

Lester Patrick of the Rangers had long since retired as an active player when his team skated out against the Maroons two nights later. Little did he know that he was about to become the central figure in one of the most amazing sports performances ever.

In the second period, Nels Stewart rifled a shot that caught goalie Lorne Chabot flush in the eye. Chabot was taken to hospital and Patrick immediately asked Eddie

Gerard, the manager of the Maroons, for permission to use Alex Connell, the great Ottawa goaltender, as a substitute. Gerard refused. Patrick, fuming, decided to put on the pads himself. He had done the same thing on two or three occasions before, but never with so much at stake. The silver-haired Patrick was 44 years old, and the fans alternately hooted and cheered when he shuffled onto the ice.

When play began Patrick amazed the fans with his agility. Throughout the rest of the game and into overtime he handled 18 shots and was beaten only once. At 7:05 of the first overtime period the Rangers broke through and scored. The exhausted Patrick was mobbed by his players and escorted to the dressing room. It is strange but fitting that Patrick, who made many outstanding contributions to the game, will always be remembered more for his play as a substitute Stanley Cup goaltender than for anything else. It was one of hockey's most electrifying occasions.

The Rangers dropped the next game with minor-league goalie Joe Miller in the nets, but with Chabot back in harness they won the following two games and skated off with the Stanley Cup.

One remarkable record established during this season belonged to goaltender Alex Connell of the Ottawa Senators, who played six consecutive games during the season without allowing a single goal. His record shutout sequence reached 446 minutes and nine seconds.

1928–29

The game of hockey opened up during the 1928–29 season when the rules were changed to allow forward passing in all three zones. Before this a forward pass was allowed only in the defending and center zones.

Goaltender Lorne Chabot went from the New York Rangers to the Toronto Maple Leafs in exchange for John Ross Roach. Meanwhile the Boston Bruins unveiled Cecil "Tiny" Thompson. Thompson, who had performed brilliantly in goal at Duluth and Minneapolis, was embarking on a spectacular career with the Bruins that would cover the next decade. He was to win the Vezina Trophy four times over that span, a record that stood until 1949, when Bill Durnan of the Canadiens won it five times.

The Maroons underwent an expensive rebuilding campaign in Montreal in an effort to win fans away from the popular Canadiens. Money was no object and the Maroons molded a powerful club. They bought Hooley Smith for $22,500 and Dave Trottier for $15,000. Dunc Munro was purchased for $8,000 and Reg Noble for $7,000. Nels Stewart and Babe Seibert received huge bonuses for signing. But despite this impressive lineup, the Maroons still finished last in the Canadian Division while the Canadiens finished on top.

Ace Bailey of Toronto won individual scoring honors that season, with 32 points, three ahead of Nels Stewart of Montreal. Boston finished on top of the American Division, four points ahead of New York.

A new playoff system was devised in which the first-place finishers in each division would meet in one series while the second-place finishers were meeting in another. In series A the Boston Bruins polished off the Montreal Canadiens in three straight games with Tiny Thompson recording shutouts in two of them.

In series B between the Rangers and the Americans, only one goal was scored. The first game was a scoreless tie and the second went 29 minutes and 50 seconds into overtime before the Rangers beat goalie Roy Worters to win the round.

In the Stanley Cup finals, a best-of-three affair, the Rangers had as much trouble beating Thompson as had the Canadiens. Boston won the series two straight, taking the first 2–0 and the second 2–1. In five playoff games, Thompson's record was three shutouts and his goals-against average was .60.

The 1928–29 season was called "the year of the shutout" and the man who scored a record number of them was diminutive George Hainsworth of the Canadiens. Hainsworth, over the course of the 44-game schedule, had blanked the opposition in no less than 22 games. No player has since come close to that mark. Perhaps no player ever will.

IV

THE THRIVING THIRTIES

New Faces, New Growth, 1929–1939

In the decade between the stock-market crash and the outbreak of World War II, professional hockey grew and changed and attracted thousands of new fans. New players like Charlie Conacher, Busher Jackson, Murph Chamberlain, Turk Broda and Syl Apps arrived on the scene. Established stars like King Clancy and the older Patricks stopped playing but did not terminate their association with hockey. A broken leg ended the career of the Stratford flash, Howie Morenz, the career of the great goaltender, Charlie Gardiner, was cut short by a brain hemorrhage and, in the most celebrated incident in NHL history, Ace Bailey nearly lost his life.

It was also the end of an era for hockey in Ottawa. Beset by financial difficulties, the Ottawa Senators gave up their franchise in 1934 and ended the city's association with major-league hockey which had dated back to before the turn of the century. The shorter-lived Montreal Maroons and Pittsburgh Pirates also disappeared, but the sorely troubled New York Americans managed to stave off final disaster for a few more years when the league itself took over the team.

Conn Smythe defied the cryers of doom and the Depression to build his Maple Leaf Gardens in record time, with an unprecedented assist from the construction unions. The schedule was increased to 48 games, making sportswriters wonder how the players could ever keep up the pace. Mud Bruneteau ended the longest game in NHL history with a tally at 176:30 and the fans began the pleasant custom of keeping the pucks that were fired into the crowd.

1929–30

Thanks largely to the efforts of Conn Smythe, hockey interest in Toronto began building in the late twenties and, after half the games had been played during the 1927–28 schedule in the old Arena Gardens, Smythe found himself turning people away at the gate. The capacity of the arena on Mutual Street was only about 8,000 and Smythe felt that a building seating at least 12,000 was necessary to make his team a paying proposition.

He had architects draw up plans for Maple Leaf Gardens. When financing became a major problem, Smythe turned to the trade unions and bartererd stock for labor. It was a brilliant solution. Six months later Smythe had his new ice palace and the workers who had kept their stock earned thousands of dollars in dividends.

With the new construction project under way, the Toronto team played their last season in the Arena Gardens. Charlie Conacher, a powerful rookie, was brought up from the junior ranks and scored a goal on his first shift in NHL play.

On December 7, Harvey Jackson, a classy left-winger was signed by the Leafs. He joined two of his former junior teammates, Conacher and Joe Primeau on a line. Jackson was only 18 years old, the third youngest player ever to join the NHL up to that time. King Clancy and Hec Kilrea of Ottawa had been a few months younger than Jackson when they had broken in.

This was the season in which the first face mask appeared in the NHL. Clint Benedict of Ottawa suffered a broken nose when one of Howie Morenz's shots hit him in the face. In the next game he appeared wearing a crude face mask and in so doing set a precedent for the major league.

One of Toronto's players that year was Art Duncan, who had been playing professional hockey since 1914. He was to be coach of the Leafs in the following season before they made their debut in the new Maple Leaf Gardens. After outstanding military service in World War I, Duncan played on the coast and once led the Western League in scoring—the only time a defenseman had ever accomplished such a feat.

Cooney Weiland, the Boston Bruins' clever center, led the NHL point getters in 1929–30 with 73 points in the American Division. He was the top goal scorer, too, with 43 goals, two more than his teammate Dit Clapper. The Bruins set an NHL record when they went 23 games without a loss. The oddity of the season was Lester Patrick's order to all his players to drink a glass of hot water every morning upon rising whether they liked it or not.

In the playoffs Boston eliminated the Montreal Maroons in the first series, while the Canadiens advanced to the final series by defeating the New York Rangers. The Canadiens' "little men of steel" weren't given much chance against the Bruins, who had won the American Division by 30 points. But they played first-class hockey and polished off the Bruins 3–0 and 4–3 to take their first Stanley Cup since 1924. Three veterans of that 1924 team—Morenz, Joliat and Mantha—were still with them.

1930–31

The Stanley Cup champion Canadiens were a powerhouse again in the following season, as were the Boston Bruins. Howie Morenz led the Canadiens to a first-place finish in the Canadian Division and won the Hart Trophy. He was a dashing center, able to lift the spectators from their seats with his electrifying rushes.

On the eve of the 1930 season, Conn Smythe spent a small fortune in order to obtain King Clancy of the Ottawa Senators. Smythe thought so highly of the aggressive little

Ottawa defenseman that he paid the Senators $35,000 and traded Art Smith and Eric Pettinger to them. The Senators had never dreamed that Smythe would put such a premium on a player who was often called "150 pounds of muscle and conversation" and who had already played in the NHL for nine seasons.

While insisting that he never skated away from a fight, Clancy sometimes found novel methods of avoiding them. One night in Boston he pushed Eddie Shore into the boards, and while Shore hated being bumped by anyone, this humiliation from a 150-pounder was too much. The Boston defenseman jumped to his feet, dropped his gloves and cocked his fist to throw a punch. Clancy immediately grabbed the bare hand, shook it warmly and said, "Why, hello, Eddie. How are you tonight?" Even the belligerent Shore had to laugh.

With Day and Clancy as leaders for Toronto and the "Kid Line" of Charlie Conacher, Busher Jackson and Joe Primeau controlling the puck as have few lines in hockey history, the Leafs appeared to be equal in strength to the teams from Montreal. But although they finished ahead of the Maroons that season, they couldn't catch the mighty Canadiens.

The Pittsburgh Pirates, winners of a mere five games in 1929–30, had been shifted to Philadelphia, where Benny Leonard the prizefighter was running the show. The team had some good players, but they finished the season with a record-low total of 12 points, after winning four games and tying four. The owners lost over $100,000 and the team dropped out of the league at the end of the season.

In the playoffs, Chicago defeated Toronto in series B and the Rangers ousted the Maroons in series C. The Blackhawks then moved into the finals against the Canadiens by eliminating the Rangers with two straight shutouts.

Series A had been a battle between the first-place finishers, the Boston Bruins and the Montreal Canadiens. Three of the five games went into overtime before the Canadiens ousted the Bruins three games to two. It was in the second game of this series that Art Ross pulled his goaltender, Tiny Thompson, in the last minute of play and threw on an extra forward in an unsuccessful attempt to score. This "amazing maneuver," as it was called in the next day's papers, marked the first time in Stanley Cup play that a goalkeeper had been pulled from the nets.

The surprising Hawks gave the Canadiens a real battle for the Stanley Cup. Johnny Gottselig scored an overtime goal to tie the series at 1–1 after Canadiens took the opener. Another overtime goal by Cy Wentworth put the Hawks in front two games to one. Then the Canadiens, who had entered the series with Armand Mondou, Howie Morenz, Battleship Leduc and Pit Lepine all out with injuries, began to roll as their stars returned. They won the Cup by taking the next two games. Howie Morenz scored the final goal of the series and Aurel Joliat played one of the greatest games of his long career.

The Ottawa Senators won only 10 games in 1930–31 and fell into the basement of the Canadian Division. The Senators were granted a one-year suspension of their franchise and joined Philadelphia on the sidelines. This left the NHL with eight teams, four in each division.

1931–32

The 1931–32 season saw the beginning of the 48-game schedule, despite dire predictions from many hockey followers that "the players will never be able to stand the pressure of more games."

Before the start of the season, Conn Smythe landed young Syd Howe on loan from the defunct Philadelphia club. Harold Darragh was picked up from Boston for the waiver price and Frank Finnigan was obtained from Ottawa.

The construction of the new Maple Leaf Gardens was under way and whenever it was discussed someone would always say, "Smythe won't be able to finance it," or, "If he does, he'll never have it ready for the November opening," or, "You can't tell me he'll ever fill the place." Some said he would never build a winning team. Smythe was determined to make these doubting Thomases eat their words.

The completion of the Gardens was an engineering miracle. On April 1, the houses and stores on the property were torn down. On June 1 the steam shovels took over and on November 12, right on schedule, the Gardens was open for business. A capacity crowd of 13,542 turned out to witness the Leafs and Chicago play the first game in the new arena, but Chicago, never a winner on Toronto ice in the past, spoiled the opener for Toronto fans by beating the Leafs 3–1.

Having silenced his critics on three counts, Smythe now set about molding a Stanley Cup winner. He offered the Montreal Canadiens $75,000 for Howie Morenz but was turned down. He made an effort to purchase Johnny Gottselig from Chicago, but Bill Tobin, the Blackhawks' manager wanted Clancy and Conacher in return. Smythe sent him a note to the effect that Santa Claus lived in the North Pole, not in Maple Leaf Gardens.

When the Leafs skidded to last place after a half-dozen games, Smythe decided to replace coach Art Duncan with Dick Irvin, who had been fired by Chicago the preceding season. With Irvin at the helm, the Leafs leaped from last to first place within a month. They couldn't keep pace with the Canadiens, however, and finished second in the Canadian Division.

Bill Cook of the New York Rangers scored 34 goals to share the NHL lead with the Leafs' Charlie Conacher. Frank Boucher, Cecil Dillon, Bun Cook and Art Somers accounted for most of the scoring as the Rangers took first place in the American Division.

The Leafs disposed of the Chicago Blackhawks in one semi-final series while the Montreal Maroons eliminated the renamed Detroit Falcons. In the third series the Rangers beat the Canadiens three games to one. Then the Maroons and the Leafs battled it out for the right to meet the Rangers. Dick Irvin changed his lines rapidly, and this tactic paid off for the Leafs. When the second game went into overtime, the Leafs, who appeared to be fresher than the Maroons, won at 17:59.

The finals opened in New York and the Leafs swept to the Cup in three straight games. It was the first time in Stanley Cup history that a team had won the final series with three straight games. The Leafs scored six goals in each game, winning 6–4, 6–2 and 6–4. Sportswriters later referred to it as "the tennis series." Conn Smythe's vow that he would some day build a hockey club that would be better than the one he had put together in New York before he was fired, had finally been fulfilled. One man who was there to help celebrate that victory was Frank Selke, a man who preferred to keep in the background but who was a vital member of the Leafs' organization. Steeped in hockey knowledge since his early days in Kitchener, Selke had been of great assistance during the building of the Gardens and he played a major role in the molding of the Cup winners. Years later, he would be called upon to rebuild the Montreal Canadiens into the mightiest powerhouse ever to perform in the NHL.

1932–33

The Boston Bruins, winners of their division title by 30 points in the 1929–30 season, had fallen all the way to last place in 1931–32, so Art Ross had made some changes before the new schedule got under way. He secured Nels Stewart from the Montreal Maroons and thick-set Billy Burch from the New York Americans. With Eddie Shore about to embark on his finest season, the Bruins were soon on their way up the ladder again.

Lester Patrick's New York Rangers also landed a well-known former Maroon, Babe Seibert. They placed Seibert on a line with Cecil Dillon, whom Patrick once described as "possibly the greatest I've ever seen," and a youngster named Carl Voss. Voss was soon to move on to Detroit and by the season's end he was named the outstanding rookie in the league.

The Maroons had two fine-looking prospects in their lineup: Hugh Plaxton, the star of Canada's 1928 Olympic team, and Mickey Blake, from whom the Maroons expected great things.

Ottawa, as promised, resumed play in the NHL and called back players they'd loaned to other clubs. Syd Howe, Hec Kilrea and Frank Finnigan, all natives of Ottawa, returned home and the Senators obtained Cooney Weiland from Boston. Weiland turned out to be their top scorer, but the Senators' comeback still earned them no more than last place in the Canadian Division.

The season was little more than a month old when Colonel John Hammond resigned his position as president of the New York Rangers hockey club. His place was taken by Lester Patrick, who had been coach of the Rangers since 1926.

Cecil Hart, who had guided the Canadiens since 1925, was replaced by former Canadiens star Newsy Lalonde, and Tommy Gorman took over as coach of the Chicago Blackhawks, replacing the deposed Emil Iverson. Major Frederic McLaughlin, then owner of the Hawks, changed coaches more often than Tommy Manville changed wives. From 1926 to 1940 he changed coaches 14 times, and even hired a publicity man and a baseball umpire to run his team.

The Leafs and the Maroons fought it out for the championship of the Canadian Division, with the Leafs finishing on top by four points. Busher Jackson won his second straight scoring title in the Canadian circuit and Bill Cook of the Rangers took his second straight for the American Division.

Detroit and Boston finished with identical records: 25 wins, 15 losses and eight ties. The Bruins, who had the better goals average, met Toronto in series A. Four of the five games went into overtime, but the last one, which began on April 3, 1933, and finished well into April 4, will live long in the memory of those who saw it.

The game was scoreless after 60 minutes and remained scoreless after the first overtime period. Then came a second, a third, a fourth and even a fifth overtime. After the first 100 minutes of extra time, Conn Smythe and Art Ross asked president Frank Calder if they could halt play and resume the following night. Their request was turned down. It was then suggested that a coin be tossed to determine the winner. The players were willing, but the fans voiced their displeasure. Calder then proposed that the two goaltenders be removed, but few thought much of that idea.

At 4:46 of the sixth overtime period, the Leafs' Andy Blair intercepted a pass from Eddie Shore and fed the puck to little Ken Doraty, who raced in to score. The time of the goal was 164:46. Doraty would have been forgotten by most of today's fans if not for the goal that ended the longest overtime game played up to that season.

The weary Leafs didn't have time to celebrate. As series winners they had another game to play later the same day in New York. They proved to be easy pickings for the Rangers in the opening game of the finals and they never recovered. Bill Cook's overtime marker in the fourth game was the clincher. It gave New York a 1–0 decision on Toronto ice. Cook's play and that of his brother Bun and Frank Boucher, three players Conn Smythe had corralled for New York years earlier, proved how sound his judgment of hockey talent had been.

1933–34

All the events in the 1933–34 season were overshadowed by the dramatic incident which took place in the Boston Garden on December 12, 1933, in a game between the Bruins and the Toronto Maple Leafs. On the morning of the game, a Boston paper ran a story quoting Eddie Shore as saying that, after trying to play gentlemanly hockey during the early part of the schedule, he would return to the rough-and-tumble style which had established him as one of the most feared, and brilliant, defensemen in the league. The quote, accurate or not, was repeated to him on many subsequent occasions.

The Bruins enjoyed a two-man advantage at one point in the game and Ace Bailey, in a penalty-killing role, did some fancy stick handling to kill time. Finally, Eddie Shore snared the puck and rushed up the ice. But he was knocked down in the Leafs' zone, behind Bailey who had his back to Shore. Shore leaped up and charged Bailey, flipping him high in the air. Bailey's head hit the ice and he lay motionless, severely injured. Leafs' tough guy, Red Horner, skated up to Shore and knocked him unconscious with one punch. Shore recovered quickly, but Bailey hovered close to death for several hours after emergency surgery in a Boston hospital. He pulled through but never played again.

Two months later, a benefit game for Bailey was held in Toronto between the Leafs and a team of NHL All-Stars. Bailey and Shore met for the first time since the incident and shook hands at center ice. The ovation that followed lasted for several minutes.

Toronto won the Canadian Division of the NHL without much trouble and Detroit finished on top of the American Division. Charlie Conacher topped the Canadian Division scorers with 32 goals and 20 assists, while linemates Joe Primeau and Busher Jackson finished right behind him for a one-two-three Leafs' sweep. In the American Division it was Frank Boucher of the Rangers at the head of the point-getters' list, followed by Marty Barry of Boston and Cecil Dillon of the Rangers in a tie for second place, with Nels Stewart of Boston one point behind them.

Detroit eliminated Toronto in the playoff semi-finals, while the Blackhawks first ousted the Canadiens and then the Maroons to reach the finals against Detroit.

That final series between Chicago and Detroit truly belonged to Charlie Gardiner. Always a great player, at 30 he was the outstanding netminder in hockey and had been on every All-Star team since the NHL had started naming them in 1931. Only once was he relegated to a second-team berth.

Chicago, which had not won a game in Detroit since February 1930, scored a 2–1 overtime victory there in the first game and two nights later won again, 4–1. Detroit closed the gap in Chicago by winning 5–2. But, in what proved to be the final game, Mush March of Chicago took a pass from Doc Romnes at 10:05 of the second overtime period and the Hawks clinched their first Stanley Cup with a 1–0 victory.

In eight games of Stanley Cup play, Charlie Gardiner had lost a game, tied one and recorded two shutouts. As a reward, his teammate Roger Jenkins wheeled him in a wheelbarrow through the Loop section of Chicago. Eight weeks later Gardiner collapsed in Winnipeg and three days after that he died of a brain hemorrhage.

1934–35

Ottawa was through as a member of the NHL. The once mighty Senators gave up the fight to keep big-league hockey in Canada's capital and the franchise was transferred to St. Louis, along with most of the players. Carl Voss, who had played with Detroit and Ottawa, was to be the leading point getter and a promising youngster named Bill Cowley came down from Ottawa to try his hand at professional hockey with the Eagles. Another Ottawa player, Syd Howe, divided the season between St. Louis and Detroit and blossomed into one of the finest players in hockey. He led the American Division in scoring that year with 47 points. His teammate Scotty Bowman scored the first penalty-shot goal in the NHL against Alex Connell of the Maroons. In mid-season Howe and Scotty Bowman were purchased from St. Louis by Detroit for $50,000.

Tommy Gorman, fresh from coaching the Chicago Blackhawks to a Stanley Cup victory, was hired by the Montreal Maroons and Clem Loughlin took over in Chicago. Another Patrick entered professional hockey when Lester inserted his son Lynn into the Ranger lineup. Meanwhile, Frank Patrick became coach of the Bruins and Art Ross moved into the front office.

It was during this season that observers noticed that the fans were keeping the pucks that went into the crowd. Normally four pucks—which had been frozen before a game to lessen the bounce—had been sufficient for the average game, but when the fans began to keep pucks for souvenirs, more and more had to be prepared. Today, three to four dozen pucks are frozen by the home club prior to each NHL game.

Sportswriters and sportscasters had developed some habits, too. Hockey writers often referred to the goal area as an "igloo" or a "citadel." Sometimes it was a "cord cottage" or "hempen hut" and more often a "net," "cage," or "twine." The hockey stick was a "cudgel," "war club," "hickory" or "wand." A player didn't shoot the puck, he "rifled" it, "whipped" it, "steamed" it or "burned" it. The puck itself was a "disc," a "doughnut," a "rubber" or an "old boot heel." When a sportswriter wrote, "Old sorrel-top got the thumb from Odie the arbiter," any fan worth his salt knew that Red Horner had been penalized by referee Odie Cleghorn.

Charlie Conacher of the Leafs ran away with the scoring title in the Canadian Division that season, finishing with 26 goals and 21 assists for 57 points, 13 more than linemate Busher Jackson. Larry Aurie trailed Syd Howe by a single point in the American Division.

Jackson played one game to remember on November 20 in St. Louis. He connected for four goals in the third period to set an NHL record. Frank Boucher captured the Lady Byng Trophy for the seventh time in eight years and was awarded permanent possession of the award.

Toronto, paced by the Kid Line, swept to first place in the Canadian Division, while Boston nudged out Chicago by a single point to win the American Division title.

In the playoffs, the Leafs swept the Bruins aside in three straight games while the Maroons advanced to the final series after victories over Chicago and the New York Rangers. In the final round, the Leafs proved to be no match for the Maroons and the hot goaltending of Alex Connell. Connell limited the Leafs to a mere four goals in the series as the Maroons won three straight games. The usual ovation descended upon the new champions at the final buzzer, with the biggest cheer reserved for Connell who leaned wearily on his net and cried.

1935–36

In 1935 the NHL bought out the St. Louis club and announced that the league would operate as an eight-club circuit. Eighteen of the 23 St. Louis players were distributed to other clubs. One of the best, Bill Cowley, moved on to Boston, where he was to become a great star.

In Chicago, netminder Lorne Chabot injured his knee, but Clem Loughlin said he wasn't too concerned because a rookie named Mike Karakas, who had been discarded by Detroit, "was a real humdinger." Karakas, up from Tulsa, became the talk of the league when the season began and he won his first four starts.

In January, Boston purchased Flash Hollett from Toronto for $11,500 and Chicago traded Howie Morenz to the New York Rangers in return for Glenn Brydson. The Rangers made some mid-season changes, too, and called up Mac Colville, Alex Shibicky and Babe Pratt from Philadelphia.

Late in the season Tiny Thompson became the first NHL goalie to earn an assist on a scoring play when he passed the puck up to Babe Seibert who scored for Boston. Other goalies had set up scoring plays and Brophy, a netminder for Westmount and Montreal in the Canadian Amateur Hockey League, had actually scored in both 1905 and 1906. However, that was not in the NHL.

A rookie who began to show flashes of brilliance late in the season was Hector "Toe" Blake of the Canadiens, but it was another rookie who stole the thunder in the playoffs.

In the first game of the semi-finals, played in Montreal, the Wings and the Maroons battled through 60 minutes of scoreless hockey and, like the Leafs and Bruins of a few seasons earlier, went five overtime periods with neither Lorne Chabot of the Maroons nor Normie Smith of Detroit giving away anything. Finally, at 2:25 A.M., after 176 minutes and 30 seconds of hockey, Modere "Mud" Bruneteau fired a shot from 25 feet out that beat Chabot. Bruneteau had spent most of that season with the Red Wings' farm team, the Detroit Olympics of the International League. His name is still in the records as having scored the goal which won the longest game in the history of major-league hockey.

In the semi-finals between Boston and Toronto, the Bruins won the first game of the two-game series 3–0 and the Leafs were on the ropes when they played back on home ice. It was in this game that Eddie Shore lost his temper and the Bruins lost the series.

The Bruins scored first in the second game and led in total goals 4–0. Then Shore was given a penalty by referee Odie Cleghorn. While he was off the ice the Leafs scored twice in less than a minute on goals by Clancy and Conacher.

Shore came back angrier than ever and, when Horner banged in a goal from the crease, Shore exploded. He protested that Horner had been in the crease and he banged his stick on the ice. King Clancy sidled up to Shore and said, "You were robbed, Eddie. Horner *was* in the crease. What's more that blankety-blank referee gave you the cheapest kind of penalty before we scored those two early goals. If I were you, I wouldn't take that kind of nonsense from anybody." While he was talking, King placed the puck on Shore's stick. Shore, fuming, glared at Clancy, then at Cleghorn, and his temper won out. He took the puck and fired it at Cleghorn, catching the startled referee in the backside.

Cleghorn whirled around and threw Shore off with a 10-minute misconduct penalty and, from that moment on, the Bruins were lost. Paced by Charlie Conacher, who scored three goals, the Leafs went on to an 8–3 win and took the round by eight goals to six.

The New York Americans eliminated Chicago 7–5 in total goals and they, in turn, were defeated two games to one by Toronto.

In the battle for the Stanley Cup between Detroit and Toronto, Bucko McDonald scored a goal for the Red Wings and kept the Leafs off balance with his rugged checking, as Detroit won the opener 3–1. Then the Red Wings made a rout of the second game, winning 9–4. The Leafs scored a 4–3 overtime thriller in game number three, but the Wings won their first Cup ever with a 3–2 victory in the fourth game.

1936–37

The Stanley Cup champion Detroit Red Wings have always produced fine goaltenders. Normie Smith played superbly for the Red Wings in the 1935–36 season and in the fall of 1936 the Wings signed Jimmy Franks. They had two other top prospects in Earl Robertson and Walter "Turk" Broda.

Toronto, unlike Detroit, could never seem to raise a quality goaltender in the Leaf system. They saw Broda play for the Detroit Olympics and learned that either he or Robertson was available for $8,000. The Leafs chose Broda.

In New York, Murray "Muzz" Patrick, Lester's son and Lynn's brother, was thinking of a professional boxing career. As the amateur heavyweight champion of Canada, he had offers to become Manhattan's "white hope," but he soon passed up the offers to sign on with the Rangers.

Gordon Drillon, signed by Toronto at the close of the preceding season, was a fine-looking prospect and a young McMaster University grad, Sylvanus Apps, back from the pole-vaulting event at the Berlin Olympics, also signed with the team.

Joe Primeau announced his retirement that season and the famous Kid Line was broken up. But a once-famous line was restored in Montreal when the Canadiens purchased Howie Morenz from New York and placed him with Aurel Joliat and Johnny Gagnon.

The Bruins were sold that year. Charles Adams sold out to his son Weston and Art Ross.

The New York Americans came under league control early in the season. Because of financial troubles, the hockey governors declared the Americans' hockey franchise forfeited. They announced that the team would operate with Red Dutton as manager and Frank Calder as team adviser. Big Bill Dwyer was allowed to retain an interest in the Americans with the league running the organization until such time as he could get back on his feet financially. He lost at least five million dollars in ten years.

The Maroons generously gave Hooley Smith an outright release after nine years of service and the Bruins snapped him up. Smith had been a 19-goal man the year before.

Suddenly, early in the season, King Clancy retired. On November 24, after 15 seasons in the big time, one of the greatest little gamecocks that hockey had ever seen called it a day. Clancy was 33 years old and, although he was through as a player, his value to hockey had barely been tapped.

Turk Broda was playing so well for the Leafs that George Hainsworth was sold to the Montreal Canadiens to replace the injured Wilf Cude.

Howie Morenz, delighted to be back in the Montreal Forum, was ablaze on the comeback trail. One night he caught his skate in a rut as he was being checked in the corner. A bone snapped in his leg and Morenz was through. On March 8, hockey fans everywhere were stunned to hear of the sudden death of Morenz while he was still in hospital. Concerned over the broken leg he'd suffered and fretful for the future, Morenz's heart had given way. Two days later 25,000 fans filed past his coffin at center ice in the Montreal Forum. He had scored 270 goals in his brilliant career, the same total as his linemate Aurel Joliat.

It was a year of injuries. Charlie Conacher and Toe Blake were out with broken wrists, Buzz Boll with a broken arm and Larry Aurie with a broken leg. Eddie Shore had a bad back and was ordered to take a long rest by the team doctor.

Russ Blinco made history by becoming the first National Leaguer to wear glasses during a game. It brought to mind players of an earlier era, notably Frank McGee of Ottawa, a great scoring star despite blurred vision in one eye, and Leo Reise, another "one-eyed" star performer.

It was one of the finest seasons for rookies. The Leafs had Apps, Drillon, Fowler, Hamilton and Davidson. Neil and Mac Colville joined the Rangers, along with Phil Watson and Babe Pratt. Pete Palangio and Hal Jackson were the bright youngsters in Blackhawk colors. Ray Getliffe scored 16 goals for Boston and a kid named Milt Schmidt began to look like a comer for the Bruins.

Major McLaughlin of Chicago caused a stir late in the season when the Blackhawks employed five American-born and trained players in an NHL game against the Boston Bruins. It had been the major's dream to discard his Canadian hockey pros some day and stock his team completely with American-born athletes. But Boston beat Chicago 6–2 and the newcomers were on the ice for all six goals. Art Ross of the Bruins was infuriated by McLaughlin's experiment and demanded that Chicago lose its franchise. "It's the most farcical thing ever attempted," he said. The experiment was short-lived. It was obvious to all who saw them play that the five new Blackhawks could not keep step in the NHL.

Sweeney Schriner of the Americans finished the season with a drive to win his second scoring title in a row, equaling Charlie Conacher's two straight championships.

The Calder Trophy for the best rookie of the year was awarded for the first time and Syl Apps of the Leafs, who finished a single point behind Schriner in scoring, was the recipient.

The Canadiens edged the Maroons for first place in the Canadian Division by a single point and Detroit won the American Division. Detroit and the Canadiens split four games in the opening round of the playoffs. The Wings, with strong men Marty Barry, Herbie Lewis and Syd Howe up front, squeezed the Canadiens out of the picture with a 1–0 overtime win in the deciding game.

The Rangers defeated Toronto with two straight victories and then disposed of the Maroons, who had eliminated the Shore-less Bruins, with a pair of shutouts by Davey Kerr.

In the finals between New York and Detroit, Lynn Patrick scored twice in the opener which was won by New York 5–1. Substitute goaltender Earl Robertson of the Red Wings, filling in for the injured Normie Smith, was brilliant in the second game which went to Detroit 4–2. In the third game, rookie Neil Colville, wearing heavy gear to protect a fractured jaw, scored the only goal as the Rangers won 1–0. Detroit turned the tables in the next game by the same 1–0 score when Marty Barry, the 31-year-old sharpshooter, scored from an almost impossible angle. Barry scored twice more in the fifth and deciding game and again Robertson was a standout. The Wings won the series and in his excitement Jack Adams fainted.

After the series, the Wings kidded the Leafs about their early-season selection of Broda over Robertson, but over the long haul Broda was to prove himself to be a tremendous bargain.

1937–38

Earl Robertson, the toast of Detroit in April 1937, when the Red Wings won the Stanley Cup from the Rangers, soon found that heroics in the spring meant nothing in the fall. Norm Smith, the Wings' regular goaltender, was healthy again and Robertson was sold to the New York Americans. He was so good there that the veteran netminder, Roy Worters, decided to call it a career.

The Chicago Blackhawks had gone for an incredible three seasons without changing coaches, until Clem Loughlin handed over the reins to "Bald Bill" Stewart, the National League umpire, turned hockey referee, turned coach. Baldy Cotton announced his retirement from pro hockey, and Hap Day, a Leafs' leader for 10 years, was sold to the New York Americans along with Jack Shill.

A rookie named Bryan Hextall was in the Rangers' lineup when the league opened its 20th season. Erwin "Murph" Chamberlain, a bashing 22-year-old rookie, signed with the Leafs and was later joined by the colorful Bingo Kampman on the Toronto roster. King Clancy was signed as coach of the Montreal Maroons, but his release from the Leafs was contingent upon his not being a playing coach.

A benefit game was played in Montreal in memory of Howie Morenz. About 8,000 fans attended and a large sum of money was turned over to his wife and their two children.

Conn Smythe liked the looks of Lester Patrick's son Lynn and offered Lester $20,000 for the youngster. Lester said he'd think it over.

After Christmas Syl Apps of the Leafs was named Canada's outstanding athlete in a nation-wide poll. It was the first time in history a hockey player had been so honored. A few days later King Clancy was fired by the Maroons. Then in January, Toronto supporters got a shock when the Leafs' team doctor ordered complete rest for the Big Bomber, Charlie Conacher. Conacher, in fact, was ordered to retire.

In March, Muzz Patrick was called up to the Rangers from Philadelphia. The Rangers were looking for additional strength to challenge the Bruins for first place in the American Division, but the new line in Boston, consisting of Bobby Bauer, Milt Schmidt and Woody Dumart, was going at a great clip and Boston won the division by seven points over the Rangers.

Toronto took the Canadian Division with 57 points, eight more than the Americans and the Canadiens who tied for second place.

The Leafs, with Broda in peak form, eliminated the Bruins in three straight playoff games, while the Americans were ousting the Rangers two games to one. Chicago upset the Canadiens by the same margin and followed up with a series victory over the Americans.

Suddenly the Hawks, winners of only 14 games in regular-season play, found themselves in the finals against Toronto. The Leafs were favored in every department when the series began. Mike Karakas tried to fit his broken toe into a skate prior to the first game, but the Chicago goalie couldn't secure a fit. Coach Bill Stewart had to find a last-minute substitute. He wanted Dave Kerr of the Rangers, but Conn Smythe said no.

After a lengthy search, Alfie Moore, a minor-league goaltender who lived in Toronto, was located and brought into the Chicago dressing room just before game time. Stewart made no attempt to hide from Moore that he was a last resort. But Moore went out and played the best game of his otherwise undistinguished career, giving up one goal as the Hawks won 3–1. On his way off the ice he thumbed his nose at the Leafs' bench.

Moore was taken to Chicago for the third game and awarded a suitably engraved watch in recognition of his services to the Hawks. He did not play again in the series as Calder, the league president, ruled him ineligible after the first game. Paul Goodman, the property of the Hawks, was pressed into service for the second game, again at the last minute. He could not duplicate Moore's feat, and the Leafs won.

By the third game Karakas was back in action and the Hawks won on a disputed goal by Doc Romnes with less than five minutes left to play. Cully Dahlstrom, Carl Voss, Jack Shill and Mush March connected for the Hawks in the fourth game. Gord Drillon was the only Leaf player to beat Karakas, and the lowly Hawks took the Stanley Cup. Bill Stewart, the former baseball umpire, had coached his team to a world championship in his first try as a coach.

The Chicago owners pounded Bill on the back and told him what a great job he had done. The next year they fired him.

1938–39

The Montreal Maroons, in financial difficulty and losers in their long battle with the Canadiens for Montreal fan support, were granted the right to suspend operations for one year before the 1938–39 season began. This came after the governors had rejected an application by Tommy Gorman to move the club to St. Louis.

The Canadiens made changes. They let Aurel Joliat, Pit Lepine and Marty Burke go and picked up six Maroons: Stew Evans, Cy Wentworth, Bob Gracie, Jimmy Ward, Herb Cain and Des Smith. The Blackhawks acquired Baldy Northcott, Earl Robinson and Russ Blinco. These sales in effect confirmed the reports that the Maroons would never operate again.

The blue lines were widened to 12 inches and the penalty-shot rule was changed to allow the player taking the shot to move right into the goal mouth if he desired. In former years, a player taking a penalty shot was forced to shoot from behind a line on the ice and remain behind the line after shooting—a most difficult feat.

Jack Adams of Detroit purchased Charlie Conacher for "a very high sum," believed to be $16,000. The money was to be paid in three installments and on condition that the 29-year-old Conacher, who had been so ill the year before, remained in good health.

In the Leafs' camp, Don Metz, the leading scorer in the Ontario Hockey Association the year before, was attracting a lot of attention. Sid Abel impressed the Detroit brass with his play and another Conacher, Roy, looked sharp for Boston. The Bruins sold Leroy Goldsworthy and Art Jackson to the Americans.

On the humorous side, Muzz Patrick and Art Coulter became the first bearded players on record. They let their whiskers grow in order to collect a $500 wager from Lester Patrick.

Bucko McDonald, benched in Detroit, was purchased by Toronto. Eddie Shore finally signed for the maximum league salary of $7,000, and Detroit purchased an aging 34-year-old Tiny Thompson from Boston for $15,000. Thompson was replaced in the Bruin nets by a 23-year-old rookie, Frankie Brimsek, called up from Providence. Brimsek showed he belonged by starting off with three straight shutouts. In the first month of play he was beaten only once in 10 starts and chalked up six shutouts in seven games.

A number of early-season injuries prompted the newspapers to start demanding "cleaner play."

Toe Blake of the Canadiens won the scoring crown with 47 points, while the sensational Brimsek won both the Calder and Vezina trophies. Boston won the league championship in a walk, outpointing the second-place Rangers 74 to 58.

Mel Hill, rejected by the Rangers a few months earlier, was the Bruins' overtime star in a thrilling series between Boston and New York. Hill, a 10-goal scorer during the regular season, earned the nickname "Sudden-Death" Hill when he scored overtime goals in three playoff games against his old mates. Hill's third game-winner came in the seventh game of the series after 48 minutes of overtime.

Toronto ousted the Americans with 2–0 and 4–0 shutouts, while Detroit was eliminating the Canadiens with two games to one. Toronto then took Detroit with an overtime victory in the third game of their best-of-three series.

The Leafs were no match in the finals for Sudden-Death Hill and the powerful Bruins. Boston took the series four games to one. The Bruins were delighted with the play of youngsters Milt Schmidt, Bobby Bauer and Woody Dumart who had become one of the most potent lines in hockey. They earned the name "Kraut Line" because of their Germanic background in Kitchener, Ontario. During World War II, the name would be changed to the "Kitchener Kids" due to anti-German sentiment.

V

HARD TIMES AT MID-CENTURY

The War Years and After, 1939–1950

As it did every other segment of North American life, World War II drastically affected the game of hockey. Many great or potentially great careers were at best interrupted or at worst terminated as players enlisted in the armed forces and others were frozen in essential war work and forbidden to cross the border to play. Experts have been arguing ever since as to whether some of the records set in that era would have been established had the caliber of the opposition been finer. Yet who could take away from the achievement of the great Rocket Richard in scoring 50 goals in 50 games in 1944–45 or his still-standing playoff scoring record of 12 goals in nine games set the year before.

No overtime became the rule as a wartime measure to ensure that trains would be caught, and the face of the game changed completely with the institution of the center red line, something that returning players in the postwar era would have to adapt to or pass from the scene.

Unquestionably the war hastened the demise of the staggering New York Americans. It also reduced the New York Rangers to such desperate straits that Lester Patrick must have bitterly regretted having been dissuaded from his original plan to suspend operations until the end of hostilities. But, with the blessings of the Canadian and American governments, which both declared hockey essential to national morale, and the cheers of an ever-increasing number of rabid fans, hockey carried on.

The game lost one of its greatest architects and greatest friends in 1943 with the death of Frank Calder, who had been the NHL president since the league's inception in 1917.

The Montreal Canadiens arrested their downward slide which had begun after their last Stanley Cup in 1931 and, under the tutelage of Dick Irvin, became the great powerhouse of the fifties and sixties.

Hap Day's Toronto Maple Leafs established Stanley Cup records along the way, too. They made the greatest comeback in Cup history and Hap Day achieved the distinction of coaching five Stanley Cup winners in eight seasons.

It was an era of great lines from the Kraut Line of Bauer, Schmidt and Dumart, the Production Line of Abel, Lindsay and Howe, and the powerful Punch Line of Blake, Lach and Richard. Goalie Bill Durnan set a record winning four Vezina trophies in a row (not to be smashed for a dozen years) and Turk Broda, the first Toronto goalie ever to win a Vezina, was fighting the well-publicized "battle of the bulge" at the end of the decade.

The first annual All-Star game was instituted in 1947 and a pension fund for hockey players was instituted in the same year. And everyone said the mayhem on the ice, which often involved fans as well as players, was getting worse than ever.

1939–40

When World War II was declared in September 1939, the National Hockey League was only weeks away from opening its 48-game schedule. Hostilities in Europe had little immediate effect upon the personnel and operating system of the pros. There were, however, ominous signs that brilliant careers would be disrupted, perhaps even snuffed out forever.

From November to March seven teams, the Chicago Blackhawks, the New York Americans, the Montreal Canadiens, the New York Rangers, the Toronto Maple Leafs, the Boston Bruins and the Detroit Red Wings, competed for the league championship and berths in the Stanley Cup playoffs.

Under the management of Art Ross and the coaching of Cooney Weiland, the well-knit Boston Bruins ended as champions with 67 points, three ahead of the second-place Rangers. Milt Schmidt, Woody Dumart and Bobby Bauer made NHL history by copping the first three positions in the league's individual scoring race. Schmidt was the head man with 52 points.

Other Bruins who contributed to the cause on a magnificent scale included goaltender Frank Brimsek, a man who dealt in shutouts and was one of the few American-born players in the NHL, defenseman Dit Clapper, who ultimately starred with the team for a total of 20 years, and Eddie Shore, a scarred warrior who gave limited aid until his trade on January 25, 1940, to the New York Americans. In the off season, Shore had become owner and manager of the Springfield Indians, which made it necessary he play only home and playoff games for the Boston team. Augmenting the scoring punch of the Kraut Line were Bill Cowley, Herb Cain and Roy Conacher.

The playoff system of that era included every team but one. As the team in the cellar, the Montreal Canadiens were eliminated from the playoffs while the six top clubs paired off in sequence. Thus, there were five series, ranging alphabetically from A to E.

In series A, the mighty Bruins were polished off in six games by the second-place Rangers who received an automatic bye into the finals. Meanwhile, Toronto and Detroit disposed of their respective first-round opponents, the Blackhawks and the Americans, and then met in series D, a somewhat bloody encounter which proved that not all wars are fought in foxholes.

This was a best-of-three game series which Toronto won handily through the superb goaltending of Turk Broda, the strong defensive work of Bingo Kampman, Red Horner and Reg Hamilton, plus the picturesque rushes of a blue-line rookie named Wally Stanowski, who was so colorful he even had admirers in rival rinks.

The cakewalk Toronto experienced in the series with Detroit was not repeated against Lester Patrick's Rangers. New York's lineup oozed class, from netminder Dave Kerr to the defense of captain Art Coulter, Muzz Patrick, Ott Heller and big Babe Pratt. When Ranger goals were needed they frequently came from the sticks of Neil and Mac Colville, their linemate Alex Shibicky or from the unit of Phil Watson, Bryan Hextall and Lynn Patrick. If they had an off night there were always Clint Smith, Wilf Hiller and Kilby MacDonald, a 28-year-old who won the Calder Trophy that spring. The Leafs bowed out in six games, three of which went into overtime. It was to be New York's last Stanley Cup victory.

The season of 1939–40, the first with guns booming in Europe, was to be the most tranquil of the war years in the NHL.

1940–41

On July 19, 1940, the first step in a movement to have pro-hockey players volunteer for military training was taken by Conn Smythe. Letters were mailed to all members of the Maple Leafs team urging them to enlist immediately. Meantime, players in other teams were joining the units of their choice.

This was the summer that Dick Irvin resigned as Toronto's coach to assume the same duties in Montreal, while Hap Day became his successor with the Leafs. Irvin announced he was aiming for a fourth-place finish. Ebbie Goodfellow was named the playing coach of the Detroit Red Wings, leaving manager Jack Adams free to attend to Detroit's widespread farm system.

Toronto optioned Murph Chamberlain to the Canadiens in May for $7,500 and he flourished with his new club. In late October the Canadiens dickered with the CAHA for permission to sign defenseman Ken Reardon and center Johnny Quilty, both aged 19.

The Canadiens had a large training camp contingent which included 30 amateurs, among them Elmer Lach, Joe Benoit and Bill Durnan. The first two were signed, but Durnan couldn't beat out goalie Bert Gardiner. Young Johnny Quilty had no difficulty making the team but Reardon failed, playing only two games.

The Canadiens missed Irvin's goal of fourth place by 12 points, but were only one point behind fifth-place Chicago who had 39. Quilty became the youngest winner of the Calder Trophy, beating out Johnny Mowers, the rookie goalie for Detroit. When asked the pre-season question of who would be the league's top rookie, Irvin had placed Quilty's name in a sealed envelope.

The Boston Bruins, league champions of 1940–41, were dominant throughout the season, although they ended only five points ahead of Toronto. With 62 points, Bill Cowley was an easy scoring champion. His nearest rivals, Bryan Hextall, Gordie Drillon, Syl Apps, Lynn Patrick and Syd Howe, were all grouped together with 44 points each.

Chicago counted heavily on rookie Johnny Mariucci, a first-string end on the University of Minnesota football team who had played defense on the college hockey team. Also in camp were the Bentley brothers, Doug and Max, who had played portions of the preceding season with the Hawks, plus 19-year-old Bill Mosienko.

The Bruins enjoyed considerable success in 1940–41 as they swept to the regular-season title. They set a pair of records, playing 15 games on the road without a loss over one stretch and then playing 23 games without a loss during another.

Turk Broda of the Leafs captured the Vezina Trophy on the final night of the season. It marked the first time a Toronto goaltender had won the award.

Toronto met Boston in series A of the Stanley Cup semi-finals, which went seven games, one of them an overtime contest. Toronto was injury-riddled from the onset of the playoffs, but showed surprising strength. Before the series ended in Boston's favor, Bobby Bauer had sustained a skate wound on his instep and Bill Cowley had twice damaged a knee ligament.

An unheralded hero of the final game was Mel Hill, a utility forward who usually served as a right-winger. Hill had made a mid-season request for permission to wear glasses on the ice, because he couldn't see the passes his Bruin mates were sending his way. With his glasses his sight was good enough that night to put the puck in a tiny area uncovered by Broda, thus sending the Bruins into the Cup finals.

And when they took on Detroit, the Bruins swept to the Cup in four straight games.

1941–42

The NHL, which came into being during World War I, was to celebrate its 25th anniversary on November 22, 1941, under the cloud of a second conflict which greatly changed the league's composition.

In joining the armed forces for the second time in his life Conn Smythe, then 47, gave up all rights as general manager of the Leafs and Maple Leaf Gardens. E. W. Bickle became the Gardens' vice-president and a few weeks later Frank Selke assumed the job of general manager.

When Red Dutton assembled his Americans for what turned out to be their last training camp, Busher Jackson spurned Dutton's contract terms. Jackson bacame one of the longest holdouts on record. It ended on January 5, when he was sold to Boston. At the end of the season the Americans would lose Charlie Conacher, who retired.

Art Ross and Lester Patrick engaged in a heated pre-season dispute over the rights to Angus "Scotty" Cameron, a tall center who had played as an amateur with the New York Rovers. On September 14, Ross walked out on a governors' meeting. A month later he resigned as a league governor. His colleagues shed no tears when they accepted his resignation. Calder had turned down Ross' official protest and awarded Cameron to the Rangers.

This was a season that produced many goaltending changes. Dave Kerr, New York's Vezina winner of 1939–40, retired before the start of the season at the age of 31. The Rangers replaced him with Winnipeg-born Jim "Sugar Jim" Henry. The Canadiens started out the campaign with Bert Gardiner in goal, but on December 6 Paul Bibeault of the Washington Lions was elevated to Montreal. Bibeault had played in one game against the Leafs the previous season and that was the only contest the Canadiens had won from Toronto. Sam LoPresti was Chicago's netminder, while Mowers, Brimsek and Broda worked for Detroit, Boston and Toronto respectively.

The league introduced two types of penalty shots. A minor penalty shot was one taken from a line 28 feet out from the goal. A major shot, awarded when a player was tripped from behind on a breakaway, allowed the shooter to skate right in on goal.

The New York Rangers were surprise first-place finishers. Ranger star Bryan Hextall won the scoring race with 56 points, two more than teammate Lynn Patrick.

Second-place Toronto met New York in series A of the playoffs, a thriller which was ultimately won by the Leafs in six games. Once Toronto had registered their third win in four games, Frank Boucher observed, "They used two goaltenders against us and they were too much." He was referring to the remarkable defensive display given by Bucko McDonald. The Red Wings, meanwhile, ousted the Canadiens and then the Bruins, who had knocked out Chicago.

Before the Leafs took on fifth-place Detroit in the Cup finals, an unidentified Toronto representative remarked, "It's a shame that two great clubs like the Rangers and the Leafs should be beating their brains out in this semi-final round in order to go up against Boston or Detroit, who don't belong in the same category."

The Wings, with a lineup that appeared mediocre compared to Toronto, swamped the Leafs in the first three games by scores of 3–2, 4–2 and 5–2. It was public knowledge that before the fourth game Hap Day would make drastic changes, but few were prepared for the benching of Drillon and McDonald, who had played so well against the Rangers. McDonald's successor was rookie Bob Goldham while Don Metz took Drillon's berth. Metz scored three goals that night and Toronto won 4–3.

Following that win with 9–3 and 3–0 victories, the Leafs paved the way for a sensational seventh game which saw the Wings panic and make player changes. On the night of April 18, 1942, Toronto won the Cup from the courageous fifth-place club. Described as the wildest Stanley Cup series on record, the last game was played in Toronto before 16,218 fans, the largest Canadian gathering yet for a hockey game. Veteran Sweeney Schriner led the Leafs to the Cup with two goals in a 3–1 win. This series marked a record for a comeback in Stanley Cup competition—one that has never been duplicated.

1942–43

By the early weeks of this new season, the NHL had lost 90 of its players to the armed forces, regular or reserve, but with the blessing of the Canadian and United States governments, which decreed the game essential to national morale, professional hockey carried on. This was to be a season which would produce controversy, bitter feelings, tragedy and, occasionally, an all-for-one unity.

In October, Red Dutton's New York Americans were asked to leave the NHL, partly because their lease was to expire with Madison Square Garden and also because the team, always weak, would be weaker still with so many players in the armed forces.

In November, league president Frank Calder announced the abolition of overtime in scheduled games so that teams would be sure to catch their trains without delay.

Art Ross, who managed the Boston Bruins, fought for the squads to be cut to 13 players. The final decision was to pare down to 14 players including the goaltender. No team needed to have more than 12 men in uniform before a game.

The season of 1942–43 was the start of an upsurge for the Montreal Canadiens that was to make them one of the flashiest and most powerful teams in the NHL.

The NHL race was a continual nip-and-tuck battle with the playoff berths undecided until the final game of the schedule. The exciting race bore out the pre-season prediction of Toronto writer Ted Reeve who had written: "In some respects this will be one of the most entertaining seasons in NHL history. Things couldn't be more uncertain if they were going through the schedule on roller skates."

Detroit not only won the league title but the Stanley Cup as well. Most of their strength was defensive, since only Syd Howe was among the top dozen scorers. Johnny Mowers became the Vezina Trophy winner with only 124 goals against him.

Toronto, with Hap Day at the helm, pulled themselves together from a wobbly start which saw Syl Apps temporarily demoralized without his old partner Gord Drillon, who had been traded to Montreal. But things got worse for Toronto when Apps sailed into a goal post in Maple Leaf Gardens one night in January and fractured his right leg. He was out for the balance of the season.

Continuing to hold the Leafs together were Turk Broda and a defense of Reg Hamilton, Babe Pratt and Bucko McDonald. Forwards Carr, Schriner, Taylor, Davidson, Kennedy, Poile and Stewart were later joined by youngsters Jackie McLean and Jackie Hamilton. Gaye Stewart was an easy winner of the Calder Trophy with 21 of the 27 voting sportswriters giving him first-place votes; Montreal's Glen Harmon ranked second.

Harmon, who was frozen in his job as a full-time war-industry worker, pulled the Canadiens' defense together, sent the team on a winning streak and was credited with helping them make the playoffs.

In that season Irvin introduced a trio he called the "Punch Line," which was comprised of Toe Blake, Elmer Lach and Joe Benoit, a right-winger from Trail, B.C. He also introduced a newcomer, Maurice Richard, who played in only 16 games before being injured. (In 1967 Frank Selke, Jr., revealed that Montreal had tried to trade Maurice Richard to New York during his rookie year in return for Phil Watson, but the deal fell through.)

The Bentley brothers, Max and Doug, dominated the league scoring with Doug winning the championship. On January 26, the Hawks trounced the floundering Rangers 10–1 with the Bentleys and Bill Thoms collecting 18 points as a unit, 13 of them going to the brothers. Max tied the NHL record of seven points in one game when he got four goals and three assists. The record was tied again on November 5, when the Red Wings defeated the Rangers 12–5, with Carl Liscombe getting seven points.

For Bill Cowley, who had been the scoring champion and winner of the Hart Trophy in 1940–41, the season of 1942–43 was almost as rewarding. While he failed to topple his own 1940–41 record of 45 assists, he was able to duplicate it.

In late January, Frank Calder was heading a meeting of NHL governors in Toronto when Hap Day noticed that Calder was in pain. As two or three governors moved to his assistance, he assured them he was all right. Then he rose to his feet and exclaimed, "My God, there is something wrong." In a short time it was announced he had suffered a heart attack.

Red Dutton, en route to Montreal at the time, was appointed as temporary president with the blessing of Art Ross, who suggested that Lester Patrick and Ed Bickle act as his advisers. So Dutton became head man of the league which he had been kicked out of only months earlier. It is doubtful that he accepted the post for any reason other than his long-standing and deep friendship with Calder. When Dutton had been manager of the Americans, Calder had been president of the club as well as president of the league.

A far-sighted man, Calder had confided to his associates years before that he was grooming Clarence Campbell to succeed him as NHL president, a job then paying $12,000 per year. At the time Calder was stricken, however, Campbell was overseas. Less than two weeks after the heart attack, Calder died.

Detroit eliminated Toronto four games to two in one semi-final series, while the Boston Bruins ousted the Montreal Canadiens four games to one. Then the Red Wings, paced by the scoring of Carl Liscombe and Sid Abel, took the Boston Bruins four straight in the finals. Johnny Mowers shut out the Bruins in the last two games.

1943–44

By now the war had ravaged the NHL teams until some of them were mere ghosts of what they had once been. Teams jockeyed for players and wangled deals to get armed-forces rejects and teenagers. The Rangers were so hard hit that in October they made it known that they would like to fold for the duration of the war. But Lester Patrick, against his better judgment, was persuaded to ice a team.

Goaltending was the major problem for the Canadiens. Regular netminder Paul Bibeault had joined the army the preceding summer. They had called up Bert Gardiner, who had been on loan to Chicago, and also had in camp Bill Durnan of the Quebec Hockey League's senior Montreal Royals and 17-year-old Gerry McNeil of the junior Quebec Aces. The Canadiens started training later than any of their rivals, completing the task in 10 days. They held practice drills at night to enable war workers on the roster to take part.

Despite their loss of personnel, the Leafs had gone to camp with a promising assortment of players. Veteran Bob Davidson had been appointed captain in Syl Apps' absence and he headed a contingent of pros which included All-Star right-winger Lorne Carr, Bucko McDonald, Ted Kennedy, Don Webster, Jack Ingoldsby, Jackie McLean and Jackie Hamilton. Goalie Turk Broda was about to enter the navy or the army. Oddly enough, the chief contender as his replacement was 35-year-old Benny Grant, who had first attempted to become Toronto's goalie 15 years earlier in 1928.

Because of the scarcity of players, the NHL clubs developed their own ruthless methods of gaining recruits. Boston squabbled with Montreal over the services of netminder Bert Gardiner, with Art Ross winning the battle. Meantime, Phil Watson of the Rangers was frozen in an essential war job in Montreal and was refused permission to play hockey in New York. Several teams sparred for Watson's services, but the dickering ended when the Canadiens offered Dutch Hiller and Charlie Sands to the Rangers in a type of lend-lease exchange.

The fact that New York won only six games out of the entire 50-game schedule and had a whopping 310 goals scored on their porous defense, indicated Patrick's wisdom in wishing to temporarily fold. When the Rangers opened the season they had only five holdovers from their team of the preceding season. For the third consecutive year they introduced a new goalie, this time rookie Ken McAuley. Some of Patrick's desperation was showing when coach Boucher sent out a 145-pound center, rookie Don Raleigh, who was only 17 years old and far out of his depth against the more experienced Toronto players. An 8–3 lacing from the Red Wings one night later prompted their coach, 42-year-old Frank Boucher, to announce his comeback plans.

On November 7, the Rangers met the Blackhawks in New York to open their season before their home fans. A sell-out crowd, many of whom had not seen Boucher play before his retirement years earlier, gave him a fine ovation. He was back in his old center-ice position with a couple of wingers who were babies when he had begun his pro career. He set up one goal and scored another, but Chicago won 4–3. Boucher's return lasted for 15 games and produced four goals and 10 assists.

In 1943–44, the center red line was introduced to hockey, along with a new face-off rule. Both were received with mixed feelings, perhaps because the unpopular Art Ross had had a hand in the changes. Frank Selke was quoted as saying, "Art Ross writes the rules and then lies awake nights figuring ways to circumvent them. It is an old Russian custom and I, for one, am sick of it. The NHL is following Ross like sheep jumping through a gate. The red line has turned hockey into a farce." Yet, despite the criticism, more people paid to watch the games than in any other comparable period in NHL history.

An NHL record was toppled on January 8, 1944. Babe Pratt came up with six assists as the Leafs whipped the Bruins 12–3. Then, on February 3, 1944, Syd Howe, a veteran Red Wing, scored six goals as Detroit humiliated New York 12–2 in the Olympia. Howe's feat smashed a record of five goals set in 1917 by Harry Hyland of the Montreal Wanderers and equaled eight times since.

A quiet surprise was the showing of the Montreal Canadiens, who went 14 games before being defeated in November by the Bruins. Bill Durnan, 29 and untried, got the season's first shutout, allowing only one goal in weekend games against Detroit. He was not only a standout goalie during this season, but compared with the pre-war best.

Durnan's job was made easier by the defensive play of Leo Lamoureaux, Butch Bouchard, Glen Harmon and Mike McMahon. Up front, Blake, Lach, Richard, Fillion, Getliffe, Chamberlain, O'Connor, Majeau and Heffernan kept up enough pressure on the opposition to lead the team to the NHL title with 83 points and a total of 234 goals.

The Canadiens won the league title for the first time since 1931, and when the schedule ended on March 19, Montreal, Detroit, Toronto and Chicago were in the playoffs. Herb Cain of Boston was the scoring champion and Bill Durnan won the Vezina Trophy. Durnan lost the Calder Trophy to Gus Bodnar who, with 62 points, set a record for points by a rookie and broke another record by scoring the fastest goal by a rookie (after 15 seconds of play in his first game).

In the first game of the Leaf–Canadien series the weakest Leaf contingent in years won 3–1, handing Montreal their first home-ice loss all season. Paul Bibeault, picked up in mid-season by Toronto, was sensational as the Canadiens outshot the Leafs 61 to 23. The second game, played March 23, was a 5–1 victory for Montreal, with Maurice Richard getting all five goals and all of the post-game "three stars." The Canadiens won the next two games in Toronto and, when the series went back to Montreal for what turned out to be the final game, they swamped the Leafs 11–0. The rout was a record for modern Stanley Cup play.

Chicago offered almost no opposition to the Canadiens, who swept to the Stanley Cup in four straight games. They had suffered only five defeats in the entire season. Richard established an all-time scoring record in Stanley Cup play with 12 goals in nine games.

1944–45

Early in the season, Red Dutton, still acting as NHL president, offered to resign, but was dissuaded by the league governors. A number of candidates had been nominated for the job, which now paid $15,000 instead of the $12,000 earned by the late Frank Calder.

Except for the absence of Mike McMahon, Gerry Heffernan and Phil Watson, who had gone back to the Rangers, the lineup of the Canadiens was relatively unchanged from the previous season. Paul Bibeault, still legally the Canadiens' property, was recalled from Toronto. The Leafs dickered with Montreal over Bibeault's services, but their offer to buy was declined. They ended up using rookie Frank McCool.

The Detroit Red Wings were introducing three newcomers: Ted Lindsay, Jud McAtee and Steve Wochy. Connie Dion, the smallest goalie since Roy Worters, started out the season, but was replaced by Normie Smith. In mid-December 17-year-old rookie Harry Lumley was promoted from Indianapolis.

The New York Rangers had more fire in their 1944–45 play, but not much more success. They went the entire campaign without the aid of Bryan Hextall. The Saskatchewan War Mobilization Committee refused to allow him to leave Canada because he was claiming exemption as a farmer. This ruling also affected Doug Bentley and George Allen.

In late December Boston had won only eight games and Art Ross, Sr., termed his Bruins as, "The worst team I ever saw."

Paul Thompson's Blackhawks ended the season just one point ahead of the last-place Rangers. With Mike Karakas in goal and an assortment of veteran and fringe players they had little success.

Late in January the Gardens welcomed Conn Smythe back to his old job. He had been seriously wounded overseas and was now out of the army. A week later Smythe visited Montreal and commented on Maurice Richard: "He looks like Morenz from the blue line in." On December 28, the Rocket collected five goals and three assists to set a new record of eight points when the Canadiens beat Detroit 9–1 in Montreal. Richard went on to set another remarkable scoring record by becoming the first player to score 50 goals in one season. This feat was accomplished in a 50-game schedule. His linemate Elmer Lach became the league scoring champion that year with 80 points—26 goals and 54 assists.

On December 17, Major Frederic McLaughlin, former president of the Blackhawks and the man who gave them their name, died at the age of 67. Ownership of the team went to his 16-year-old son William.

When the schedule ended on March 19, the Canadiens were champions with 80 points, far ahead of Detroit and Toronto. Bill Durnan was an easy winner of the Vezina Trophy. Rookie Frank McCool, who starred for the Leafs, was his nearest rival. Montreal's Punch Line, consisting of Richard, Lach and Blake, duplicated the feat of the Kraut Line, finishing one, two and three in scoring.

The third-place Leafs seemed no match for the Canadiens in the semi-finals, but in the first game Ted Kennedy golfed a shot that resulted in a 1–0 Leafs win. Toronto won the second game 3–2. The Canadiens then took a 4–1 decision, lost the fourth game 4–3, but came back with a decisive 10–3 victory in the fifth on Forum ice led by Richard's three goals. The spine-tingling sixth game went to the Leafs by a 3–2 score.

"Those last two minutes seemed like a lifetime," sighed Hap Day. In the meantime, the Bruins surprised Art Ross by forcing the Red Wings to seven games before being eliminated in the semi-final round.

During the schedule, the Wings had beaten the Leafs in eight out of 10 games. This Detroit aggregation, the highest scoring group in team history, was shocked when they lost the Stanley Cup in five games while suffering three consecutive shutouts. Toronto won the first game 1–0 on Sweeney Schriner's goal. The second game, a 2–0 victory, was highlighted by McCool's superlative goaltending. Game three, won 1–0 on Bodnar's goal, was McCool's third shutout and gave him an all-time Stanley Cup netminding record.

1945–46

With players returning to the NHL at a rapid rate, the 1945–46 season was one of the most interesting campaigns since the war had weakened the caliber of play. The players filtered back all through the season. Syl Apps and the Kraut Line got back in the fall while Frank Brimsek was still aboard a U.S. ship in Tokyo Bay. Bob Carse, originally missing in action, then a prisoner of war, took time off to recover from his experiences.

With an abundance of goalies in the NHL, where previously there had been a scarcity, Lester Patrick's announcement that he was considering using two netminders drew interest and mild amusement. Patrick had at least three goalies at his disposal, while the Leafs had four and the Canadiens owned at least nine. By early November, Frank Boucher was rotating Charlie Rayner and Sugar Jim Henry. Three seasons earlier he had predicted a hockey system that would see the substitution of goalies during a game, much in the manner of changing forwards or defensemen. Boucher termed the 1945–46 brand of hockey as "Americanized," meaning it was played under the same hectic, speedy conditions which Americans were said to live.

Despite a solid basic team, for the first time in 16 years the Leafs failed to get into the Stanley Cup playoffs. Broda, McCool and Gordie Bell each had a turn in goal and Conn Smythe fingered a weak defense as the chief cause of failure. But he foresaw no improvement before 1948. "At the moment the only Leafs in the minors who impress me are Jim Thomson, Gus Mortson and Joe Klukay," he commented.

Frank McCool returned to his Calgary home by November 1 after a salary conflict. He reportedly asked for $5,000 and was offered $500 less. The Toronto management indicated he had left because of a bad case of ulcers. Terms were reached before the season ended, but it was McCool's last campaign in the NHL.

The news that rocked the NHL in 1945–46 was the expulsion of Toronto's Babe Pratt on January 29 for wagering on games. There was no evidence that Pratt had bet against his own team, but he had violated the rules against gambling. He also admitted to Dutton that an unsuccessful attempt had been made to bribe him to throw a game. Pratt, who was then 30, was reinstated on February 14, after a 16-game suspension, when the league governors responded to Dutton's appeal for leniency.

In February 1945, Lester Patrick, 62, retired as manager of the Rangers and Frank Boucher, his star pupil, succeeded him. Even with an improved roster, the Rangers finished last. Their highest point getter was Ab Demarco, who finished seventh in the scoring race. Bryan Hextall had been forced to miss the entire season due to a liver complaint and defenseman Muzz Patrick, hampered by a knee injury, played only 24 games then retired.

The Canadiens finished on top of the regular schedule with 61 points. With Max Bentley winning the scoring championship (nine points ahead of the Leafs' Gaye Stewart whose 37 goals was tops in the league), the Blackhawks squeezed into third place—three points behind Boston and three ahead of Detroit. The semi-final round of the playoffs between Montreal and Chicago was almost uneventful with the Canadiens winning in four straight games. Series B between Boston and Detroit went five games before the Bruins won.

The finals, which went five games, three of them into overtime, were lively and hard fought. Boston, with Brimsek back in goal and a lineup that included Johnny Crawford, Bep Guidolin, Don Gallinger, Terry Reardon, Pat Egan and Herb Cain, offered stiff resistance. The first game was won by the Canadiens 4–3 on a spectacular goal by Richard in overtime.

Game number two was a repeat of the first, except that Montreal's Jimmy Peters got the overtime winner and the score was 3–2. The Bruins blew a fine chance to draw the series closer in the third game when they played a badly crippled Canadiens club. Bouchard left the game with a knee injury after three minutes of play, Toe Blake was sidelined with a recurring back injury early in the third period, Harmon played with a bad wrist and Chamberlain was handicapped with injured ribs. But the Canadiens still won 4–3.

Boston finally won an overtime contest when, after each side had missed at least five wide-open chances, Terry Reardon scored. But Montreal completely overpowered Boston in the fifth and final game, winning 6–3. Toe Blake scored the winner and Elmer Lach spearheaded the attacks by the Punch Line.

1946–47

The accent was on youth in 1946–47, with most teams trying to blend their veterans with newcomers.

Detroit disposed of Mud Bruneteau, Syd Howe, Carl Liscombe and Joe Carveth and rookie Gordie Howe was inserted into the Detroit lineup.

The Leafs made some drastic changes. Babe Pratt, their highest-paid player in 1944–45, was sent to Boston. Gus Mortson and Jim Thomson grabbed blue-line jobs. This was also the first NHL season for Bill Barilko, Howie Meeker and Vic Lynn.

Chicago's youth movement provided quantity, but not results. Consequently, they ended in the cellar. They promoted Bill Gadsby, Frank Ashworth and Ralph Nattrass. Emile Francis, 19, was signed with 19 games remaining in the schedule.

Even Dick Irvin made changes in his Cup-holding Canadiens, adding Roger Leger, Leo Gravelle and George Allen. Irvin was reunited with Frank Selke who, at 53, assumed the Montreal managerial post on July 10, 1946, a week after the resignation of Tommy Gorman.

The Bruins were inclined to spurn youth for experience. They made Bobby Bauer captain after he reversed his autumn decision to retire and got top efforts from Crawford, Henderson, Guidolin, Egan, Brimsek and the Kraut Line. Herb Cain, the NHL's top scorer in 1943–44, went to the minors.

In New York, Frank Boucher welcomed back Bryan Hextall, who had been absent all the preceding season. New York had a youthful unit in Rene Trudell, Church Russell and Cal Gardner, and Boucher was about to get his first full season from defenseman Hal Laycoe.

On September 4, 1946, Clarence Campbell, 41, succeeded Red Dutton as NHL president. A former referee, Campbell had just returned from overseas where he had risen to the rank of lieutenant colonel in the Canadian Army.

In 1946–47 plans were laid for the annual All-Star game, the first of which was to be played in the fall of 1947. Considerable discussion began among individual clubs regarding plans to establish a pension fund for NHL players, which became effective on October 1, 1947.

Rules regarding the Calder Trophy for the league's outstanding newcomer were changed to recognize players who participated in 20 games or less in the previous season. Previously, men who had participated in three or more games were ineligible.

Overshadowed by the point-for-point stretch drive of Max Bentley and Maurice Richard, with the Chicago forward winning out by a single point, was the surprising and steady climb of Detroit's Billy Taylor. He finished third in the scoring race only eight points behind Richard. On March 16, 1947, Taylor ran wild in a 10–6 win over Chicago and collected seven assists, which was logged as a modern record for the most assists in one game.

Veteran Bill Cowley broke an all-time NHL scoring record on February 12, when he gathered a goal and an assist to raise his scoring total to 574 points, two above the former mark held by Syd Howe, who had retired. The game in which Cowley set his record was preceded by a colorful ceremony honoring Dit Clapper, coach of the Bruins, who had officially retired after a 20-year NHL playing career. At the end of the season Cowley also retired.

Even the lowly Blackhawks managed to set a record for attendance as 20,004 thronged into the Chicago Stadium on February 23 to see them lose to Boston.

This was a venomous season in the NHL as far as brawls and verbal battles were concerned. A bitter feud developed between the Leafs and the Canadiens, and it worsened when Elmer Lach collided with Don Metz in a game in Montreal on February 7. Lach was carried from the ice with a fractured skull. Metz received a minor penalty on the play but Lach was finished for the season. There was a wild riot in New York on March 16 when the Canadiens beat the Rangers 4–3. The ice was a mass of wrangling players, many of whom hit each other on the head with their sticks.

Second-place Toronto met fourth-place Detroit in series B of the semi-finals and the Leafs won the first game 3–2 on Howie Meeker's overtime goal. The Wings came back to even the series by crushing the Leafs 9–1. The third game, won by Toronto, exploded into a riot when an argument between Howe and Mortson led to a battle that overflowed into the aisles. The Leafs took two more games to knock the Wings out of the playoffs.

It took the Canadiens six games, two of them overtime encounters, to dispose of Boston. Then came the battle between Toronto and Montreal. The Canadiens breezed to an easy 6–0 victory in the opening game, but lost 4–0 in the second, which saw Richard banished with a 20-minute match-misconduct penalty for a head injury he inflicted on Ezinicki. Earlier in the game the Rocket had already been assessed a major penalty for felling Vic Lynn. The next day Clarence Campbell announced that Richard had been suspended for one game and fined $250, a fine which included the automatic $100 assessment which goes with a match penalty. Hurt in the first period when he tore his knee ligaments in a collision with Gus Mortson, the Rocket said, "I simply lost my temper."

Despite the 4–2 score for Toronto, the third game was a close battle. The Leafs drew a 3–0 lead, but the Canadiens scored twice in a third-period comeback. Kennedy's goal, with less than a minute remaining, killed their drive.

A thrilling overtime goal by Apps won the fifth game for Toronto, 3–2. Ted Kennedy's winning goal in a 2–1 victory brought the Stanley Cup to Toronto on April 19. The win was termed a modern hockey miracle, because the Leafs were the youngest Cup winners in NHL history.

1947–48

In October 1947, the first annual All-Star game, aimed at building up the players' pension fund, was played in Toronto between the Cup-holding Leafs and an aggregation of All-Stars coached by Dick Irvin. The game was won by the All-Stars 4–3, but was marred when Bill Mosienko of Chicago fractured his left ankle after being body checked by Jim Thomson. All-Star teams had been selected since 1931, and one All-Star game had been played in 1934 for the benefit of Ace Bailey, but 1947 was the start of a new tradition.

Trades were one of the main topics of the 1947–48 season, with a surprise deal being an off-season swap between the Canadiens and the Rangers. Montreal gave up Buddy O'Connor and Frank Eddolls for Hal Laycoe, Joe Bell and George Robertson. The Red Wings traded Billy Taylor to Boston for Bep Guidolin. Taylor had given the Red Wings excellent service in 1946–47, but he changed uniforms just one day before the new schedule opened.

Conn Smythe attempted to swing a deal in late October with Bill Tobin. On November 3, Chicago accepted Gus Bodnar, Ernie Dickens, Gaye Stewart, Bud Poile and Bob Goldham for Max Bentley, the league's scoring champion, and Cy Thomas. Clarence Campbell said, "It's the biggest trade in the NHL for a long, long time and only goes to emphasize the worth of such a player as Bentley."

On December 31, 1947, Charlie Conacher, who had been coaching the junior Oshawa Generals, took over the coaching duties of the last-place Blackhawks as a replacement for Johnny Gottselig, who then became manager. Conacher's pro-coaching debut on New Year's Eve was ruined by a 4–0 defeat in Detroit where the Wings were also being guided by a rookie mentor, Tommy Ivan.

It was evident throughout the season that Montreal and Chicago stood a good chance of missing the playoffs. Chicago's position wasn't surprising since they were the cellar team of 1946–47, but the Canadiens had been the regular-season champions of the past year. The Canadiens were struggling to get out of fifth place on January 11, when Toe Blake, their 35-year-old captain who had played superbly all season, suffered a double fracture of the right ankle when checked by New York's Bill Juzda. The injury ended his playing career.

Because he was coaching a loser, Dick Irvin was lampooned by home fans, one of whom threatened to burn down the Forum if Irvin was on the bench for the next

Saturday home game. To show they were behind their leader, the Canadien players wore bright-red firemen hats in a pre-game warm-up in Toronto. But the "firemen" couldn't catch fire and Montreal ended four points behind New York.

On February 24, Clarence Campbell began an intensive investigation into rumors that at least two NHL players had gambled on games in which they had played. Most of the probe took place in Detroit, because the police in that city were said to have wiretapped the conversations of a big-time gambler named James Tamer. Thirteen days later Campbell expelled Billy Taylor of the Rangers and Don Gallinger of the Bruins on charges of being associated with gamblers. Campbell emphasized that no other NHL players were involved and that no fix of a game was attempted by any player. The expulsion and suspension of Taylor and Gallinger for life were the most severe penalties ever handed out.

By mid-season there had been 400 more minutes of penalties than over the same period in the previous campaign. Toronto's Bill Ezinicki was branded as the league villain after a body check he gave Edgar Laprade of New York.

Syl Apps, who had retired in the spring of 1947, was back in a Leafs uniform at the start of the new season after yielding to the persuasion of the management. He retired permanently in April 1948.

Coach Frank Boucher had been touting Don Raleigh as the likely rookie winner when the 21-year-old newcomer broke an all-time record for speedy assists by picking up three assists in only one minute and 21 seconds against the Canadiens. But it was Detroit's Jim McFadden who won the Calder Trophy.

The duel for the league scoring championship between Elmer Lach and his former teammate Buddy O'Connor, both centers, had a thrilling finale when Lach nosed out O'Connor by one point. It was a great comeback for Lach after missing half of the past season due to a fractured skull.

It took five games for the Leafs to eliminate Boston in their semi-final series. The highlight was a melee late in the third game, won by Toronto 5–1, which gave the Leafs a 3–0 lead in the round. Boston fans swarmed onto the ice attacking Leafs players. Bill Ezinicki and Grant Warwick started the rough play, but the main bout was between Harry Watson and Murray Henderson, who retired to the dressing room with a broken nose. In comparison, the Ranger–Red Wing series was played quietly and cleanly, with Detroit winning in six games.

Toronto skated away with the Stanley Cup in four straight games. The Leafs held Detroit's vaunted Production Line to a single goal in the finals.

1948–49

With Syl Apps definitely in retirement, the Maple Leafs made an off-season trade to get a replacement. They had hoped to get Ed Sandford from the Bruins, but Art Ross wouldn't deal so the Leafs sent Stanowski to the Rangers for Cal Gardner.

Having missed a playoff berth in the spring of 1948, Frank Selke began a swift rebuilding job on the Canadiens. In August there was pessimism when it was learned that a back injury might end Ken Reardon's career. Doug Harvey, a rookie from the Montreal senior Royals, was signed as defensive insurance, but Reardon was able to play for two more seasons.

The Ranger club suffered a severe jolt in October when four of its players—high scoring Buddy O'Connor, Frank Eddolls, Edgar Laprade and Bill Moe—were involved in a car accident near Rouse's Point, New York. All four were unconscious when admitted to hospital. The player most severely injured was O'Connor, who sustained broken ribs. The Rangers sagged throughout the season, largely because of these and other injuries, and ended in the league cellar. In December, desperate for help, Frank Boucher sent Elwyn Morris and Eddie Kullman, plus a large amount of cash, to Providence for rookie defenseman Allan Stanley. A few days later Boucher, who had served as New York's coach, relinquished his duties and brought in Lynn Patrick as his replacement. Patrick, at 36, became the NHL's youngest coach. Boucher, 47, continued with New York and managed the Ranger farm system, which included eight teams.

The Bruins, on their way to a second-place finish, were flying by late November. Much credit was given to Milt Schmidt, Ed Sandford, Grant Warwick, Frank Brimsek and the most improved third line in hockey. The Bruins were getting mileage from Ed Kryzanowski, Paul Ronty, Jimmy Peters and Pete Babando.

In September, Don Gallinger, suspended the previous March and hopeful of winning an appeal and rejoining the Bruins, was officially barred forever from the NHL. In making this announcement public, Clarence Campbell declined to name the charges against him. In November a non-fraternization law was issued which warned players of opposing teams not to mingle.

Charlie Conacher's Blackhawks ended the schedule in fifth place, but only seven points behind Toronto. A February feud developed between Conacher and the Leafs arising from a game in which Chicago's Red Hamill axed Toronto's Vic Lynn. Conacher branded the Leafs as the "league's cry-babies" after they claimed an "unprovoked attack."

A league record was smashed on November 25 when 10 major penalties were called on the Leafs and the Canadiens in Montreal. The old record, established February 13, 1932, involved the Leafs and Montreal Maroons.

Toronto and Montreal became embroiled again in early January, when the main event was between Cal Gardner and Kenny Reardon. Campbell clamped down on the stick swingers, suspending them for a game against one another. He fined Gardner $250 and Reardon $200. The incident had been building up for two years, ever since Reardon had lost some teeth and required 14 stitches after being cut by Gardner's stick.

Between fights there was the occasional amusing incident in the NHL. The wife of Montreal defenseman Glen Harmon owned a popular hat shop and Mrs. Butch Bouchard, wife of the Canadiens' captain, admired a certain hat in her store. Harmon appointed himself delivery boy and toted the hat to the Forum. He turned it over to Bouchard, warning him not to look at the expensive price tag. When Bouchard peeked and demurred at the cost, Harmon offered to let him have the hat free of charge if he scored two goals that night. Although Bouchard had only scored four goals in all of the previous season, he rose to the challenge. The outcome of the game was Bouchard 2, Detroit 0. Harmon had lost a hat.

The season of 1948–49 was a particularly rough one for Montreal's Elmer Lach. He suffered a jaw fracture on December 11 in a game against Chicago, wore a steel brace that clamped his jaws together and lost 10 pounds while on a liquid diet. He recovered, returned to the lineup and sustained another jaw fracture in March.

Bill Durnan, who had to be coaxed into playing another season with the Canadiens after the home fans jeered him in 1947–48, set a new modern record for NHL goaltending on March 9 in Chicago. Durnan had a string of four straight shutouts and 283 minutes and 45 seconds of scoreless play going into the Hawks–Canadiens game. He held the Hawks scoreless in the first period, but his streak ended at 5:36 of the second period when Gaye Stewart scored. That gave him 309 minutes and 21 seconds without a goal being scored against him, surpassing the 290-minutes-and-12-second mark set by the Hawks' Charlie Gardiner in 1930.

Detroit's Jack Adams spoke as a prophet in 1948–49 when he said, "There's not enough money in the NHL to buy Gordie Howe. He's the greatest young player I ever saw."

Despite being in fifth place, the Blackhawks held the two top spots when the scoring race ended. Roy Conacher was the champion, with Doug Bentley his runner-up. For the fifth time in six seasons Bill Durnan captured the Vezina Trophy.

Detroit, with a strong, well-balanced team, had to fight seven games before getting past the Canadiens in the Stanley Cup semi-finals. One stumbling block was rookie Gerry Plamondon, Montreal's top playoff scorer, with five goals and one assist.

By disposing of Boston in five games and polishing off Detroit in four straight, Toronto's Hap Day established a remarkable coaching record of five Stanley Cups in eight seasons. In the finals the desperate Wings even had an oxygen tank on their bench, a last-ditch move by Detroit executives who borrowed the equipment from the junior Montreal Royals. Detroit's 27-year-old Bill Quackenbush became the first defenseman to win the Lady Byng Trophy, polling 52 points out of a possible 54.

1949–50

In an attempt to capture the Stanley Cup in the 1949–50 campaign, the Detroit Red Wings exploded two NHL deals on August 16. They sold Bud Poile to New York, his fourth NHL team, for an undisclosed amount of cash. Then they sent All-Star defenseman Bill Quackenbush and forward Pete Horeck to Boston for forwards Pete Babando and Jimmy Peters, plus defensemen Clare Martin and Lloyd Durham. Detroit's manager Jack Adams said, "We want the Stanley Cup. We have defensemen but we don't have forwards. You can be sure I hate to lose Quackenbush."

Later, the Boston Bruins sold their former prize goaltender, Frank Brimsek, to the Blackhawks for a large, undisclosed sum of money. Brimsek had become unhappy as a Bruin and his place was being taken by rookie Jack Gelineau, who was to become the Calder Trophy winner that year. George "Buck" Boucher, the elder brother of Frank Boucher and coach of the Allan Cup champion Ottawa Senators, signed a one-year contract to coach the Bruins when Dit Clapper resigned unexpectedly at the end of the 1948–49 schedule.

Except for minor changes, the Canadiens announced that they had a stand-pat club. Elmer Lach, besieged by injuries, had retired in the spring but he ended his retirement in the fall at 31 years of age.

In October the Rangers signed rugged defenseman Gus Kyle from the Regina Capitals with a view to teaming him with Allan Stanley. In less than a month of action, Kyle, an ex-Mountie who had no previous pro experience, had added backbone to the

Ranger blue line. There was even a chant of, "Stop the Rangers or they'll win the Stanley Cup," an unheard-of theme for the doormats of the league.

It was in December that Frank Boucher, head man of the Rangers, stated, "The red line should be taken out of hockey." Because he was a member of the rules committee, he was rebuked by Campbell for speaking publicly on the matter. Boucher immediately offered his resignation, but Campbell asked him to reconsider.

Campbell, in his fourth year as league president, must have found the 1949–50 season as trying as some of his experiences in the war. On February 9, Charlie Conacher, Chicago's coach, was in trouble on two fronts. The Hawks absorbed a 9–2 beating in Detroit and Conacher became incensed when Doug Bentley was felled in a collision with George Gee. He exchanged hot words with referee Chadwick when the latter declined to call a penalty. Conacher then grabbed the official and continued the discussion at close range.

Afterwards, Detroit writer Lew Walter attempted to interview Conacher in the Hawks' dressing room. Conacher reportedly blew up, criticized the writer's past stories and then knocked him to the floor. By March, Conacher had been fined $200 for his attack on Walter and the writer had dismissed his court action against the Chicago coach.

Earlier, Campbell had had another mess to sort out. When the Canadiens lost 4–1 in Chicago on November 2, 1949, a wild melee broke out between Billy Reay, Leo Gravelle, Ken Reardon and a number of Hawks' fans. One fan even chased Reardon across the ice. The game was held up for 20 minutes by the outbreak, which threatened to bring even more spectators on to the ice. Campbell commented that, "fans should leave the fights to the players. There's ample protection for the patron if he stays in the seat allotted to him." The fracas ended with the three Canadiens' players being arrested. Reardon and Gravelle were jailed for one hour and released on $200 bonds. There were no charges against Reay.

Late in November, the slumping Leafs, who had picked up only eight out of a possible 26 points, so exasperated Conn Smythe that he benched Turk Broda with an order to drop seven of his 197 pounds, snapping, "We're not running a fat man's team." The next day he engineered a trade with the Cleveland Barons for the rights to Al Rollins, a slim goaltender. Additionally, Gil Mayer was recalled from Pittsburgh for immediate netminding duties. He, too, was on a diet—but he was trying to *gain* weight.

On December 5, weighing eight ounces less than mandatory, Broda was back in Toronto's nets. Montreal's Dick Irvin lauded Smythe's actions, but Frank Selke differed: "We don't make spectacles of our players," he stated. "When they get older, naturally they get heavier."

Chicago, who had made it to fifth place the previous season, slipped back into the cellar in 1949–50. No blame was attached to either Conacher or Tobin. The trouble lay in the lack of a farm system. This situation stemmed from the late Major McLaughlin's unwillingness to groom his own talent. After a scouting trip to see what might be available to the Hawks, Conacher was evidently disenchanted and he resigned at the end of the schedule.

It was on January 5, 1950, that the Montreal Canadiens marked their 40th anniversary in hockey with their first win of the season over the Bruins. In a pre-game ceremony, Newsy Lalonde, Jack Laviolette and Art Bernier, all members of the first Canadiens' team, were introduced to the crowd.

Clarence Campbell was busy on March 1 imposing a $1,000 fine on Montreal's Kenny Reardon to keep the peace in a verbal extension of his feud with Cal Gardner. This development was induced by a magazine article in which Reardon was quoted as saying, "I'm going to see that Gardner gets 14 stitches in the mouth. I may have to wait a long time but I'll get even."

The final games of the schedule saw a quick surge by Montreal move them over Toronto and into second place by three points. Detroit already had the championship locked up and the Rangers had a seven-point edge on the fourth berth. The Rangers, who were about to take on the Canadiens in the semi-finals, were relieved to get Edgar Laprade, the club's top scorer and playmaker, back into action after he had missed a number of games with a torn knee cartilage.

Penalties to the Canadiens (five of them to Reardon) and the brilliance of New York's Charlie Rayner in goal led to a 3–1 victory for the Rangers in the first game. In the second contest New York grabbed a 3–2 win and another injury was added to Montreal's growing list. With 15 seconds left in the game, Reardon was carried off the ice on a stretcher suffering from a dislocated left shoulder. The day before he had received a telegram from his sister in Regina wishing him a happy 29th birthday. The address on the telegram read: "Care of penalty box, Forum."

Game three was just as disastrous for the Canadiens, who were easily defeated 4–1, mainly on the strength of three goals by Pentti Lund. The surprise move of the series came on April 4, the morning of the fourth game, when Bill Durnan asked Irvin to use understudy Gerry McNeil in the nets. Durnan explained that he was suffering from bad nerves and the effects of an injury he had sustained a month earlier in Chicago. It was also known that his right hand, which had bothered him all season, would need to be frozen if he played. It was Elmer Lach's overtime goal that kept the Canadiens in Cup contention and made Durnan the happiest man in the rink. McNeil, who hadn't played in a couple of weeks, was nervous but good enough to be one of the stars.

Five rookies—McNeil, Tom Johnson, Paul Meger, Bobby Frampton and Bert Hirschfeld—lined up with the Canadiens for game five. The changes didn't help. The Rangers, well coached by Lynn Patrick, stormed to a 3–0 triumph.

Detroit faced the Leafs in their series knowing Toronto had defeated them in 11 straight playoff games and had knocked the Wings out of contention in three consecutive seasons. Toronto's domination continued with a 5–0 opening victory. The score was overshadowed, however, by a devastating injury to Gordie Howe, the Wings' leading scorer, who was carried off bleeding on a stretcher after a third-period collision with Toronto captain Ted Kennedy. Preliminary examinations brought discouraging conclusions. Howe had a deep cut near his right eye, a fractured nose, a possible fractured cheekbone and a possible fractured skull. After a team of doctors performed a 90-minute operation to save his life, Howe's condition was described as serious, but team physician Dr. C. L. Tomsu said, "The outlook is good." At noon on March 29, the big right-winger was pronounced out of danger, and from then on his progress was rapid and satisfactory. Most Detroit fans blamed Kennedy for a deliberate injury, but Clarence Campbell made it clear that the game officials had completely absolved Kennedy.

The Wings squared the series in the second game, one which resembled a vendetta as they bludgeoned their way to a 3–1 victory. Kennedy, already suffering from a charley horse, came out of the game with a black eye and cut lip. He was the chief target of

Detroit players and fans. President Campbell, an observer at the game, warned of fines and suspensions if the feuding didn't stop.

When the third game was played on Toronto ice, it was a tame affair with only three penalties. Toronto won 2–0. Critics termed it, "Hockey as it should be played." Then Detroit tied the series in game four when Leo Reise scored in the second overtime period. It was a 15-foot freak shot, but it earned a 2–1 win.

Ivan called up the Wilson brothers, Larry and Johnny, for the fifth game, but they couldn't spoil Broda's 2–0 shutout as Toronto recaptured the series lead. The Wings evened the series again with a strong 4–0 win in the sixth game. It was another overtime goal by Leo Reise that demolished the Leafs 1–0 and ended the spell they held over Detroit. "It has been a long reign," Conn Smythe declared.

With a circus taking over Madison Square Garden, the homeless Rangers elected to play their "home games" against Detroit in Maple Leaf Gardens where the SRO sign was hung up early. No one other than avid New York supporters seriously thought that a fourth-place team would threaten Detroit, but New York pushed the series to a full seven games, three of them going into overtime.

After two games the series was deadlocked and the Wings benched four players: Pete Babando, Steve Black, Marcel Pronovost and Larry Wilson. An SOS was sent out for Terry Sawchuk, Clare Raglan, Al Dewsbury, Gord Haidy and Doug McKay. In game three Detroit outclassed New York 4–0. The Rangers came back with two overtime victories, but the Wings were able to achieve a 5–4 win in game six.

Detroit won the Stanley Cup by a 4–3 score on April 23. In the second overtime period Pete Babando sank the winning goal. He had been one of the men Adams had obtained from Boston in the fall when he wanted to create a Cup-winning team.

VI

A TALE OF TWO CITIES

Detroit and Montreal, 1950–1960

There were six teams in the league during the 1950s, but never before nor since were two cities so dominant for a comparable length of time. For seven straight seasons, ending with 1954–55, the Detroit Red Wings won the National Hockey League Championship. In 1955–56, the Montreal Canadiens were the champs of the regular season, losing out to Detroit in 1956–5′, but taking the Prince of Wales Trophy for the rest of the decade.

The list of Stanley Cup winners tells a similar story. From 1949–50 through to the 1959–60 season, Detroit and Montreal won 10 of 11 Stanley Cup championships—Detroit dominating early in the decade and Montreal in the latter stages.

The Chicago Blackhawks and the New York Rangers were the perennial cellar dwellers of the decade. Even with the help of a hypnotist for one season, the Rangers made the playoffs only three times and the Blackhawks were last for six out of seven years—that is until 18-year-old Bobby Hull broke into the league in 1957–58 and led the scorers two seasons later to help the Hawks finish third.

Two players dominated the decade: Maurice Richard of Montreal, the dynamic scorer, and Gordie Howe of Detroit, the perfect player. Arguments still persist as to who was the brighter star. In the 1950–51 season, Richard became the highest scorer in Canadiens' history with his 271st goal and Howe earned his first of four straight scoring championships, an honor Richard never achieved. During the decade, the older Rocket was on seven All-Star first or second teams; Howe was on nine. But statistics didn't tell the whole story. No witness will forget Richard's goal against the Bruins in the 1952 playoffs while he played with six stitches in his head, nor will they forget his four goals in one game in the 1957 playoffs or his constant tiffs with players, officials and fans.

These were years of growth and prosperity for the NHL. In 1952 Cleveland almost

58

joined the league and in 1959 San Francisco and Los Angeles were rumored to be on the verge, although the NHL owners did not encourage these attempts. One change of front-office management took place when Jim Norris, Jr., and Arthur Wirtz took over the Blackhawks in 1952, but this was "in the family" since they had been associated with Detroit.

The players started to get a better deal in the 1950s. The NHL pension plan, with assets of over half a million dollars, was revised in 1957 with more benefits for the players. The players' cut of the Stanley Cup playoffs was increased and an owner-player council was established by the owners. However, they did not recognize the Players' Association formed in 1957 with Ted Lindsay of Detroit as president. The idea of an association subsided for the time being.

The interest of the fans increased substantially throughout the decade, particularly with the advent of television. By 1957 games in all six cities were telecast. But in the history of hockey spectator interest has never become so inflamed as it was on St. Patrick's Day, 1955, the night of the "riot."

In Boston on March 13, 1955, Rocket Richard attacked Hal Laycoe with his stick and struck linesman Cliff Thompson with his fist. Clarence Campbell quickly suspended Richard for the remainder of the season, including the playoffs. At the time Richard was almost assured of his first league scoring championship. In the next few days team-mate Boom Boom Geoffrion overtook Richard and won the scoring crown by one point.

On St. Patrick's Day, the Canadiens met Detroit at the Forum. Montreal fans, incensed over the suspension of their hero, gathered outside the building in mid-afternoon. Some carried banners and demanded, "We want Campbell." In the middle of the first period Campbell arrived at the game and was pelted with eggs, tomatoes and pickled pigs' feet. A young hoodlum approached Campbell, offered his hand in a friendly way, then punched the league president.

A tear-gas bomb, thrown from behind one goal, landed on the ice and the fire director ordered the building cleared. While panic was narrowly averted inside the Forum, a mob outside the arena, spurred on by teenagers, became angry and then uncontrollable. Screams and shouts filled the air and rifle shots smashed through the Forum windows. The mob swept down Ste. Catherine Street, damaging cars, ripping through stores and looting and burning private property. Campbell, spirited out of the Forum, was lucky to escape with his life. But he was not persuaded to rescind the Rocket's suspension.

1950–51

The face lifting for the NHL's 1950–51 schedule began weeks before the October 11 season opening, the earliest in league history.

On July 1, 1950, Lynn Patrick was lured back from premature retirement by Boston's Art Ross as successor to coach George "Buck" Boucher. Ross announced that Patrick was being groomed to handle Bruin managerial chores by 1952–53.

Conn Smythe, who was ailing during the 1949–50 campaign, gave up some of his duties at the end of that season. Hap Day, a five-time Stanley Cup winner in the 10 years he had coached the Maple Leafs, moved up as acting general manager while Joe Primeau assumed the coaching duties.

In July the biggest trade in the history of the NHL was completed. Detroit had swapped five of their players for four from Chicago. The champion Wings had given up goalie Harry Lumley, defensemen Jack Stewart and Al Dewsbury, center Don Morrison and left-winger Pete Babando, whose overtime goal had captured the Stanley Cup for them the previous April. In return Detroit received goaltender Jim Henry, defenseman Bob Goldham and forwards Gaye Stewart and Metro Prystai. In a separate deal they got Vic Stasiuk for Lee Fogolin and Steve Black. Hawks' president Bill Tobin felt his organization had outsmarted the Red Wings, but time showed that Detroit would benefit more in the long run.

The Toronto management became disenchanted with Bill Ezinicki, who was traded to Boston along with Vic Lynn for Fern Flaman, Phil Maloney and Kenny Smith. The Leafs also got the rights to Leo Boivin, then a Port Arthur junior. At the same time the Bruins sent Ed Harrison and Zellio Toppazzini to New York for Dunc Fisher, a forward who had led the Rangers' playoff scoring the previous spring.

By November the Rangers were stumbling along in such luckless fashion that more aid had to be called in, but not in the form of new players. Dr. David F. Tracy, a psychologist and hypnotist, was retained to instill confidence in the players—something he had failed to do in an earlier experiment with baseball's St. Louis Browns. The first night he worked with them, the Rangers played their 13th straight game without a win.

Despite constant tampering with the lineup, the revamped Wings set a record for the most points compiled by a team in one season. In the 70-game schedule they won 44, lost 13 and tied 13 for an impressive 101 points. All this was accomplished with rookie goalie Terry Sawchuk in their nets.

Toronto got off to a flying start, going undefeated in their first 11 games. Al Rollins, more impressive in each outing, was part of a two-platoon netminding system with Turk Broda. It was Smythe's aim to have his rookie and veteran netminders be double winners of the Vezina Trophy. The award eventually went to Rollins, who played in 40 games compared to Broda's 31 games.

By December 5, Toronto was completely dominating the league with a comfortable lead over the other five teams. Bentley, Sloan and Kennedy were leading the point race and Broda paced his rivals in shutouts. But Detroit zoomed ahead late in the season, with the Leafs ending in second place with 95 points. Except for Chicago, piloted to last place by Ebbie Goodfellow, the other three clubs were clustered together. Montreal and Boston eventually nudged New York into fifth place.

The Canadiens were still injecting youth into their 1950–51 lineup. Besides 23-year-old goalie Gerry McNeil, they had added Paul Masnick and Tom Johnson, whose first fight was a brawl in Maple Leaf Gardens on January 24 with Ted Kennedy. Calum MacKay had been held over from the previous season and they dug into their amateur ranks for Bernie Geoffrion.

Detroit announced that Bert Olmstead, their newly acquired left-winger, had been traded to the Canadiens for Leo Gravelle and an undisclosed amount of cash. Paired with Lach and Richard, Olmstead became the first man to click with them since Toe Blake had rounded out the Punch Line. The Rocket spurted forth with 13 goals in nine games.

This was a particularly hectic and rugged season. On February 3 the Blackhawks went wild in Toronto while losing 6–3 to the Leafs. Coach Goodfellow defied referee

Hugh McLean's order to leave the bench, thus contravening a rule which states that a manager or coach, so ordered by an official, must not direct his team's play. Goodfellow was subsequently fined $250 by Clarence Campbell, a figure Bill Tobin considered "pretty stiff."

A more disturbing exhibition occurred on January 25 in Detroit when Boston's Bill Ezinicki fought with Ted Lindsay for more than three minutes. It ended with the Bruin player prone on the ice, bleeding profusely from a cut above the ear; Lindsay was cut above the right eye and on the hand. Each player was suspended for three games and fined $300.

March was a busy month for Clarence Campbell, who fined Maurice Richard $500 for "conduct prejudicial to the welfare of hockey." This related to a scuffle in New York's Picadilly Hotel on the morning of March 4, when Richard, incensed over what he felt was an undeserved game-misconduct penalty in Montreal the previous night, grabbed referee Hugh McLean by the neck or tie. No punches were thrown but considerable profanity filled the air.

The Stanley Cup series A pitted Dick Irvin's "kids" against the mighty Red Wings. The third place Montreal team knocked off Detroit in six games. In game one the Canadiens twice battled from behind to tie Detroit and send the game into four overtime periods, with the Rocket eventually scoring the winner. The second game ended exactly the same way, the Rocket striking in the third overtime.

In game three, Gordie Howe connected for the first Wings' goal in 218 minutes and 42 seconds of play against the Canadiens. When Detroit won 2–0 someone said, "Class will tell."

When Detroit evened the series on a 4–1 score they became heavy favorites to win it all. But a red-hot band of 10 inspired Hab rookies helped deflate the Wings 5–2, although it was said that Richard's flattening of Ted Lindsay with one punch turned the tide. A 3–2 win for the Canadiens in Montreal before a frenzied crowd sent the Wings home stunned and deflated. "It's unbelievable but it's true," said Detroit manager Jack Adams.

Toronto eliminated Boston easily to enter the finals with Montreal, which turned into a series of five overtime games. The opening game saw the Leafs' Sid Smith whip in the winner at 5:51 of the first overtime period. Richard was the hero in overtime once more when he sank the Leafs 3–2 in a stirring battle. Game three in Montreal was also broken up in overtime by Ted Kennedy to give the Leafs a 2–1 win. And the fourth game, played in Montreal, was ended by Harry Watson as the Leafs won 3–2.

Game five was the most dramatic of all, breaking all records for sheer tension. Montreal had the game almost cinched at 2–1 when the Leafs yanked their goalie and Tod Sloan scored at 19:28 of the third period. This set the stage for two minutes and 53 seconds of overtime, before a Bill Barilko slapshot won the Cup for Toronto. Barilko died tragically in a plane wreck the following August.

1951–52

As the 1951–52 season progressed, Toronto felt the absence of Barilko on defense and in February promoted Jim Morrison from Pittsburgh. He had joined the Leafs' chain a month earlier when an angry Art Ross shook up his fifth-place Bruins by trading

Morrison to Toronto for Fleming Mackell and elevating Real Chevrefils and Leo LaBine. A few days later George Armstrong joined the Leafs from Pittsburgh. Much traded Gaye Stewart packed again, this time going to New York while Detroit received Tony Leswick.

On August 20, the largest cash deal for players in NHL history was revealed when the Blackhawks bought six players from Detroit for $75,000. That surpassed the $35,000 Toronto had paid for King Clancy in the 1930s. In getting Jim McFadden, George Gee, Jimmy Peters, Clare Martin, Clare Reglan and Max McNab, the Hawks had a total of 19 former Red Wings in their fold.

The Leafs welcomed King Clancy back into their organization after a 14-year absence. His new role was as talent developer for Toronto through his coaching job at Pittsburgh.

Royalty entered the hockey scene in both Toronto and Montreal when Princess Elizabeth and Prince Philip attended a game in each city during October. The flamboyant Maurice Richard should have been the star of the Canadiens–Rangers game with his two goals, but the usually self-effacing Floyd Curry stole Richard's thunder by scoring three.

The Rocket did dominate two mid-week contests between Toronto and Montreal. On Wednesday in Toronto he threatened to hit a fan in a rail seat and he got into a real fracas the following night. He was in the penalty box, sitting out two majors and a misconduct for fighting with Fern Flaman, when he unleashed his Sunday punch at Bill Juzda, who was standing too close to the box. The Leafs' player lay face downward for almost a minute. Richard was tossed out of the game.

In December 1951, the Rangers lost another coach. This time Neil Colville, only 37, was quitting because of the team's poor showing and the fact that his health was so poor he was on a milk diet. Fifty-three-year-old Bill Cook stepped in as Colville's replacement and New York wound up in fifth place with 59 points.

A couple of records were set in this season. On March 23, in a game against the Rangers, Bill Mosienko of Chicago sparked a five-goal third-period burst as the Hawks won 7–6. Mosienko scored three goals in 21 seconds on netminder Lorne Anderson, breaking a record set in 1938, when Carl Liscombe of Detroit collected three goals in one minute and 52 seconds. Another league record was set when Elmer Lach picked up a goal and three assists in a 7–0 win over Chicago, boosting his total points to 550.

When the schedule ended in late March, the Detroit Red Wings—with Howe and Lindsay leading the point getters and Sawchuk winning the Vezina—were heavy favorites to take the Stanley Cup. Toronto had the dubious privilege of meeting the Wings in the semi-final round and bowed out in four consecutive games.

Meanwhile, the Canadiens and Boston were battling seven games for the chance to meet Detroit. With Richard leading them, the Canadiens sped to a 5–1 win in their opener. The second game was a 4–0 victory, thanks largely to Bernie Geoffrion, who scored three goals. It was a costly win, because Ken Mosdell, who scored the other goal, fractured his leg. The Bruins came back with a 4–1 win, then tied the series on April Fool's night with a 3–2 victory. They followed that up with a 1–0 win. Lynn Patrick joyfully predicted, "The Habs are dead." Two nights later Montreal's Paul Masnick scored in overtime to sink the Bruins 3–2.

Then came the most dramatic goal of the series, a Rocket Richard special in the seventh game. The score was tied 1–1 in the second period when Richard was crashed to the ice by Leo LaBine. He was taken to the Forum clinic to get six-stitches in his head and was in a foggy state when he returned to the ice. Late in the third period the Rocket took a Bouchard pass, went past four Bruins, warded off Bill Quackenbush with sheer strength, then hooked a short, one-handed shot past Sugar Jim Henry. A four minute ovation followed the goal and later Lynn Patrick commented, "A truck wouldn't have stopped Richard."

Detroit not only stopped Richard, but stymied the entire Canadiens' team, disposing of them in four straight games, just as they had handled Toronto. That was a feat never before accomplished in the history of the NHL's best-of-seven series, which had been introduced in 1939. The Wings swept the series by scores of 3–1, 2–1, 2–0 and 3–0. Wings' checkers held Richard scoreless, while Howe and Lindsay scored five of the 11 Detroit goals between them. Jack Adams called his club the greatest Detroit team of all time.

1952–53

The NHL almost had a seventh team in their group in 1952–53. The Cleveland Barons were accepted on May 14, with the proviso that they deposit $425,000 to show good faith, prove that they had sufficient working capital to consort with the established teams and make sure that 60 percent of their shareholders resided in Cleveland.

With all the stipulations met, or so he thought, Jim Hendy triumphantly showed up at the June governors' meeting. He was greeted warmly but suspiciously, on the grounds that the franchise was in debt for the money he had raked up. The governors felt the amount was too great to pay back in two years and suggested the city try again at a later date.

On July 29, Chicago announced the signing of Sid Abel, who had captained three Stanley Cup winning Red Wing teams, to a two-year contract as playing-coach. Bill Tobin stressed that he had sought Abel strictly as a coaching replacement for Ebbie Goodfellow, but Abel insisted he could aid the Hawks by playing.

Rumors became fact when on September 11 two former Red Wing officials, Jim Norris, Jr., and Arthur Wirtz, were revealed as Blackhawk executives. Norris became chairman of the board while Wirtz took over Tobin's presidency. Tobin moved down to general manager and vice-president. Norris immediately got together with Conn Smythe in September to swing a four-for-one deal. Goaltender Harry Lumley went to the Leafs. The Hawks demanded Cal Gardner, Gus Mortson, Ray Hanningan and Vezina Trophy winner Al Rollins. The always popular Lumley had been sought by the Leafs for some time. Norris and Wirtz felt their acquisition should provide the power to get the Hawks into the playoffs, which it did.

The Leafs added Ron Stewart, Bob Hassard, Leo Boivin and Eric Nesterenko to their roster. Injuries riddled Toronto for most of the season, with George Armstrong starting out with a pre-season shoulder separation. The worst blow was a shoulder separation to Ted Kennedy, sustained in a fracas with Boston's Milt Schmidt.

Detroit was still the dominating force in 1952–53, but their grip was weakening. In August the Wings gave up veteran Leo Reise for New York's Reg Sinclair, as well as a cash payment and an amateur defenseman. In December their ace left-winger, Ted Lindsay, scored his 200th goal against New York's Charlie Rayner.

With the death of the elder James Norris in December, his daughter Marguerite moved into the Wings' office as president and Jack Adams assumed more authority.

Art Ross, who seldom went out on a limb with predictions, warned the rest of the league that his rebuilt Bruins were comparable to his 1942 squad. The team was built around goalie Jim Henry and a defense of Bill Quackenbush, Hal Laycoe, Bob Armstrong, Warren Godfrey and Jerry Toppazzini, a forward who served as fifth rearguard. Up front they had Schmidt, Sandford, McIntyre, Peirson, Red Sullivan and Woody Dumart. The Bruins ended with 69 points in a tie with Chicago, but gained third place on an extra victory.

In January the Rangers purchased the suspended Pete Babando from Chicago and merged him with former junior stars who had just turned pro. Harry Howell and Andy Bathgate had been signed while Aldo Guidolin came up from the Valleyfield Braves. Nothing helped, however, and the Rangers ended up last with 50 points.

The injection of youth into the Canadiens' lineup during previous two seasons made them strong second-place finishers with 75 points and eased the burden of the veterans. Maurice Richard got off to a roaring start in October by scoring two fast goals against the Maple Leafs, which brought his total to 324, the same as record-holding Nels Stewart. The pressure was removed from the Rocket on November 9 in Montreal when he fired in his 325th goal. It had taken Nels Stewart 15 seasons to amass his total, while Richard had done it in 11.

Television moved into Maple Leaf Gardens in 1952–53 with the telecast starting at 9:30 P.M., catching action midway in the second period. In December the smallest turnout for a Red Wing visit to Toronto was noted with concern. A year earlier Clarence Campbell had been quoted as describing television as, "The greatest menace of the entertainment world." There was speculation that the absent standees were watching from their living rooms.

The 1952–53 schedule ended on a dramatic note as the Leafs made a desperate and unsuccessful effort to capture a playoff berth. This was the season that Gordie Howe threatened Richard's 50-goal record, but fell one short at 49.

Since Detroit had required only eight games to take the Cup the previous year, they were favored to dispose of Boston easily in the semi-finals. A 7–0 clobbering of the Bruins in the opening game supported the theory. But the Bruins fought back and handed Detroit their first setback in 10 playoff games as Jim Henry made 43 saves in a 5–3 win. It took a total of six games before Boston vanquished the Wings and went into the finals. Detroit outshot Boston in the six games, 228 to 140, but Henry was superb.

Meanwhile, the Canadiens were having a harder time getting past the Blackhawks. Gerry McNeil, like his predecessor Bill Durnan, was suffering from nerves and was replaced by Jacques Plante with Chicago leading 3–2 in games. The Canadiens won two straight and took the series four games to three.

Boston, after their stunning upset over Detroit, also encountered goaltending problems in the finals against Montreal. Sugar Jim Henry became ill and was replaced by Hershey's Gordon "Red" Henry early in the second game. Boston took only one game and 35-year-old center Elmer Lach fired the Stanley Cup winning overtime goal on a pass from Richard in the fifth game, won by the Canadiens 1–0.

1953–54

The New York Rangers, tired of being the league pushovers, made a determined effort in the summer of 1953 to build up their team for the new campaign. A waning box-office interest spurred them to purchase Max Bentley from the Maple Leafs, obtain his brother Doug on a trial basis and persuade Frank Boucher to handle the dual role of manager-coach. In December, Boucher handed the coaching job over to Muzz Patrick. The Bentley brother combination didn't last long. Doug played in 20 games, collecting two goals and 10 assists, then quit. Max got 14 goals and 18 assists in 57 games.

In July, the Rangers obtained goalie Johnny Bower from Cleveland. Bower was to dislodge the Calder Trophy holder, Lorne Worsley, from the nets. By August they had engineered another transaction by trading Ed Slowinski and Pete Babando to the Canadiens for defenseman Ivan Irwin.

Before the schedule opened on October 8, the earliest start in league history, New York signed Ike Hildebrand and 20-year-old Camille Henry. A week later Boucher predicted that "Henry could be the rookie of the year." He was. New York ended fifth, but their attendance zoomed.

Boston managed to gain fourth place in 1953–54. From the beginning of the season they were plagued by injuries to key men. Hay Laycoe was the first to fall, then Chevrefils broke a leg, Quackenbush fractured an ankle and Schmidt was sidelined for some time.

The hapless plight of Chicago became so acute in 1953–54 that rumors spread of their pending withdrawal from the league. The five other teams heard the sos and plans were laid to help bolster the club. The Hawks secured Jack McIntyre and Ike Hildebrand, who had earlier gone to minor affiliates of Boston and the Rangers. Kenny Wharram was elevated from Quebec, while Lou Jankowski and Pete Conacher were playing full NHL schedules for the first time.

A pessimistic Conn Smythe predicted the Leafs would end in the cellar and they surprised him by grabbing third place. The only rookie in their lineup was fiery Bob Bailey, who teamed as center for Rudy Migay and Eric Nesterenko. Jimmy Morrison was hailed as coming into his own while Ron Stewart's penalty killing caught the eye of new coach King Clancy, who had succeeded Joe Primeau when he retired for business reasons in March. George Armstrong had shown so many attributes that Conn Smythe, who once vowed that Syl Apps' number-10 sweater would never again be worn, decided Armstrong was worthy of wearing it.

For Detroit, who again won the league championship, Earl Reibel was a bonus. With 15 goals and 33 assists to put him in the top 10 scorers, the Wings were touting Reibel as the only logical recipient of the Calder Trophy. At 23, he made an excellent partner for Howe and Lindsay. The Wings clinched their sixth straight title with five games remaining in the schedule and could indirectly thank Toronto for some of their good fortune. In their first five trips to the Olympia, the Leafs were shut out, going scoreless there for over 300 minutes.

The Montreal Canadiens had a similar hold over the Rangers, who waited until February 1954 to gain their first Forum win since April 6, 1950. The Canadiens had finally landed Jean Beliveau in the fall, but the high-priced rookie got off to the same sort of start Maurice Richard had encountered in his initial year. In early October, Beliveau picked up the first injury of his hockey career, a cracked fibula he received in Chicago. That, plus other mishaps, forced him to miss 26 scheduled games and kept his points to 13 goals and 21 assists. Referring to the broken leg Richard had suffered in his rookie season, Beliveau commented, "If mine turns out like his, this will be really worthwhile." Beliveau was the most-publicized junior player of all time, a giant center who was idolized in Quebec City. He had played a year with the Quebec Seniors before turning professional with the Canadiens.

President Campbell had fewer fines to levy in this season than he had in some of the others, although Bernie Geoffrion kept him busy. In November the Canadien winger was fined $250 for charging referee Frank Udvari into the boards. The following month Campbell suspended Geoffrion for eight games against the Rangers for his part in a stick-swinging duel with New York's Ron Murphy on December 20. Murphy, who suffered a fractured jaw in the fracas, was suspended for five games.

Fourth-place Boston won 32 victories, the largest number achieved by a Bruin team since the 1938–39 season, a year they finished in first place.

Gordie Howe was again the scoring champion with a commanding lead over Maurice Richard. Toronto's Harry Lumley won the Vezina Trophy by a single point over Detroit's Terry Sawchuk.

Boston offered scant resistance to the Canadiens in their Cup semi-final series and bowed out in four straight. Detroit handled Toronto almost as swiftly, but needed five games to do the job.

Then there was a titanic struggle between Detroit and Montreal which went to seven games. With slumps and injuries to consider, Irvin had to shake up his team for this series. The Punch Line had gone pointless against Boston while their teammates had supplied the scoring power. Then they were held scoreless in the first game against the Wings, but the Rocket later clicked for three goals.

It was in the fifth game of the series that Irvin played his longest hunch. Jacques Plante, who had moved up from Buffalo in February to replace the injured Gerry McNeil, had suddenly lost his playoff touch. Irvin called in the rusty McNeil and apparently suggested he play that night or terminate his career with the Canadiens. McNeil responded with a sensational 1–0 demonstration and the game was won in overtime by Ken Mosdell.

When Detroit won their sixth Stanley Cup on Friday, April 16, in the Olympia it was on the strength of an overtime goal by Tony Leswick, an angle shot which went in off of Doug Harvey's left glove. McNeil was inspired all night and Terry Sawchuk's performance was flawless.

1954–55

Trades were a highlight of the 1954–55 season. In May, the Canadiens gave Dick Gamble and the rights to Eddie Dorohoy of the Victoria Cougars to New York in exchange for Hy Buller, a defenseman.

Tommy Ivan, who had guided Detroit to six championships and three Stanley Cups, was appointed manager of the Blackhawks in July. No one was displaced when Ivan took over, since the post had been vacant for some years. Before the season began, Chicago's Sid Abel bowed out as coach while Frank Eddolls moved behind the bench. Ivan's spot with the Wings was filled by Jimmy Skinner.

Conn Smythe finally gave up on Danny Lewicki, who had fluctuated up and down from Pittsburgh, and sold him to the Rangers. Smythe traded Fern Flaman back to Boston for Dave Creighton.

Boston's Johnny Peirson, a consistent 20-goal scorer, decided to retire at the age of

29. He had attended McGill University in Montreal and was about to enter his father-in-law's business.

Gerry McNeil, who had replaced Bill Durnan in Montreal's nets when his nerves forced him into retirement, was quitting for health reasons. Four seasons of facing NHL opponents had strained his nervous temperament to the limit so he stepped aside for calm, colorful Jacques Plante.

Finding someone to fill the void left by the retired Elmer Lach was a big chore for the Canadiens. A leading candidate was Jackie Leclair, a 25-year-old rookie acquired by the Canadiens when they gave Brian Cullen to the Leafs.

The campaign to help the Blackhawks continued in 1954–55. Toronto contributed Dave Creighton and Harry Watson. Montreal supplied Bucky Hollingworth, Johnny McCormack, Paul Masnick and outstanding rookie Ed Litzenberger. Detroit contributed Metro Prystai, but got back Lorne Davis who had been another addition from Montreal. Others who eventually went to Chicago were Frank Martin, Pete Conacher, Bob Hassard, Ray Timgren, Red Sullivan, Dick Gamble, Ike Hildebrand and Bill Gadsby.

Jim Norris sought a farm club and in January he bought the Buffalo Bisons for $150,000. That was the first move towards establishing an extensive farm system, something the Blackhawks had never had. The Hawks gave up Bill Gadsby and Pete Conacher to the Rangers in mid-season, much to the dismay of Chicago fans, and received Nick Mickoski and Allan Stanley in return. Stanley had been in and out of a Ranger uniform a year earlier due to the hostile attitude of the New York fans. In less than a month both Stanley and Mickoski were favorites of Hawk supporters.

The platoon system of goaltending was getting a grip in the NHL this season as Chicago called up Hank Bassen from Buffalo as a relief man for Al Rollins. In the fall Lorne Worsley won back his netminding job from Johnny Bower, who had displaced him in the preceding season. Bower went to Vancouver where a youngster named John Ferguson hung around the team and helped with the sticks. Boston searched for someone to alternate with Sugar Jim Henry and gave Ray Gariepy to Toronto for 20-year-old John Henderson. In January Henderson had the best netminding record in the NHL. He lost only three of 14 games.

The Bruins got a new coach when Milt Schmidt took over from Lynn Patrick. Earlier in the season Schmidt had scored his 229th goal, the highest in Boston history. Fern Flaman, originally a Bruin, was brought back into the fold when the Leafs accepted Dave Creighton in exchange during an off-season deal. Rookie Don McKenney contributed 22 goals and 20 assists and played for a time with Doug Mohns and Murray Costello, who had been obtained from Chicago in exchange for Lorne Ferguson.

The Rangers took on more color. On October 27, Lou Fontinato was elevated from Vancouver to replace the injured Allan Stanley. In February, Bill Ezinicki joined the Rangers for 15 games, coming up from Vancouver as the Rangers sent Jack McLeod plus a cash payment in return. Larry Popein, Dean Prentice and Ron Murphy were mixed with other sophomores and rookies. The club made it to fifth place but didn't gain the playoff berth they had been aiming for since 1949.

Gordie Howe went into his worst scoring slump in nine years. He started the season fast with 20 goals in his first 37 games, but then collected only four in the next 17 games. In November his linemate, Ted Lindsay, scored the 250th goal of his career. With only five games remaining in the schedule the Wings signed defenseman Larry Hillman, 18 years old and the youngest player in the league.

On February 1, Conn Smythe stepped down as general manager of the Maple Leafs and handed the position over to Hap Day, promising he would still "take an interest" in the running of the Gardens. Smythe, then 60, retained the presidency of the team. Toronto's grasp on third place was flimsy the night of March 12 when they lost Tim Horton, one of their best defensemen. Horton suffered a broken leg and a broken jaw in a collision with New York's Bill Gadsby in Maple Leaf Gardens.

Ted Lindsay of Detroit was given a 10-day suspension for striking a spectator with his stick in a game in Toronto on January 22. The incident occurred after Eric Nesterenko and Gordie Howe scuffled along the boards and the fan grabbed Howe's stick. As Howe pulled away, the spectator reached over the boards in an effort to hit him. Lindsay, who was 30 or 40 feet away, rushed forward and struck the fan.

The Canadiens were tough playoff opponents even though Richard had been suspended in March after the action that caused the "riot." Montreal was able to eliminate Boston in five games. Coach Dick Irvin set a precedent for playoff strategy when he alternated two goaltenders, Plante and Charlie Hodge, in the first two games, which the Canadiens won handily. In the fourth game Jim Henry sustained a fracture of the upper jaw and cuts over his left eye after being hit by a hard shot from Calum MacKay late in the third period. He returned to play out the last few minutes of the game, but afterwards announced his upcoming retirement. Henderson was in the nets for the fifth and deciding game.

When the Leafs met the Red Wings in their series they were without Tim Horton. Toronto had the lowest goal production in the league and an indifferent power play. Detroit had no difficulty winning the minimum four games.

The seven games of the final series between the Canadiens and Red Wings were rough, fast and without overtime. Montreal lost the first two games on Olympia ice, but tied up the series in Montreal. It was in this series that the Canadiens snapped a 15-game record winning streak by Detroit, a string of victories that had begun on February 27 and continued until April 7. But that wasn't good enough. With two goals in Detroit's 3–1 win, Alex Delvecchio was the hero of the seventh and Cup winning game.

1955–56

In May 1955, Dick Irvin left Montreal and signed as coach of the Chicago Blackhawks. In replacing Frank Eddolls, whom he had coached as a rookie on the Montreal defense, Irvin said, "We're going to shoot for third place." Irvin was returning to his first NHL club, the one he captained in 1926 when Chicago first entered the league. He was appointed coach in 1929 and was later dropped in favor of Godfrey Matheson in 1931–32.

Toe Blake, a 14-year veteran with the Canadiens, was named as Irvin's successor on June 8. Blake was Selke's personal choice over Billy Reay and Roger Leger, who had also been candidates. When he officially accepted the job, Blake said one of his greatest ambitions had been realized.

Two weeks after Irvin's appointment the Blackhawks sent Gerry Toppazzini, Bucky Hollingworth, Johnny McCormack and Dave Creighton to Detroit for Tony Leswick, Glen Skov, Johnny Wilson and Benny Woit. This was designed to give Irvin the kind of material he needed to mold together a contending team.

Before Detroit had finished bartering they had only nine players left from their Cup-holding team of the previous spring. Jack Adams swapped the classy Terry

Sawchuk, Vic Stasiuk, Lorne Davis and Marcel Bonin to Boston for Bruin captain Ed Sandford, Real Chevrefils, Norm Corcoran, Warren Godfrey and Gilles Boisvert. Sawchuk was the current Vezina Trophy winner, but had showed nervous strain and Adams was apparently disenchanted with him. Glenn Hall, who had substituted briefly in the 1954–55 season, was brought up as Sawchuk's successor.

Sandford's stay with the Wings was brief. The season wasn't a month old before he was shipped to Chicago in exchange for Metro Prystai.

A summer change in the New York front office saw Muzz Patrick step up as manager and introduce ex-Ranger Phil Watson as coach. Harry Howell became the club's eighth captain and those close to the scene predicted, "This is the Rangers' year." With Andy Hebenton promoted from Vancouver and producing 24 unexpected goals, plus a healthy production from Bathgate, Creighton, Lewicki, Prentice and Murphy, the Rangers clicked for 203 goals and finished third.

Before Toronto began their 70-game schedule, Hap Day handed King Clancy a fighting slogan of "Guts, Glamor and Goals." Billy Harris, a fragile, 20-year-old center from the Toronto junior Marlboros, had been signed as a possible replacement for the retired Ted Kennedy. Dick Duff and Earl Balfour were added. In all, Toronto introduced 16 rookies with seven gaining permanent berths.

The Red Wings had their worst start since 1938 and slid quickly into the cellar. In a desperate move, Red Kelly was moved to the forward line to inject scoring punch, but only on a temporary basis. With coach Jimmy Skinner juggling his lineup, the Wings came out of their slump with enough power to gain second place, but well behind the Canadiens. Most of Detroit's offensive power was generated by Howe, Lindsay, Delvecchio and Reibel. In October, captain Ted Lindsay surpassed the mark set by Aurel Joliat as the highest scoring left-winger, by collecting his 271st goal. In February, Gordie Howe became the third player in NHL history to score 300 goals, thus joining Nels Stewart and Maurice Richard.

For a rookie coach Toe Blake manipulated the Canadiens like a veteran. He had invited 54 men to training camp and retained three rookies: Henri Richard, Claude Provost and Jean Guy Talbot. Gerry McNeil attempted a comeback, but couldn't displace Jacques Plante. Butch Bouchard, who had announced his retirement, changed his mind and remained as captain. By mid-February the Canadiens had virtually clinched the NHL championship, largely on the goals of Beliveau, Richard, Olmstead and Geoffrion. Between them they had amassed 128 regular schedule goals.

The 1955–56 season was not without its fights, but the disturbances were minor compared to some seasons. One of the most astounding incidents was the 22 minutes in penalties picked up by Red Kelly in one period. In Detroit on October 16, Kelly became enraged at Toronto's Eric Nesterenko. Besides a minor and two majors, Kelly drew a misconduct, more penalty minutes than he had served in all his past eight seasons in the league.

The Boston Bruins were pushed into fifth place by the surge of the Rangers, but they were contenders until the finish, ending only two points behind fourth-place Toronto. Terry Sawchuk was accepted with enthusiasm by Bruin fans. He gained nine shutouts and his presence in a Boston uniform undoubtedly accounted for an increased attendance. But the Bruins slumped so badly that Johnny Peirson, who had retired to go into business, returned to offer his services. He took part in 33 games and scored 11 goals and got 14 assists.

Although Chicago finished sixth for the third consecutive year, most experts conceded that they were a vastly improved team under Irvin's hand. The coach himself had visions of second place as late as December. The Hawks' downfall could be attributed to injuries to key players. The trouble began when defenseman Gus Mortson entered a Boston hospital for emergency surgery and missed several games. Filling in as team captain was Harry Watson, who in turn was replaced by defenseman Lee Fogolin. In Fogolin's initial game as captain he had no *C* on his sweater and, therefore, the officials would not recognize his status. A makeshift job with adhesive tape served for the rest of the game, but when he played his next contest he sported an 18-inch *C*—large enough for the poorest eyes to recognize.

When the season ended the Canadiens held the NHL championship with 100 points and took most of the individual awards. Yet King Clancy, whose Leafs lost to Detroit 4–1 in the Cup semi-finals, predicted the Wings, with Calder Trophy-winner Glenn Hall in the nets, would be too strong for Montreal.

The only game the Canadiens lost to the Rangers in their semi-final encounter was the second one, playing against rookie netminder Gordie Bell. Bell was 31 and playing in the Quebec League when he got the call to replace Worsley, who was out for the season with torn knee ligaments. In posting a 4–2 win, Bell helped the Rangers snatch their first Forum victory since January 30, 1954.

In the same number of games—five—the Canadiens overcame Detroit to win the Stanley Cup for Toe Blake in his rookie season. Having outscored New York 24–9 in their series, Montreal went on to out-score Detroit 18–9. The only game the Wings won was the third one by a 3–1 score. Red Kelly, who was hit by a Sid Smith shot in the mouth in the final game of the Toronto series, was playing with 12 stitches in his face and minus several teeth. He was also on a liquid diet and was weakened by the loss of 12 pounds. Still, Kelly scored the first Wings' goal and rallied his teammates to a win.

Beliveau scored the opening goal in what proved to be the final game, his 59th goal of the year, including 12 in the playoffs.

1956–57

In the annual All-Star game preceding the regular season, Rocket Richard, newly elected captain of the Canadiens, and Ted Lindsay were the goal scorers as the All-Stars and the Canadiens battled to a 1–1 tie.

In Montreal a fan named Tom Donohue complained to police that thieves had invaded his home and made off with $385 worth of season tickets for Montreal games. Nothing else was touched. It was another indication of the soaring popularity of hockey.

American hockey fans were able to tune in to hockey on their television sets for the first time this season. CBS-TV began telecasting games on Saturday afternoons from the four American cities in the league and many predicted that hockey would soon rival the popularity of baseball and football among American viewers.

In mid-January Terry Sawchuk was in the news after an earlier lengthy illness. In a dramatic move he quit the Boston hockey club and went into hiding. The Bruins' Milt Schmidt called up Norm Defelice to replace Sawchuk and denied that he'd called Sawchuk a quitter. On the day he quit, Sawchuk's name appeared on the mid-season

All-Star team. He was suspended by Boston and he threatened to sue four Boston papers for saying nasty things about him. With Sawchuk on the sidelines, Boston bought the rights to Don Simmons from Springfield and Simmons took over from Defelice. The following season saw Sawchuk back with Detroit.

The floundering Toronto Maple Leafs unveiled an 18-year-old rookie, Frank Mahovlich, a 200-pound center called up on a three-game basis. Mahovlich made his big-league debut on March 20, 1957, and delighted Toronto fans with his speed and playmaking ability.

Throughout the regular schedule, Detroit was once again the class of the league, although they floundered against Boston in the playoffs. On March 17, the Red Wings won their eighth league title in nine years by beating the Canadiens 2–1.

The playoffs got underway and Rocket Richard, the 35-year-old wizard, scored the winning goal in overtime as the Canadiens ousted the New York Rangers in one semi-final series 4–1.

The Boston Bruins stunned the Detroit Red Wings in the other series, whipping the Wings decisively 4–1 in games. In the finals, Richard stole the spotlight again in game number one. The Rocket scored four times as Montreal took the opener 5–1. After the game, Don Simmons said of Richard's outburst, "It was humiliating." Beliveau's goal in the second game gave Montreal a 1–0 victory and a two-game edge in the series.

It was Geoffrion's turn in game number three. The Boomer scored twice in a 4–2 Montreal victory. Jack Bionda gave Bruin fans a rare chance to cheer when he flattened the Richard brothers, one after the other. Fleming Mackell kept Boston in the series in the fourth game, scoring both goals in a 2–0 Bruin win. Mackell's second goal was into an empty net as Richard scurried back too late, prompting one wag to report, "They've finally found the Rocket's weakness. He can't play goal."

The Canadiens breezed to another 4–1 Cup victory in game number five. Rookie Andre Pronovost, along with veterans Dickie Moore, Bernie Geoffrion, Donnie Marshall and Floyd Curry, scored for Montreal as the Bruins were beaten 5–1.

Near the end of the season the Toronto team announced plans for the next year. Conn Smythe recommended that Howie Meeker be retained as coach, King Clancy be retained to "do nothing" again next season and George Armstrong be named the new Leafs' captain. Smythe said he'd have a statement about Hap Day's position with the club in a day or two, but Day beat him to the punch by announcing that he was no longer available for further hockey employment with the Leafs.

1957–58

In September 1957, Senator Hartland Molson announced that he had bought controlling interest in the Canadien Arena Company, which owned and operated the Montreal Forum and the Montreal Canadiens. Senator Molson bought 60 percent of the shares from Senator Donat Raymond. The price was not announced but it was estimated at between $4 million and $5 million.

The same day, Ted Lindsay, traded in the off-season from Detroit to Chicago, announced that the NHL Players' Association planned court action against the league "to gain our rights." The suit was for $3 million. The Players' Association, of which Lindsay was president, had been refused recognition by the league.

Before the season began, Foster Hewitt, the voice of hockey in Canada, handed over the play-by-play job to his son Bill, and the CBC announced that the Hot Stove League, a long-time intermission fixture on radio and television, would be dropped with the coming season.

The schedule was barely underway when Rocket Richard scored his 500th NHL goal. Richard immediately dedicated the puck to the memory of the late Dick Irvin, "The man who taught me everything I know about hockey." Irvin had died in May, after 30 consecutive seasons in the NHL, 26 as coach and four as a player.

In Detroit Jack Adams saluted Richard's achievement, then said, "Someday our big number nine, Gordie Howe, will join Richard in the 500-goal circle." At the time, Howe, 29 years old, had 354 goals.

In November the Detroit players handed the Players' Association a crushing body check when they announced that they were no longer a part of the group.

An injury threatened to end Rocket Richard's career in November. His Achilles tendon was almost completely severed by Marc Reaume's skate and, at the age of 36, many fans thought he would call it a day.

A big, blond kid named Bobby Hull was the talk of Chicago. Not since Ted Kennedy had entered the league had a youngster looked so talented at such an early age. Hull was only 18.

Montreal's Jacques Plante drew attention to himself by wearing a novel plastic face mask in practice sessions.

After the New Year, Rudy Pilous took over the Chicago coaching reins from Tommy Ivan, who carried on as Chicago manager.

A speedster from Fredericton, New Brunswick, Willie O'Ree, became the first black player to make the NHL when he performed for Boston against Montreal on January 18 in Boston.

Boom Boom Geoffrion was the leading goal scorer in February with 27 when he collided with Andre Pronovost in practice. Geoffrion suffered a ruptured bowel and underwent major surgery.

The Toronto Maple Leafs finished last for the first time in history and Wren Blair was rumored to be the man Stafford Smythe wanted to take over as the new Toronto manager.

Dickie Moore played the last five weeks of the season with a cast on his right wrist but he still won the scoring title with 84 points.

It was Montreal's year. The Habs beat Detroit four straight in one semi-final series. Richard, who missed 42 regular-season games, pulled his team from a 3–1 deficit in the final period of the fourth game. The Rocket scored a hat trick to pace the Habs to a 4–3 win. It was his 1,000th game in the NHL.

Boston walloped New York 8–2 in the final game of their best-of-seven series. The Bruins took that one in six games.

In the finals, Boston and Montreal were tied 2–2 in games when Richard cut loose again. He scored one of his patented overtime goals in the fifth game to sink the Bruins. The Rocket had only two shots on goal all night but he connected on the one that counted.

Geoffrion, back in shape after his operation, fired two goals in the sixth game to help the Canadiens to a 5–3 victory and the Stanley Cup.

1958–59

The June 1958 intra-league draft was one of the most active in years. The Rangers lost five men and were compensated by $75,000. Chicago took defenseman Jack Evans. The Canadiens grabbed Danny Lewicki and Dave Creighton, Boston drafted Guy Gendron and Gord Redahl. The Canadiens lost Bert Olmstead and Gerry Wilson to Toronto. Olmstead reported late, due to an assault case in Vancouver, but even at 31 he was a great asset to Toronto. In other moves Chicago took Earl Balfour from Toronto and Al Arbour from Detroit, Boston snared Earl Reibel from Chicago and Toronto sold Tod Sloan to Chicago.

In August the Leafs signed 33-year-old goaltender Johnny Bower to a two-year contract. Assistant team manager Punch Imlach, a new addition to the front office, flew to Saskatoon to personally cinch the pact. Staff Smythe predicted, "Bower could be worth 10 points to us." Further changes were made in October. Defenseman Jim Morrison, long ago destined to move on, was traded to Boston with cash for 32-year-old Allan Stanley and rookie Carl Brewer was signed on his 21st birthday.

Montreal coach Toe Blake looked over the 56 candidates he had in camp and observed, "This is definitely the strongest bunch I've seen in my four years as coach at the camp." Out of the newcomers he had selected center Ralph Backstrom, who went on to score 18 goals and 22 assists and grab the Calder Memorial Trophy.

The Blackhawks, coached by Rudy Pilous, considered center ice their weak spot. With Glenn Hall in his second season as a Hawk and newly acquired Dollard St. Laurent to go with Arbour, Pilote, Evans and Vasko on defense, the Hawks loomed strong behind the blue line. Up front Chicago had sophomore Bobby Hull, Murray Balfour, Kenny Wharram, Ted Lindsay, Tod Sloan and Glen Skov. As further insurance, left-winger Danny Lewicki was purchased from the Canadiens for the $15,000 waiver price.

Phil Watson's Rangers were hopeful that Eddie Shack would be the top rookie in 1958–59. His elevation was designed to help add muscle to a lightweight team.

This was to be a rough season for Sid Abel's Red Wings, who were about to slip down to the cellar from the third spot they had held the previous season, despite Gordie Howe's 32 goals.

Jack Adams called the Boston Bruins "a strong defensive team that could give the Canadiens trouble." They had the "Uke Line" and four players who surpassed the 20-goal mark, with Don McKenney leading the way with 32. Don Simmons was in goal, surrounded by defensemen Hillman, Flaman, Boivin, Armstrong and Morrison.

On November 21, Punch Imlach was promoted to the rank of general manager of the Leafs, authorized to make whatever changes were necessary. A week later Billy Reay was fired and Imlach was handling the dual role of manager-coach with Olmstead as a temporary playing-coach.

In a 6–1 win for the Canadiens over the Rangers in late February, the biggest mass brawl on Forum ice in years suddenly broke out. The game was held up 15 minutes as players engaged in savage fighting.

Two weeks later another brawl erupted, this time in Toronto between the Rangers and the Leafs. It was sparked by Lou Fontinato's cross-check of Larry Regan, a player the Leafs had acquired from Boston in January for the $15,000 waiver price. Then a fan attempted to attack Fontinato in the penalty box. When his teammates dashed to his rescue the Leaf bench emptied after them. The final score was 5–0 for Toronto.

In November, the Rocket scored the 600th goal of his career, including playoffs, when he connected against the Rangers in New York. On January 9 in Montreal, he collected his 525th regular-schedule goal in a 3–0 win over the Leafs. Meanwhile, his arch rival Gordie Howe collected his 400th goal in a December tie in Montreal.

At 37, Richard sustained a broken ankle in January 1959, which was slow to mend. He was out of action for three months, returning without practice during the playoffs. Another star who was out for the entire season was Chicago's Stan Mikita, who suffered a dislocated shoulder.

Termed the "Cinderella Team," the Leafs battled to the last game of the season to edge their way into the playoffs by a single point over New York. The disappointed Rangers, who were almost assured of a playoff berth and had sold tickets two weeks earlier, had to refund thousands of dollars. Muzz Patrick and Phil Watson singled out Lorne Worsley as the man most responsible for their team's slump in the last 10 days, when they lost six out of seven games.

Imlach predicted the Leafs would oust Boston in six games, but it took them seven and some were hectic. Pinch hitter Harry Lumley was pressed into the nets for Boston in the opening game and guided them to a 5–1 victory. Game two went to Boston on a 4–2 score. The Leafs stormed back to tie the series, with Ehman as the spark plug in the third game and Mahovlich the overtime scorer in the fourth. It was Johnny Bower, termed a miracle man, who aided the Leafs in their third straight win. "And I was going to bench him in favor of Ed Chadwick," shuddered Imlach. Boston fought back to even the series and force a seventh game, but their injuries made them easier prey for Toronto. With Ehman getting the winner, the Leafs went into the finals on a 3–2 win.

The Canadiens took a two-game lead over Chicago in their semi-final series. They not only lost the third game 4–2, but lost their star center, Jean Beliveau, with a fractured spine. Ken Mosdell was called up from the Montreal Royals as his replacement. Before 17,538 home fans the Hawks tied the series. The Canadiens won the fifth and sixth games 4–2 and 5–4.

In the sixth game, Junior Langlois of Montreal allegedly tripped the Hawks' Bobby Hull, but referee Red Storey failed to call a penalty. Three fans rushed out of their seats to pour beer on Storey's head and knocked him to the ice. Debris littered the ice as the game was held up 25 minutes. Because Storey felt his actions had not been upheld by the league president, who had reportedly criticized him, Storey refused to continue to work as an NHL official. His resignation on April 7 made the front pages.

With the Rocket back, but Beliveau out, the Canadiens took on the Leafs and eliminated them in five games. The score of the opening game was 5–3 for Montreal, but an optimistic Imlach figured the champs were on their way out. His theory was shattered when his team lost 3–1, despite Bower's outstanding display. An overtime goal by Duff in the third game provided Toronto's only victory. A 3–2 Canadien win, followed by a 5–3 decision, permitted Montreal to create history as they won an unprecedented fourth successive Stanley Cup. Thus Toe Blake became the first coach to guide his team to four championships in a row.

1959–60

In the June draft, Boston plucked Autry Erickson from the Hawks, Charlie Burns from

Detroit and Bruce Gamble from the Rangers. No one paid much attention when the Wings snatched Gary Aldcorn from Toronto until he was placed on a line with Gordie Howe and ended up with 22 goals and 29 assists.

New York reportedly got the "cream of the crop" when they snared Brian Cullen and Ian Cushenan. This was the season that New York vowed they would make the playoffs no matter how many changes were needed. The Rangers had counted heavily upon Eddie Shack in his rookie season, but he didn't earn a single vote for the Calder Trophy. With goalie Lorne Worsley in and out of hot water, the Rangers employed more netminders than usual, including Marcel Paille, Al Rollins and Jack McCartan. In November 1959, with coach Phil Watson in hospital for his ulcer, Alf Pike was hired to handle the team and Watson was relegated to look after the Ranger farm system. New York ended the season in last place with 49 points.

The new whip cracker of the league was Punch Imlach. In September there was the rumor of a possible Leafs revolt in a dispute over fatter contracts. Imlach commented, "If they strike I'll replace them with players from our minor teams." The gossip faded and the men signed. By December the big disappointment was the dismal play of Frank Mahovlich with only three goals in 22 games. He ended the 70 games with 18 goals and 21 assists.

The big news among goalies was Jacques Plante's decision to wear a face mask of his own design. Coach Toe Blake was at first dubious and then disenchanted by the decision. Lorne Worsley candidly stated he'd never cover his face. In January, after observing Plante over half the schedule, Terry Sawchuk figured the mask wouldn't last. "I wouldn't want to wear one regularly," he stated. Using the best possible means of squashing all the doubters, Plante won the Vezina Trophy.

Managing director Frank Selke found it easy to sign up his employees. Toe Blake inked a three-year coaching contract while Rocket Richard signed for his 18th season. In November, for the third consecutive winter, Richard was severely injured. This time a flying puck smashed his left cheekbone, putting him out for a month. At 38, some observers felt he was finished, but on April 14 it was captain Richard who accepted the Stanley Cup on Toronto ice from Clarence Campbell.

The Blackhawks did some juggling in 1959–60, moving Bobby Hull from center to left wing and inserting rookies Murray Balfour and Bill Hay into their lineup. Once owned by Montreal, the latter two players had been termed Hab castoffs, a remark which annoyed Frank Selke. He pointed out that the Canadiens could only protect 18 men and it was only fair to let two fine prospects go to a club that needed help. Before long the unit of Hull, Balfour and Hay was being hailed as the "Million Dollar Line."

Boston ended the season in fifth place, but one of their players, Bronco Horvath, lost the scoring title to Bobby Hull by only one point. The 39 goals and 41 assists picked up by Horvath was his greatest NHL output. Despite Boston's defensive weakness, coach Milt Schmidt singled out Don Simmons for individual praise and noted that his play had improved since he had begun wearing a face mask.

The Red Wings experienced a mediocre season. For a time Gordie Howe and the entire club slumped. Then on January 13, Howe's 436th career goal ran his point total to 945 in regular-schedule games to tie Maurice Richard's record. On February 4, manager Jack Adams traded Red Kelly and forward Bill McNeill to the Rangers for Bill Gadsby and Eddie Shack. Angered by the manner in which the trade was engineered, Kelly adamantly refused to go to New York and retired. For personal reasons,

McNeill, whose wife had died a few months earlier, also retired rather than take his two-year-old daughter to New York.

By Wednesday, February 10, Red Kelly was a Maple Leaf and defenseman Marc Reaume was a Red Wing. With King Clancy using Irish persuasion, Kelly was induced to come out of retirement and the Wings were convinced they could bolster the hole made on their blue line by acquiring Reaume.

On January 6, fierce stick-swinging action broke out between Bobby Hull and Lou Fontinato in a game in New York. Using their sticks as bayonets the duel became so rough that officials and players hesitated to restore order. Also in January, Carl Brewer shoved Toronto's penalty time-keeper Jack Hewit and then pushed him in the face. Brewer was serving a misconduct penalty at the time for swearing at referee Eddie Powers and locking the penalty-box door when the period ended so that league officials could not get to their dressing room.

Topping the league with 92 points to Toronto's 79, the Canadiens went into series A against Chicago as heavy favorites, although Blake warned that the Hawks would be tough. With Hull sidelined with a throat infection, the Canadiens scored a 4–3 win in the opener. The line of Jean Beliveau, Bernie Geoffrion and Marcel Bonin paced Montreal.

The second game went to Montreal by the same score, but it was accomplished the hard way—in overtime. Doug Harvey pulled off the winning goal and vindicated himself for being the goat on Bill Hay's game-tying goal with 62 seconds left in the third period. A decisive 4–0 victory clinched game three for Montreal with a makeshift line of Ralph Backstrom, Don Marshall and Billy Hicke leading the attack. Infuriated Hawk fans bombarded the ice with boards, sandbags and paper as the disorganized home team failed to get a shot on Plante in the final 10 minutes. A 2–0 win on March 31 swept Chicago aside and thrust Montreal into the finals.

The Toronto–Detroit semi-final series opened on March 23, with goals by Gordie Howe and Len "Comet" Haley providing a 2–1 win for Detroit. With Larry Regan providing the spark, game two went to the Leafs by a 4–2 score. The incentive that spurred the team was the $1,250 lying in the middle of the dressing-room floor after the team's pre-game warm-up. It had been put there by the psychology-conscious Imlach, along with a message on the dressing-room blackboard which read: "'Take a good look at center of the floor. This represents the difference between winning and losing."

Thoughts of the loot may have carried over to the next night in Detroit, when the game went into three overtime periods before Frank Mahovlich scored his second goal of the night in a 5–4 victory. Playing a big part in the series against his old mates, Red Kelly set up the winning goals in the second and third games. The Wings evened the series in game four on a goal from Jerry Melnyk in overtime, with Toronto's Ron Stewart in the penalty box.

The fifth game ended with Toronto winning 5–4. The hero was defenseman Allan Stanley, who cut loose with two goals and assisted on two others. Stanley had scored only three goals in 40 previous Cup games. Overcoming a 2–1 deficit going into the third period of game six, Toronto ousted Detroit from the playoffs with a 4–2 win. It was Pulford who paced them with two goals, but Frank Mahovlich who scored the winner.

With the Leafs all healthy and riding the crest of Johnny Bower's classy goaltending, they met the Canadiens, who were supposedly less formidable because Beliveau,

Bonin and Harvey were hobbling. A 3–0 shutout for Montreal was the result of the opener as Henri Richard picked up a goal and two assists.

Using strong defensive tactics in game two, the Canadiens edged the Leafs by 2–1 in a dull contest. Then they came up with a 5–2 win in the third game. Phil Goyette collected two goals, the aging Rocket scored his first goal of the playoffs and Henri Richard and Don Marshall completed the scoring.

Imlach had hopes that the Leafs might come back, but a resounding 4–0 whacking knocked them out of contention and gave the Canadiens their fifth consecutive Stanley Cup. This marked the second time that a club had swept to the Cup in eight straight games. Detroit had done it back in 1952.

VII

THE MONEY YEARS

Prosperity and Expansion, 1960–1970

Although the expanded NHL did not become a reality until the 1967–68 season, much talk and behind-the-scenes maneuvering took place during the sixties. Clarence Campbell persistently squashed expansion rumors, which most often involved Los Angeles and San Francisco, but it was only a matter of time before money talked. Television revenue and the upsurge in attendance throughout the league, setting new records year after year, could not go unnoticed. Nor could big offers, such as $1 million for Mahovlich made by Chicago's Jim Norris in 1962 or other big-money deals indicating the prosperity of the clubs.

Finally formal discussions about expansion started in 1965, and on February 8, 1966, Clarence Campbell announced that the following centers would have teams: Los Angeles, San Francisco, St. Louis, Pittsburgh, Philadelphia and Minnesota. Acceptance of Jack Kent Cooke's Los Angeles bid was unexpected, as was the inclusion of St. Louis, which had made no formal application. The omission of Vancouver, which rankled many Canadians, was excused on the grounds that Vancouver would add no new television audience. Vancouver's bid for a franchise was also said to be poorly prepared.

The cost of each franchise was $2 million payable to each original club, for which the new members would get 20 players each from the old clubs.

Working quickly, the new clubs began to line up front office men. The St. Louis Blues signed the proven Lynn Patrick as general manager and Scotty Bowman as coach. Minnesota chose Wren Blair as manager-coach. The Philadelphia Flyers signed Bud Poile as manager and Keith Allen as coach. The Pittsburgh Penguins hired Jack Riley with Red Sullivan as coach. San Francisco and Los Angeles made no final arrangements in this period.

For four out of the first seven seasons of the sixties, the Montreal Canadiens finished on top of the league, continuing their dominance of the late fifties despite the retirement of Rocket Richard. In the Stanley Cup playoffs they did not fare as well, winning only in 1964–65 and 1965–66, with the Toronto Maple Leafs taking the rest, except for a 1960–61 upset by Chicago.

These were years of team play, with players of each club vying for scoring honors and defensive laurels, but one star led the rest—Bobby Hull of Chicago. Hull had the most goals of any player for 1961–62, 1963–64, 1965–66 and 1966–67, including a record-breaking 50 in 1961–62 and the all-time high of 54 in the 1965–66 season.

Howe continued his amazing career, notching his 600th NHL goal in 1965, winning the new Lester Patrick Award in 1966 and being chosen for every All-Star team of the period.

1960–61

The Silver Fox of hockey, Lester Patrick, died on June 1, 1960, in a Victoria, B.C., hospital at the age of 76. Patrick had run the gamut of hockey from player, coach and manager to the vice-presidency of Madison Square Garden in his long career with the Rangers. At the time of his death his younger son, Muzz, was vice-president and general manager of the Rangers while Lynn held a similar position with the Boston Bruins.

After the June draft meeting in Montreal there was the usual changing of team sweaters for a number of players. Boston took two minor-league defensemen, Ted Green and Tom Thurlby, plus forward Jimmy Bartlett. Parker MacDonald was drafted by Detroit, while Toronto grabbed Guy Rousseau and defenseman Larry Hillman. Detroit traded Jim Morrison to Chicago for Howie Glover and a day later Morrison was drafted by the Rangers, who also claimed Billy McNeill and Ted Hampson. Montreal sent Ab McDonald to the Hawks for Glen Skov and Terry Gray plus a cash payment. In an involved scheme, Bob Courcy, Cec Hoekstra and Reg Fleming were allowed to leave the Canadien chain and go to Chicago.

In July, with 14 consecutive seasons behind him, left-winger Ted Lindsay of the Hawks announced his retirement. He had participated in 999 league games and set a record for left-wingers with 365 goals. During his career he had served 1,623 minutes in penalties.

Rocket Richard debated whether or not to attempt a 19th season with the Canadiens. He was out of condition, slightly overweight and had been much injured. On September 15, Richard regretfully announced his decision to retire and become Montreal's goodwill ambassador. He had set 17 records, played in 978 league games and 133 playoff contests. For 16 consecutive campaigns he was selected on one of the two All-Star teams. Only one achievement eluded him—he never won the NHL scoring championship.

Veteran Bert Olmstead and defenseman Tim Horton were holdouts for Toronto. Forward Johnny Wilson asked to be traded when he balked at demotion to the minors. He was concerned because his iron-man record of having played in 580 straight league games would be broken. Dick Duff also differed with Imlach over salary and became the last Leaf to sign. A November trade saw Toronto send Wilson and Pat Hannigan to the Rangers for Eddie Shack, a brilliant junior who had only been mediocre in the NHL up to this time. Shack wanted to escape New York, whereas Wilson and Hannigan wanted regular work.

Injuries played havoc with all teams in 1960–61. For Toronto, only Frank Mahovlich, Bob Baun and rookie Dave Keon played the full schedule. Out of the entire league only 21 players dressed for all 70 games. Chicago's valuable "Scooter Line" of Kenny Wharram, Ab McDonald and Stan Mikita was broken up when Wharram sustained a fractured jaw. Toe Blake lamented that his Canadien roster was never intact. New York had to get along without Lorne Worsley and Lou Fontinato.

Toronto went through three goalies sidelined with injuries: Bower, Gerry McNamara and Cesare Maniago. Pulford, Allan Stanley, Red Kelly, Eddie Shack and George Armstrong gave Imlach plenty of lineup miseries.

Toronto and Montreal dominated the headlines for two reasons. They battled to the season's end for the league championship, which the Canadiens won by two points. Then there was an individual scoring duel between Frank Mahovlich and Bernie Geoffrion, which was not immediately evident since another Canadien, Dickie Moore, was leading the pack with 21 goals in November. Moore eventually finished with 35.

Helped by a fantastic 18 goals in 11 games, Geoffrion scored his 50th goal in the Montreal Forum on March 16 against Toronto's Cesare Maniago while rival Mahovlich went pointless. The fans thundered their approval as Geoffrion joined the Rocket's elite circle and garnered the scoring title with 95 points over teammate Beliveau's 90 and Mahovlich's 84.

Ten years earlier Geoffrion had vowed to his bride, the former Marlene Morenz, "Someday, I'll score more goals than your father did." On December 7, 1960, in Maple Leaf Gardens, he rapped in two goals—his 270th and 271st—which respectively tied and surpassed the goal output of Howie Morenz.

Detroit opened their first season in 15 years without Gordie Howe, who had been injured in the All-Star game in Montreal. But their big gun recuperated quickly and on December 1, in a game against Boston at Detroit, he boosted his total points, including playoffs, to 1,093, two more than the record once held by Maurice Richard.

Brawls, threats and fines played a major part of the 1960–61 season as the league raked in money from the offenders. An early October game between Boston and Detroit was delayed 10 minutes by a wild, swinging free-for-all. On October 19, Montreal charged that Mahovlich had deliberately shot a puck at Henri Richard's eye. In another Montreal–Toronto encounter, on December 1, Henri Richard, who scored with goals and punches, collected 29 minutes in penalties and a $50 fine. Punch Imlach openly taunted referee Frank Udvari for "The worst officiating I've ever seen since I came to the NHL." In February referee Eddie Powers was hit by a puck after calling a disputed goal for the Leafs.

A brawl in January between Toronto and New York ended with defenseman Lou Fontinato in hospital for surgery to close a deep skate gash. It was alleged he had been kicked by a Leafs' player.

One of the worst fights of 1960–61 erupted on Toronto ice when the Hawks and Leafs clashed in mid-March. This one started when Pilote hit Shack with his stick and both benches cleared. In an unusual procedure, four policemen stepped on the ice to separate combatants.

It was a bleak season for Boston. The Bruins ended in the cellar with only 46 points.

Both coach Milt Schmidt and manager Lynn Patrick denied rumors that their jobs were insecure. To spread their scoring punch the Uke Line of Vic Stasiuk, Johnny Bucyk and Bronco Horvath was broken up in December. A month later it was permanently disrupted when Stasiuk and Leo Labine went to Detroit for Murray Oliver, Gary Aldcorn and Tom McCarthy.

The plight of the fifth-place Rangers was not much better. Coach Alf Pike was fired in March.

The opening game of the series A semi-finals between Montreal and Chicago saw the Canadiens make a strong comeback to win 6–3, but three of their players, Bill Hicke, Don Marshall and Jean Beliveau, were injured. Montreal representatives cried "dirty hockey." With Ed Litzenberger breaking up the second game late in the third period the Hawks tied the series on a 4–3 win played under less violent circumstances.

A marathon third game, which went into three overtime sessions, was won by Chicago on Murray Balfour's backhand shot. Coach Blake's temper sizzled so hotly over an injury to Geoffrion and the officiating of Dalt McArthur that he took a swing at the referee. His rash action cost him $2,000. In game four the Canadiens fired 60 shots at goalie Glenn Hall, 52 of them in the first two periods. The Canadiens romped to a 5–2 victory and evened the series.

The Hawks came back with a pair of shutouts and eliminated the champion Canadiens in six games. In a desperate effort to get into the final game, Geoffrion disregarded medical orders and removed the cast from his injured knee.

Canadiens' manager Frank Selke had accolades for Glenn Hall, whom he congratulated. Maurice Richard termed the series the dirtiest he had ever witnessed.

Series B between Toronto and Detroit went five games before Toronto was ousted. The only Leafs' win was a 3–2 overtime decision on George Armstrong's goal.

An all-American final brought hockey fever to Chicago. The opener went to Chicago 3–2, a win they salvaged after holding a 3–0 first-period lead. Sawchuk was injured early in the game and had to be replaced by Hank Bassen. With Howe shadowing Hull, Detroit won the second game 3–1. Game three went to Chicago 3–1 after the Hawks were instructed to use their weight. Coach Pilous had also told them to get rid of their "Howe complex."

Detroit came back to win game four 2–1 and deadlocked the series again. Tommy Ivan and Pilous made remarks about the officiating which cost them fines of $300 and $200 respectively. The last two games went to the Hawks 6–3 and 5–1 and the Stanley Cup went to Chicago for the first time since 1937–38.

1961–62

A long-awaited hockey dream came true on August 26, 1961, when Prime Minister John Diefenbaker formally opened the new $500,000 International Hockey Hall of Fame at the Canadian National Exhibition in Toronto. On the opening day, which saw the captains of the six teams raise their club pennants on flag poles, the new building boasted 89 members, 43 still living.

One of Montreal's greatest defensemen, Doug Harvey, signed a three-year contract as playing-coach of the New York Rangers on May 31. At 36, he became the league's youngest coach and reportedly received an $81,000 contract. As compensation for releasing Harvey to the Rangers, the Canadiens received defenseman Lou Fontinato.

There was plenty of action at the annual June draft as the Canadiens took Cesare Maniago from the Leafs for the $20,000 waiver fee. Then they sent defenseman Junior Langlois to the Rangers for defenseman John Hanna. New York traded Bill Gadsby, 34, to Detroit for defenseman Les Hunt.

With Phil Watson having signed as Boston's new coach, Bronco Horvath was up for grabs because Watson regarded him as a moaner. The Hawks took Horvath while the Bruins claimed Earl Balfour from Chicago. Boston also acquired Pat Stapleton and Orland Kurtenbach. The Hawks traded captain Ed Litzenberger to Detroit for Gerry Melnyk. Al Arbour was picked up by the Leafs when the Hawks left him unprotected.

Under Phil Watson's handling the Boston Bruins floundered all season, winning only 15 games and ending the season with a pitiful 38 points. They struggled along with Don Head, Bruce Gamble and Ed Chadwick, allowing a whopping 306 goals.

Toronto ended up second with a 10-point lead over Chicago. Mahovlich was far off the pace he had set during the previous schedule, scoring 33 goals in 70 games.

Chicago's Bobby Hull went on a goal-scoring rampage that netted him 50 goals in 66 games. At 23, and in his fifth NHL season, Hull's record-tying goal came in the last game of the schedule and tied him with Andy Bathgate of the Rangers for the scoring title. The league awarded them both $1,000, but gave the Art Ross Trophy to Hull since he had more goals than Bathgate.

Although the Canadiens took the league championship with a comfortable 13-point margin there was grumbling that the team wasn't as formidable as in the past. They were the highest-scoring team in the league and allowed so few goals behind agile Jacques Plante that he won the Vezina Trophy. They also had rookie Bobby Rousseau, a speedy right-winger, who took the Calder Trophy.

In New York, rookie player-coach Doug Harvey got 26 wins out of his Rangers and took the last playoff berth. Harvey's perfect passes aided the scoring of Bathgate and the team was setting a torrid pace at the box office.

The fourth-place Red Wings took New York to the wire in the playoff race and ended only four points behind them. Alex Delvecchio was enjoying his best NHL season. Hank Bassen was a competent back-up man for Sawchuk, while Gadsby and Stasiuk added a steadying influence. Often described as both an asset and liability was defenseman Howie Young, who stayed in the lineup for 31 games.

This was the campaign in which Gordie Howe collected his 500th regular-season goal, a feat he accomplished on March 14 in New York. In the preceding November he had taken part in his 1,000th NHL game. Not a bad clip for a player often referred to as elderly.

By guarding Chicago's nets for the full 1961–62 schedule, Glenn Hall, known as "Mr. Hockey," kept intact his iron-man record of not having missed a game since he broke into the NHL as Detroit's regular goalie in 1955–56.

Brawls were less prevalent in this schedule, but injuries were numerous. Lorne Worsley suffered a pre-season concussion. Tom Johnson almost lost an eye when struck by teammate Lou Fontinato's stick in a game in Toronto. Bert Olmstead sustained a broken shoulder while Pierre Pilote had a shoulder separation. All season players from various teams were going in and out of hospital.

In November 1961, Conn Smythe, the man who built Maple Leaf Gardens, officially stepped aside to be succeeded as president by his son Stafford. The elder Smythe remained as chairman of the board of directors. To purchase majority control of the Gardens, Stafford Smythe, John Bassett and Harold Ballard turned over a two million dollar check to Conn Smythe. Ballard replaced the younger Smythe as chairman of the Leafs' hockey committee.

Red Kelly, having made a successful conversion from Detroit's defense to Toronto's forward line, announced on March 14 that he would stand for the Liberal nomination of the Toronto riding of York West at the conclusion of the hockey season. He ultimately won the seat and effectively combined hockey with politics.

The odds were with Montreal and Toronto that they would knock out their opponents in the semi-finals. The Leafs, facing the Rangers who weren't assured of a playoff berth until the 69th game of the schedule, ran into tough opposition and took six games to eliminate New York. Worsley was superb in goal for the Rangers, especially in the fifth game. Tied 2–2 at the end of regulation time, the game went into two overtime periods before Kelly snared the puck from under the prostrate Worsley and fired in the winner. Worsley later conceded that that moment had been his most heartbreaking experience in hockey. When he skated out as the game's second star behind Kelly, the goalie received a standing ovation. He had kicked out 56 shots in 84 minutes.

The series between the Canadiens and the Hawks was taken 4–2 by the Hawks after dropping the first two. Montrealers remembered when the Canadiens had been shipping players to Chicago to build up the Hawks. Now they were victims of their own generosity.

Toronto was the 8–7 favorite to take the champion Hawks in the Cup finals. With energetic fore-checking and precision play, Toronto won the first game 4–1 and shaded Chicago 3–2 in the second game, which they never appeared in serious danger of losing.

It was a different band of Hawks' players who greeted the Leafs in Chicago for the third and fourth games. With Mikita as the most prominent Hawk forward, the Leafs' team was downed 3–0 in the third encounter. Game four was Chicago's as Hull and Fleming looked after all the goals in a 4–1 win. A Hull shot caused Bower to pull a groin muscle in the first period and sent him into a Chicago hospital. Toronto recaptured the lead with a convincing 8–4 win paced by Bobby Pulford's three goals in game five. With Don Simmons in goal, 14,129 fans chanted, "Go, Leafs, go." Eddie Powers refereed with a firm hand and the game became wide open with end-to-end rushes.

On April 22, Toronto dethroned the Hawks in the Chicago Stadium with Dick Duff scoring the winning goal in a 2–1 decision. For the first time in 11 years the Stanley Cup returned to Toronto, after a record 87 penalties in six games. Leaf defenseman Tim Horton established a record by gathering 12 assists in 13 playoff games, the most ever picked up by a rear guard.

1962–63

A long-familiar figure was missing from the scene when the 1962–63 schedule opened. After 35 years as coach and general manager with Detroit, Jack Adams resigned in April 1962 to become president of the Central Professional Hockey League.

In June, when Jim Norris of the Blackhawks was among the 13 new additions to the Hockey Hall of Fame, history was made with the first father-and-son combination gaining entry. Several years earlier Jim Norris, Sr., was entered in the builders' section.

In July, Doug Harvey emphatically stated he was through as New York's playing-coach in order to spend more time with his family. He signed a lucrative one-season contract as a player, leaving Muzz Patrick in the double role of manager-coach. On December 28, Red Sullivan was named New York's coach, but it was too late for Sullivan to get the Rangers into the playoffs.

Sid Abel, who had inherited Jack Adams' job as general manager of the Wings, removed the C from Gordie Howe's sweater, made Alex Delvecchio captain and appointed Howe assistant coach. Terry Sawchuk, who had gone maskless for 11 seasons, decided to wear a face protector in 1962–63.

It came as something of a surprise when Toe Blake turned down Montreal's offer of a three-year coaching contract and settled for a one-year pact to launch his eighth coaching season. Montreal missed first place by three points to Toronto and finished a mere two points behind Chicago, despite goalie Jacques Plante's asthma, Tom Johnson's fractured cheekbone, which put him out for the year, and Lou Fontinato's dislocated and fractured neck, which ended his career. Replacements for the injured defensemen were Terry Harper and Jacques Laperriere, who were hailed as promising but too green for immediate stardom.

It wasn't an entirely dismal season for the Canadiens, since Henri Richard emerged as the league's superlative playmaker with 50 assists and center Jean Beliveau became the sixth-highest scorer of all time in January when he hit the 300-goal mark.

The Boston Bruins, who had been in the cellar the season before, had only one win in 14 games when Phil Watson was fired and Milt Schmidt took over as coach. Although they didn't make the playoffs, the Bruins were strengthened by Dean Prentice, acquired from the Rangers for center Don McKenney, and got good support from Tommy Williams of Duluth, Minnesota, the first U.S. player to really stick in the NHL since Frank Brimsek made goaltending headlines.

The amazing iron-man record of goaltender Glenn Hall was brought to an end in November when he left the nets suffering from a strained ligament in his back. He had participated in 502 consecutive games, 553 if the playoffs were counted, before Denis DeJordy took over. Hall recovered to win the Vezina Trophy for the season.

New York's Lorne Worsley had troubles of a different sort. He was called upon to stop 269 shots in the span of six games.

In October, Montreal's Gilles Tremblay and Chicago's Reg Fleming engaged in a stick-swinging duel. Both were suspended for three games, which meant a pay loss of approximately $750 each. On March 5, when the Canadiens played at Detroit, right-winger Bernie Geoffrion found it didn't pay to hurl his stick and gloves at referee Vern Buffey. President Campbell suspended him for five games, which meant a financial loss of about $2,000.

In the playoffs, series A between Toronto and Montreal was won by the Leafs in five games against the weakened Canadiens.

When Chicago took the first two games from Detroit on Chicago Stadium ice they were running true to form. They were powerful and well balanced, but the one big worry after an indifferent season was Bobby Hull's health. He had a shoulder injury which almost kept him out of the opening game and in the second meeting suffered a broken nose and a cut on his face which required 10 stitches. But Hull missed only one of the next four games, which the Wings won to sweep into the finals against Toronto. By scoring five goals in a losing cause, three of them in the last game, Hull showed bravery beyond the call of duty.

Toronto took care of Detroit in five games, despite the efforts of Howe, the year's top scorer, and never appeared in serious danger. They won the first two games, dropped the next, then easily took the last two. It was not a particularly exciting series.

1963–64

Dissatisfied with the way the Blackhawks blew their chance of winning the NHL title in 1962–63, management fired 48-year-old Rudy Pilous, their coach since January 4, 1958. His successor, 44-year-old Billy Reay, had performed with the Canadiens, coached Toronto and was coaching the Buffalo Bisons of the AHL when the announcement was made.

The summer trade that caught hockey fans napping was the swap between the Rangers and the Canadiens—Lorne Worsley, along with Dave Balon, Leon Rochefort and Len Ronson, went to Montreal for Jacques Plante, Don Marshall and Phil Goyette.

In the June draft Boston picked up Tom Johnson of the Canadiens and New York's Andy Hebenton. For problem player Howie Young, the Red Wings obtained goalie Roger Crozier and defenseman Ron Ingram from Chicago. The Leafs brought up Jim Pappin from Rochester and he played 50 games for the Toronto club.

A renovation was made to the NHL waiver rule in October which put coaches in the driver's seat and players on the spot. It was decided that a player could be demoted at any time and waivers were necessary only if the player was not on the 20-man protected list submitted at the June meetings.

The early-season experts eyed the Blackhawks as the team to beat on the grounds of balance and depth, with Hall in goal and Hull's offensive punch.

The highest rating given to the Montreal Canadiens was fourth place. Dickie Moore, a left-winger with 12 years of exceptional service, retired. But Toe Blake had Balon, Bryan Watson and flamboyant John Ferguson, obtained earlier from Cleveland to add muscle. Worsley had been slated as the regular goalie, but lost his job through injury to Charlie Hodge, who was the goalkeeper for 62 games and won the Vezina Trophy. Staging a race with the Hawks, the Canadiens took the league title by one point.

This was the season the Rangers planned to go places. Bathgate was slated for a hot scoring year. Plante was going to lead them out of the cellar and Harvey was back on the blue line. But Harvey was given his outright release after 14 playing years while Bathgate had the worst slump of his NHL career.

Since Toronto had been making overtures to Bathgate for a couple of seasons this was an auspicious time for them to make a sales pitch. Before the February 23 trading deadline arrived, the barter was concluded. Dick Duff, Bob Nevin, Arnie Brown, Rod Seiling and Bill Collins were sent to New York while Don McKenney and Bathgate became Leafs.

Punch Imlach scoffed at suggestions that he'd just taken a shortcut to the Stanley Cup. Tongue in cheek, he claimed if he were that clairvoyant he'd snare the Cup every spring. The Leafs did go on to win the Cup and the presence of the two former Rangers helped a great deal.

Gordie Howe was in the news again. He tied Maurice Richard's 544 goal record on October 28 in the Detroit Olympia against Worsley of the Canadiens. On November 10, again in the Olympia against Montreal, Howe sank goal number 545 to become the all-time scoring champion.

Some other records that were tied or established included Terry Sawchuk's participation in his 804th game. It broke the mark previously held by Harry Lumley by one game. Then on January 18, Sawchuk picked up his 95th shutout in a 2–0 win over Montreal, a feat no other goalie could match.

The record Boston's Andy Hebenton set on December 4 against the Blackhawks dealt in durability rather than goal scoring. At 34, he took part in his 581st straight NHL game, dethroning Johnny Wilson, who had participated in 580 consecutive games.

In trying to curb brawling on the ice, Campbell aimed hard at the pocketbook and, by the middle of the season, had garnered $5,000 in fines. For failing to control their men, coaches Imlach and Reay were fined $1,000 while 22 players paid fines of $100 each after a December Leafs–Hawks fight in Chicago.

The semi-final series between the third-place Leafs and the first-place Canadiens was a struggle to the finish, with Toronto coming out on top after seven games. The opener went to Montreal 2–0 with Charlie Hodge and Boom Boom Geoffrion leading the way. It took a couple of veterans, Johnny Bower and Red Kelly, to reverse procedure in the second meeting, squeaking out a 2–1 victory for Toronto. In this game Gilles Tremblay of Montreal suffered a broken ankle. The series continued with each club winning, then losing, until Toronto scored a 3–1 decision to eliminate Montreal from the playoffs.

The fourth-place Red Wings took seven games to dispose of the second-place Blackhawks and they did it the hard way, having to call upon 21-year-old Bob Champoux, a greenhorn netminder, when Sawchuk was hurt in the second game. Howe and Ullman accounted for 11 of Detroit's 24 goals in the series.

The Leafs and Wings also went the limit of seven games in the final. Toronto grabbed the lead by winning the opener 3–2, but Detroit hustled back to take the next two games. It was newcomer Andy Bathgate who scored the winning goal for Toronto in game four to even the series. Then the determined Wings clicked for a 2–1 victory.

The sixth game was stacked with drama. Defenseman Bob Baun was taken from the ice on a stretcher with an injured ankle and there was doubt that he'd return. But when the game went into overtime Baun was the hero who scored the sudden-death goal that saved Toronto from oblivion. With Brewer, Baun and Kelly all requiring needles to deaden their pain, the Leafs handed Detroit a decisive 4–0 defeat in the seventh game to win their third consecutive Stanley Cup.

Only after the series would Baun consent to have his ankle x-rayed and, as he suspected, the pictures revealed a cracked anklebone.

1964–65

The 1964–65 schedule brought about some sweeping changes in the NHL. It was a season packed with sadness, surprises and optimism.

The Montreal Canadiens lost the services of two solid contributors to their past success. Frank Selke retired as managing director of the team. He was later succeeded by Sammy Pollock, who had worked his way up through the Canadiens' chain. Bernie Geoffrion ended speculation about his future when he retired to become coach of the Quebec Aces of the AHL.

There were several deals in the off season and many calculated risks of leaving players unprotected were successfully pulled off, but the occasional one backfired. Obliged to protect Roger Crozier, the Red Wings gambled on leaving goalie Terry Sawchuk unprotected. Punch Imlach drafted him for $20,000.

The Hawks were the big dealers. To land Doug Mohns they gave the Bruins Reg Fleming and Ab McDonald. Then they sent Murray Balfour and Mike Draper to Boston for Jerry Toppazzini and Matt Ravlich. Later, Ron Murphy and Autry Erickson went to Detroit for John Miszuk, Ian Cushenan and Art Stratton.

Besides Sawchuk, the Leafs drafted Dickie Moore whose legs, they felt, might stand up for one more season. At 33, Moore had been off skates for a year so his future was debatable.

Detroit picked up Gary Bergman, Murray Hall, George Gardner, George Harris and Fred Hilts. Ted Lindsay's four-year retirement ended in October when he decided to rejoin the Wings so he could officially end his career with Detroit. Lindsay had been a Blackhawk when he quit in 1960.

It didn't take long for Lindsay to get into his familiar rut. He re-established his feud with the Maple Leafs' Dickie Moore for 38 games, found it didn't pay to tangle with young Ted Harris of the Canadiens and had tiffs with league officials. In mid-season the 39-year-old winger, after a verbal battle with referee Vern Buffey, was assessed a misconduct and a game misconduct. Declining a private hearing with Clarence Campbell, a customary procedure under such circumstances, Lindsay talked loosely of the president's "kangaroo court." That action called for a written apology and a $75 fine. With 14 goals and 14 assists, along with 173 minutes in penalties in 69 games, Ted Lindsay had, indeed, made a remarkable comeback.

Rookie Roger Crozier was one of the hottest Wings until just past mid-season when he had a temporary lapse. Anxious to find someone to back up their southpaw gem, the Wings sought Ed Giacomin from Providence and were staggered when the asking price was $75,000. Detroit didn't buy.

Crozier went to Florida for a few days' rest and when he returned the Wings clicked their way to the NHL title, thanks to defensive work by Bergman, Barkley and Gadsby, plus the offense of Ullman, Howe and Delvecchio.

No matter how the Rangers maneuvered they couldn't assemble a playoff team. New York inserted Arnie Brown and Rod Seiling on their defense. Dick Duff wasn't happy as a Ranger and was sent to the Canadiens for Bill Hicke. In yet another move, Emile Francis was made general manager after serving as assistant manager to Muzz Patrick since 1962. Patrick moved up to become vice-president of the new Madison Square Garden.

Toronto slid to fourth place in the final standing with a team that didn't quite jell as a group but sparkled individually. Ron Ellis and Pete Stemkowski added a touch of new blood. If Roger Crozier's superlative play hadn't earned him the Calder Trophy, Ellis would have taken it. Frank Mahovlich, Dave Keon and Red Kelly were the high point getters for the team. Kelly's contribution was given under adverse circumstances since he divided his time between politics and hockey. Sawchuk and Bower made a scintillating goaltending combination that won them joint possession of the Vezina Trophy, a feat never before accomplished.

Always good on paper, the Blackhawks never quite matched that image on the ice, much to the disgust of Jim Norris, who made threats, and Billy Reay, who made player changes. Bobby Hull went into a scoring slump that produced only one goal in 20 games. Then Glenn Hall, who had proven he was an iron man, requested a mid-season holiday and was replaced by Denis DeJordy. The best Chicago could do was gain third place even though Phil Esposito, a young center they counted on heavily, came through with 23 goals. Hoping a second Hull would produce like the first one, the Hawks signed Dennis Hull, who played in 55 games and scored 10 goals.

Injuries riddled the teams during the 1964–65 season, which was probably one reason why the clubs lacking depth struggled for playoff berths. Dean Prentice was sidelined for a year with a fractured vertebra. Alex Delvecchio, who scored his 270th goal to tie the record of Morenz and Joliat, suffered a broken jaw. Bobby Rousseau had a shoulder separation, Doug Mohns broke a bone in his foot and Kenny Wharram fractured a jaw bone, to mention only a few of the mishaps.

The repercussions of Toe Blake's 1963 blast at referee Eddie Powers were still heard this season. After quitting because the league failed to support him, Powers brought suit, which was eventually dropped when he accepted a settlement and an apology from Blake in November 1964.

In February 1965, 58-year-old Carl Voss, for 15 years the overseer of NHL officials, announced his retirement. He was succeeded by Ian "Scotty" Morrison.

Again the league doormats, the Boston Bruins accepted their fate with almost optimistic grace. They were openly disappointed at the showing of new acquisition Ab McDonald, but agreeably surprised by the improved deportment of Reg Fleming, who settled down and scored 18 goals.

The second-place Canadiens introduced two newcomers: Yvan Cournoyer, destined to become a fantastic power-play scorer, and defenseman Ted Harris. Worsley was seldom heard from as Charlie Hodge maintained the style that had made him the talk of the league in 1963–64. Claude Provost was the big scorer for the Canadiens, getting an impressive 27 goals. Montreal, it was said, had a number of weak points. However, they were strong enough to win the Stanley Cup in the spring.

Series A of the playoffs, between first-place Detroit and third-place Chicago, got underway with Detroit winning two games. But the Hawks won the next two games to even things up. The Red Wings took game five, but lost game six to the brilliance of Hall and the scoring of the "Scooter Line" of Mohns, Mikita and Wharram. The final game was all Chicago's as Bobby Hull connected for his eighth playoff goal in the seven game series. The score was 4–2.

Series B between second-place Montreal and fourth-place Toronto broke into instant warfare and was totally unlike the cleanly played contests between Chicago and Detroit. In the opening game, which went to the Canadiens 3–2, the busiest man on the ice was referee Vern Buffey, who called 75 minutes in penalties. Leaf defenseman Kent Douglas was given a match penalty after attempting to decapitate Dave Balon. A strong defensive game and three goals were all the Canadiens needed to beat the Leafs in their second meeting. Nineteen penalties were served in this 3–1 game.

Dave Keon was the hero of the third game which Toronto won 3–2 in overtime. It was Andy Bathgate, in disfavor with the fans, who got the goal that sent the game into overtime. Red Kelly's two goals in a clean, but hard-fought contest led Toronto to a 4–2 victory in the fourth game. When the teams went back to Montreal a 50-foot slap shot

Low boards and high snowbanks surround the McGill University rink in Montreal, circa 1880. Some historians credit McGill students with originating the game.

Lord Stanley of Preston, Canada's sixth governor general, donated the Stanley Cup in 1893. He never saw a playoff game for the trophy that bears his name.

Montreal Amateur Athletic Association. The first winners of the Stanley Cup in 1893.

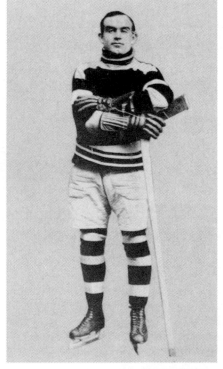

In 1905, the Dawson City Nuggets journeyed four thousand miles from the Yukon to Ottawa to play for the Stanley Cup. The Nuggets lost by the largest margin ever despite the heroics of seventeen-year-old goalie Albert Forrest, the youngest goalie ever to play for the Cup.

Cyclone Taylor, professional hockey's original superstar. Legend has it he scored a goal while skating backwards.

The last photo of Newsy Lalonde as a player, taken when he tried a comeback with the New York Americans in 1937, thirty-two years after turning professional.

Hockey Hall of Fame

Bill Galloway

Alex Connell set an NHL *record in 1927–28 when he played 461 minutes, 29 seconds without being scored on.*

Coach Lester Patrick achieved everlasting fame when he played goal at the age of 44 in a Stanley Cup playoff game during the 1927–28 season.

Bill Galloway

On defense, no Bruin was better than Eddie Shore until Bobby Orr.

King Clancy was an All-Star defenseman who was once called "150 pounds of muscle and conversation."

Dubbed the "Stratford Streak," Howie Morenz was the fastest skater of his day.

Aurel Joliat in the Montreal Canadien dressing room. Friend and teammate Howie Morenz occupied the other chair until his sudden death in 1937.

Toronto's "Kid Line": Charlie Conacher, Joe Primeau and Busher Jackson. They paced the Leafs in the thirties.

Boston's famous "Kraut Line" of Bobby Bauer, Milt Schmidt and Woody Dumart.

Detroit's Ted Lindsay, a member of the famed "Production Line" with Gordie Howe and Sid Abel (not seen), chases a puck in front of Leaf goalie Ed Chadwick.

"Billy the Kid" Taylor was suspended for life by the NHL for associating with gamblers. Taylor was later reinstated and was a big league scout for many years. He died in June, 1990.

Moscow 1950. The Soviet Union's Central Red Army Club skates on artificial ice for the first time on a rink 40 × 42 feet.

Bill Barilko's final goal. His dramatic overtime goal won the Cup for Toronto in 1951. Barilko died in a plane crash a few weeks later.

by Bobby Rousseau beat Bower at 7:30 of the third period and won the game. Beliveau's insurance goal in the dying second made the score 3–1.

The highlight of the sixth and final game was Claude Provost's overtime goal at 16:33 of extra time. It was a costly victory since it sent the Canadiens into the finals without defenseman Jacques Laperriere, out with a broken ankle.

To help fill the gap made by Laperierre's absence, the Canadiens called up Noel Picard and opened the Cup series against the Hawks on an auspicious note, winning 3–2 on Cournoyer's goal. A 2–0 win in the second game, with Lorne Worsley playing in the first Cup final of his checkered career, gave the Canadiens a commanding role in the series. But the underdogs fought back and Chicago won the next two games to tie up the series.

Charlie Hodge was in goal and the Montreal power play clicked as the Canadiens took the next game 6–0. Jean Beliveau contributed two goals with Duff, Rousseau, Richard and Tremblay providing the others. The desperate Hawks gave themselves a reprieve in the sixth game by winning 2–1 before 20,000 deliriously happy home fans. The game was marked by a stormy first period, highlighted by hostilities between Stan Mikita and Terry Harper. The Canadiens won the final game 4–0 in the Montreal Forum on May 1, inspired by the line of Duff, Beliveau and Rousseau and the shutout performance of Worsley.

A new award, the Conn Smythe Trophy, was presented to the NHL in 1964 by Maple Leaf Gardens, to be awarded to the most valuable player for his team in the entire playoffs. The first winner of the award was the Canadiens' captain, Jean Beliveau, the man who scored the Cup-winning goal in the seventh game.

1965–66

A pre-season trade saw the Leafs send Andy Bathgate, Billy Harris and Gary Jarrett to Detroit for Marcel Pronovost, Autry Erickson, Eddie Joyal, Larry Jeffrey and Lowell MacDonald.

The Rangers traded Providence goalie Marcel Paille, Aldo Guidolin, Don McGregor, plus an unnamed player for netminder Ed Giacomin, who had spent five seasons with the Reds. By trade and draft the Rangers swelled their ranks with Cesare Maniago, Ray Cullen, Johnny McKenzie and Gary Peters.

The constantly trading Red Wings picked up Ken Stephanson, Ab McDonald and Bob McCord from Boston in exchange for Al Langlois, Parker MacDonald, Ron Harris and Bob Dillabough. They added Bryan Watson, a tough little defenseman, in the draft.

In an effort to strengthen their defense, the weakest link in their team, Chicago drafted the small but skillful Pat Stapleton, left unprotected by Toronto.

Boston was guided by the astute Hap Emms, who had been appointed team manager in the spring. At 60, Emms had a successful career behind him as a coach of juniors and was noted for his stern disciplinary actions.

After 12 seasons in the NHL Jacques Plante, a 36-year-old goalie with seven Vezina Trophy wins to his credit, called it quits. Plante once said of goaltending:

> How would you like it if you were sitting in your office and you made one
> little mistake. Suddenly a big red light went on and 18,000 people jumped

up and started screaming at you, calling you a bum and an imbecile and throwing garbage at you. That's what it's like when you play goal in the NHL.

It was good news for the Leafs when Red Kelly gave up politics in the fall of 1965 to concentrate on hockey. But a couple of unpleasant jolts were in store for Punch Imlach. Defenseman Bob Baun stalked out of camp after failing to reach salary terms, but gave in later and went on to a disappointing season. The unpredictable Carl Brewer announced his retirement and returned to the University of Toronto.

Ted Lindsay officially retired again and this time made it stick. Defenseman Tom Johnson, who had slowed up, was given his unconditional release by Boston.

Despite a concerted effort by the Rangers to make the playoffs they slid downwards into last place. Rod Gilbert, one of their top scorers, was lost for a year due to back surgery.

The Rangers needed some muscle so Emile Francis traded Johnny McKenzie to Boston for Reg Fleming. Francis, slightly bigger than a jockey, needed some muscles himself on November 21 when he attacked a goal judge in New York and some belligerent fans joined in.

The Rangers used three goalies in 1965–66: Ed Giacomin, Cesare Maniago and Don Simmons. When their combined efforts failed, Francis chose the route taken by many losing managers. He fired the coach—in this case Red Sullivan.

The biggest news story of 1965–66 was Bobby Hull's scoring spree, despite being hampered by a knee injury. In January he scored his 300th NHL goal. On March 2, 1966, the powerful winger hit the 50-goal plateau for the second time in his career by scoring on Detroit's Hank Bassen. On March 12, Hull made New York's Cesare Maniago the victim of his 51st goal. The fantastic Hawks' player went on to score an all-time record 54 goals and 43 assists to win the Art Ross Trophy handily.

It was a mixed season for the Red Wings. Their ace forward Gordie Howe created history on November 27, 1965, by scoring his 600th NHL goal when Detroit lost 3–2 to the Canadiens. Later, Alex Delvecchio, another old reliable, scored his 300th goal. Fighting off pancreas trouble, goalie Roger Crozier had his off nights. Stalwart defenseman Doug Barkley was hit in the eye by Doug Mohns' stick, suffered a detached retina and was forced to retire.

There was a pre-season warning against stick swinging, calling for an automatic $200 fine, but it didn't make a very deep impression on some NHL wage earners. It cost Ranger Reg Fleming $275 for swinging at ex-teammate Ted Green and for accidentally cutting linesman Brian Sopp. A Canadiens–Rangers melee swelled league funds by $300. Then Kent Douglas of Toronto was on Campbell's carpet for pushing linesman John D'Amico and tossing a punch at an official.

When the Leafs went into a tailspin in the first half of the schedule, Stafford Smythe stated that some of the jobs would be spread among the Leaf hockey committee, leaving Imlach with less responsibility for the farm clubs he had been supervising. Some observers felt Imlach had swallowed a small plate of crow when he had to recall Eddie Shack from Rochester, where Shack had been sent in the fall as a disciplinary measure. The fact that Shack returned and scored 26 goals made others think that Imlach had used skillful psychology.

With Boston and New York as playoff onlookers again, the Stanley Cup semi-finals opened on April 7 in Montreal and Chicago.

The Canadiens encountered a Leafs team that had banked on Allan Stanley's injured knee holding up, but his knee gave in in the opening game, won 4–3 by the Canadiens. Game two also went to Montreal on a 2–0 victory and was a peppery affair with a total of 26 penalties handed out.

A 4–1 score for the Canadiens in the third game wasn't unexpected, but the brawling was, as eight new playoff records were established. To control the combatants, referee Art Skov called 35 penalties totaling 154 minutes. With the teams playing two men short for almost all of the first period, it took 65 minutes to complete the 20 minutes of official action. In a less rambunctuous fourth game the Canadiens spotted Toronto a 2–0 lead and then overwhelmed them with a 5–2 defeat.

The first four games between Detroit and Chicago were evenly split, with the Wings getting the immediate edge. The attack in game five was engineered by Normie Ullman, who paced his Detroit teammates to a 5–3 win with a pair of goals. Having acquired Dean Prentice from Boston and then getting two goals from him in game six, the Wings were indirectly obligated to the Bruins for surging into the finals on a 3–2 victory.

With Roger Crozier hot, the Red Wings handed the startled Canadiens two defeats in a row by scores of 3–2 and 5–2. The hungry Detroit team was on the trail of its first Stanley Cup in 11 years. But the next four games were a clean sweep for the Canadiens, culminating with Henri Richard's overtime goal in game six. Roger Crozier won the Conn Smythe Trophy, although some felt that J. C. Tremblay or Jean Beliveau had earned it in a winning cause.

1966–67

The pre-season activity mainly concerned expansion plans, but in the meantime, the old teams of the NHL had their own business to look after.

Thinking youth might appeal to youth, the Boston Bruins signed 33-year-old Harry Sinden to succeed Milt Schmidt as coach. Then they went after their highly prized junior prospect, defenseman Bobby Orr, an 18-year-old sensation. Orr's father and lawyer Alan Eagleson negotiated his first contract for a reported $70,000 at a time when the average annual salary was $15,000. If Boston had any misgivings about Orr's ability they were soon dispelled. Despite missing nine games through a knee injury, Orr was the third-highest scorer on the Bruin team. He won the Calder Memorial Trophy in a breeze and got a berth on the All-Star team.

With Bernie Parent and Ed Johnston sharing the goaltending job and a potentially impressive defense in rookie Joe Watson, tough sophomore Gilles Marotte and rugged Ted Green, the Bruins looked as though they might go places. They did, right back into the cellar. Their forwards couldn't muster enough scoring punch to offset the 253 goals their opponents scored against them.

In the draft, Orland Kurtenbach and Al MacNeil went to the Rangers. Toronto took Johnny Brenneman from New York but lost Wally Boyer to the Blackhawks, who needed center strength because of the supposed retirement of Bill Hay.

Having severed his coaching connections with the Quebec Aces, Bernie Geoffrion's two-year retirement as a player ended in mid-summer when he signed a three-year contract with the Rangers. His 17 goals and 25 assists in 58 scheduled games surpassed what the public expected of him and often made him a thorn in the side of his old mates, the Canadiens. With tremendous performances from two other ex-Montrealers, Phil Goyette and Don Marshall, a good recovery by Rod Gilbert from spinal surgery, plus the fine defensive work of Arnie Brown, Harry Howell and goalie Ed Giacomin, the Rangers rose to fourth place and, at last, a spot in the playoffs.

Toronto's Terry Sawchuk had off-season surgery on his long-ailing back, but he started the season and seemed better than ever, until he entered a Toronto hospital in early December with suspected disc trouble. In all, Sawchuk participated in only 27 scheduled games, but he came back brilliantly to get his 100th career shutout and star in the playoffs. With all NHL teams now employing the two-goalie system, there is little chance of any goalie ever matching Sawchuk's record.

Frank Mahovlich was a Leaf holdout who succumbed to a reported $35,000 contract for one year. Carl Brewer cropped up in troublesome fashion again. This time he sought reinstatement as an amateur so he could join Canada's national team. It was a move Imlach opposed, but negotiations between lawyer Alan Eagleson, the Gardens and the league eventually brought approval for the move.

This was the toughest season Punch Imlach had ever experienced in the NHL. His team had gone on a disturbing 10-game losing streak amid rumors that Punch was on the way out. Just as his team was coming out of the slump, Imlach was hospitalized. With King Clancy at the helm, the team surged to nine victories out of 12 games and produced a potent trio in Pulford, Stemkowski and Pappin. Gossips muttered that the squad wouldn't play for Imlach. When he returned he steered them to third in the league, then to the Stanley Cup.

Bill Hay and Glenn Hall announced their retirements, but money brought them both back to the Hawks, playing as though they had never been away. Always powerful offensively, Chicago's weakest spot had been on the blue line. This was rectified in 1966–67 with the addition of husky Ed Van Impe, the hitting of Doug Jarrett and the improved play of Pat Stapleton, enough of a change to gain first place for the season.

The champion Canadiens embarrassed Toe Blake. Woefully weak at scoring, the team temporarily dipped into the league cellar for the first time since 1948, but rallied to finish second. John Ferguson set a team record as the most penalized Canadien, taking the dubious honor away from Lou Fontinato. A high stick almost cost Jean Beliveau the sight in one eye early in the year. He missed several games and fell one goal short of attaining his 400th goal. The most pleasant surprise for Blake was the outstanding play of rookie goalie Rogatien Vachon, called up from the minors to replace Worsley, who had been hit in the face by an egg thrown in New York.

Tempers frayed easily in this season. The usually placid Bobby Hull, possibly remembering the shadowing he'd received from Detroit's Bryan Watson in past playoffs, cut loose on the pesky Red Wing in November and 18 stitches were required to close the wound around Watson's eye. In a February game in Boston Garden there was a slugging match between Bobby Orr and Ted Harris which Orr won handily. On February 5, John Ferguson went berserk in the Detroit Olympia and knocked down the glass partition in the penalty box after a fight with Gary Bergman and Bryan Watson. Another time Ferguson hit linesman Brent Casselman and was suspended for three games. Bernie Geoffrion was suspended for three games for a similar action.

Busher Jackson's death in Toronto on June 25, 1966, sparked sadness and anger in those who had admired him in his heyday. He had dreamed of being entered in hockey's Hall of Fame, an honor bestowed upon many of his old teammates, but his friends said it was denied him due to disapproval of his personal lifestyle.

On February 20, 1967, Gordie Howe, who seemed to have collected every award available, became the second winner of the Lester Patrick Trophy, an award for outstanding contributions to hockey in the United States.

When the 1966–67 schedule came to a close on April 2, the Chicago Blackhawks had a 17-point lead over the Canadiens, their nearest rivals. For the first time in 40 years the Hawks won the NHL title, with Hull scoring 52 goals. Mikita won the scoring race, however, with 35 goals and a record 62 assists. He also won the Lady Byng and Hart Trophies, becoming the first player to win three major awards in a season.

Drawing Chicago as semi-final opponents hardly seemed like a lucky break for Toronto, but with a magnificent effort from their goalies the chore became easier. Bobby Hull's power play goal proved to be the Chicago winner in a 5–2 opener. The goaltending of Sawchuk won game two for the Leafs and an all-round team effort gave them the third contest. Game four went to Chicago 4–3, but Glenn Hall stopped Jim Pappin's shot with his face and required 25 stitches. Terry Sawchuk was rushed into Toronto's nets after Bower started game five and became shaky. Sawchuk thwarted the Hawks while his teammates outsmarted them 4–2. Then in the next game a rookie with a famous name, Brian Conacher, whipped in the first two playoff goals of his young career and shot Toronto into the finals on a 3–1 victory.

Because the Ranger team was husky and filled with desire it looked as though the Canadiens might have a battle on their hands in the other semi-final series. But Montreal won four straight games and made it look easy even though a couple of games were taken the hard way. John Ferguson, usually more at home in the penalty box, scored the winning goals in the second and fourth games.

The final encounters between the Canadiens and the Leafs were fast, rugged and featured wide-open hockey. Montreal soundly trounced Toronto 6–2 in the opener, but the Leafs came back, somewhat unexpectedly, with two wins, one of them being a 3–0 shutout. The other was won 3–2 on Bob Pulford's overtime goal in one of the most exciting games ever played. In the fourth game Terry Sawchuk looked wobbly after he replaced Bower who had been hurt in the pre-game practice. With Backstrom and Beliveau each scoring a pair of goals, Montreal came through with a decisive 6–2 victory.

Back in Montreal for game five, the Leafs came up with a strong team effort to defeat the Canadiens 4–1 and take the edge in the series. Then with a combination of age and youth, they overpowered Montreal 3–1 and won the Stanley Cup in front of their home crowd. Pappin got his seventh goal of the playoffs, Sawchuk stopped a barrage of 41 Canadiens' shots and Armstrong scored the insurance goal into an empty net. Toronto owned the Cup for the 11th time.

1967–68

With the NHL's golden anniversary season behind it, the circuit looked forward to double the fun in the season ahead. The reason?–expansion. A new era began with the birth of six new franchises. The NHL embraced teams in a Western Division composed of the California Seals, the Minnesota North Stars, the Los Angeles Kings, the Philadelphia Flyers, the St. Louis Blues and the Pittsburgh Penguins.

According to a poll conducted among leading hockey writers and broadcasters, the Chicago Blackhawks would repeat as first-place finishers in the Eastern Division. In the fledgling Western Division, the poll predicted a strong finish by the California Seals, with Philadelphia and Minnesota not far behind. Six months later, when the Hawks finished fourth in the East, 14 points behind first-place Montreal, and California finished dead last in the West, the pollsters were left wondering where they went wrong.

Jacques Plante's return to netminding was a brief one. Hired to coach California Seal goaltenders while the team was in the middle of contract negotiations with Charlie Hodge, Plante found himself more interested in playing that tutoring. On September 21, Plante returned to the nets. After the Seals lost 3–1 to the Kings, with two of the goals scored against him, Plante mysteriously left the club and returned to his sales job in Quebec, using a family illness as his excuse.

Detroit's Sid Abel was also on the move—from behind his team's bench. The general manager of the Red Wings said that Baz Bastien, his assistant, would coach the team and that Abel would consult with Bastien on game strategy while watching from the stands.

To prevent hockey great Gordie Howe from deteriorating, Red Wing president Bruce Norris insisted on a clause in Howe's contract that would force him go to Florida if the Wings felt he needed a rest during the season.

Due to the NHL's expansion from six to 12 teams, the 1967–68 regular-season schedule was the most extensive in the history of the league. Each team would play 74 games. The schedule was comprised of 444 games, compared to the 210-game schedule of the last 10 seasons when the six teams played 70 games each.

All indications were that Boston's Milt Schmidt had outsmarted Chicago's Tommy Ivan in the blockbuster deal between the Bruins and the Hawks. Phil Esposito, Ken Hodge and Fred Stanfield went to Boston in return for Gilles Marotte, Pit Martin and Jack Norris. It was Schmidt's first official move as general manager of the Bruins. Schmidt was very happy with the deal, as Esposito and Stanfield played excellent hockey for the Bruins and quickly became their most productive forwards.

Two weeks after the start of the league's expansion season, the Los Angeles Kings, destined to finish last in the new Western Division according to the experts, were the only undefeated club remaining in the 12-team league.

The St. Louis Blues launched a new era of major-league hockey on October 11. Before the home opener, Guy Lombardo and his Royal Canadians played sweet melodies from rinkside while TV personality Arthur Godfrey skated a duet with figure-skating queen Aja Zanova. The Blues tied the North Stars 2–2 with a dramatic goal late in the game. Seth Martin tended goal for the Blues when Glenn Hall fell victim to a hand infection. Months earlier, 34-year-old Martin was billed as the best amateur goaltender in the world after his spectacular play for Canada's team in the world championships. After a strong recommendation by Scotty Bowman, the Blues signed Martin to a contract.

October 18, 1967, was an historic night in Portland, Oregon. Andy Hebenton of the Portland Buckaroos ended his iron-man streak of 1,062 consecutive games without a single miss, when he was kept out of the lineup to attend his father's funeral. It was the first time Hebenton had missed a hockey game since March 8, 1952, when he was with the old Victoria Cougars in the Western Hockey League. The streak included 216 games in the Western League, 630 consecutive NHL games with New York and Boston and 216 games back in the Western League.

On November 28, St. Louis Blues' general manager Lynn Patrick announced the trade of top goal scorer Ron Stewart to the New York Rangers. In return, the Blues received forward Gordon "Red" Berenson and defenseman Barclay Plager, brother of the Blues' Bob Plager. After 16 games in which St. Louis had a record of four wins, two ties and 10 losses, Lynn Patrick decided it was time for him to hand over one of his duties. Patrick remained as general manager and his top aide, Scotty Bowman, took over as coach. It marked the beginning of one of the most successful coaching careers in NHL history.

To the surprise of many, Larry Zeidel, a pro for 17 years and the leader of three minor leagues in penalty minutes, caught on as a defenseman with the Philadelphia Flyers. In the off-season, Zeidel spent $150 and prepared a glossy resumé extolling his virtues as a player and hockey executive. When Philadelphia said they were interested and Cleveland would not release Zeidel, the resourceful player arranged a conference call and quickly talked the deal into completion. To that point in his career, Zeidel had spent nearly 2,500 minutes in the penalty box, time equal to more than 40 full games. He had been away from the NHL since 1954.

The Blues, meanwhile, were resurrecting another oldtimer, Dickie Moore. Moore had retired from the Canadiens in 1963 and tried a comeback with the Toronto Maple Leafs in 1964, but was able to play only 38 games due to a knee injury suffered before the season got going.

Frank Mahovlich was out of the Leaf lineup and in hospital for an 11-game stretch beginning on November 2. He received treatment for extreme tension and nervousness.

In December, the longest consecutive shutout streak in 12 years—three straight games—was recorded by goalie Cesare Maniago of the Minnesota North Stars. Maniago had recorded only two shutouts in $51\frac{1}{3}$ NHL games prior to the 1967–68 season and carried a string of 183 minutes 32 seconds of shutout hockey into the North Stars' next game.

In the minors, hot-tempered, 36-year-old Bob Bailey of the Dayton Gems went berserk in a game against Fort Wayne and for the second time in his career attacked an official. Commissioner Andy Mulligan banned Bailey for the rest of the year. John Brophy, defenseman of the Long Island Ducks, was suspended for at least a month and fined $100 by Eastern Hockey League president Tom Lockhart. Brophy blew his top after receiving a misconduct penalty from referee Bill Pringle and knocked him twice to the ice in a game with New Haven. A few days later, Brophy was named coach of the Ducks for the rest of the Eastern Hockey League season.

This season saw the opening of several new arenas. Prior to the opening of the $18-million Forum in Southern California in late December, the $6-million Metropolitan Sports Center opened in Bloomington, Minnesota, and the $12-million Spectrum opened in Philadelphia. The opening of New York's new Madison Square Garden Center, costing $25 million, would soon follow.

When Jack Kent Cooke, owner of the L.A. Kings, opened the Forum for hockey business on December 30, NHL president Clarence Campbell called it "a fantastic building, the finest sports emporium in creation." Canadian actor Lorne Greene emceed the opening, witnessed by the largest crowd ever to see a hockey game in the U.S. west. They also witnessed a horrible performance by the hometown Kings, who lost 2–0 to the Philadelphia Flyers.

In January, Montreal's Jean Beliveau surpassed Maurice Richard as the highest scoring Canadien of all time. Beliveau collected four assists in a win over Minnesota. That gave him 967 points, including 411 goals. Richard retired in 1960 with 965 points, of which 544 were goals.

NHL president Clarence Campbell handed Bert Olmstead of the Oakland Seals a $200 fine for chasing a fan around the Boston Garden with a hockey stick. Campbell said that Olmstead had no business leaving the bench and pursuing the fan. Going on the ice raised Olmstead's fine to $250. This was the same amount Campbell had charged Montreal's Toe Blake a few days earlier for chasing referee Bill Friday on the same Boston ice to protest a call.

January 13 proved to be a tragic day for Bill Masterton and the Minnesota North Stars. An injury resulting in death occured for the first time in the NHL's 51-year history when Masterton died from a blow to the head after being body-checked heavily by two Oakland players during a game with the Seals. Minnesota manager-coach Wren Blair said he was convinced it was not a dirty play.

As the Toronto Maple Leafs hit the halfway mark of the season, Mike Walton had scored 22 goals, 19 of which had been achieved in the Gardens. During one stretch Walton was chosen as one of the three stars in seven consecutive games.

A future NHL star continued to attract attention in U.S. college hockey. Cornell (27–1–1) won the NCAA championship in 1967 with a good portion of the credit going to young Ken Dryden, the goalie from Islington, Ontario, who turned in a 1.48 goals average. Dryden was hot again this season and chalked up five shutouts in 13 games. His goals-against average was 1.31.

The Oakland Seals made four player deals with the Detroit Red Wings, sending defensive ace Kent Douglas to Detroit in exchange for center Ted Hampson, left-wing John Brenneman and defenseman Bert Marshall.

By February, the Montreal Canadiens had extended their unbeaten streak to 13 games and had won nine straight. NHL records showed it had been 13 years since a league team was that hot. Much of the credit for the streak that brought the Habs from last to first place belonged to 21-year-old Rogatien Vachon, who was up for the NHL's rookie award. The Habs won another three games before the Rangers stopped their streak at 16.

Johnny Bower, 44, sport's most amazing antique, was named the All-Star NHL goaltender in mid-season voting and was a contender for the Vezina Trophy. But the old goalie refused to shovel snow. "It's dangerous for men in my age bracket," he quipped. Bruce Gamble, secured from the minor leagues two years earlier by Punch Imlach of the Leafs, was proving to be an outstanding backup goalie for Bower.

Stafford Smythe, representing the Leafs at a governors' meeting, predicted that helmets would be mandatory in the NHL. He ordered all players in the Toronto Marlboros' organization to begin wearing them immediately.

On February 11, the doors of the old Madison Square Garden closed after 43 years of exciting sports history. Some 60 past and present National Hockey League greats were on hand to pay their final tribute to the old Garden.

When Jim Anderson was called up to Los Angeles from the minor leagues he was 37 years old, the oldest rookie in the NHL. He played six games without scoring a goal, but finally in his seventh game he scored. The next day he was sent back to the minors.

In Grenoble, France, the Soviet Union captured their third gold medal in four tries since entering international hockey. The Soviets defeated Canada 5–0 in the final game of the 10th Winter Olympics. Canada settled for a third place bronze medal behind Czechoslovakia.

Bert Olmstead, coach of the Oakland Seals, turned over his coaching duties to top aide Gordon Fashoway in order to watch the Seals from a new perspective. He said, "I was sick and tired of looking at them and I'm sure they were sick and tired of looking at me. I had to get off the bench to keep my sanity."

In mid-February, Boston's Bobby Orr had surgery to remove the medial cartilage from his left knee. According to Dr. Ronald Adams, the Bruins' team physician, the operation was badly needed and a success. There was a chance that Orr would return late in the season.

In late February, Gordie Howe, only weeks shy of his 40th birthday, reached the 30-goal plateau for the 12th time in his amazing career. But the Wings were in decline. Sid Abel, the Detroit manager-coach, blamed expansion and the NHL Players' Association for the Red Wings' fall. "Players are fat in the pocketbook," said Abel. "They know damn well they have you over the barrel. They know if they don't play here, they'll play somewhere else because there are 12 teams in the NHL now." He also said that players were protected by the Players' Association in that if they were sent back to the minors they would receive the same salary they were earning in the major league.

A multi-player swap rocked Toronto and Detroit. Punch Imlach's four-for-three trade with the Detroit Red Wings, in which Frank Mahovlich was the main figure, was a desperation move to get the slumping Leafs into the playoffs. The defending Stanley Cup champions shuffled Mahovlich, 31, off to Detroit along with centers Peter Stemkowski, Garry Unger and the NHL rights to defenseman Carl Brewer. In return they received veteran center Norm Ullman, Paul Henderson and Floyd Smith.

On March 3, Jean Beliveau became the first Montreal Canadiens' player in history to score 1,000 points, when he scored a goal against Detroit at the Olympia. He joined the only other player at the time to reach 1,000—Gordie Howe.

When fierce winds blew the roof off the $12-million Spectrum in Philadelphia, the Flyers were without a home for the rest of the season. They were forced to play their remaining "home" games in Toronto and Quebec. On March 7, after one Flyer "home" game in Toronto against Boston, NHL president Clarence Campbell handed out suspensions after a vicious stick-swinging outburst by the Flyers' Larry Zeidel and Boston's Eddie Shack. Zeidel was suspended for four games as the aggressor, while Shack, as the retaliator, was suspended for three games. They also received $300 fines.

The NHL board of governors turned down a suggestion that players wear their names on the back of their sweaters.

As the Pittsburgh Penguins reached the end of the regular season, they reflected on some surprising developments. First, the team's leading scorer, Andy Bathgate, was a player almost passed over in the expansion draft. He was considered to be washed up. Second, goalie Joe Daley, whom the Pens selected first in the draft, wound up playing with Pittsburgh's farm team at Baltimore. Third, the player who emerged not only as the regular goaltender but also as one of the best goalies in the league turned out to be Les Binkley, a grey-haired, near-sighted 31-year-old rookie who was already owned by the club before the draft.

A troubled Oakland club was faced with the possibility that it would end up in Vancouver if and when the NHL's board of governors gave their consent. Labatt

Breweries of Canada announced that they had completed negotiations to purchase a controlling interest in the Seals. The sale was contingent upon the franchise being moved to Vancouver.

The Philadelphia Flyers were also having troubles that could have ultimately led to the Flyers moving to another location unless the city reopened the $12-million Spectrum arena after its roof damage.

Minnesota general manager-coach, Wren Blair, offered U.S. Olympic team defenseman Lou Nanne "an eight-game tryout with the North Stars anytime he wants it." Then Blair added, "I don't think we can afford to pay Lou what he's presently making in four jobs [envelope salesman, University of Minnesota freshman coach, semi-pro hockey player and part-time television sportscaster] but there is an open slot on the roster and we hope he sees fit to fill it." Nanne decided against joining the Stars for their game against Pittsburgh, but he indicated that he might reconsider his decision before the start of the 1968–69 season.

When the regular season ended, Chicago Blackhawks' center Stan Mikita gained $1,250 as the NHL's leading scorer. It marked the fourth time in five seasons that Mikita had won the Art Ross Trophy as scoring champion. He collected 87 points, three more than runner-up Phil Esposito of the Bruins.

In the final meeting between the Montreal Canadiens and the Detroit Red Wings, Bobby Rousseau of the Habs scored a goal that was worth $47,250. It was the game winner in a 7–4 victory and assured Montreal of a first-place finish. That meant the Prince of Wales Trophy and 21 units of $2,250 each for the team.

The spring of 1968 was a time of racial unrest and violence. Much of it occurred in some of hockey's major cities and involved the postponement of three Stanley Cup playoff games. The wave of rioting also forced postponement of playoff games in the Central and American hockey leagues.

In series A, the Montreal Canadiens swept their best-of-seven quarter-final with Boston in four straight games. It was the third consecutive year that Montreal had won the opening series in four games.

In series B, the Chicago Blackhawks defeated the New York Rangers four games to two. The Hawks, down 2–0 in the series, rallied for four straight wins to defeat the Rangers and move on to meet the Habs in the best-of-seven semi-final.

In series C, The St. Louis Blues used a pair of veteran playoff competitors—Doug Harvey and Dickie Moore—to defeat Philadelphia four games to three and set up an expansion final against the Minnesota North Stars.

Meanwhile, in series D the North Stars came through with a victory over the L.A. Kings in the seventh and deciding game to win their Western Division semi-final playoff series.

In the semi-finals of series E, Montreal almost made it eight straight playoff games without a loss. The Blackhawks' only win was a 2–1 victory in game four.

In series F, which went to seven games, the Blues trailed Minnesota 3–0 with time running out in the final game. Suddenly the Blues caught fire. They scored four straight goals to win 4–3 and advance against Montreal.

In the finals, the Canadiens eliminated the Blues in four games to capture the Stanley Cup. J.C. Tremblay emerged as the hero of the last game, as he set up the tying goal and scored the winner in the Habs' 3–2 victory. It was the 13th time in modern hockey history, which dates from 1927, that Montreal had won the trophy.

After the Canadiens' Stanley Cup victory, Hector "Toe" Blake retired as coach of the Montreal club. He had starred as a player for 13 years and had coached for another 13 years. His team had just won their 13th Stanley Cup in the modern era and they had done it in 13 games. Perhaps Blake was a superstitious man. As a coach Blake's record was matchless. Since he took over in 1955–56 the team had won eight Stanley Cups and chalked up nine first-place finishes.

1968–69

Four NHL teams acquired new coaches for the 1968–69 season—a 76-game schedule, the longest in league history. It was a season of record-smashing performances.

At 29, Claude Ruel became the league's youngest coach when he was signed to replace Toe Blake who retired from Montreal at the conclusion of the 1967–68 season. Bill Gadsby was chosen to succeed Sid Abel as Detroit's coach, Bernie Geoffrion was signed to handle the New York Rangers and Fred Glover would coach the Oakland Seals. In November John Muckler was called up from Memphis to coach the Minnesota North Stars.

On January 17, Geoffrion collapsed in his team's dressing room after a game in Oakland and was replaced by Emile Francis, who announced that Geoffrion would work for the organization in another capacity. On January 19, John Muckler was replaced by Wren Blair after the North Stars went on a 14-game winless streak.

The NHL had made an off-season decision to have the annual All-Star game be an East-West contest. It was played on January 21 in Montreal's Forum and ended in a 3–3 tie.

The board of governors made a summer decision to establish the Clarence S. Campbell Bowl in honor of the league's president. The trophy was to be awarded to the team ending in first place in the Western Division. The Philadelphia Flyers were the first recipients.

A highlight of the summer draft was the St. Louis Blues' acquisition of goaltender Jacques Plante. Plante made a stunning comeback and combined with Glenn Hall to jointly win the Vezina Trophy at the end of the schedule.

George Armstrong, Toronto's captain, announced his retirement prior to the start of the schedule in October, but reversed his decision in December.

Bobby Hull announced his retirement in early October after a contract dispute with Chicago management. On October 13, he signed a three-year contract at a reported $100,000 per season.

A notable deal saw goaltender Terry Sawchuk go to Detroit from Los Angeles in exchange for Jim Peters. Bob Baun and Ron Harris were traded to Detroit by Oakland for Gary Jarrett and Doug Roberts. Before the trading deadline, Brit Selby and Forbes Kennedy were sent to Toronto by Philadelphia for Bill Sutherland, Gerry Meehan and Mike Byers.

Gordie Howe scored his 700th goal on December 4 in Pittsburgh, Jean Beliveau's 500th goal was scored in Minnesota in October, while Norm Ullman collected his 350th goal on January 4 in Toronto.

Punch Imlach's job as manager-coach of the Leafs appeared to be in jeopardy in December when the Leafs' brass held closed sessions regarding the team's low standing in the league. He received a vote of confidence, however. His team made the playoffs in fourth position but suffered a disastrous quarter final against Boston, who eliminated them in four straight games. Imlach was fired on April 6 by Stafford Smythe, immediately after the fourth game. The move upset many fans and delighted others. Jim Gregory took over as general manager of the Leafs while John McLellan was named coach.

The Boston Bruins and Montreal Canadiens jockeyed for first place in the Eastern Division for most of the season, but were frequently short of manpower.

Chicago's Bobby Hull sustained a fractured jaw on December 25, but missed only one game and scored a record 58 goals.

The fate of the Oakland Seals was in doubt due to a lack of attendance and uncertainty over the ownership of the franchise.

The St. Louis Blues clinched first place in the Western Division early in the schedule and ended with 88 points, a comfortable 19 points ahead of the Seals.

The Montreal Canadiens officially won the Eastern Division championship. They ended the season with 103 points to Boston's 100 points for their greatest total ever. It was the 18th time they had finished on top.

On January 2, Red Berenson of St. Louis became the second NHL player to score six goals in a single game. He accomplished this in an 8–0 win over Philadelphia. Twenty-four years earlier, in 1944, Syd Howe of Detroit had set the modern-era record with six goals in one game.

When Chicago defeated Detroit 9–5 on March 30 in Chicago, Pat Stapleton's six assists tied the league record for assists by a defenseman, set by Babe Pratt of Toronto in 1944. Stapleton's 50 assists established another record.

Leaf rookie defenseman Jim Dorey established two records in his second NHL game. Playing against Pittsburgh in Toronto on October 16, he totalled 38 minutes in penalties, the most any player had ever compiled in a single game, before he was ejected by referee Art Skov. The eight separate penalties he incurred were also a record.

Two rookies held the spotlight in the Western Division. Danny Grant of Minnesota and Norm Ferguson of Oakland both scored 34 goals to tie a record set by Nels Stewart in 1925–26. Grant edged Ferguson for the Calder Trophy.

Bobby Hull, Phil Esposito and Gordie Howe became the first NHL players to surpass 100 points in a season. It was Howe's finest season in points. He collected 103 and he set a record for right-wingers by assisting on 59 goals, breaking Andy Bathgate's mark of 58.

The line of Mahovlich, Howe and Delvecchio set a line record for goals with 118 and amassed 254 points, but it was the Boston Bruins who smashed the most records. Esposito set a record for goals by a center with 49, breaking Jean Beliveau's record of 47 set in 1957. His 77 assists, also a record, brought his points total to 126, breaking the total points record by a player in a single season. The line of Esposito, Hodge and Murphy collected 263 points, 37 better than the previous mark of 226. Bobby Orr set a record for goals by a defenseman when he scored 21 times. His 64 points was also a record for a defenseman.

Boston's 303 goals shattered the record set by Chicago in 1966–67. The Bruins set two other records: 497 assists, plus a total of 800 scoring points. They also went on record as the most penalized NHL team with a season total of 1,297 minutes.

A total of 40 marks were tied or broken in this record 456 game season. Forbes

Kennedy established a penalty record for centers with 219 minutes. Minnesota's Danny Grant, with 65 points, set a record for the most points by a rookie. Brad Park and Walt Tkaczuk of New York equaled the record of four for the most assists in a game by a rookie. The St. Louis Blues tied a team record when goaltenders Hall and Plante, with eight and five shutouts respectively, equaled the mark for shutouts by a team during a minimum 70-game schedule.

In the opening game of the quarter-final playoffs between Toronto and Boston, several records were tied or set. Phil Esposito's four goals and six assists equaled the playoff record set by Dickie Moore. Forbes Kennedy of the Leafs, penalized eight times, set NHL playoff records in four categories on April 2. These included the most penalties in one game (eight), the most minutes in one game (38), the most penalties in one period (six) and the most minutes in one period (34). His eight penalties broke the record of seven held by Eddie Shore and his 38 minutes broke a record held by Red Horner. The Leaf team, penalized 20 times, a set a record for team penalties in one game. The 38 penalties meted out to both teams was also an NHL record. Kennedy's actions earned him a four-game suspension and a $1,000 fine.

Boston defeated the Leafs in four straight games by scores of 10–0, 7–0, 4–3 and 3–2.

Montreal disposed of New York in four consecutive games in their first round meeting by scores of 3–1, 5–2, 4–1 and 4–3.

The most exciting playoff hockey was performed by Boston and Montreal in their semi-final series, which went six games and produced superlative goaltending. In defeating the Bruins the Canadiens entered their 20th Stanley Cup final.

In the Western Division the St. Louis Blues disposed of Philadelphia in four straight games in their quarter-final series. Meanwhile, Los Angeles and Oakland played seven games before the Kings eliminated the Seals. St. Louis had no difficulty in disposing of Los Angeles in their semi-final meeting, winning four straight games.

The Stanley Cup finals marked the second consecutive meeting between Montreal and St. Louis. The Canadiens swept the disappointing series by scores of 3–1, 3–1, 4–0 and 2–1. John Ferguson triggered the winning goal in the final game, a shot that enriched each Canadiens' player by $9,750.

After the final series, Wren Blair of Minnesota predicted a long reign at the top for Montreal. "This may be the last dynasty in professional sport now that the draft systems are balancing teams everywhere," he stated. "It's a dynasty that may last a long time. It's going to be much harder to pull down the Canadiens than either the New York Yankees or the Green Bay Packers."

Neither Blair nor anyone else could foresee that the mighty Canadiens would miss the playoffs entirely in the season ahead.

1969–70

The 1969–70 season of the NHL not only provided the longest schedule in league history with 76 games, but was packed with wild and unique happenings.

Team personnel changed drastically before and during the regular schedule. In the preceding April the Toronto Maple Leafs had fired manager-coach George "Punch" Imlach, replacing him with Jim Gregory as manager and John McLellan as coach.

After the 1968–69 playoffs Red Kelly resigned as coach of the Los Angeles Kings and subsequently signed a one-year contract with the Pittsburgh Penguins, who had earlier fired coach Red Sullivan. Hal Laycoe succeeded Kelly in Los Angeles, but after 24 games (his team won only three) Laycoe was assigned to the newly created role of director of player personnel. John Wilson was elevated from the Kings' Springfield farm team as his successor.

Keith Allen, who had coached the Philadelphia Flyers for two seasons, was made vice-president and assistant to manager Bud Poile, thus making way for Vic Stasiuk to become coach. In December, Allen became general manager after Poile was fired.

After coaching the Detroit Red Wings to two victories in the opening games of the schedule, Bill Gadsby was unexpectedly replaced by Sid Abel, who handled the dual role all season. Gadsby was assigned to scouting future prospects, but was relieved of that position at the conclusion of the season.

In December, the NHL granted conditional franchises to Vancouver and Buffalo to enter the league in the 1970–71 season, at a cost of $6 million each.

Vancouver, planning to operate under the name Canucks, signed Bud Poile as manager and Hal Laycoe as coach. Buffalo, to be known as the Sabres, signed Punch Imlach as manager-coach.

In late December, Charlie Burns, a playing member of the North Stars, was named Minnesota's coach when ill health forced Wren Blair to relinquish his double role.

The Oakland Seals, in deep financial trouble since expansion began, presented coach Fred Glover with a three-year contract.

Twenty NHL linesmen and referees, led by lawyer Joe Kane, a former CHL president, demanded that the league recognize their association by threatening to strike and boycott the officials' special fall training camp. The league refused, but a seven-point program was agreed upon, and the strike was averted.

Hockey's Hall of Fame inducted Red Kelly, Bryan Hextall, Sid Abel, Bruce Norris, Al Leader and the late Roy Worters.

The pre-season exhibition games were rampant with brawls, but the most serious was a stick-swinging duel on September 21 in Ottawa between Boston's Ted Green and Wayne Maki of St. Louis. Hit by Maki's stick, Green was rushed to hospital for immediate five-hour brain surgery. Other operations followed, including the insertion of a steel plate in his skull.

The stiffest suspensions in NHL history followed this incident. Maki's suspension was for 30 days, Green's for 13 games, if and when he returned to action. Assault charges were laid against both players, the first in hockey history but both men were exonerated in Ottawa court hearings.

Kenny Wharram of the Hawks suffered a heart attack at training camp in September. Although he recovered he did not return to hockey.

The Blackhawks relied heavily upon rookies, several of whom were recent graduates of college hockey from the University of Denver. They also secured the services of goaltender Tony Esposito by drafting him from the Montreal Canadiens in the preceding summer.

When Normie Ullman signed for a reported $57,000 he became the highest paid player in Toronto's history until defenseman Tim Horton was lured out of retirement by an $84,000 contract.

Goaltender Marv Edwards and forward Bob Barlow, both 34, became the oldest rookies in NHL history. Johnny Bower, who started the season as an active Maple Leaf and the oldest player in the league, retired to serve the team as a scout for goaltenders.

New York drafted Terry Sawchuk from Detroit as goalie insurance for Ed Giacomin. Shortly after the schedule ended Sawchuk was hospitalized for stomach surgery and died on May 31 from cardiac arrest.

The schedule opened on October 11, with a record number of rookies entering the league. In a crackdown on stick swinging, brawling and the molesting of officials, Clarence Campbell imposed lengthy suspensions and heavy fines against players committing such offenses.

Several scoring milestones were registered. Gordie Howe scored his 800th goal into an empty net in St. Louis on October 19, Dean Prentice of Pittsburgh scored his 300th goal on November 1, Bobby Hull registered his 500th goal on February 21 in Chicago and Alex Delvecchio became the third player in league history to attain 1,000 points.

Goaltender Lorne Worsley, inactive since December when he retired after dissension with Montreal management, was permitted to join Minnesota late in the season for future considerations.

The Los Angeles Kings, wading through a dismal season, made many changes. But their trades did not help them. The team set a record for the most losses (52) in league history, tied for the most home losses (22) and tied for the most road losses (30). The Kings also went winless for 20 games, one less than the NHL record held by New York and Chicago.

From November 15 to the first week of March, the New York Rangers held sole possession of first place and established themselves as a powerhouse. Receiving excellent performances from defensemen Brad Park and Jim Neilson, solid goaltending from Ed Giacomin, who participated in 70 scheduled games, and an unexpected bonus from the play of rookie Bill Fairbairn, the Rangers set a record by scoring in their 118th consecutive game.

When they toppled from first place, giving way to Boston, injuries to Park and Neilson were contributing factors. In an effort to quell their slide, the Rangers acquired Tim Horton from Toronto in March in exchange for five players to be named at a later date. They also obtained forward Ted Irvine from the Kings in return for Real Lemieux and Juha Widing, a promising rookie.

When the Montreal Canadiens fell from their throne and missed the playoffs for the first time in 22 years, it was blamed on a combination of internal strife, suspensions and injuries, particularly a broken leg for Serge Savard. Coach Claude Ruel, distressed by Montreal's play after a three-game losing streak, volunteered to resign, but his proposal was rejected.

The Philadelphia Flyers, who had not missed the playoffs since they entered the NHL, came up with a rookie discovery in 20-year-old Bob Clarke, a center who was unique because he was diabetic. Excellent crowd support and fine work by goaltender Bernie Parent and defenseman Ed Van Impe failed to get the Flyers into the playoffs. Their undoing was in setting a record of 24 tied games, thus ending the season with 58 points, the same number as the Oakland Seals. Philadelphia's fewer wins dropped them into fifth place.

Red Kelly's coaching was credited with getting Pittsburgh into the playoffs for the first time. A revamped lineup that included rookie Michele Briere (who died following a car accident in May 1970) moved the Penguins into permanent possession of second place in the Western Division.

Scotty Bowman's St. Louis Blues won the Western Division championship and set a precedent by using a three-platoon goaltending system, utilizing the talents of Jacques Plante, Ernie Wakely and Glenn Hall.

The loss of Ted Green and injuries to many Boston players failed to slow down the Bruin team. Led by defenseman Bobby Orr, the club smashed records. Their 81 power-play goals eclipsed the old record of 70 set in 1965–66 by Chicago. Orr not only broke the record for the most goals in a season by a defenseman when he scored 33, but set another one with his 87 assists and became the fourth player in league history to register 100 points when he ended the schedule with 120. He became the first defenseman to win the scoring championship and was ultimately the recipient of the Smythe, Hart and Norris trophies. He was also a member of the first All-Star team.

Chicago, originally rated as a tail-end contender, came to the fore through the goaltending of Tony Esposito. He set a record for modern netminding with 15 shutouts, erasing Harry Lumley's 16-year mark of 13 shutouts. Additionally, Esposito won the Vezina and Calder trophies.

A greenhorn defense and a weak offense mired the Leafs in the cellar throughout most of the season. They ended with 71 points, 21 behind their nearest rivals.

By Sunday, April 5, the Detroit Red Wings, bolstered by the return of Carl Brewer, who had been obtained earlier from Toronto, assured themselves of third place with 95 points. The Rangers and Canadiens both ended with 92 points and the same win-loss records, but New York got the playoff berth on the strength of having scored two more goals than Montreal. Boston and Chicago wound up with 99 points each but Chicago had five more wins than Boston and took the championship.

In the Eastern playoffs Chicago met Detroit in series A and defeated them in four consecutive games. Series B between Boston and New York was won by the Bruins in six games in the liveliest series of all. Two goals by Bobby Orr in the final game of the series served to emphasize his role as leader of the club.

In the Western Division, series C between St. Louis and Minnesota went six games with the Blues winning. The Pittsburgh Penguins swept to a four-game win over Oakland in series D, which involved one overtime game.

Series E saw Boston knock off Chicago in four straight games. A goal by Johnny McKenzie late in the third period sent the Bruins into the finals against St. Louis. Series F involving St. Louis and Pittsburgh went six games before the Blues won. On April 28, in a 5–0 victory, goaltender Jacques Plante set a playoff record of 14 shutouts in his career, erasing the record of 13 he shared with Turk Broda.

In the finals, the Boston Bruins defeated the St. Louis Blues in four straight games. In the opening contest, played in St. Louis on May 3, Jacques Plante was knocked unconscious by a slapshot from Fred Stanfield's stick. His goaltending mask saved him from possible death. He received a concussion and did not return to action. On May 10, after 40 seconds of overtime in the Boston Garden, Bobby Orr fired in Derek Sanderson's pass for a 4–3 win. Boston had won the Stanley Cup for the first time since 1941.

Phil Esposito and Bobby Orr had each set two records in the playoffs. In scoring 20 points Orr had shattered Tim Horton's previous record of 16 points set in 1962. His nine playoff goals had broken the previous mark of five set in 1938 by defenseman Earl

Seibert of Chicago. Phil Esposito's 27 playoff points surpassed the previous record of 21 held by Stan Mikita. His 13 playoff goals bettered the 12-goal record shared by Maurice Richard and Jean Beliveau.

On May 14, Boston coach Harry Sinden announced his retirement from hockey in favor of an executive position with an industrial firm in New York State.

Ned Harkness, a 48-year-old native of Ottawa, Ontario, and hockey coach at Cornell University, made NHL history by signing to coach the Detroit Red Wings for a reported $50,000.

Red Kelly renewed his contract with Pittsburgh, becoming manager as well as coach.

Phil and Tony Esposito also made hockey history by becoming the first brother combination to be named on the first All-Star team.

At the June draft meeting in Montreal, the Buffalo Sabres and Vancouver Canucks stocked their teams with players considered dispensable by the established clubs. Buffalo won first choice in the amateur draft and Punch Imlach quickly selected Gilles Perrault, the star and captain of the Montreal Junior Canadiens. Vancouver then took Dale Tallon, a top-rated forward defenseman with the Toronto Marlboros.

VIII

THE CHANGING FACE
OF HOCKEY

The Early Seventies, 1970–1976

1970–71

With Buffalo and Vancouver gaining admission via an entrance fee of $6 million each, the NHL became a 14-team two-division league. All but three of the teams were U.S. based.

Colorful Punch Imlach, previously of the Toronto Maple Leafs, was named coach and general manager of the Buffalo entry, while Hal Laycoe became pilot of the Canucks. In other coaching moves, Tom Johnson replaced Harry Sinden at Boston, Larry Regan took over from Johnny Wilson in Los Angeles, Al Arbour replaced Scotty Bowman behind the bench in St. Louis and Jackie Gordon took the coaching reins from Charlie Burns in Minnesota. The latter reversed the usual procedure by reverting from coach to player.

Gilbert Perreault, the graduating junior sensation, was reportedly signed to a $55,000-a-year contract by Buffalo. Dale Tallon was said to be getting a similar amount from the fledgling Vancouver Canucks. Such big salaries for untried rookies brought a warning from Chicago's outspoken center, Pit Martin, that proven NHL veterans would demand huge increases. No sooner had he said it than Stan Mikita, Harry Howell, Jean Ratelle, Vic Hadfield and Derek Sanderson, among others, became holdouts on their clubs.

In California, Charles O. Finley, a self-made millionaire who rose from a job in the Gary, Indiana, steel mills to become one of America's top insurance executives, bought the Oakland Seals for $4.5 million. He renamed them the California Golden Seals. Finley, who also owned the Oakland Athletics of the American League in baseball, thought the Seals would become winners. Instead, they finished dead last in the NHL's West Division and set a new record for futility by losing 53 games in the season.

The Hall of Fame admitted defensemen Bill Gadsby and Tom Johnson, while shutting out Doug Harvey, and also brought in oldtime scoring star Cecil "Babe" Dye. The latter was the second most accurate goal-getter in NHL history, with 200 goals in just 271 games.

Hockey was saddened by the passing of ex-goalie Paul Bibeault, 51, son-in-law of Frank Selke, Sr. Cy Denneny, 78, an oldtime great with the Ottawa Senators, also passed away. Newsy Lalonde, a Hall of Famer in both hockey and lacrosse, died at the age of 83. Michel Briere, 20, an outstanding rookie with the Pittsburgh Penguins, was hospitalized as the result of a car crash. Almost a year later he died without having ever regained full consciousness.

Boston defenseman Ted Green, who'd been almost fatally injured in a stick-swinging brawl and had been out of hockey for a year, returned to action on the Bruins' defence.

The NHL increased the schedule to 78 games, the longest in its history, limited the curvature of the blade of hockey sticks to one-half inch and announced that referees would wear orange-colored armbands to distinguish them from linesmen. The NHL clubs, in turn, announced that teams would wear white uniforms at home and colored sweaters on the road. Apparently it was easier to keep colored sweaters clean on the increasingly long road trips. The NHL also ruled that players with two years' service in pro hockey at any level could not be sent to the minors without waivers from other NHL clubs.

In a somewhat overdue spirit of forgiveness, the league lifted the lifetime suspensions of Billy Taylor and Don Gallinger. Both were banished 22 years earlier for allegedly betting on games in which they played. Taylor had performed with Toronto and other NHL teams; Gallinger had played with Boston.

The Chicago Blackhawks, moving to the NHL's Western Division after having won the league title in the East for the second time in their long history, petulantly declared that they would not return the Prince of Wales Trophy to the East. "Let them get a new trophy to signify first place in the East," said Chicago president Bill Wirtz. "We won this one fair and square and we're taking it with us." Most people thought Wirtz was kidding. The Hawks were also thought to be far too strong for West Division competition, which consisted of expansion teams, and they proved it by finishing a full 20 points ahead of runner-up St. Louis. Bobby Hull, the celebrated "Golden Jet" of the Hawks, fired career goals number 545 and 546 against Vancouver on February 14, 1971, to pass retired Maurice "Rocket" Richard as the game's number-two goal getter on the all-time scoring list.

Gordie Howe, the greatest scorer in NHL history, was moved back to the Detroit defense by new coach Ned Harkness. The experiment didn't work, however, and Howe was returned to right wing.

It was a tough season for the Red Wings. Carl Brewer, who'd signed a 1970–71 contract, walked out before the schedule began, leaving them vulnerable on defense. Brewer, a brilliant but temperamental player, had done the same thing to the Toronto Maple Leafs in 1964–65. Detroit, also having goalie problems, went on to suffer the worst defeat in their long history when they were bombed 13–0 by the Maple Leafs in mid-season. Internal strife ripped the club apart. Sid Abel, longtime coach and manager and a former playing hero on the team, walked out. Abel said he "could not accept this club any longer, nor its coach, Ned Harkness." The latter, who'd had an enviable coaching record in U.S. college ranks, moved up to replace Abel as general manager. Former defenseman Doug Barkley became coach. The Wings continued to reel through the season, however, and wound up last in the East—one point behind new entry Vancouver—and posted the worst record in their existence: 22 wins, 45 losses, 11 ties.

Dick Duff, who confided to friends that he'd lost $60,000 in the stock market, was traded to the Los Angeles Kings by the Montreal Canadiens. Eddie Shack, "The Entertainer," went to the Buffalo Sabres from L.A. Years before, while coaching the Toronto Maple Leafs, Punch Imlach had banished Shack, saying, "I can't afford entertainers. I need hockey players." Now, with newly franchised Buffalo, Punch could pay the price.

Around the league a number of oddities occurred; some were tragic and some comical. In British Columbia, Roy Spencer, the 59-year-old father of player Brian Spencer, was killed in a shoot-out with police outside a TV station. He opened fire after protesting the station's decision to carry a Vancouver vs. California hockey game, rather than the Toronto–Chicago contest in which his son was playing. In Montreal, defenseman Serge Savard broke his left leg for the second time in less than a year, and it was said his career was over. Big Jean Beliveau became only the fourth player in NHL history to score 500 goals. Later, a "Jean Beliveau Night" was staged in Montreal. Hundreds of thousands of dollars were raised for underprivileged children.

In Pittsburgh, the Mellon Bank sued the Penguins for payment of a $3.6 million debt, following which the league took the club over. Subsequently, a group of businessmen bought the franchise for $7 million.

The Vancouver Canucks, averaging close to capacity in their first season, converted to a public company and shares were snapped up. The Canucks also figured in a hockey milestone. They were the scheduled opponents of the Montreal Canadiens in a March game in the Forum which had to be postponed on account of a snowstorm. It was the first time a Montreal game involving the Canadiens had been postponed in 54 NHL seasons.

The Boston Bruins went on a season-long rampage and set 37 different team records. Center Phil Esposito shattered marks with an amazing 76 goals and 152 points. He set nine different individual records. Gilbert Perreault set a new record for goals by a rookie when he fired his 35th versus St. Louis in March. Al MacNeil became the first Maritimer to coach an NHL team when he took over from Claude Ruel behind the Montreal Canadiens' bench. Michel Plasse of the Kansas City Blues in the Central League, became the first pro netminder to score a goal when he laced one into an empty net in a game against Oklahoma. Unfortunately, the building was almost as empty as the net for Plasse's historic effort. Only 850 fans were there.

Noel Picard, the stalwart St. Louis defenseman, was embarrassed when he sat on the Boston Bruins' bench by mistake. Punch Imlach was warned by the NHL to stop writing items in a syndicated column which were detrimental to his former Toronto club. Bruce Norris, the Detroit Red Wings' owner, rewarded his team and their families with a Florida vacation, despite a horrendous season. A Boston radio station held a "Date Derek Sanderson" contest and got over 13,000 entries. The contest was won by a 76-year-old grandmother.

The Boston Bruins, easy winners of first place in the East during the regular season, were victims of a stunning upset by the Montreal Canadiens in the playoffs. Ken Dryden, a towering, six-foot-four-inch newcomer in the Canadiens' nets, was the chief architect of the Bruins' defeat. A 23-year-old law student who was still completing his studies at Montreal's McGill University, Dryden went on to win the Conn Smythe Trophy for MVP of the playoffs, as the Canadiens won the Stanley Cup.

To win the Cup, the storied Habs followed their upset win over Boston with a tough, hardwon victory over the Minnesota North Stars in the "cross-over" semi-final round. It marked the first time that an East Division winner and a West Division winner had clashed in a playoff semi-final. The North Stars had qualified by besting St. Louis, four games to two. In the companion series, Chicago swept past the Philadelphia Flyers four games to none, then eliminated the New York Rangers in six games to qualify for the finals against Montreal.

In a brilliantly played series which went the full seven games, the Canadiens edged the Hawks with Henri Richard scoring the tying and winning goals in the deciding contest. Richard thus vindicated himself after having blasted coach Al MacNeil. Frank Mahovlich was another brilliant figure for the Habs, setting a new playoff record with 14 goals along the way. The real hero, however, was Ken Dryden, who was being dubbed the "discovery of the decade."

1971–72

Two of the greatest players in hockey—Gordie Howe and Jean Beliveau—announced their retirements just before the new season got underway.

Howe, 43, had completed an incredible 25 years with the Detroit Red Wings, during which time he had virtually rewritten the record book. He had played more seasons, more games and scored more goals, assists and points than any other player in NHL history. He also won more Hart and Ross Trophy awards, made more All-Star teams and played in more All-Star games than anyone else.

Beliveau, 40, had played for 18 seasons with the Montreal Canadiens. No other center in history had scored as many goals and only Howe had more points.

The rules committee of the NHL announced that, henceforth, the third man into an altercation on the ice would be hit with an automatic game misconduct penalty. It was a laudable move, aimed at curtailing the endless brawls that had marred games in previous seasons. There was also to be a change in the format for Stanley Cup playoffs. Teams finishing first in each division would meet the fourth-place finishers. Second place teams would clash with those ending third. The old system had been first vs. third and second vs. fourth. The new plan provided all clubs with a greater incentive for finishing as high as possible in the standings.

The Hall of Fame finally got around to admitting Harvey "Busher" Jackson, left-wing star on the old Toronto Kid Line. Also inducted was the late Terry Sawchuk, plus oldtime great "Cooney" Weiland. The latter was a star center on a high-scoring Boston Bruins' line in the 1930s. Another former star, Gordon Roberts, was also admitted as a player. Arthur Wirtz, the board chairman of the Chicago Blackhawks, was named to the builders' section.

Through one of Sammy Pollock's complicated deals, the Montreal Canadiens had first pick of the graduating amateurs. They choose Guy Lafleur of the Quebec Remparts, a phenomenal scorer who'd counted 307 goals in his last two years of junior hockey, including playoffs. The Canadiens, it turned out, owned no less than six of the first 25 amateur choices. The second choice was Marcel Dionne, who went to Detroit. Jocelyn Guevremont followed and was sent to Vancouver. Gene Carr was signed by St. Louis. Richard Martin went fifth in the draft, and was grabbed by Buffalo. He wound up setting a new goal-scoring record for NHL rookies.

At training camp, Gilbert Perreault shocked the Sabres by turning up at 225 pounds, greatly exceeding his playing weight. Garry Unger shook the St. Louis brass by appearing with long, blond hair. "Unger used to go around with Miss America," noted a scribe. "Now, he looks like Miss America."

Glenn Hall, 40, announced his retirement after 16 years with Detroit, Chicago and St. Louis. George Armstrong retired for the fifth time, after 20 years in the NHL. This time he made it stick. He was just four goals short of the 300 mark. John Ferguson, "the heavyweight champion of hockey," called it quits after a hectic career with the Canadiens. Andy Bathgate, onetime superstar with the New York Rangers, who later played for several other NHL teams, also packed it in, as did Leo Boivin, the last of the real sock 'em defensemen.

The Boston Bruins lost their opener 4–1 to the Rangers. A furious Milt Schmidt, at that point still the team's general manager, cancelled all public appearances and ordered players to refuse commitments. "No, it's not a disciplinary move," he seethed. "But, believe me, we're going to concentrate on hockey around here."

The Bruins got the message and went on to post a 54–13–11 record during the season to nail down their second straight Prince of Wales Trophy as first-place finishers in the East.

The Montreal Canadiens were sold during the season for a reported $15.4 million, plus assorted fringe benefits. Among the latter was a $2.5 million saving because the sale took place just before a new capital gains tax was written into Canadian law. The new owners were Edward and Peter Bronfman of a financially prominent Montreal family, the Bank of Nova Scotia and Baton Broadcasting Ltd., of which John Bassett was a principal figure. Montreal lawyer Jacques Courtois was named president of the hockey club.

The number of coaching changes around the NHL was almost unprecedented. Scotty Bowman took over at Montreal, after having severed connections with St. Louis. He replaced Al MacNeil, whose reward for having won the Stanley Cup the previous year was a job behind the bench of the Nova Scotia Voyageurs, the Canadiens' farm club. Vic Stasiuk went to California as coach, replacing Fred Glover who was fired. Glover wound up in L.A., but was fired again at the end of the season. Stasiuk was fired by the Seals at season's end and then grabbed a berth with Vancouver. Johnny Wilson took over for Doug Barkley in Detroit. Billy McCreary became coach in St. Louis, but was fired on Christmas Day and replaced by Al Arbour. As the season progressed, Red Kelly asked to be relieved of the general manager-coach position in Pittsburgh in order to concentrate on coaching. Punch Imlach, 53, suffered a heart seizure at Buffalo and had to relinquish the coaching job there to Joe Crozier. In Toronto, John McLellan came down with an ulcer and was replaced behind the bench by King Clancy.

A number of players reached some important milestones. Bobby Hull scored his 600th career goal in regular season play when he beat Gerry Cheevers in the Boston net.

110

Hull had averaged better than 40 goals a season through 15 NHL campaigns. He wound up by hitting the 50-goal mark for the fifth time. Phil Esposito became the 16th player in NHL history to score 300 goals. Phil scored 66 goals for the season and 133 total points for his second straight scoring title.

The New York Rangers unveiled the trio of Jean Ratelle, Vic Hadfield and Rod Gilbert, and their scoring feats earned them the name of "GAG Line," meaning a goal a game. Hadfield had a 50-goal season. The line became the first in NHL history to have each of its members count 40 or more goals in a single season. In Buffalo, rookie Richard Martin set a new scoring record for first-year players when he finished the season with a total of 44 goals. However, another rookie, Marcel Dionne of Detroit, established a new mark for points by a rookie with 76. Brad Park, the Rangers' classy defenseman, became the first rear guard in 30 years to score two hat tricks in one season. In Minnesota, lanky Tom Reid became the first defenseman to score on a penalty shot in seven seasons.

As always, there were trades around the NHL. Some had unusual overtones. The California Golden Seals, desperately trying to gain strength, sent Gary Smith to Chicago for goalie Gerry Desjardins and two other players. Soon they discovered that Desjardins was still disabled with a broken arm, suffered the previous season. They complained to the NHL about it and the league sympathized. Chicago eventually agreed to take Desjardins back. They supplied another netminder, young Gilles Meloche, and defenseman Paul Shmyr to the beleaguered Seals. However, the Seals weren't out of the woods by any means. They traded rear guard Ron Stackhouse to Detroit for forward Tom Webster. The latter played eight games for the Seals then was hospitalized with a bad back. He was out for the season.

In other trades, Andre Lacroix went to Chicago from Philadelphia for Rick Foley and others. Bobby Rousseau, who once scored five goals in a single game but managed only four goals all through 1970–71, went to New York from Minnesota in return for Bob Nevin. Rogatien Vachon went to L.A. from Montreal for Dale Hoganson and others. Jim Roberts was dealt to Montreal by the St. Louis Blues. There was a seven-player swap between the Blues and Rangers and an eight-player deal between Los Angeles and Philadelphia. Defenseman Larry Hillman, traded to Buffalo from Los Angeles, figured that he had changed uniforms 25 times in 18 pro hockey seasons.

There was a riot in the Philadelphia Spectrum involving a game with the St. Louis Blues and the Blues' owner, Sid Salomon, Jr., accused police of brutality after they rushed onto the ice swinging clubs.

In Toronto, Stafford Smythe, whose father Conn had founded the Leafs, died at the age of 50. George Gee, an ex-player with Chicago and Detroit, collapsed and died during the intermission of a Detroit Oldtimers' game in which he'd been playing. He, too, was 50. Louis Trudel, a star with the Chicago Blackhawks in the 1930s, passed away. Herb Gardiner, a defense star with the early Montreal Canadiens, died in Philadelphia. Gardiner had been an NHL rookie at the age of 35.

Jean Ratelle, having a tremendous season with the Rangers, displaced Phil Esposito as scoring leader at the halfway mark and was threatening to become overall scoring champ when he broke his ankle late in the season. Tim Horton, upon whom the Pittsburgh Penguins had pinned their defensive hopes, also suffered a broken ankle. Bernie Parent and Denis Dupere, teammates on the Toronto Maple Leafs, were lucky to escape serious injury when the car in which they were driving was involved in a head-on collision. Parent suffered a badly scraped face. "First time I look better with my mask on," said the goalie. St. Louis defenseman Noel Picard received a badly smashed foot and ankle in an unusual horseback riding accident. Philadelphia goalie Bruce Gamble's career was suddenly terminated when he suffered a heart attack.

For the second year in a row, Boston and Chicago clinched first place in their respective divisions.

The NHL announced that each member of the Stanley Cup winning team would get $15,000, up from $7,500 in other years. Losers would get $7,500 apiece, up from $1,500. The players said they were not satisfied with the split and wanted more.

In the opening round of Cup play, Boston dumped Toronto in five games, the New York Rangers were surprise winners over Montreal in six outings, Chicago swept Pittsburgh four straight and St. Louis edged Minnesota in seven. The Bruins then eliminated St. Louis in four straight games, while the Rangers did the same to Chicago in a stunning upset. Boston won the Stanley Cup by defeating the Rangers four games to two.

Bobby Orr won the Conn Smythe Trophy as the outstanding performer in the playoffs.

There was an outcry when post-season awards were made and Montreal goalie Ken Dryden was named the Calder Memorial Trophy winner as top rookie. Many felt he was not a legitimate rookie due to his extensive service in the previous year's playoffs. Some believed the real rookie of the year was Buffalo's Richard Martin.

The season closed on a somewhat menacing note for the NHL when the upstart World Hockey Association signed several players, notably Wayne Connelly and Larry Pleau from the NHL, although U.S. Olympic team goalie Mike Curran had been their first signee. WHA officials announced that they would be in business with a 12-team operation in 1972–73.

1972–73

With stunning force, the news of Bobby Hull's defection to the Winnipeg Jets of the World Hockey Association swept through the hockey world prior to the start of the new season. Hull, the revered "Golden Jet" of the NHL, signed a $2.75 million contract as playing-coach. "With the signing of a star of Bobby Hull's magnitude," said a WHA spokesman, "our league has achieved instant credibility." He was right. In rapid-fire order, Bernie Parent, Johnny McKenzie, Brad Selwood, Rick Ley, Rosaire Paiement, Andre Lacroix and a clutch of others jumped from the NHL to the upstart WHA. The war for talent was underway.

The NHL, at the annual draft meetings in June, announced that two more teams—the Atlanta Flames and New York Islanders—would commence operations in the 1972–73 season. The league which had operated as a six-team outfit for a quarter of a century from 1942 to 1967 had added 10 clubs to their ranks in a five-year period.

The Atlanta Flames named Bernard "Boom Boom" Geoffrion as their coach and drafted a couple of good young goalie prospects in Phil Myre and Dan Bouchard. They also signed amateur Jacques Richard to a lucrative contract.

The Islanders inked Phil Goyette to a "multi-year" coaching pact, drafted veterans like Denis Dejordy and Gerry Desjardins to guard their nets and put Ed Westfall up front, as well as securing the services of graduating amateur whiz, Billy Harris.

In other off-season business, the Hockey Hall of Fame waived the normal waiting period and admitted Gordie Howe and Jean Beliveau. In a long overdue move, they also elected Reginald "Hooley" Smith to their ranks. Smith was a member of the Montreal Maroons famed "S-Line" with Nels Stewart and Babe Seibert back in the twenties. Harry "Hap" Holmes, an outstanding netminder from the past, was also elected. Weston Adams, son of the founder of the Boston Bruins and a former president of the club, was admitted to the builders' section.

Team Canada was formed to play an eight-game series against Russia. Harry Sinden was named coach with John Ferguson as his assistant. An uproar followed the announcement that only players signed to NHL contracts could play on Canada's team. That meant Bobby Hull was excluded, as were any other WHA jumpers. Despite a strong public outcry, the NHL held firm to this rule. Bobby Orr couldn't make the team, either, due to an off-season knee operation. Still, the experts unanimously picked Canada to wallop the Russians in eight straight games.

It was a shock when Team Canada was trounced 7–3 in the opening game in Montreal and trailed 2–1–1 in games by the time the series shifted to Russia. Canadian fans booed the team in the fourth game in Vancouver, and Phil Esposito took to a microphone to blast the public for their lack of support. In Russia, Vic Hadfield, Richard Martin, Jocelyn Guevremont and Gilbert Perreault quit the team and came home because they weren't being used by coach Sinden. Then, in a fantastic windup, Team Canada rallied through the last few games to win the series by a narrow 4–3 margin in games, with one match tied. Phil Esposito and Paul Henderson were the heroes of the series, the latter scoring three game-winning goals for the highlight performance of his hockey career.

The first meeting on the ice between the newly franchised Atlanta Flames and the New York Islanders resulted in a 3–2 win for the Flames. The Orr-less Bruins, missing their super defenseman who remained sidelined with knee problems, were in fifth place after 11 games and were, according to coach Tom Johnson, "lacking desire." The Vancouver Canucks used five defensemen on a power play against Buffalo, but were nonplussed when the Sabres used four rear guards as penalty killers. A total of nine defensemen on the ice at once! Buffalo pulled a switch by going back to training camp in mid-season, when they returned to St. Catharines, Ontario, during a three-day break in the NHL schedule.

This season saw the usual shuffling of coaches from team to team, as well as a few general managers. Bob Pulford took over in Los Angeles, and actually lasted the season. Al Arbour was fired for the second time by St. Louis and was replaced by Jean-Guy Talbot. Red Kelly was fired by Pittsburgh and player Ken Schinkel took over. Phil Goyette got the heave-ho from the New York Islanders and Earl Ingarfield moved in. Tom Johnson was bounced at Boston and Bep Guidolin was stepped up from the minors to try his hand at coaching the Bruins. Garry Young was fired by the California Seals and Fred Glover took over three jobs: executive vice-president, general manager and coach.

The WHA grabbed Derek Sanderson and Gerry Cheevers, and even raided the ranks of referees to snag Bill Friday for a reported $50,000 a year. Vern Buffey was hired as referee-in-chief. Sixty-seven players had jumped form the NHL to the WHA by the time the hockey season had officially opened. Doug Harvey, an ex-NHL defense great, signed as assistant coach of the WHA Houston Aeros.

As the season moved along, players in both the NHL and WHA reached various career milestones. Stan Mikita, veteran Chicago Blackhawks' pivot, passed the 1,000-point mark in the second week of the campaign. Johnny Bucyk of the Boston Bruins hit two milestones in little more than two weeks when he clicked for his 400th career goal and then notched his 1,000th point, against Detroit. Ron Ellis became the 19th Toronto Maple Leafs player to hit the 200-goal mark and Dave Keon scored career goal number 300 against Vancouver. Alex Delvecchio, the Detroit veteran, became the all-time second-leading points scorer behind Gordie Howe and ahead of Jean Beliveau. Detroit newcomer Henry Boucha set a quick-scoring record by netting the puck six seconds after the opening faceoff. Boucha's teammate, Mickey Redmond, wound up the season by becoming the first Red Wing in history to reach or surpass the 50-goal mark. He scored 52 goals. Frank Mahovlich of the Montreal Canadiens became only the fifth NHL player in history to score 500 career goals.

During this season, NBC sports carried several regular-season and playoff games into millions of homes throughout North America. Tim Ryan handled the play-by-play of the games, Hall of Famer Ted Lindsay was the color commentator and this author conducted between-period interviews. Plans were made to introduce a cartoon character named Peter Puck to the intermissions as a means of explaining hockey's rules and fundamentals to the vast U.S. television audience.

Bobby Orr announced that he had become engaged to a Florida schoolteacher, then celebrated the news by assisting on six goals against Vancouver to tie an NHL scoring record for defensemen. Carol Vadnais, a Boston defenseman, had an unusual experience during the season when he was mistaken for a bank robber and arrested in Philadelphia. Bill Flett of the Philadelphia Flyers grabbed headlines when he took to the ice with a flowing beard to match his long hair and moustache.

Death claimed some former hockey greats. Within a month, Bill Durnan, Turk Broda and Doug Bentley had passed away. Durnan, 57, and Broda, 58, former goaling greats with the Canadiens and Maple Leafs respectively, died within two weeks of each other. They had been rival greats during the 1940s, but were longtime friends off the ice. Durnan was a six-time winner of the Vezina Trophy. Bentley, the older brother of the famed combination of Doug and Max Bentley, had been a member of Chicago's celebrated "Pony Line" with Billy Mosienko as the other forward. Death also claimed Jack Crawford, 56, a former Bruins' defenseman, and Weston Adams, 68, ex-president of the Bruins who had been elected to the Hall of Fame at the start of the season.

In Boston, Derek Sanderson returned to the Bruins after having curtailed his WHA deal with the Philadelphia Blazers. Milt Schmidt, a 36-year veteran of the Boston organization, said he'd quit the club at the end of the season. In Pittsburgh, the Penguins wowed their followers with a line of Schock, Schinkel and Shack, before Schinkel moved up to become coach. The Vancouver Canucks were in near open rebellion against the tough tactics of coach Vic Stasiuk. In Montreal, there was a dressing room altercation in which Henri Richard slapped Serge Savard in the face. Denis Dupere walked out on the Maple Leafs and disappeared for a week. On the lighter side, in Rochester American League goalie Gaye Cooley had a face mask made with a smile on it.

The Montreal Canadiens clinched first place in the East, losing only 10 games along the way, while the Chicago Blackhawks were first-place finishers in the NHL West. In the WHA, the New England Whalers wound up atop the East Division while the Winnipeg Jets headed the West in that league.

In the NHL playoffs, Montreal ousted Buffalo in their first-round series while the Rangers surprised Boston, who lost Phil Esposito with a damaged knee. Chicago dumped St. Louis in their opening round while Philadelphia took care of Minnesota.

Montreal then eliminated Philadelphia in five games in the semi-final "crossover" round, while Chicago did the same to New York. The Canadiens wrapped up their most successful season in history with a Stanley Cup triumph over the Hawks in six games. Several players had a shot at the Conn Smythe Trophy as the result of outstanding play, but Yvan Cournoyer topped them all. He set a playoff scoring record with 15 goals.

No sooner had the final buzzers sounded than the post-season maneuvering began and some of the developments were shockers. The NHL announced that Washington and Kansas City would be admitted to their growing family in 1974–75 and Milt Schmidt revealed that he would be general manager in Washington. Sid Abel announced he would leave St. Louis to become general manager at Kansas City. Detroit fired coach Johnny Wilson and replaced him with Ted Garvin, from their minor-league affiliate, the Port Huron Wings. Vancouver dumped their coach, Vic Stasiuk. Jacques Plante stunned Boston by suddenly defecting to the WHA to become general manager of the Quebec Nordiques. Henri Richard, captain of the Montreal Canadiens, let it be known that he had a solid $200,000 offer to jump to Houston of the WHA. The Canadiens quickly signed him to a two-year contract for a comparable amount. Marc Tardif, the young Canadiens' winger, did jump. He joined the Los Angeles Sharks of the WHA. Dale Tallon was traded by Vancouver to Chicago for Gary Smith and Jerry Korab, after Tallon had hinted he, too, might defect.

For the first time in hockey history, the NHL held its amateur draft separate from the regular June meetings. Denis Potvin, a rear guard from Ottawa who'd broken Bobby Orr's scoring record for defensemen in the junior ranks, was the first pick. He went to the New York Islanders and quickly signed for an astronomical sum. Tom Lysiak, Dennis Ververgaert and Lanny McDonald were next in line and they went to Atlanta, Vancouver and Toronto respectively, for equally huge amounts.

The biggest and most shocking news of all, however, concerned the WHA's signing of Gordie Howe and his two sons, Mark and Marty. All three signed with the Houston Aeros, providing the fledgling league with perhaps the biggest coup of all.

To the NHL, which had seen the season begin with the defection of Bobby Hull, the news of the Howes' jump came as a stunning blow. Obviously shaken, the NHL governors met in private to determine ways and means of coping with the unexpectedly strong challenge posed by the WHA. An attempt to actually talk merger with the upstart league was sidetracked when the NHL Players' Association let it be known that they would launch a suit against the NHL if such a move took place.

Fifty-six years old in 1973, the NHL admittedly had problems but was moving resolutely forward to meet the challenge of what was becoming known as the game's new era.

1973–74

On September 13, 1973, Montreal's Sam Pollock received a call from his goaltender

Ken Dryden. A brilliant performer in the previous regular season and playoffs, Dryden stunned Pollock and the entire hockey world with his decision to retire, at least for the forthcoming season. Dryden was quitting to article for a Toronto law firm, as he was unhappy with the terms of his $80,000-a-year contract when other goalies in pro hockey were making up to $200,000 a year. Despite this loss, the Canadiens were picked by most of the experts to finish on top in the East Division, followed by the New York Rangers and the Boston Bruins.

In the West, Chicago was the choice for first place, with the Philadelphia Flyers and the Minnesota North Stars close behind.

It didn't take Phil Esposito long to make his scoring presence felt as the new season got underway. The Boston sharpshooter scored his 400th career goal in the NHL opener against Vancouver. Esposito figured in five of six goals as the Bruins whipped the Canucks 6–4—not bad for a guy who wasn't supposed to start skating until mid-season because of summer surgery on a gimpy knee.

Goalie Bernie Parent returned to the Philadelphia Flyers with much fanfare and recorded back-to-back shutouts over the Leafs and the Islanders.

Two imports from Sweden, Inge Hammerstrom and Borje Salming, easily won regular berths on the Toronto roster. In fact, Salming's play was on a par with the Islanders' brilliant rookie defenseman Denis Potvin.

Goalie Gary Smith, signed by Vancouver in an off-season deal with Chicago, gave the Canucks the most dependable goalkeeping the club had enjoyed in its three-year history. When Smith arrived in Vancouver he announced to a press gathering: "Everything you've heard about me is true. I'm a fantastic goaltender."

A few days after Buffalo's Punch Imlach called his centerman Gilbert Perreault "the best player in hockey today," Perreault was sidelined with a broken leg.

After the Detroit Red Wings lost nine of their first 12 games, Red Wing captain Alex Delvecchio replaced Ted Garvin as coach of the team, thus ending Delvecchio's illustrious 23-year playing career.

In November, Boston's Bobby Orr picked up seven points in a 10–2 Boston win over the Rangers to set a record for most points in a game by a defenseman. During an 8–0 Bruins win over Detroit, Orr collected his 453rd career assist to break another record held by Doug Harvey. In 18 seasons Harvey had garnered 452 assists, tops for a defenseman until Orr passed him in just seven seasons.

Coach Jack Gordon of Minnesota, unable to get his club rolling, called for relief. Parker MacDonald moved up from the North Stars' New Haven club of the American League to replace Gordon. Gordon said, "My nerves were shot. It was getting so bad I couldn't even hold a cup of tea in one hand."

Bobby Clarke at 24 became the youngest captain in NHL history. The two oldest were Johnny Bucyk of Boston, 38, and Montreal's Henri Richard, 37.

In December, Derek Sanderson rejoined the Boston Bruins after a conditioning stint with the Boston Braves in the AHL. While with the Braves, Derek drew an all-time attendance record at Springfield where 2,000 fans had to be turned away at the gate.

November 28 was Frank Mahovlich Night at the Montreal Forum. Mahovlich was honored for bettering Jean Beliveau's 507 career goals.

There was an ugly incident in Philadelphia just before Christmas. Rookie defenseman Barry Cummins of the Seals was cut under the eye by Bobby Clarke's stick. Cummins suddenly swung his stick and struck Clarke over the head, slicing him for 20 stitches and knocking him to the ice. Bill Flett of the Flyers wheeled and attacked

116

Cummins. Bob Kelly led a band of Flyers off the bench and soon Cummins was under a herd of enraged Flyers. He emerged, groggy and bloody, and was handed a match penalty. Later, president Clarence Campbell suspended Cummins for three games and fined him $300. Cummins subsequently phoned Clarke at home and apologized. "He sounded really sick about what happened," said Clarke.

Phil Hoene of the Kings, a rookie who would score one of his career total of two NHL goals on a penalty shot, was reported to be the first player ever to make a penalty shot goal his first. Not so. Ralph "Scotty" Bowman of the St. Louis Eagles scored his first NHL goal on a penalty shot in 1934.

By mid-season, Emile Francis had taken over the coaching duties of the Rangers again, replacing Larry Popein. After a newsman wrote that Marcel Dionne wanted to leave Detroit because of its homicide rate and because some of his teammates were not producing, Dionne threw a towel at him and threatened, "I'll get you! I'll get you!"

Bobby Orr established another record when he scored his 200th goal against the Rangers. No other defenseman had ever topped this.

The Vancouver Canucks fired coach Bill McCreary and moved Phil Maloney into the coaching chair. When Maloney was asked his opinion of long hair, he said, "I don't care if a player wears his hair down to his knees and paints it green as long as he produces on the ice."

The Canadiens again honored a player. This time, captain Henri Richard was saluted with a special night.

The 27th annual All-Star game, played in Chicago, was won by the West All-Stars, spearheaded by Garry Unger of St. Louis, the game's most valuable player.

By February, controversial Ned Harkness was through in Detroit. Harkness resigned as general manager of the Wings, ending a turbulent four-year career. He was replaced on a temporary basis by assistant general manager Jimmy Skinner.

Marc Boileau, coach at Fort Wayne of the International Hockey League, moved into Pittsburgh to replace Ken Schinkel as coach of the slumping Penguins.

In the early morning hours of February 21, veteran Buffalo defenseman Tim Horton was racing his Italian-made sports car back to Buffalo after a game in Toronto. Police said Horton's car reached speeds in excess of 100 miles an hour when it left the highway and crashed. Horton was killed instantly. Punch Imlach, Horton's coach, said, "He was the backbone of our team in Buffalo. It's a terrible loss, not only to his family and his team, but to the game of hockey."

It was a busy season for trades. By the time the trading deadline rolled around, only five clubs had not been involved in deals—Montreal, Philadelphia, Chicago, California and the New York Islanders. Close to 50 players were involved in the swapping.

Colorful Derek Sanderson found himself in the Bruins' doghouse late in the season. During a west-coast trip, Derek was involved in a fist-fight with teammate Terry O'Reilly in the club's dressing room. Then, after missing a team flight, Sanderson was suspended by the Bruins for the rest of the season. Harry Sinden, the Bruins' general manager, said it was unlikely that Sanderson would ever play again for the Boston club. Sanderson's comment was, "Yeah, I'm probably through in Boston. But then, so is Bep Guidolin. He won't be back either."

By the end of the regular 78-game schedule, the experts who'd picked Montreal and Chicago to head their respective divisions were wishing they'd given more attention to Boston and Philadelphia.

As the eight playoff teams prepared for the race to the Stanley Cup, fans were still buzzing over Marcel Dionne's goal. The Detroit center scored against the Blackhawks with only 66 seconds left in the regular season and forced Chicago and Philadelphia into a tie for the Vezina Trophy, each club with 164 goals against. For the first time in the 48-year history of the award, two names would be inscribed—Tony Esposito and Bernie Parent.

Boston center Phil Esposito became the second player in NHL history to capture four straight point-scoring titles and·five in his career. Gordie Howe had skated off with six. Esposito did, however, become the first player to lead the NHL in goals for five straight seasons. He tallied 68. Four Bruins finished on top of the individual scoring race. Esposito collected 145 points, Orr was second with 122, followed by Ken Hodge with 105 and Wayne Cashman with 89.

There were four 50-goal scorers, another league record. Esposito (68) and teammate Hodge (50) were joined by Buffalo's Richard Martin (52) and Detroit's Mickey Redmond (51).

THE PLAYOFFS

Toronto met Boston, the East Division champions, in series A. The Bruins pushed the Leafs aside in four straight games, with Ken Hodge scoring an overtime winner in the final match at Toronto.

In series B between the Rangers and the Canadiens, the Rangers became giant killers for the third consecutive season by eliminating the Habs four games to two.

Series C matched the West Division champion Philadelphia Flyers and the fourth-place finishers, the Atlanta Flames. The Flyers won the first two games on home ice and then moved into Atlanta for the wildest weekend of their season. In game three Don Saleski scored a goal, his first in 32 games, as the Flyers triumphed 4–1. Atlanta goalie Dan Bouchard, infuriated by a disputed goal in this game, attacked referee Dave Newall and swung his stick at linesman Neil Armstrong, receiving only a misconduct penalty.

After the game, Flyer coach Fred Shero was mugged. Shero remembers waking up in his hotel room, bruised and bloody with his glasses broken. No money was taken from him. "I don't remember anything about what happened," he said. Shero was hospitalized for the Flyers' fourth straight win, a game Dave Schultz ended with an overtime goal.

After taking the first two games from Los Angeles on home ice in series D, the Blackhawks scored an amazing victory in the Forum. They managed only 10 shots on goal, only three shots in the final two periods, and won the game 1–0. The Kings came back to win 5–1 in game four, but the Hawks wrapped up the series with a 1–0 shutout in game five.

In the semi-finals, Philadelphia ousted the Rangers in seven games. The Flyers squeaked through with a 4–3 victory in the final game at the Spectrum. In game four of the series, defenseman Barry Ashbee suffered an eye injury when struck by a Dale Rolfe slapshot. The injury marked the end of Ashbee's playing career.

The other semi-final series saw the Boston Bruins surge past the Blackhawks in six games. Greg Sheppard's goal from a near-impossible angle with 1:49 left to·play won game six for the Bruins 3–2 and allowed Boston to advance against Philadelphia in the finals.

The final playoff series leading to the Stanley Cup in May 1974 will be remembered more for drama and tension than for big moments on the ice. Would the Flyers become the first expansion club to skate off with the coveted trophy? Would the constant brawling throughout the series taint hockey's premier event, showcased coast to coast on NBC television?

Bobby Orr was the hero in game one. Orr scored a game winner with just 30 seconds left to play. An overtime goal by Bobby Clarke gave the Flyers a 3–2 victory in game two. Back at the Spectrum, the Flyers won twice by scores of 4–1 and 4–2. But the Bruins roared back with a 5–1 win to stay alive. In game six, the Flyers received an assist from Kate Smith who was a surprise visitor to the Spectrum. Kate sang "God Bless America" before the game and then cheered mightily for the team which had adopted her. There was only one goal scored. Rick MacLeish, who paced all playoff scorers with 13 goals and nine assists, deflected Andre Dupont's shot past Gilles Gilbert in the first period. The Flyers made that goal stand up and a last-minute drive by the Bruins was frustrated when Orr was penalized for holding Clarke with 2:22 left to play. After the game there was a celebration in Philadelphia that matched the celebrations following VE and VJ days after World War II.

Goalie Bernie Parent was awarded the Conn Smythe Trophy as the most valuable performer in the playoffs. "To play here, and win like this," said Bernie, "it's the greatest feeling in the world."

1974–75

During the summer hockey meetings in Montreal, seven new members were elected to Hockey's Hall of Fame. Tommy Ivan, the dapper general manager of the Chicago Blackhawks and a veteran of 27 years in hockey as an executive, the late Charles Hay, one-time head of Hockey Canada, and former referee-in-chief Carl Voss were named to the builder's section of the Hall. Former players elected included Dickie Moore, a Montreal scoring star, Art Coulter, captain of the Rangers in the forties, the late Billy Burch and the late Tommy Dunderdale.

Punch Imlach of Buffalo made it clear how he felt about the inroads the WHA clubs were making on the NHL member teams. He sent out letters to all NHL clubs giving them permission to sign any Buffalo-owned player who jumped to the WHA. If the NHL teams were successful in luring a player back, Punch agreed to accept the normal waiver price — $40,000 for a player who had been in the NHL before he jumped, $20,000 for a player who had been in the minors. "We've got to start fighting fire with fire," said Punch.

NHL president Clarence Campbell was resentful of Ontario attorney William McMurtry's allegations that the NHL was resposible for most of the fighting in amateur hockey. He also disagreed with the claim that the NHL sold violence to uninitiated audiences in the United States to the detriment of the basic skills of the game. McMurtry headed a government inquiry into violence in hockey.

In Washington, Milt Schmidt was busy shaping the Washington Capitals. Schmidt shelled out an estimated $2.5 million to sign the Caps' first five draft choices before Washington's expansion twin, Kansas City, had signed even one. The top amateur choices in Washington's camp were Greg Joly, a defenseman from the Regina Pats, and Mike

Marson, a rugged winger from the Sudbury Wolves. Marson was billed as the second black player in NHL history. Jimmy Anderson was signed as coach of the Capitals.

In Kansas City there was concern that the team would lose first-round pick Wilf Paiement to the WHA. Alan Eagleson, Paiement's lawyer, called the scouts' offer "nothing short of an insult" and said he intended to make Paiement "the highest-paid graduating junior in history." Paiement eventually signed a contract rumored to be in the $500,000 bracket.

The league decided to use the names of trophies and members of the Hockey Hall of Fame to identify its new 18-team, two-conference, four-division setup. One two-division group was named the Prince of Wales Conference, the other the Clarence Campbell Conference.

In the Campbell Conference were the Lester Patrick Division (Atlanta, the New York Islanders, New York Rangers and Philadelphia) and the Conn Smythe Division (Chicago, Kansas City, Minnesota, St. Louis and Vancouver). The Prince of Wales Conference included the James Norris Division (Detroit, Los Angeles, Montreal, Pittsburgh and Washington) and the Jack Adams Division (Boston, Buffalo, Toronto and California). Fans complained it would take them years to remember all the divisions and conferences and where each team fit in.

Players and fans alike were intrigued with the idea of being able to see replays of key situations on giant screens in at least one major-league arena—the Capital Center outside Washington.

New coaches in the NHL (aside from Jimmy Anderson in Washington) included Floyd Smith, who replaced Joe Crozier at Buffalo and Don Cherry who was signed by Boston. Guidolin moved from Boston to Kansas City.

The new season was just one day old when Henri Richard threatened to retire. Richard was miffed when he learned he was sitting out Montreal's home opener. Richard's number, but not his name, was listed with the other Hab non-starters and he stormed out of the dressing room. He felt his coach Scotty Bowman should have handled the situation with more diplomacy. Richard missed one practice, gained great support from the Montreal press and returned to the club.

Rookie Danny Gare of Buffalo scored a goal 18 seconds after the puck was dropped during his first shift. The NHL record for the fastest goal by a rookie was a 15-second goal by Gus Bodnar, set in 1943.

Early in the season, Boston's Bobby Orr and Chicago's Stan Mikita slashed at each other with high sticks. Mikita infuriated Boston coach Don Cherry when he said, "Bobby stayed on the ice after he served his penalties. That shows you who's running the show in Boston. It's Orr ... not Cherry. And when baby [Orr] doesn't get his way, he throws a fit ... ."

Cherry replied, "I only wish I'd had one man to send out there after Mikita, someone to send him back to Czechoslovakia in a coffin."

Before the end of October, Lou Angotti had resigned as coach in St. Louis. He was replaced by Garry Young, formerly of the California Seals.

Guy Lafleur of the Canadiens was off to his best start ever and there was talk that he had finally arrived as a big league star.

It was noted that more U.S. born and trained players were involved in pro hockey than ever before. Approximately 30 Americans were employed in the NHL and the WHA.

Early in November, Chicago veteran Chico Maki announced his retirement. Henri Richard of Montreal suffered a broken ankle. Dale Tallon of Chicago was sidelined with a dislocated hip and Bobby Rousseau of the Rangers underwent a back-fusion operation and was out for the season. Wayne Cashman of Boston was hospitalized with a disc problem in his back. The Leafs lost defenseman Ian Turnbull with torn knee ligaments. Then Rod Seiling of the Leafs, acquired earlier in a trade with Washington, suffered a similar injury. Walt Tkaczuk of New York broke his leg, Ron Harris of the Rangers went out with a broken hip socket and Dale Rolfe broke his foot. Atlanta's Bobby Leiter also broke a leg.

In Philadelphia, Don Saleski was in a slump. After laboring through 31 games with one goal, he was hearing boos. Then, during a fashion show on the Spectrum ice, his wife Mary Ann was also booed while modeling a fur coat. Flyer captain Bobby Clarke was incensed. "Anybody who boos a player's wife has to be missing some marbles," he said.

The Blues and the Rangers celebrated the approaching New Year with a wild, bench-clearing brawl that resulted in a total of 246 penalty minutes, a record for one game.

On December 26, the Washington Capitals called up center Bill Riley from Dayton of the International League and the Caps became the first NHL club to dress two black players for a league game.

On January 4, Dave Forbes of Boston was assessed a match penalty by referee Ron Wicks for deliberately injuring Henry Boucha of Minnesota with the butt end of his stick. Boucha suffered a serious eye injury and required several operations to restore full vision. Forbes was suspended for 10 games, the third most severe penalty ever handed down by Clarence Campbell. What's more, Forbes was indicted on a charge of aggravated assault, a charge that carried a prison sentence of up to five to 10 years, depending on the circumstances. The trial would take place months later.

The Montreal Canadiens went 22 games without a loss and were only two games shy of a record when they ran into a fired-up Toronto club. The Leafs beat the Habs 5–3 to end the streak.

The annual mid-season All-Star game, held in Montreal, was one of the dullest in years. It matched the Campbell Conference against the Wales Conference. Broadcasters called the teams the "Wales and the Campbells."

Tommy Ivan, general manager of the Blackhawks and former NHL referee Bill Chadwick were selected for the 1975 Lester Patrick Awards given for outstanding service to hockey in the United States.

In mid-February, the Washington Capitals replaced coach Jim Anderson with Red Sullivan. Atlanta fans were still getting over the shock of Boom Boom Geoffrion's sudden departure. Geoffrion had quit as coach of the Flames but refused to give a reason. He was replaced by Fred Creighton, who moved up from the Omaha Knights.

A new Stanley Cup playoff system for the 1974–75 season allowed 12 teams to qualify for the post-season action. The first three teams in each division would earn playoff positions, with the top team in each division getting a bye through the first round. Eight second and third place teams in each division would be matched in a best-of-three first-round series. Of these clubs, the team with the most points would meet the team with the least points. The team with the second-highest point total would meet the team with the second lowest, and so on.

In March, ice problems plagued the New York Rangers. First Brad Park stepped in a rut in the poor ice and strained his left knee. Then Dale Rolfe fell while skating alone, pitched into the boards and suffered a compound fracture of his ankle. The injury ended Rolfe's hockey career.

Henry Boucha, still bothered by blurred vision, returned to the Minnesota lineup late in the season to play defense for a few games.

Pittsburgh's Ron Stackhouse tied a league record for assists in one game by a defenseman (6) when the Penguins walloped Philadelphia 8–2. In a March game, Bobby Orr slapped in his 38th goal of the season, breaking his own record for most goals by a defenseman. He now headed for a sixth straight 100-point-plus season. In Detroit, Marcel Dionne snapped Gordie Howe's club-assist record (59) and season-point record (103) with a dozen games left to play.

Red Sullivan's stint as coach of the Washington Capitals was short-lived and he resigned before the season ended. He explained, "My old stomach can't hack it anymore. I'm going back on the road as a scout." Milt Schmidt was forced to move behind the bench of a team that had just lost a record 61 games.

With the playoffs in mind, the Buffalo Sabres went looking for goaltending help. They acquired Gerry Desjardins from the WHA Baltimore Blades. Desjardins claimed his contract was breached when the Michigan Stags moved to Baltimore.

Montreal's Guy Lafleur broke one of the oldest club records in the NHL when he scored his 51st goal of the season. The 50-goal record was set by Rocket Richard in 50 games, 30 years and 12 days earlier. It was tied in 1960–61 by Boom Boom Geoffrion, who did it in 64 games.

The defending Stanley Cup champions, the Philadelphia Flyers, closed the regular season with a tremendous rush, winning 12 and tying two of their final 14 games to finish on top, ahead of both Buffalo and Montreal. All three clubs finished with 113 points, but the Flyers had the most victories (51). Montreal lost the least number of games (14) and led in goals scored (374). Philadelphia allowed the fewest goals against (181) and goalie Bernie Parent was declared the Vezina Trophy winner.

Boston's Bobby Orr won his second NHL scoring title with 135 points. Phil Esposito topped the goal scorers with 61. Pierre Lorouche was the high-scoring rookie with 68 points but lost out to Eric Vail of Atlanta in the Calder Trophy balloting. Vail had scored 39 goals. Dave Schultz of the Flyers was again the league bad man with 478 penalty minutes.

For the first time in league history, seven players had scored 100 or more points. They were Bobby Orr (135), Phil Esposito (127), Marcel Dionne (121), Guy Lafleur (119), Peter Mahovlich (117), Bobby Clarke (116) and Rene Robert (100).

THE PLAYOFFS

The best-of-three elimination series involving eight teams proved to be a disaster for three of the NHL's playoff favorites. The Los Angeles Kings, who were at or near the top of the standings for most of the regular season, were bounced by the Toronto Maple Leafs. The upstart New York Islanders edged the Rangers to the sidelines 2–1 in games. The deciding game was won in overtime by Jean Paul Parise after just 11 seconds, a playoff record. The Chicago Blackhawks lost the opener to Boston then bounced back to win the next two. Pittsburgh eliminated St. Louis in two straight games.

Pittsburgh appeared to be well on the way to advancing after winning the first three games of their quarter-final series with the Islanders. Then the Islanders stormed back with one of the most brilliant comebacks in league history. The Isles won four straight and took the seventh game 1–0 on Ed Westfall's third-period goal. Not since the 1942 playoff season, when the Toronto Maple Leafs had roared back with four straight wins against Detroit to take the series 4–3, had a team shown such a playoff comeback.

Buffalo had little trouble ousting Chicago 4–1 in games, while Montreal eliminated stubborn Vancouver 4–1. the Canucks' lone win snapped a 28-game winless streak (lasting five seasons) against Montreal. Philadelphia captured four straight from the Toronto Maple Leafs.

In the semi-finals, the Canadiens met the Sabres and Philadelphia faced the "Cinderella" Islanders.

Montreal had not won a game from Buffalo in five regular season tries and Buffalo took the first two games from Montreal. But the Habs came up with big wins on home ice. Back in Buffalo, an overtime goal by Rene Robert gave Buffalo a 3–2 lead in the series. The Sabres came up with hot goaltending in game six to win 4–3 and advance to the finals.

Meanwhile, the never-say-die Islanders produced another astounding comeback against the mighty Flyers in the other semi-final series. After dropping the first three games, the Isles dug in and refused to bow out. They won the fourth game, then the fifth and the sixth and the Flyers went back to Philadelphia to regroup. Kate Smith was also called upon to sing "God Bless America" prior to the deciding game. The Islanders finally ran out of miracles as Rick MacLeish scored three times and the Flyers triumphed 4–1.

The Stanley Cup finals matched Buffalo's brilliant scoring line, the "French Connection," against the solid goaltending of Philadelphia's Bernie Parent. The unquestionable victor was Parent, whose six-game performance earned him the Conn Smyth Trophy as MVP in the playoffs.

The Flyers captured the first two games at the Spectrum but ran into stubborn opposition back in Buffalo. Rene Robert's overtime shot gave Buffalo game three. The Sabres also took the fourth game 4–2. The Sabres had little confidence as they skated out for game five in Philadelphia. After all, they had not won at the Spectrum since coming into the NHL five years earlier. The result was an easy 5–1 win for the Flyers. Tough guy Dave Schultz was a surprise hero with two goals.

In game six, coach Floyd Smith started Roger Crozier in goal in place of Desjardins, who had been less than spectacular in the previous game. Both Crozier and Parent were brilliant through two periods. At the 11-second mark of the third period, Bob Kelly came from behind the net to slip the puck behind Crozier. Late in the period Bill Clement added an insurance goal. The Flyers won the game 2–0, the series 4–2, plus the Stanley Cup. Again there was a wild celebration in Philadelphia when the Flyers returned home.

1975-76

When the Philadelphia Flyers finally finished the longest NHL season in history with a Stanley Cup victory over Buffalo, there was little time for hockey men to enjoy post-season vacations. June draft meetings were followed by moves designed to strengthen clubs for the onrushing new season.

The New York Rangers handed Ron Stewart a two-year contract as coach. The 42-year-old Stewart promptly stated, "I'm not here to be a three-month coach." As it turned out, Steward did survive three months but not much longer. He was counting heavily on two ex-Toros of the WHA, Wayne Dillon and Pat Hickey, and goalie John Davidson, who had been acquired from St. Louis in return for Ted Irvine, Jerry Butler and Bert Wilson.

Marcel Dionne, who finished the previous season with 121 points, third in the individual scoring race, was available to the highest bidder. Toronto made a strong attempt to get Dionne but he signed a long-term contract in the million-dollar range with Los Angeles. The Kings compensated Detroit with players Terry Harper and Dan Maloney, with Harper balking at the move.

Jack Evans, coach of the year with Salt Lake City in the CHL, moved up to coach California. San Francisco businessman Mel Swig purchased the Seals and outlined long-range plans to move the club from Oakland to San Francisco once a new arena in San Francisco was completed.

At the June meetings, Clarence Campbell admitted he was hoping the league would soon find a man to replace him.

Greg Neeld, chosen in the fourth round of the amateur draft by Buffalo, was crushed when the NHL's board of governors voted against him in his bid to seek NHL employment. Neeld, who had lost the sight of one eye in a freak accident in junior hockey, displayed a new mask and face guard which he claimed was "foolproof" and would protect his good eye. But the governors upheld a rule which denied any player with only one eye the right to perform in the NHL. Neeld threatened to sue the league when the decision was announced.

Three modern-day stars and two players from a bygone era were inducted into Hockey's Hall of Fame in August. Glenn Hall, Pierre Pilote and George Armstrong were the trio of "moderns," while Gordie Drillon and "Ace" Bailey were the oldtimers.

Bill Clement, who scored the final goal of the 1975 Stanley Cup finals, was traded to Washington from Philadelphia for a first-round choice in the 1976 amateur draft.

Ted Harris took over as coach of the Minnesota North Stars.

Phil Esposito signed a multi-year contract with the Bruins and told the press, "I signed for two and a half times less than an offer I had from the WHA."

Toronto fans were shocked when flashy forward Ron Ellis announced his retirement. The 30-year-old winger said he simply wanted to spend more time with his family.

The league decided to put a stop to players bickering with officials and stalling during games by introducing tough new rules. Only captains would be allowed to discuss a ruling with an official, and then only if the captain were invited to discuss the call. Alternate captains were thought to be unnecessary and their role became a part of hockey history.

A blow to the Bruins was the loss of Bobby Orr. The great defenseman underwent surgery for the fourth time on his knee before the start of the season and was not expected back for two months. The Piladelphia Flyers, like the Bruins, lost a key player when Bernie Parent suffered a neck injury. Doctors predicted that Parent would be out for several weeks.

In midsummer, Sport Systems Corporation of Buffalo, with Jeremy Jacobs as their chief spokesman, announced the acquisition of the Bruins and the Boston Garden for $10 million. The three brothers from Eggertsville, New York—Max, Jeremy and Lawrence Jacobs—were the new owners of the Bruins.

The NHL and the National Hockey League Players' Association signed an historic agreement as the new season began. The acceptance of the free-agent clause was the key point in sealing a five-year collective bargaining agreement between the parties. The pact stated that in future when a player had played out his option, the NHL club for which he had performed would have to be compensated before he could perform for another team in the league. The agreement was highlighted by the players' recognition that "the owners have the right to compensation." It marked the first time in pro-sports history that equalization or compensation was recognized by the players and achieved through collective bargaining.

Meanwhile, rookie Bryan Trottier, just 19, was the talk of the early season. Trottier had scored a hat trick in his second game with the Islanders.

When the Rangers faltered, Emile Francis placed the entire club on revocable waivers. "That's Emile's way of telling us he'll listen to offers for any of us," said one veteran. Then Francis traded goalie Gilles Villemure to Chicago for Doug Jarrett. He placed Ed Giacomin on waivers and Giacomin wound up in Detroit in return for $30,000. Popular Derek Sanderson was shipped to St. Louis in return for a draft choice. Giacomin returned to Madison Square Garden a few days later and earned a standing ovation when he starred in a 6–4 Red Wing victory.

Boston's Johnny Bucyk joined the select 500-goal club when he rapped in a milestone goal against St. Louis. Bucyk, 40, became the seventh player to reach the 500-goal plateau.

In a mammoth trade, Phil Esposito and Brad Park switched uniforms, as did Carol Vadnais and Jean Ratelle. The transaction moved Boston's great scorer Esposito and defenseman Carol Vadnais to New York in return for Park (who had been booed at times by Rangers fans) and Ratelle. Rookie Joe Zanussi was also shipped to Boston. Espo said he was shocked. "There should be a rule," he insisted, "protecting veterans from trades after a player has been with a team five or seven years." Park, who wore New York's sweater number two for years, grabbed number 22 with the Bruins. "I'm going to be twice as good here in Boston," he explained.

Bobby Orr returned to the Bruin lineup, but only for 10 games. In that stretch he scored five goals and assisted on 13 others. Then one day he stepped out of a car and his bad knee locked. "The maddening thing is that it was feeling so good," said Orr as he was wheeled back into surgery. His fifth knee operation followed his fourth by only two months.

Garry Young became the second coaching casualty of the season when he was released as coach of the Blues just before Christmas. Lynn Patrick, the first man to coach the Blues, took over on an interim basis. Doug Barkley was axed at about the same time by Detroit and Alex Delvecchio moved in as both coach and general manager.

125

Goalie Gilles Gratton jumped from the WHA Toronto Toros to the St. Louis Blues and back again, all in a matter of weeks. A St. Louis official told Gratton he should see a psychiatrist.

"I did," was the answer.

"What did he tell you?" asked the official.

"He said I was a genius," said Gratton, smiling. Before the year was over, Gratton had found his way to the New York Rangers.

The Rangers, befuddled throughout the season, were the victims of a 7–3 shellacking at the hands of the touring Soviet Army Team in the first game of an eight-game international series. The touring Soviets awed some 17,000 New York fans with pinpoint passing and brilliant skating.

On New Year's Eve Montreal fans witnessed one of the greatest games in years when the Canadiens and the Red Army club fought to a 3–3 deadlock. Tretiak was phenomenal in the Soviet nets as the Canadiens outshot the Soviets by a wide margin.

The final match of the tour pitted the Stanley Cup champion Philadelphia Flyers against the Red Army on Sunday, January 11. "I hate the sons of bitches," said Flyer captain Bobby Clarke prior to the game. "They complain about the ice, the practice time. They show up late, they don't like our gifts. They're always trying to play with our minds. But that won't work with our club. We've got 20 guys with no brains."

Clarke and the Flyers checked the army into the ice in the final match, winning 4–1. For a time it looked like the series might never be completed. The army team skated off the ice midway through the first period when they objected to an Ed Van Impe check on Valeri Kharlamov. There was consternation among the fans and veiled threats of non-payment of a $200,000 guarantee to the Russians if they didn't return. Finally the game continued. After a 16-minute delay, the Soviet players agreed to play but the momentum after that was all Philadelphia's.

"We're the world champs," said Fred Shero succinctly. "If they had won then they'd be the world champs. It's as simple as that." Still, the two Soviet clubs had five wins, two losses and a tie to show for their widely publicized tour.

Owner Ed Snider of the Philadelphia Flyers was upset with writers who criticized the Flyers' tactics in the final game with the army team. Dave Anderson of the *New York Times* described the Spectrum as "the cradle of licensed muggings." He also wrote, "the Flyers' victory was a triumph of terror over style." He added that Flyer fans would "cheer Frankenstein's monster if he could skate."

Snider said:

> People who see all our games know we're not a dirty team. Millions of people wanted us to win this game. I don't think we played as rough as some of our league and playoff games. What right do writers have to decide what is good hockey? If they don't like our style, they don't have to come to the games!

With mid-season approaching, the Rangers decided their player trades hadn't been too successful, so club president Bill Jennings fired popular Emile Francis as general manager. Francis was replaced almost immediately by former Montreal hardrock John Ferguson, who just as promptly fired coach Ron Stewart and accepted the coaching position himself. The St. Louis Blues also named a new coach, Leo Boivin, who served an unusual three-week apprenticeship under Lynn Patrick to become the Blues' ninth coach in nine years. Another coaching casualty was Pittsburgh's Marc Boileau who was fired by club president Wren Blair when the Pens went into a seven-game slump. Blair named former Pittsburgh coach Ken Schinkel as interim pilot of the Penguins.

The Washington Capitals fired Milt Schmidt, the man who had molded their expansion team, and hired Tommy McVie from the International Hockey League as coach. Early in Feburary, Bep Guidolin resigned as coach of Kansas City after a dispute with general manager Sid Abel. Guidolin exploded after Abel vetoed a move to send defenseman Larry Johnston to the minors.

One bright spot in the Detroit picture was the play of goalie Jim Rutherford. Rutherford tied a Red Wing club record when he chalked up three consecutive shutouts, blanking Washington, Toronto and Minnesota.

The annual All-Star game was a dull affair for the second year in a row. The best from the Prince of Wales Conference trimmed the Campbell Conference selects 7–5. Pete Mahovlich won a new $8,000 car as the top star of the game. He promptly sold the car and split the profits with the other five Canadiens who had played in the contest.

Goalie Gerry Cheevers, on the fourth year of a seven-year contract with the Cleveland Crusaders of the WHA, secured his release from the Crusaders and joined the Boston Bruins, his old club, for a salary far less than his $200,000-a-year income with Cleveland.

For almost two months, the Washington Capitals tried vainly for a victory then, after 25 games without anything to celebrate, the Caps beat the Rangers 7–5. The 25-game winless streak was a record in futility.

On February 7, the Boston Bruins were hoping to extend their seven-game winning streak at Maple Leaf Gardens. Instead, they ran into Darryl Sittler of the Leafs, who turned in a scoring performance never seen before in NHL play. Sittler went on a scoring spree with six goals and four assists, all at the expense of rookie Boston goalie Dave Reece, and the Leafs won 11–4. Sittler's 10 points broke by two the record for points in a game. The original mark was set by Rocket Richard of Montreal in December 1944 during a 9–1 victory over Detroit, when he got five goals and three assists. Years later, Bert Olmstead, another Canadien, tied the mark with four goals and four assists in a 12–1 Montreal rout over Chicago.

Two other milestones were reached in the same game. Johnny Bucyk of the Bruins passed Alex Delvecchio, moving into second place on the all-time list of career point scorers, and Jean Ratelle of the Bruins scored his 350th career goal.

Stan Mikita of the Blackhawks, a 35-year-old veteran known for his charitable work, and Bruce Norris, in his 21st season as president and owner of the Red Wings, were named as recipients of the 1976 Lester Patrick Awards for outstanding service to hockey in the United States. Later, Al Leader, former Western Hockey League president, joined Mikita and Norris as a Patrick Award winner.

In Detroit one night, the Blackhawks were preparing for a game with the Red Wings when they received a welcome visitor. Former Hawk Chico Maki, who had retired several months earlier when his son was badly injured in a farming accident (his son lost four toes and required several operations) came around to say hello. Before he knew it, Maki had agreed to a comeback with the Hawks.

Dan Maloney of Detroit was ordered to stand trial for assault causing bodily harm as a result of his alleged assault on Toronto Maple Leafs defenseman Brian Glennie during a game played earlier in the season. A witness for the court said that Maloney had struck

127

Glennie from behind, felling the Toronto player and giving him a mild concussion. Maloney pleaded not guilty and elected to be tried by a judge and jury. The trial was set for April 5, one day after the regular season ended.

Maloney wasn't the only worried Red Wing. Star forward Mickey Redmond had missed much of the season with leg and back problems. "The damage is serious and I might not play again ... ever," said Redmond as he embarked on an intensive therapy program.

As the season headed into its final month, the Wings traded speedy Bill Hogaboam to Minnesota for veteran center Dennis Hextall. Then the Wings stopped Philadelphia's unbeaten streak at 23, leaving the Flyers to share the unbeaten record with the 1940–41 Boston Bruins, who had also gone for 23 games without a loss.

When Flyers' coach Fred Shero was asked how he felt about failing to set a new record he said, "If I'd really wanted to win that game do you think I'd have started Bernie Parent?" Parent, after missing most of the season, was just getting back into shape and showed little of the form that had earned him the Conn Smythe Trophy the preceding spring.

The North Stars raved over an acquisition from the U.S. Olympic team. Steve Jensen, from nearby Plymouth, Minnesota, starred for the U.S. Olympians in two victories at Innsbruck after leading Michigan Tech to the national collegiate championship in 1975.

The Montreal Canadiens finished the regular season with a record 127 points and were considered the team capable of stopping Philadelphia from grabbing its third straight Stanley Cup.

THE PLAYOFFS

Altanta, Vancouver, Pittsburgh and St. Louis all fell early in the Stanley Cup playoffs. The Flames lost their best-of-three preliminary round to Los Angeles, the Canucks bowed to the Islanders, the Penguins were ousted by the Leafs and the Blues were pushed aside by Buffalo.

In quarter-final play, the Boston Bruins struggled through seven games before eliminating the Los Angeles Kings 4–3 in games. Game six, a 4–3 overtime win for the Kings, was said to be the most exciting game ever played in California. Kings' fans gave their team sustained applause that continued long after the players had left the ice. Boston won game seven 3–0 to advance to the semi finals.

Montreal had little difficulty with Chicago, capturing four straight games. The Sabres swept the first two games of their series with the Islanders and Buffalo fans started talking Stanley Cup. They recalled how close the Sabres had come one year earlier. But the Islanders received standout goaltending from Billy Smith and brilliant leadership from Denis Potvin, who scored a point in every game. They bounced back to win four in a row and end the Sabres' season.

Toronto fans, pleased with the Leafs' performance during the regular season and through the three-game series with Pittsburgh, would have been content with a win or two against the defending-Cup champion Flyers in the quarter finals. They never anticipated a bitter seven-game series that created headlines on the front pages of newspapers as well as in the sports sections. The opening games went according to form as the Flyers won twice on home ice. Then all hell broke loose at Maple Leaf Gardens.

In game three, a three-and-a-half-hour marathon, the Leafs scored five power-play goals while the Flyers chalked up a record 28 penalties. The Leafs won 5–4. Three Flyers—Don Saleski, Joe Watson and Mel Bridgman—were charged with criminal offenses as a result of incidents that occurred during the game. Carrying out Ontario Attorney-General Roy McMurtry's orders to clamp down on hockey violence, police charged Saleski and Watson with assault and possession of a dangerous weapon (a hockey stick) after an incident in the penalty box that involved players, fans and police. When Bridgman battered star Leaf defenseman Borje Salming in a one-sided fight, he was charged with assault causing bodily harm. I have been involved in broadcasting sports for three decades, yet consider this game to be the most difficult and controversial one I have ever broadcast.

In game four, Salming drew a three-minute ovation after he scored a dazzling goal to help sink the Flyers 4–3. Saleski scored three times in game five to give the Flyers the series lead, but tempers erupted again in Toronto during game six. The teams totalled 185 penalty minutes — 94 to the Leafs and 91 to the Flyers.

Darryl Sittler stuck to hockey and rifled five goals past Bernie Parent to tie Rocket Richard's long-standing playoff goal-scoring record and lead his team to an 8–5 victory in game six. Another penalty box incident produced yet another charge by police officials. The game was almost a carbon copy of game three. Fans shouted obscenities at the Flyers. Dave Schultz was jostled by a fan as he left the ice. Bob Kelly hurled his hockey glove into the crowd and it struck an usher in the face. Schultz accused Tiger Williams of biting him on the cheek during a scrap. Brian Glennie stopped a shot and suffered a broken jaw. And Red Kelly claimed that the Leaf win was due to pyramid power. He pointed to special pyramids he'd placed under the Leafs' bench and said, "They produced the miracle." Kelly's pyramids were no match for the explosive Flyers in game seven, however. Five second-period goals by the Flyers helped push the Leafs aside 7–3.

Philadelphia met Boston in semi-final play and lost the opener at home 4–2. It marked the first home loss for the Flyers in 24 games. With Wayne Stephenson replacing Bernie Parent in goal, the Flyers took game two in overtime on Reg Leach's goal. Two more Flyer victories in Boston almost eliminated the Bruins and Reg Leach pushed them over the brink almost single-handedly with a five-goal outburst in game five. Leach ripped five shots past Gilles Gilbert to tie the Richard–Sittler record. Philadelphia won 6–3 and Boston fans turned to basketball for their sports entertainment. Their Celtics provided some consolation by winning the NBA championship.

Meanwhile, the Montreal Canadiens were enjoying good fortune against the highly regarded Islanders. The Canadiens took the first three games by close scores, then dropped game four, 5–2. It turned out to be the only loss the Canadiens suffered in their race to the Stanley Cup. Montreal's Steve Shutt scored twice in game five and the Habs' fierce checking and outstanding defensive play mesmerized the Islanders. Montreal won 5–2.

Most observers predicted a long series on the eve of the Flyers–Canadiens confrontation. Game one saw the Canadiens muster a strong comeback to win 4–3 just when overtime appeared imminent. Guy Lapointe drilled a low shot past Wayne Stephenson with less than two minutes left, to clinch it for Montreal. In game two, the Flyers' top line of Bill Barber, Bobby Clarke and Reg Leach was held to just three shots on goal, as Montreal won again by a 2–1 score. Leach had his consecutive game-scoring streak halted at 10. "Things will be different back in Philadelphia," promised Leach.

Leach connected for two first-period goals at the Spectrum, but Steve Shutt matched him with a pair for Montreal. Again, when it appeared that the teams might require overtime to settle matters, Pierre Bouchard swatted a long shot past Wayne Stephenson to give the Habs a 3–2 decision and a 3–0 lead in the series. "I've scored two goals this season and both were game winners," bragged Bouchard. Desperate, the Flyers called on Kate Smith to help them out. When Kate warbled "God Bless America" at Flyer games, Philadelphia almost always won. Her record was 47–4–1.

But even Kate couldn't save the Flyers. After Reg Leach potted his record-breaking 19th playoff goal in the first minute of play, Shutt and Bouchard shot the Canadiens back into the lead. Then Barber tied the score. Cournoyer, Lafleur and Mahovlich whipped pucks past Stephenson in the final 40 minutes, while superb defensive play kept the Flyers in a constant state of frustration. The final score was Montreal 5, Philadelphia 3.

It took the Canadiens just 13 games to win their 17th Stanley Cup of the modern era. Losing coach Fred Shero offered a post-series comment on the Canadiens' strength:

> You've got to give Sam Pollock a lot of the credit. When the NHL expanded in 1967 six clubs had the same opportunity to make sure they remained strong. But it looks like Sam was the only one to use his noodle. This is Montreal's sixth Stanley Cup since then and from what the Canadiens showed us in this series, there'll be lots more coming up.

Reg Leach, named the Conn Smythe Trophy winner, added his praise. "The Canadiens have one helluva great team," said Leach. "They've got guys who skate 400 miles an hour and there's no way we could keep up with them."

IX

A NEW LEAGUE

The WHA Muscles In, 1972–1976

1972–73

NHL moguls, after watching their league dominate professional hockey for over half a century, treated the upstart WHA like a pesky nuisance—one that might cause some aggravation and leave a trail of unpaid bills and broken promises before disappearing like melting ice in the summer sun.

WHA officials, on the other hand, were gleefully looking forward to October 11, 1972—opening night. The Alberta Oilers would meet the Ottawa Nationals and the Quebec Nordiques would visit Cleveland.

With name players like Bobby Hull, Bernie Parent, Johnny Mackenzie, J. C. Tremblay and Gerry Cheevers under contract, and over 60 other NHL stars, WHA organizers were well satisfied with the prospects for the 12-team circuit.

The league was divided into two divisions, East and West. Experts looked over the roster of unfamiliar names and picked the teams to finish in the following order:

EAST DIVISION	WEST DIVISION
1. New England	1. Minnesota
2. Philadelphia	2. Alberta
3. New York	3. Winnipeg
4. Cleveland	4. Los Angeles
5. Quebec	5. Chicago
6. Ottawa	6. Houston

For a time, it appeared that judges and lawyers might become as famous as the players. When the Boston Bruins tried to restrain Gerry Cheevers and Derek Sanderson from jumping, a U.S. federal judge refused to prohibit the pair from joining their chosen WHA clubs. In another ruling, a Chicago court judge issued a restraining order against Bobby Hull of the Winnipeg Jets, but also ruled that Hull could work out with the Jets pending the outcome of a hearing in Chicago in which the Hawks were taking legal action against the Jets.

The new league was eager to get the NHL into a court showdown over the NHL's reserve clause which bound a player to a contract until he obtained his release from the NHL team. There was no shortage of copy for hockey writers as opening night approached.

In New York, the Raiders introduced Alton White, the first black player in New York hockey history. In Philadelphia, Johnny Mackenzie, the playing coach of the Blazers, suffered a broken arm in a pre-season game. Derek Sanderson was named captain of the Blazers and Andre Lacroix spent several days locked in a bank vault in an effort to promote the club.

The WHA's pre-season experimental shootout received its first test on October 3 when the Houston Aeros edged the Minnesota Saints 7–6. Don Grierson, a journeyman minor leaguer, emerged as the hero of the premier overtime test when he scored the deciding goal after 18 penalty shots. The teams were tied 4–4 after regulation time and when they failed to break the deadlock in a 10-minute overtime period, the teams went into their shootout. With the visiting team receiving the first free shot, each team proceeded with designated players firing in turn at the goalie. Jim Johnson and Ted Hampson scored for the Saints and Larry Lund and Murray Hall for the Aeros to keep the score deadlocked at 6–6. Then Grierson drilled one into the net to make it 7–6 and when Minnesota's Terry Ball missed on the Saints' chance to equalize the score, the Aeros became the ultimate winners. The shootout experiment was later abandoned.

Opening night in Philadelphia turned out to be a nightmare for the hometown Blazers. The ice surface in the newly furbished Convention Hall was deemed unsafe and unplayable and team owner Jim Cooper had the unenviable job of telling 5,000 first-night fans there would be no game. The fans reacted by throwing souvenir hockey pucks at Cooper, who beat a hasty retreat.

Former NHL great Rocket Richard retreated almost as quickly from the WHA coaching ranks. After coaching Quebec through the first two league games for a win and a loss, the Rocket took a week off to "think things over," then decided the pressures of coaching weren't for him.

Los Angeles opened at home on Friday the 13th and promptly lost to Houston 3–2. Over 10,000 fans saw the pucks bounce like rubber balls on the poor ice. During one intermission workmen flooded the surface and a black liquid oozed out from the Zamboni. Terry Slater, the Los Angeles coach, wearing a multi-colored jacket, a pink shirt, maroon pants, white tie and white shoes attracted more attention than most of his players. Slater told reporters he had also appeared behind the bench wearing a tuxedo and had once plugged a referee's whistle with cotton and dumped a pail of water on a player who was not "up" for a game.

The Philadelphia Blazers lost Bernie Parent for a month with a broken anklebone and created a hockey first when they won only one game and lost two general managers. Murray Williamson quit the same day the Blazers called a news conference to announce his appointment and his successor, Dave Creighton, bowed out when the team went to 1–8. Johnny Mackenzie requested relief as player-coach and was replaced behind the bench by Phil Watson.

CBS television in the United States and the CBC in Canada announced plans to telecast WHA games. Both networks expressed confidence in the future of the league.

In November there was good news for Bobby Hull and other players who jumped leagues. A ruling by Judge Leon Higginbotham in a Philadelphia district court placed an injunction against any NHL club prohibiting them from enforcing the controversial reserve clause. The reserve clause had given the NHL a virtual monopoly on the professional hockey talent pool. So Hull, Cheevers, Tremblay and others were now legally entitled to play for their new teams in the WHA. Bobby Hull, finally able to play for Winnipeg, drew large crowds. He played his first WHA game in Quebec and over 10,000 fans turned out, almost double the normal attendance.

Two franchises thought to be stable, New York and Philadelphia, found themselves in trouble before 20 games had been played. The Raiders, who were paying $22,000 just to stage each home game at Madison Square Garden, were averaging only about 4,800 fans per game. Jim Cooper, founding father of the Blazers, called it quits and sold out to trucking magnate Bernard Brown. One of the most expensive Blazers, Derek Sanderson, was nursing a sore back and joined Johnny Mackenzie on the sidelines. Philadelphia was 3–17 when Cooper bowed out. The Blazers hit a new low two months into the season when only 790 fans paid to see Philadelphia defeat New York by 3–1.

Edmonton's Jim Harrison took the WHA scoring lead in late November and then fractured a kneecap when he slammed into a goalpost.

The first hat trick in the brief history of the Los Angeles Sharks was scored by forward Gary Veneruzzo. General manager Dennis Murphy rewarded him with a trip for two to Hawaii.

Midway through the first season, WHA president Gary Davidson predicted a rosy future for the league. "Average attendance has been above 5,000," he said. "That's about 1,000 more than we hoped for. We're three to five years ahead of where the ABA and the American Football League were at this point in their history."

The most successful franchises appeared to be New England and Quebec. The Whalers were drawing around 10,000 a game and the Nordiques about 7,000. Quebec fans, however, did not appear too interested in the mid-season All-Star game held in that city. Only 5,000 turned out to witness it.

In Minnesota, the Fighting Saints opened their posh new ice palace, the St. Paul Civic Center, and 11,000 fans took in the inauguration.

By February Derek Sanderson had severed his ties with the Philadelphia Blazers. The Blazers gave Sanderson his release and paid him a reported $1-million settlement on his whopping 10-year contract that called for $2.4 million. Sanderson had played only eight games and was picking up $2,300 a day in salary without even donning skates.

There were some strong individual performances during the season. Philadelphia's Danny Lawson scored five goals in one game and later New York's Ron Ward matched that output. Jim Harrison of Edmonton came back from his injury and collected 10 points in a game against the Raiders, with three goals and seven assists.

In mid-February, Bill Hunter, vice-president of the Edmonton Oilers, stepped in to replace Ray Kinasewich as coach of the team. The slumping Chicago Cougars were cheered by the news that the team was going after Chicago Blackhawks' stars Stan Mikita and Pat Stapleton.

Danny Lawson, whose best previous goal-scoring effort in the NHL was 10 goals with Buffalo, became the league's first 50-goal shooter. Philadelphia's Lawson hit the plateau during a game with Ottawa on February 22.

Late in February, Harry Neale joined the Minnesota Fighting Saints as coach. Glen Sonmor, who was coach and general manager of the Saints, revealed that he would now be free to spend more time setting up a development league for the WHA.

The New England Whalers and the Winnipeg Jets emerged as the divisional champions at the conclusion of the regular schedule. The Whalers wound up with 94 points, five better than Cleveland in the East Division. In the West, the Jets finished with 90 points, eight points better than second-place Houston.

An extra game was needed to decide the fourth playoff berth in the West after Alberta and Minnesota had finished with identical records. Minnesota won the showdown game 4–2.

Philadelphia's Andre Lacroix scored 50 goals and 74 assists to capture the WHA individual scoring crown.

THE PLAYOFFS

Bernie Parent stunned Philadelphia fans during the playoff series with Cleveland when he walked out on the team on the eve of the second game. The goalie, on a five-year $750,000 contract, claimed the Blazers had not deposited the final $100,000 insurance on his salary. He decided not to play and the Cleveland Crusaders quickly polished off the weakened Blazers in four straight games.

New England eliminated Ottawa 4–1 in the other East Division series. In the West, the Winnipeg Jets flew past the Fighting Saints in five games and Houston required six games to oust the Los Angeles Sharks.

Winnipeg went on to sweep the Houston Aeros aside in four straight, while Jack Kelley's New England Whalers disposed of the Cleveland Crusaders in five games.

The Whalers, paced by Larry Pleau, who registered 12 playoff goals, rolled to a 4–1 victory and the Avco Cup in their best-of-seven championship series with the Jets. Familiar names like Rick Ley, Ted Green, Brad Selwood, Jim Dorey and Tom Webster were instrumental in the victory over Bobby Hull and the Jets.

Toward the end of the season several developments made news. Jacques Plante said he was joining the Quebec Nordiques as general manager and coach. Plante was offered a 10-year contract to jump the Boston Bruins, for a reported $1 million plus. The Ottawa Nationals were purchased by Toronto sportsman John F. Bassett, Jr., for $1.8 million and were moved to Toronto. The Philadelphia Blazers were purchased by Vancouver industrialist Jim Pattison. He said he would have the team in Vancouver by the following season. Cincinnati, tired of waiting for an NHL franchise, joined the WHA and gladly paid the $2-million entry fee.

Houston rocked the hockey world in a post-season move when they boldly signed the teenage sons of Gordie Howe, Mark and Marty, and then convinced Gordie himself to join the Aeros. Gordie was reported to have been offered a $1-million package spread over four years. Mark, 18, and Marty, 19, were signed by the Aeros amid charges that

Houston had violated the pro-amateur hockey agreement that existed between the pros and the Canadian Amateur Hockey Association. The WHA claimed that both boys were American born and not governed by the CAHA edict.

The two top WHA scorers were traded—New York swapped Ron Ward to Vancouver for Andre Lacroix. In other moves, the Los Angeles Sharks plucked a big shooter from the Montreal Canadiens when they signed moody Mark Tardif to a three-year contract. Minnesota signed the Walton brothers, Mike (Boston) and Rob (Seattle) and defenseman Rick Smith from the California Seals. Pat Stapleton and Ralph Backstrom moved from the Chicago Blackhawks of the NHL to the Chicago Cougars. Stapleton replaced Marcel Pronovost as coach of the Cougars. Veteran rear guard Harry Howell accepted a position with the New York Raiders and retired defenseman Carl Brewer signed with the Toronto Toros.

Having survived one season, WHA officials confidently faced season number two.

1973–74

It didn't take long for Gordie Howe to prove he still had his goal-scoring touch. Howe, on the ice for the first time in a WHA game after a two-year retirement, scored on his first shot after just 21 seconds of play in an unusual pre-season game. Actually, it was more of a pre-season free-for-all with four teams engaged in a six-period game at Madison Square Garden. The New York club (renamed the Golden Blades), the New England Whalers, the Houston Aeros and the Winnipeg Jets were involved in the unique attraction which drew a disappointing 7,000 fans. Joining Howe in the Houston lineup were sons Mark and Marty. It marked the first time a father-and-sons combination had played together in major professional hockey. Bill Dineen, the Aeros' coach, said, "Old Gordie's in great shape. He'll score 35 goals for us this season."

In mid-September the WHA granted franchises to Phoenix and Indianapolis. Along with Cincinnati the new franchise holders made plans to play in 1974–75.

There was optimism expressed on several fronts. In Quebec, coach Jacques Plante was beaming over the play of NHL jumpers Réjean Houle, Dale Hoganson and Serge Bernier. In Toronto, coach Billy Harris sang the praises of two rookies, Wayne Dillon and Pat Hickey. Pat Stapleton, the new playing-coach in Chicago, figured his club would be in the playoffs. There was word from Edmonton that Jim Harrison was playing so well that Ben Hatskin, owner of the Winnipeg, Jets, would gladly trade Bobby Hull for him. "Of course we can't trade Bobby," said Hatskin. "Don't forget he's our coach. But we'd sure love to have Harrison."

In Los Angeles, Dennis Murphy assured everyone who would listen that the Sharks "would not leave Los Angeles, no matter what."

WHA officials were pleased with their sudden-death overtime rule during regular-season games. During their first season 64 of the league's 468 games went into overtime and 45 were settled with extra play. The NHL carded 624 games and 87 failed to produce winners. (The NHL had abandoned overtime play years earlier.)

The New York Blades were in deep financial trouble and there was doubt the team would remain in New York.

After much speculation, Gary Davidson stepped down as president of the WHA. The 39-year-old founder of the league said he would concentrate his efforts on the World

Football League, which he claimed would open the following season.

Ron Ward, the second-best scorer in the WHA in year one, was traded from Vancouver to the Los Angeles Sharks and placed on a line with Marc Tardif, the former Montreal Canadien.

Jim McMasters, the young defenseman who had been compared to Bobby Orr a few months earlier, was shipped from Cleveland to Jacksonville of the AHL. So much for comparisons.

Early in December, the New York Golden Blades waved goodbye to Gotham and moved to Cherry Hill, New Jersey, and a tiny 4,000-seat arena, the former home of the Jersey Devils of the defunct Eastern Hockey League. Harry Howell was named new coach of the team while Camille Henry, the former coach, stepped up to the assistant general-manager's office. The Blades also changed their name to the Jersey Knights.

Andy Bathgate took over as coach in Vancouver, replacing Phil Watson, who was once Bathgate's coach with the New York Rangers of the NHL. Watson moved up to become general manager of the Blazers.

The Los Angeles Sharks made a couple of moves. Ted McCaskill stepped up from his playing role to become coach, replacing Terry Slater who accepted the general manager's job. Dennis Murphy left the general manager's desk in Los Angeles in order to become the interim WHA president.

By Christmas the Toronto Toros' young owner, John Bassett, was busy inspecting sites for his $18-million arena and he talked about bidding for Leafs' stars Paul Henderson and Jim McKenny. Eventually the arena plans were scrapped and the following season would find the Toros moving from the antiquated Varsity Arena in Toronto to Maple Leaf Gardens, with a fat rental fee going to Maple Leaf Gardens' president Harold Ballard.

There was little cause to celebrate the New Year in New England. Attendance was down at the Whalers' games. It dropped from an average 8,000 to 4,000 in less than a season and team officials contemplated a move elsewhere.

Marc Tardif, the quiet winger with Los Angeles, made a surprising prediction in mid-season. "Next year," he stated, "Frank Mahovlich will leave the Montreal Canadiens and join the Toronto Toros."

A story from Los Angeles revealed that general manager Terry Slater hit the roof when new coach Ted McCaskill (with a 6–1 record) walked in and suggested some player changes. The first player he wanted to move out was Slater's brother. Ted McCaskill's stint as coach of the Los Angeles Sharks was short lived. In mid-February Terry Slater was back behind the bench and McCaskill returned to the playing roster. Insiders predicted that the Sharks would be moved to Detroit for the following season with former NHL great Ted Lindsay signing on as coach and general manager.

Playing before a crowd of over 13,000 in St. Paul, the East Division beat the West 8–4 in the second annual WHA All-Star game. Mike Walton from Minnesota scored a hat trick for the West.

Former NHL iron man Johnny Wilson was introduced in January as the new general manager and coach of the Indianapolis team. Wilson promised to have a team ready for play the following season. Indianapolis was building a new 18,000-seat downtown arena.

Dennis Murphy was winning plaudits for his work as WHA president. Ben Hatskin, chairman of the board of trustees, said of Murphy's efforts: "The man is tireless. The best thing we did after signing Howe and Hull was to make Dennis president. You don't know the mess we had to clean up after Gary Davidson left."

In late February, Ron Ward was on the move again, this time to Cleveland. Ward was traded for a pair of wingers, Bill Young and Ted Hodgson. At the time of the trade Ward had only 35 points. The year before he had tallied 118 points in 77 games for the New York Raiders. Another scoring star, Jim Harrison, was feuding with his boss, Bill Hunter, and his days in Edmonton appeared to be numbered. Harrison entered hospital for spinal disc surgery and accused Hunter of reneging on an agreement to renegotiate his contract.

The Minnesota Fighting Saints were drawing only half the number of fans needed to break even. Their owners said flatly that the team would be moved if attendance did not pick up. The Saints also gave a tryout to Fern Tessier, just out of prison after serving an 11-year stretch, but he wasn't quite good enough to rate a contract.

The New England Whalers were headed for the East Division championship and in early March they announced that they would move from Boston to Hartford, Connecticut, in April and play their playoff games in the 5,900-seat Springfield Coliseum. The new Hartford Civic Center would be ready for the Whalers early in 1975.

One team without problems was Houston. Gordie Howe's inspiring leadership vaulted the Aeros into first place and an easy West Division championship.

Referee Bill Friday was furious early in March after he refereed a game between Chicago and Quebec. Learning that the Cougars had used suspended player Connie Forey, Friday said, "If I'd known who that guy was skating around out there, it would have been his gear off or mine." Forey had been suspended by the Western Hockey League for slugging and injuring referee Malcolm Ashford. His suspension was for part of one season and all of the 1973–74 season. In addition he was ordered to pay Ashford $10,000 in damages. After his lone appearance in Chicago, Forey was banned from further WHA play.

Four outstanding rookies in the league were Claude St. Sauveur of Vancouver, Mark Howe and Andre Hinse of Houston and Wayne Dillon of the Toros. Dillon was the only pro hockey player still attending high school. He was 18.

Joe Crozier, coach of the Buffalo Sabres in the NHL, was reported to be on his way to Vancouver to join the Blazers as general manager and coach prior to the 1974–75 season.

As expected, the Whalers and the Aeros finished on top of their respective divisions at the end of the regular schedule.

THE PLAYOFFS

The Houston Aeros and the Minnesota Fighting Saints breezed past their opponents in the first round of the WHA playoffs. The Aeros ousted the Winnipeg Jets in four games, while the Fighting Saints took just five games to eliminate Edmonton. Mike Walton was the Saints' scoring star with six goals and six assists in the five games.

In East Division playoff action, the defending champion New England Whalers were shunted aside by a most unlikely foe, the Chicago Cougars. The Cougars, forced to win the second-last game of the season just to make the playoffs, downed the Whalers in seven games. The Toronto Toros, meanwhile, eliminated the Cleveland Crusaders 4–1 in five games.

When Minnesota and Houston met to decide the West Division finalist, over 73,000 fans witnessed the series for an average attendance of over 12,000 per game. Houston, paced by the Howes and goalie Don McLeod, advanced to the WHA finals with a series victory, four games to two.

The surprising Chicago Cougars struggled through seven games with the Toronto Toros. The Cougars took game seven 5–2 in Toronto and prepared to meet Houston in the finals.

The Cougars, aiming for their third straight playoff-series upset, met their match in the Aeros. The Aeros were never seriously in trouble and swept the finals in four straight games. Gordie Howe said the championship was "the greatest thrill of my career. When you give up the game for a couple of years, then come back and play with your two sons and end up winning the title, that has to be the greatest."

With the playoffs over, Jacques Plante resigned as general manager and coach of the Quebec Nordiques and announced he would make a comeback as a goalie the following season with Edmonton. Plante was miffed over criticism of a $500,000 loss and the Nordiques' failure to make the playoffs.

As predicted by Marc Tardif, Frank Mahovlich left the Montreal Canadiens and joined the Toronto Toros. "They made an offer I couldn't refuse," stated Mahovlich. Paul Henderson also joined the Toros from the Leafs. Chicago lured goalie Dave Dryden away from Buffalo. Cincinnati inked another Leafs player, Mike Pelyk. Cleveland signed Al McDonough from the Atlanta Flames. Edmonton grabbed Barry Long from the Kings, Ray McKay from the Seals and Bruce McGregor from the Rangers. The New England Whalers went overseas for a brother act. They signed twins Thommy and Crister Abrahamson, two Swedish stars, to long-term contracts.

The shifts continued behind WHA benches and in the front offices. Rudy Pilous, Bobby Hull's former coach in Chicago, joined the Winnipeg Jets in a coaching capacity. As expected, and despite several denials, the Los Angeles Sharks packed up and moved to Michigan where they became the Michigan Stags. Johnny Wilson, reported to be heading up the new Indianapolis entry, wound up as coach and general manager of the Stags. Gerry Moore was named coach of Indianapolis. Terry Slater, ex-Shark general manager and coach, was signed to a similar post with the Cincinnati entry, still a season away from actual play. Sandy Hucul joined Phoenix as coach. John Hanna replaced Bill Needham as coach of Cleveland. Jean-Guy Gendron quit the playing ranks to move behind the Nordiques' bench. And when the Jersey Knights fled Cherry Hill, New Jersey, for San Diego in a franchise shift, Harry Howell simply bought a bathing suit, packed his golf clubs and suntan oil and moved with them as coach.

1974–75

When the WHA's version of Team Canada met the Soviets in the Summit Series Two, the first four games in Canada concluded on a note of sportsmanship and goodwill. But in Moscow, where the Soviets played superbly to win the series, the games were anything but friendly. Team Canada manager Bill Hunter threatened to pull his club out of the series after sloppy timekeeping by the Soviets robbed Team Canada of a 5–4 win in game seven. The Soviets threatened to pull out of game eight if Team Canada continued to "play dirty." Coach Boris Kulagin of the Soviets said Canada's Rick Ley should be thrown in jail for starting a brawl in the second game in Moscow. "We had togetherness in Canada," coach Billy Harris said, "but we didn't have it in Moscow." With the Summit Series over, the players could look forward to the start of another WHA regular season.

The defending champion Houston Aeros (minus the Howes who were in Moscow) defeated the St. Louis Blues 5–4 in the first confrontation between a WHA team and a club from the NHL. The upset took place in pre-season play. In another exhibition game, goalie Jacques Plante, now with Edmonton, suffered a broken hand.

The Toronto Toros were counting heavily on Czech refugee Vaclav Nedomansky and his fellow countryman Richard Farda.

Gordie Howe, looking ahead to his 47th birthday, said, "This is definitely the final season for me. I would have quit after last season if it hadn't been for the series against the Russians. I really appreciated the opportunity to play on a team representing my country."

On the eve of the opener the WHA decided to keep the red line in the game. In pre-season games, the red line had been eliminated in an effort to open up play.

In Winnipeg, Rudy Pilous of the Winnipeg Jets joked about attending the Berlitz school of languages. Pilous had four Swedes, two Finns and two French-Canadians on his roster.

Andy Bathgate, a longtime NHL star, had his comeback plans nixed by his doctors. A workshop injury had left Bathgate with only partial sight in one eye and he was urged to stay on the sidelines.

Two WHA cities boasted spanking new arenas. The opening of Nick Mileti's $20-million 18,000-seat Coliseum in Cleveland was spoiled when the ice machine broke down. The first-night festivities, with much fanfare and many celebrities, had to be set back three nights. In Edmonton, Bill Hunter said their Coliseum, a 16,000-seat stadium with room for expansion to 20,000, was the "the finest arena in Canada."

In what was termed the first deal between the WHA and the NHL, player Butch Deadmarsh of the Kansas City Scouts was sold to the Vancouver Blazers. Deadmarsh was reportedly headed to the Blazers anyway, having signed an off-season contract with the WHA club, but was legally bound to start the season with Kansas City.

There were early-season rumors that the Chicago Cougars would move to Baltimore and that Indianapolis would either change ownership or be taken over by the league. The league also was called on to help the Michigan Stags with financial problems.

Marc Tardif scored 11 quick goals for the Michigan Stags but his $80,000 salary was costing the Stags money they didn't have. So they traded Tardif to Quebec City for Pierre Guite, Mike Rouleau and Alain "Boom Boom" Caron.

In Chicago, some Cougar players bought a large chunk of the club. The principal investors were Pat Stapleton, Dave Dryden and Ralph Backstrom. For the first time in pro-hockey history team players owned a piece of the action.

By midseason the New England Whalers were not only well on their way to a division title but also well on their way to a new home in Hartford. The Whalers became tenants of the posh $31 million Hartford Civic Center.

It was strange but true—half a season had gone by and not a single coach had been fired. Then the axe fell. John Hanna was dismissed in Cleveland and replaced by his boss, general manager Jack Vivian. In Toronto, Billy Harris resigned as coach of the

Toros citing family problems as his reason for leaving.

Bobby Hull, in an effort to get the slumping Winnipeg Jets moving again, assumed the role of player-coach and Rudy Pilous moved upstairs as director of player personnel.

The Michigan Stags finally threw in the towel after playing to near-empty stands in Detroit's Cobo Hall. The team moved on to Baltimore and became the Blades.

Gordie Howe thrilled a crowd of over 15,000 in Edmonton when he scored one goal and assisted on another in the annual All-Star game. Howe paced the West to a 6–4 win over the East.

Bobby Hull blasted three goals past the Houston Aeros in a February game, thus becoming the first player since Maurice Richard to score 50 goals in 50 games. Hull's 50th came with just over a minute to play.

There was another hockey first in Chicago when the Cougars announced that they would refund the price of admission if the club lost their game with Joe Crozier's Vancouver Blazers. Fortunately, the Cougars won on a third-period goal by Gary MacGregor. There were just over 4,000 fans at the game.

In March, John Bassett, Jr., owner of the Toronto Toros, had almost everyone in junior hockey screaming at him when he announced the signing of 18-year-old Mark Napier to a three-year contract. Bassett's announcement appeared to go directly against a recent tentative agreement between professional and amateur hockey.

Indianapolis fans witnessed a hockey rarity when one night the home-town Racers entertained the Cleveland Crusaders. When a donnybrook erupted in the second period (three WHA penalty records were set), coach Jack Vivian of the Crusaders grabbed the sweater of player Murray Heatley. Rival coach Gerry Moore rushed over and began fighting with Vivian. Both coaches were subsequently ejected from the game.

Gordie Howe reached another milestone when he collected his 2,000th point. "Just think of it," said teammate Murray Hall, referring to Howe's feat. "A rookie breaking in would have to score 100 points a year … and do it again and again … every year for 20 years … just to come close to Howe. Impossible!"

Late in the season, daredevil Evel Knievel donned skates for a publicity stunt at Maple Leaf Gardens in Toronto. Knievel pocketed $10,000 when he beat Toro's goalie Les Binkley on two out of four penalty shots between periods.

Despite a fantastic season by Bobby Hull, the Winnipeg Jets missed the playoffs. Hull broke the major professional record for goals in a season when he potted 77. The Winnipeg line of Hull, Nilsson and Hedberg netted 363 points, 27 more than the previous pro record set by Boston's line of Esposito, Hodge and Cashman. Hedberg, with 53 goals, was the top rookie in the WHA.

THE PLAYOFFS

In the playoffs, injuries crippled the New England Whalers and allowed the Minnesota Fighting Saints to oust the East Division champions in a best-of-seven quarter-final series. The Quebec Nordiques breezed past the Phoenix Roadrunners in another quarter-final matchup. Defenseman J. C. Tremblay, a key man in the Nordiques race to the playoffs, was booed by Quebec fans. "That's it," said J.C. "I'll never finish my career in Quebec. I'll play the two years I have on my contract and then get out."

Another former NHL star, Gerry Cheevers, also heard the boos from hometown fans as Cleveland bowed to Houston in five games. Cheevers gave up 23 goals in five games.

The Toronto Toros, picked by most experts to win the Avco Cup in a pre-season poll, did not even make it to the semi-finals. The San Diego Mariners eliminated the Toros in six games.

Rookie Real Cloutier, 19, was the key performer as the Quebec Nordiques advanced to the WHA finals, pushing the Fighting Saints aside four games to two in the semi-finals. Meanwhile, the Houston Aeros swept the San Diego Mariners in four straight and then stunned the Nordiques with a similar display of power in the finals. Gordie Howe scored two goals and an assist in the last game of what he said would be his "final season."

Rookie Houston goalie Ron Grahame was presented with the Gordie Howe Trophy as the top performer in the playoffs. Mark Howe took the playoff scoring honors with 22 points.

As the players dispersed to beaches and golf courses, there was word that the Chicago Cougars franchise had been shelved by the league. The WHA was also attempting to find new ownership for the Baltimore club while Vancouver made plans to move to Calgary. Denver and Cincinnati joined the league with Cincinnati plucking Buffalo Sabres' star Rick Dudley as a "name" player.

1975–76

Prior to the start of the 1975–76 WHA regular season, the Minnesota Fighting Saints hoped to sign Bobby Orr. "We've a pretty good chance of getting him," said general manager Glen Sonmor of the Fighting Saints. The offer called for a million-dollar bonus and a contract described as a multi-million-dollar deal. Some said it was for $6.5 million. Orr, ultimately, decided to stay in the NHL and the optimism in the Saints' camp turned to despair in the following weeks.

In Houston, Gordie Howe, who had been named team president in the off season, was having second thoughts about his second retirement. "I'll play the pre-season games and the home opener, the first game in our new building," said Howe. "Then I'll hang 'em up, I guess. I'm getting too fat to play much longer." But he refused to say his retirement was definite.

Norm Ullman, with his 40th birthday approaching, signed a one-year contract with the Edmonton Oilers and Dave Keon, another ex-Leaf, agreed to play with the Minnesota Fighting Saints.

The Quebec Nordiques picked up tough guy Gord Gallant from Minnesota. Gallant's departure from the Fighting Saints was precipitated by a punch in the nose he delivered to coach Harry Neale. "We're going to be good," predicted Nordiques' coach Jean Guy Gendron. "But the Winnipeg Jets are the team to beat."

Gordie Howe, after collecting a goal and an assist in the Aeros' 5–0 opening-night win over New England, forgot about retirement, flab and fatigue and became the only playing club president in organized sport.

Gerry Moore became the first coaching casualty of the season. Moore was sacked as head coach of Indianapolis after just five games and Jacques Demers moved in to replace him.

In Winnipeg, Bobby Hull sat out a game in a one-man protest against excessive violence in hockey.

The largest crowd in Texas hockey history turned out in Houston's new $18-million home, the Summit, to cheer the Aeros to a 6–4 win over visiting Minnesota. Mark Howe treated 12,053 fans to a hat trick in the game.

Norm Ullman of Edmonton clicked for career goal 500 as the Oilers whipped Quebec 7–4. Ullman became the eighth player in history to score 500 or more goals, joining luminaries such as Gordie Howe, Bobby Hull, Frank Mahovlich, Maurice Richard, Phil Esposito, Jean Beliveau and Johnny Bucyk.

By Christmas, the Indianapolis Racers had added to their staff, signing Hall of Famer Doug Harvey as chief scout.

The Cleveland Crusaders received a gift win, thanks to the Toronto Toros. Leading 8–2 with just over a period to play, the Toros staggered. Cleveland tied the game with time running out and won it 10–9 with 20 seconds left on John A. Stewart's goal. The game produced four WHA records and tied eight other league marks.

The Toronto Toros welcomed goalie Gilles Gratton back to camp. Gratton, 23, had jumped from the Toros to St. Louis of the NHL and back to the Toros again, all in a span of a few months. The Toros also gave one-eyed Greg Neeld a chance to play pro hockey. Neeld had been performing for a semi-pro team in Reno, Nevada.

Left-winger Marc Tardif, the pride of Quebec City, was rewarded with a 10-year contract calling for some $1.5 million over its duration.

In mid-season, the Denver Spurs packed their bags and moved to Ottawa where, as the Civics, they attracted over 8,000 fans to their first game on Ottawa ice. A few days later the Civics folded, leaving the WHA with 13 survivors. Ivan Mullinex, owner of the Spurs-Civics, declared all of his players free agents after he sold Ralph Backstrom to New England, Gary MacGregor and Barry Legge to Cleveland and three or four lesser-known players to Indianapolis.

By February the Edmonton Oilers eased Clare Drake out of his coaching job and Bill Hunter, vice-president and general manager of the club, took over.

Minnesota's Curt Brackenbury set a new penalty record in a game with Phoenix. Brackenbury drew a double minor for leaving the bench, a five-minute fighting penalty, a match penalty for deliberate attempt to injure, a misconduct and a game misconduct. His 39 minutes set a league record for a single game.

Goalie Gerry Cheevers, on the fourth year of a seven-year pact with the Cleveland Crusaders, became disenchanted and jumped back to the Boston Bruins of the NHL. It was reported that Cheevers, a $200,000-a-year man, was financing some of the Cleveland players with personal loans while the team was scrounging for additional money to meet back salaries.

Taking their cues from Cheevers, Henry Boucha jumped from the Minnesota Fighting Saints to the Kansas City Scouts while Rick Smith bolted to the St. Louis Blues. The financially troubled Saints were sold to a group of Minnesota businessmen for a nominal one dollar. This was the same team that had earlier offered Bobby Orr a reported $6.5 million.

Quebec's Marc Tardif became the fastest player in pro hockey to score 50 goals and 100 points. Tardif cracked the 100-point barrier in his 55th game.

The floundering Toronto Toros fired Coach Bobby Baun late in February and replaced him with Gilles Leger.

Jim Pattison, head of the company which owned the Calgary Cowboys, noted that WHA attendance figures had jumped from 2.5 million in its first year to 4.1 million in year three. "Despite continuing rumors of the league's imminent demise, the WHA is here to stay," said Pattison.

No sooner had Pattison spoken than the Minnesota Fighting Saints closed up shop. The Saints ended a two-month financial struggle, which included three missed payrolls, when the players decided not to play any longer without pay.

Late in the season, Gordie Howe accomplished a feat that had eluded him for 28 pro season—he scored his first overtime goal as the Aeros nipped the Toros in Toronto. "I almost laughed when it went in," said Howe. "That's probably the only thing I haven't done in 28 years."

The San Diego Mariners were unable to meet player payrolls and the players on the club voted to carry on "without money in anticipation of new owners coming in."

Winnipeg, Houston and Quebec were the power teams in the WHA with all three clubs topping 100 points by the end of the regular season.

Marc Tardif of Quebec collected a record 148 scoring points and became the only major-league player to top the 70-goal plateau. He finished with 71.

THE PLAYOFFS

Violence erupted early in the WHA playoff series between Quebec and Calgary. Marc Tardif, the brilliant left-winger, was felled by a vicious charge from Calgary's Rick Jodzio. Tardif, seriously injured, was rushed to hospital with a concussion. Doctors said he was finished for the year and he was warned not to count on playing for Canada in the World Cup tournament. Criminal charges were laid against Jodzio.

Ben Hatskin, the league's chief executive officer, suspended Jodzio for the rest of the series and "possibly for all time" and suspended Calgary coach Joe Crozier for the rest of the playoff series between the two clubs. He also fined the teams $25,000 each for failing to control their players in the wildest donnybrook in the brief history of the league. Fighting was so fierce after the Tardif injury that 20 Quebec City policemen were on the ice trying to restore order.

Winnipeg's Bobby Hull, bitter about the state of hockey, talked about retiring at the end of the playoffs. "The game isn't much fun anymore," said Hull. "It's getting to be a disaster. The idiot owners, the incompetent coaches, the inept players, are dragging the game into the mud. They're destroying it with their senseless violence."

One hockey man who did quit was Bud Poile, executive vice-president of the WHA. Poile's resignation was demanded by the Quebec City Nordiques after the injury to Tardif. Poile said he was resigning in the best interests of the league.

In the playoffs, Winnipeg swept Edmonton aside in four straight games and then ousted Calgary (winners over Quebec) four games to one. New England whipped Cleveland in a best-of-five series and then eliminated Indianapolis four games to three. San Diego squeaked by Phoenix in a best-of-five series but fell to Houston, 4–2, in a best-of-seven engagement. Houston went on to oust New England while the Winnipeg Jets sat back and waited to play the winners for the Avco Cup.

Most fans anticipated a long series when the Jets and the Aeros finally clashed in the final playoff series of the year. But the Aeros turned out to be no match for the speed and hot shooting of the Jets. The Jets won four straight and captured the Avco Cup on home ice. Gordie Howe simply shook his head when it was all over. "They have one hell of a hockey team," lamented Howe.

X

THE MOVE TOWARD MERGER

One League Again? 1976–1979

In 1976, two of hockey's brightest stars disagreed sharply on the issue of a merger between the NHL and the WHA. Bobby Hull thought a merger was inevitable and would prove to be a good thing for hockey. Gordie Howe liked the attendance figures he saw in the WHA and predicted that the new league was "here to stay." Howe was supported by WHA president Bill MacFarland, who stated that his league had no interest in merging with the NHL.

Meanwhile, both leagues were forced to deal with serious in-house problems in the late seventies, most of them financial. For the first time in 40 years the NHL approved two franchise shifts, allowing the California Seals to move east to Cleveland and the Kansas City Scouts to go west to Denver. Both teams suffered in their new surroundings and when the Cleveland franchise failed to draw, it was rescued from bankruptcy by the players themselves. Dwindling attendance in Atlanta forced the Flames to seek greener pastures and there was doubt the Blues could survive in St. Louis.

Stepping in to deal with these and other problems was John Ziegler, the new president of the NHL who quickly sided with the pro-merger governors. There was a scandal involving drugs and another involving theft of players' money by an agent. Fans became more enamored of international play, especially after the excitement generated by the 1976 Canada Cup, won by Team Canada on Darryl Sittler's thrilling goal in overtime against Czechoslovakia. But some players, like Flyer captain Bobby Clarke, one of the dominant players of the era, were less concerned with international matches than they were with getting the NHL's house in order. Ultimately, a merger with the WHA seemed like a good idea to almost everyone.

1976–77

During the summer of 1976, Clarence Campbell, elected for the 31st time as NHL president, moved to eradicate the goons and intimidators in the NHL and eliminate unnecessary violence. Most believed that his actions were prompted by two main elements—a public outcry and Ontario Attorney-General Roy McMurtry's threat that law enforcement officers would lay charges against hockey players who committed on-ice assaults. Campbell's five basic rule changes included a major penalty and/or major and game misconduct to any player initiating a fight, a game misconduct for any player physically interfering with spectators, a double minor for the first player to leave the team or penalty bench during an altercation (plus a game misconduct and additional fines) and a $50 fine for a boarding check which causes injury to a player's face or head. The president of the league could also review any incident during or after a game and assess additional fines or suspensions.

The NHL Players' Association wanted to go even further towards eliminating violence. They wanted immediate game expulsion of both players involved in fights, even if they had thrown only one punch, and game misconduct penalties for stick swinging. But that was too radical a change for the owners, who defeated the proposal 13–4.

In the off season, Boston Bruins defenseman Bobby Orr became a free agent and signed a $3-million multi-year contract with the Chicago Blackhawks. The move was a bold gamble to put fans back in Chicago Stadium seats. Through club president Paul Mooney the Bruins announced that the club would file suit in U.S. district court for an injunction restraining Orr from playing with Chicago unless the Bruins received adequate compensation from the Hawks. NHL president Clarence Campbell ruled, "There is no reason in the world why Orr shouldn't play for Chicago." The Hawk players threatened to go on strike if the Bruins were successful in keeping Orr off the ice. Under a section of the NHL bylaws, the Bruins would normally be entitled to compensation, either money or players, for the loss of Orr. Campbell, however, said that the Boston club had waived arbitration on the compensation issue on June 7, noting that they "thought they had a good enough team without Orr. I guess they miscalculated." Orr's departure from Boston cost the Bruins an estimated 5,000 paying customers per game.

The grand old man of the Houston Aeros, 48-year-old Gordie Howe, started an off-season rumor. Howe said, "I'm going to play next season but my sons are going to retire." Howe did quit his job as the Houston Aeros' president, saying, "I want to have the best year I can so I'm going to concentrate on just playing."

Islander Bryan Trottier won the Calder Trophy and teammate Denis Potvin was awarded the Norris. Jean Ratelle of Boston took home the Byng Trophy, while Bobby Clarke of Philadelphia won the Hart Trophy as the NHL's most valuable player for the third time in four years.

For the first time since 1934 the league gave its approval to transfer two franchises. The California Seals moved from the west coast to Cleveland, where they became the Barons, and a Denver group purchased the bankrupt Kansas City Scouts and turned them into the Colorado Rockies.

An interesting trade saw Rangers' forward Rick Middleton go to Boston in exchange for forward Ken Hodge. The Bruins then traded Andre Savard to Buffalo in return for Peter McNab. The Canadiens announced that Rejean Houle (who had defected a few years earlier to the Quebec Nordiques of the WHA with defensemen Dale Hoganson, Jean-Claude Tremblay and left-winger Marc Tardif) would be returning to Montreal.

The big hockey event in September was the inaugural Canada Cup. To head off any recurrence of the 1972 Team Canada–Soviet series, when dissension over lineup selections swept the Canadian squad and caused a split amongst players, several members of Team Canada '76 held a team meeting to inform the players they didn't want any trouble. Players like Phil Esposito, Bobby Clarke and Gerry Cheevers told team members if they didn't like the setup they were to get out now, not later. With other stars on the team such as Bobby Hull, Bobby Orr, Guy Lafleur, Guy Lapointe, Darryl Sittler, Denis Potvin and Rogie Vachon, the Canadian squad was touted as the best ever. Canada and Czechoslovakia met in the finals and the windup match was a thriller. The gallant Czechoslovakian team fought back from a 2–0 deficit after Team Canada had driven Europe's best goaltender, Jiri Holecek, from the net. He was replaced by Vladimir Dzurilla, who days earlier had backstopped the Czechs to a 1–0 victory over Canada. Dzurilla was brilliant again, forcing the game into overtime. It was a tip from Boston coach Don Cherry, one of four Team Canada coaches, that gave Canada the victory: "Dzurilla rushes out to meet you when you get a break. Give him a move and go to the side." Darryl Sittler did just that, scoring the sudden-death overtime winner in Canada's 5–4 triumph. Scotty Bowman, the head coach of Team Canada, observed, "We have more individual ability and more experience than does Team Czechoslovakia. But they are very good and they pushed us to the wall. I'm glad it's over, and that Canada won."

The first rounders selected in the annual entry draft received close scrutiny during training camp but only a handful would blossom into stars. While Don Murdoch of the Rangers was the flashiest, Rick Green of Washington and Bernie Federko of the St. Louis Blues would prove to be the most steady.

One of the NHL's toughest and most colorful players, 35-year-old Barclay Plager, retired from St. Louis to become player-coach of the newly organized Blues' farm club in Kansas City.

Dave Schultz, 26, of the Philadelphia Flyers was traded to the Los Angeles Kings for future considerations in a move that shocked Philadelphia fans. "The Hammer," known for his aggressive play, was one of the Flyers' most popular players.

Before the first puck was even dropped to start the 1976–77 NHL season, the Toronto Maple Leafs, all the way up to president Harold Ballard, were talking about winning the Stanley Cup. Surveying his team's spirited play in the exhibition season, Ballard said he believed the Maple Leafs could be two years or less from winning the coveted cup.

Early-season attendance was down in many NHL cities, even with teams accustomed to automatic sellouts. The Minnesota North Stars, the Boston Bruins and the New York Rangers, usually well supported, all showed significant attendance drops. Rising ticket prices, the high cost of living and a more discerning breed of hockey fans were reasons given for the downward trend in NHL attendance.

With the season underway, sharpshooters began their assault on the scoring records. Rookie Don Murdoch of the Rangers scored five times in one game, equaling Howie Meeker's freshman-year feat of 1947.

Bobby Orr was temporarily out of the Chicago lineup after being examined by a Toronto surgeon who was convinced that Orr's troublesome knees could not stand up to the daily wear and tear of the rugged NHL. The surgeon suggested that Orr play only two out of three games or rest one or two days every week.

Cliff Koroll of the Chicago Blackhawks had the distinction of scoring a most memorable penalty shot. When Koroll slipped the puck past St. Louis goalie Eddie Johnston on October 24, it marked the first penalty shot scored by a member of the Hawks in 35 years. Joe Cooper had last done it in 1941 against Montreal.

The Montreal Canadiens got off to a blazing start. In the NHL's individual scoring race, the Canadiens had three players in the top four and five in the top 20. The electrifying Guy Lafleur was scoring at almost a goal-a-game pace with 10 goals in 11 starts. He also had nine assists. Just one point behind Lafleur was linemate Steve Shutt with nine goals and an equal number of assists.

Early predictions that Boston would have the best pair of goalkeepers in the league were correct as Gerry Cheevers and Gilles Gilbert were playing spectacular hockey. Teammate Peter McNab had a great start with the Bruins, with six early season goals.

In November, Ontario Attorney-General Roy McMurtry lowered the boom on the Leafs' Dave "Tiger" Williams for the 26-stitch head cut he inflicted on defenseman Dennis Owchar with his hockey stick on October 20. Williams was remanded to December 14 after he appeared at a Toronto police station to answer charges of assault causing bodily harm and possession of a weapon dangerous to the public peace. McMurtry said he was moving to prosecute Williams.

Defenseman Bryan Watson of the Detroit Red Wings was suspended by the NHL for 10 games because of his unprovoked attack on Chicago's Keith Magnuson, breaking his jaw.

For the 1976–77 season, the Amateur Hockey Association of the United States (AHAUS) ruled that members in junior classifications and below (except paid gate junior A and B teams) would be required to wear either a full face mask or half face mask with an external mouthpiece. This ruling was an attempt to reduce facial injuries, especially eye injuries. Canadian youngsters would be a year or more away from the same requirements.

With only one victory and three ties in their first nine games, the Leafs summoned Mike Palmateer from the Dallas Blackhawks of the Central League. He was so hot he pushed Wayne Thomas out of the regular goaling job and forced the club to send another goalie, Gord McRae, to the minors.

Bobby Hull, believing that the answer to better hockey would be a merger of the NHL and the WHL, said, "I believe it will happen. It's got to. We could eliminate the weak franchises in both leagues and get rid of the 100 or so jerks who just play for the money and don't put anything back into the game. We'd have something good again." Gordie Howe disagreed with Hull: "I don't think it's right for Bobby to knock the WHA because the league's been good to him. I don't agree with some of the things he said. This year the WHA's over-all attendance is up and I think the league is here to stay."

The NHL Players' Association signed a five-year agreement forbidding any merger with the WHA. Furthermore, according to WHA president Bill MacFarland, the WHA wasn't interested in merging with the NHL anyway.

Before Christmas, Wayne Stephenson, the Philadelphia Flyers' goaltender who was a sensation in the previous year's Stanley Cup playoffs, announced his retirement.

At odds with the Flyers over a new contract, he had missed all of training camp and did not appear in a regular league game after the Flyers suspended him for not showing up at practice. Stephenson would sit out the year, become a free agent and try to return to hockey the following year with another club.

The iron man of NHL linesmen, Neil Armstrong, officiated his 1,600th big-league hockey game. In his 19th season he was the second-oldest official. Matt Pavelich was in his 21st year but had 1,480 games to his credit.

The New York Rangers lost a record seven games at home. John Ferguson, the rookie general manager-coach, was having trouble rallying his youthful team. Veteran Ranger star Rod Gilbert, however, was attaining some personal milestones. He played in his 1,000th NHL game as a Ranger. He owned or shared 22 Ranger records including most goals (392), most assists (589) and most playoff goals (34). And he became the 14th player in NHL history to attain the 1,000-game plateau with the same team. Harry Howell was the only other Ranger to achieve the feat.

The Pittsburgh Penguins installed Baz Bastien as the man in charge of the club's NHL hockey operations after relieving Wren Blair of his post as president and chief operating officer.

Mid-season trades saw Detroit bad man Bryan Watson go to Washington in return for second-year pro Greg Joly, who had spent more time off the ice than on as the result of injuries. The floundering Vancouver Canucks traded John Gould to Atlanta for defenseman Larry Carriere and winger Hilliard Graves. Vancouver general manager Phil Maloney said that other deals would follow in an attempt to get the Canucks back into contention.

Bobby Orr's gimpy knees continued to give him problems. He appeared in only 12 of the Blackhawks' first 27 games and had three goals and 15 assists.

The financial structure of the Atlanta Flames was so shaky by December that Georgia Governor George Busbee and Mayor Maynard Jackson stepped in to lend a hand. Busbee and Jackson talked with representatives of 40 of the state's largest business firms and received promises of $25,000 worth of Flames tickets from each. A total of $750,000 was raised to keep the team skating for the rest of the season. Principal owner Tom Cousins said the team would be forced to consider moving if it couldn't function on a break-even basis—an average of 13,000 fans per game in Atlanta. This season's average had been 10,500.

At mid season, veteran John Bucyk of the Boston Bruins moved into fourth spot on the all-time NHL scoring list ahead of Maurice Richard when he scored his 545th career goal. The Rocket quit with 544 goals. Only Gordie Howe, Bobby Hull and Phil Esposito had scored more goals than the 41-year-old captain of the Bruins. Another scoring ace, Garry Unger of the St. Louis Blues, became the 24th player in the history of the league to score 300 goals. But he was far ahead of the pace set by most of those before him. At the time Unger was 29, and only four of the other 23 had scored their 300th goal before age 30. Those included Bobby Hull, Gordie Howe, Phil Esposito and Stan Mikita.

Emile Francis, not satisfied with his St. Louis Blues who were leading the Smythe Division, dealt Rick Smith to the Bruins for Joe Zanussi, dumped defenseman Bob Hess (once said to be another Orr) to the Kansas City farm team along with rookie Brian Sutter. He called up two of the CHL Blues' top forwards, Bernie Federko and Rick Bourbonnais. A few days later, Francis placed controversial center Derek Sanderson on waivers without recall. Sanderson said he was confident he would land with some other club.

There were three coaching changes in the New Year. Most startling was the end of the 13-year-reign of Bill Reay of the Chicago Blackhawks, who had become the dean of major-league hockey coaches. The downtrodden Hawks, suffering badly at the gate and on the ice, decided to entrust the interim coaching job to a triumvirate of players headed by veteran defenseman Bill White. Attendance in Chicago was down from a game average of 17,000 to less than 10,000, even with Bobby Orr. Elsewhere, Orland Kurtenbach returned to the Vancouver Canucks as head coach after a successful two-year sojourn in the Central League as coach of the Tulsa Oilers. He replaced Phil Maloney who had been carrying the double portfolio of coach and general manager. Maloney would stay on as general manager.

Alex Delvecchio, for the third time in four seasons, moved behind the Detroit Red Wing bench. The Red Wing general manager-coach vacated his spot in the press box on December 17 to take over the coaching duties again and immediately promised a "get tough" approach toward the players. Weeks later the Red Wings acquired their fifth coach in the previous six years when Larry Wilson stepped up from the Baltimore Clippers of the Southern Hockey League to take over the coaching reins from Alex Delvecchio. At the time Detroit was battling Washington for last place in the Norris Division, some 41 points behind the leading Montreal Canadiens.

NHL president Clarence Campbell and Alan Eagleson, president of the NHL Players' Association, talked with officials of the Soviet Union about a new hockey series that would bring together the best team in Russia and the Stanley Cup champions. A tournament in the holiday period of 1977–78 became a strong possibility. Bobby Clarke, captain of Team Canada in its Canada Cup triumph the previous fall, felt that the National Hockey League should clean up its own problems before heading into any more international competitions.

Bogged down by poor attendance, the last-place Cleveland Barons decided to fire general manager Bill McCreary and install former NHL defense star Harry Howell in the position.

Although the NHL Referees' Association was not happy with the way the NHL had been assessing fines to coaches and players for their poor conduct and verbal abuse of officials, the new rules aimed at curbing violence were effective. "The amount of publicity given to the penalties got through to the players and, except for certain hellers, did the job," said Clarence Campbell. "The total number of infractions is about the same, but the character of these infractions is vastly different." There were, however, more high-sticking incidents and Campbell conceded that some additional action might have to be taken to curb these violations.

In January, Barbara Williams was officially appointed by general manager Bill Torrey as the official power-skating coach of the New York Islanders. Coach Williams' prize pupil turned out to be Bob Nystrom. A 20-goal scorer in each of the previous three seasons, Nystrom became a threat for the 40-goal plateau.

Marcel Dionne scored his 500th career point in his 418th game. Only Bobby Orr had scored that many points in fewer games. Orr counted 500 points in 396 games. Dionne also notched his 200th NHL goal. In February, defenseman Ian Turnbull of the Toronto Maple Leafs scored five times in one game as the Leafs bombed the Detroit Red Wings 9–1. His feat was unprecedented—no other NHL defenseman in history had been able to score that many goals in one game.

In the WHA, Anders Hedberg of the Winnipeg Jets became the first player in the history of major-league hockey to score 50 goals in fewer than 50 games. Hedberg broke the record established 22 seasons before by Maurice "Rocket" Richard and matched in 1974–75 by Bobby Hull. Hedberg scored 51 goals in 49 games, collecting four goals in game number 48, four more in game 49 and three goals in game 50—a spectacular rush to the record.

The news no one wanted to hear inevitably came. "I'm finished for this season ... I just can't continue to go on the way I am," said Blackhawk superstar defenseman Bobby Orr. "I'm going to meet with my doctor and a decision will be made on my knee and what to do. If the doctor says that there's no chance for me to play again, then it will be all over. I'll have to quit hockey."

The Cleveland Barons were encountering major financial problems. The players gave owner Mel Swig an ultimatum that he either pay them their back salaries or find someone who would come up with the money. If not, the Cleveland Barons would cease to operate as a team.

The Vancouver Canucks took over Derek Sanderson's $160,000-per-year contract from the St. Louis Blues and hoped that he would give them some late-season spark to make the playoffs.

Buffalo goaltender Al Smith announced that he was retiring from hockey. The unhappy Sabre said moving around 30 times in an 11-year pro career and not getting a fair chance from the Sabres had convinced him that it was time to quit. Smith's departure was bizarre to say the least. After reporting for a game and expecting to play, Smith found out that rookie goaltender Don Edwards, recently called up from the American League, would be in net. Just before the opening faceoff, Smith skated out onto the ice, turned toward the players and club president Seymour H. Knox III, saluted, skated to the end of the rink and proceeded to the dressing room. He donned his street clothes and departed for good.

Atlanta's Tom Lysiak, who had signed a long-term contract years earlier with the Flames for an annual salary reportedly in the vicinity of $150,000, announced that he was broke and blamed his agent. He was one of the many professional athletes who alleged that player agent Richard Sorkin owed them money. Lysiak and teammates Ken Houston and Eddie Kea took legal action against Sorkin of Rockville Center, New York. It was claimed Sorkin lost hundreds of thousands of dollars of his clients' money in the stock market and at the race track. Eventually Sorkin was found guilty of fraud and sentenced to three years in jail.

Two members of the Montreal Canadiens, Yvan Cournoyer and Jacques Lemaire, climbed into hockey's select high scoring company. Cournoyer scored his 400th career goal and Lemaire came through with his 300th, ironically both on the same night in a game against Philadelphia. Rod Gilbert of the Rangers attained another major-league milestone when he collected his 1,000th scoring point in a game against the Islanders. Gilbert became only the 11th man in NHL history to reach the 1,000-point mark in his career. In the same two-week period, Gilbert went on to become the 12th player in league history to reach the 400-goal plateau. Stan Mikita of the Blackhawks became only the eighth player in NHL history to score 500 goals when he put the puck behind Vancouver's Cesare Maniago on February 27.

The St. Louis Blues struggled through their annual financial crisis. In a dramatic move, the team fired a long list of top executives, including senior vice-president Lynn Patrick, the hockey patriarch who was the first employee of the franchise in 1966, more than a year before the Blues took to the ice.

The Cleveland Barons came back from the dead with the infusion of a $1.3-million loan courtesy of the NHL and the NHL Players' Association in one of the most bizarre rescue missions ever seen in professional sports. Facing an 11th-hour decision whether to disband or continue, the Barons suddenly found themselves with enough cash to assure the club of finishing the current season. However, the 1977–78 season was still in question. Their actions saved the NHL the embarrassment of folding a franchise in mid-season for the first time in its history and it also prevented losses of revenue on games that would have been cancelled. Reaction to Alan Eagleson's infusion of $600,000 of NHL Players' Association funds into the shaky Cleveland Barons was fast and furious—and unanimously negative. All-Star defenseman Brad Park, vice-president of the Players' Association, and Bruins' player representative Terry O'Reilly were the most vociferous. "I'm very upset with the way this was handled," said Park. "How did I learn about it? In the newspaper. Terry O'Reilly wasn't informed either."

Ageless Gordie Howe brought the WHA plenty of attention when he scored his 900th career goal, making him the first man in the history of professional hockey to achieve such a plateau. Bobby Hull was second on the all-time list with 840.

The NHL Players' Association director Alan Eagleson informed his player clients that NHL teams would lose between $15 million and $18 million in this season.

At the end of the season, the Detroit Red Wings, a club that had missed the playoffs for seven consecutive seasons, hoped to regain their respectability by firing general manager Alex Delvecchio. He was replaced by Ted Lindsay, a former Detroit hockey great, who was given a five-year mandate to get the Wings out of the NHL doldrums. That year Cleveland, Colorado, Washington and the New York Rangers also failed to make the playoffs.

Jean Ratelle of the Boston Bruins reached another milestone in his career as he scored his 400th goal just before the curtain came down on the 1976–77 schedule.

The Montreal Canadiens concluded a fabulous record-breaking season during which they dominated the NHL's 1976–77 schedule from start to finish. They won the Prince of Wales Trophy, captured the individual Vezina (Dryden) and Ross (Lafleur) trophies, set 10 new NHL records and tied an 11th. They ended up as overall champions of the regular 80-game schedule, making them the favorites to repeat as Stanley Cup champions. The Canadiens lost only eight games all season and topped the Norris Division with 60 wins and 132 points. Montreal was paced by Guy Lafleur, who won the scoring title with 136 points, and Steve Shutt, who set a goal-scoring record for left-wingers with 60.

The Philadelphia Flyers won their division and conference regular-season titles for the fourth straight season. Boston edged Buffalo by two points to win the Adams Division and St. Louis captured the Smythe Division title.

THE NHL PLAYOFFS

Preliminary Round (Best of Three)

In preliminary-round play, the Islanders eliminated Chicago and Buffalo took out Minnesota, both winning the best-of-three series 2–0. The Los Angeles Kings won their series 2–1 over the Atlanta Flames and Toronto came from behind to oust the Pittsburgh Penguins 2–1.

Quarter-Finals (Best of Seven)

In the quarter-finals, Montreal swept their series against St. Louis 4–0. Philadelphia eliminated Toronto 4–2 after the Leafs opened with two straight wins at the Spectrum. The Islanders met Buffalo and took the series easily 4–0. Boston won their series against Los Angeles, 4–2.

Semi-Finals (Best of Seven)

In semi-final play, the Philadelphia Flyers were dumped from further action after four straight losses to the upstart Boston Bruins. Depending too much on an overworked Bobby Clarke and without the services of injured Gary Dornhoefer in game four, the Flyers managed only one goal in the final two games of the series. The Montreal Canadiens advanced to the finals with a 4–2 series victory over the Islanders. Bob Gainey set a record for the fastest goal at the start of a game when he scored just seven seconds into the final game.

The Stanley Cup Finals (Best of Seven)

The Montreal Canadiens—with depth, defense and discipline—swept the Boston Bruins in four straight games to win the 1977 Stanley Cup. It was Montreal's 20th Cup victory. Since 1929, Boston had played Montreal in 15 playoff series and come out winners only twice, in the semi-finals of 1929 and 1943. The cup-clinching hero was Jacques Lemaire, whose two goals in game four, including the overtime tally at 4:32, brought a second consecutive Cup to Montreal. The Conn Smythe Trophy winner was Guy Lafleur, who paced all playoff scorers with nine goals and 17 assists for 26 points, five more than runner-up Darryl Sittler of Toronto. A major reason for Montreal's success was excellent goaltending during the season and the playoffs. Ken Dryden was in goal throughout the post-season play and made his 34th consecutive playoff appearance in the deciding game.

In the WHA, Quebec captured the Eastern Division crown with 97 points. Cincinnati, Indianapolis and New England also made the playoffs in the Eastern Division. Led by the Howe family and Terry Ruskowski, the Houston Aeros took the Western Division title with 106 points. Winnipeg finished second, San Diego third and Edmonton fourth in the Western Division of the WHA.

Quebec's Real Cloutier finished atop the scoring race with 66 goals and 141 points, 10 ahead of the Jets' Anders Hedberg.

THE WHA PLAYOFFS

Quarter-Finals (Best of Seven)

In the WHA's Eastern Division, the Indianapolis Racers, coached by Jacques Demers, shocked the Cincinnati Stingers with a four-game sweep of their playoff series. Demers called it "the greatest upset in WHA history." Quebec defeated New England 4–1. In the Eastern Division final, the Racers' season ended abruptly against the Nordiques, who wiped them out 4–1. The Nords big line of Serge Bernier, Real Cloutier and Andre Boudrias made the difference.

In the Western Division, the Winnipeg Jets' seven-game series win over pesky San Diego set up a division final between Winnipeg and Houston after the Aeros had eliminated the Edmonton Oilers in five games. The Jets, paced by the high-scoring trio of Anders Hedberg, Bobby Hull and Ulf Nilsson, won the West by ousting Houston from the playoffs, four games to two. In the loser's dressing room, Gordie Howe told reporters, "I won't play next year. The body is gone."

For the first time in its five-year history, the WHA experienced an all-Canadian final for the Avco World Trophy.

Avco Cup Finals (Best of Seven)

After Winnipeg stunned Quebec 2–1 in the series opener, the Nords bounced back with a 6–1 triumph. The Jets captured game three in a 6–1 romp but faltered in game four, losing 4–2. The Nordiques, brandishing a powerful offense, ripped the Jets 8–3 in game five and needed only one more win to take the championship. In game six, the Jets humiliated the Nords 12–3, but the Quebec gunners dominated the final game, winning 8–2. The Nordiques skated off with the Avco Trophy.

Robbie Ftorek of the Phoenix Roadrunners became the first American-born player to win a major trophy when he was voted MVP of the WHA.

While the playoffs were continuing, Canada experienced its most humiliating defeat ever on the international hockey scene with an 11–1 humiliation at the hands of the Soviet Union during the World Hockey championships in Vienna. Team Canada finished the competition with a 6–3–1 record, two points behind the first-place (7–2–1) Czechs. Sweden and the Soviets each compiled a 7–3 record.

With the season over, Bobby Orr planned to undergo his sixth knee operation, which he hoped would give him more mobility and enable him to return to his hockey career the next season.

Gordie Howe's honeymoon with hockey in Houston was over. Next stop—Hartford. An agreement was reached between the Hartford Whalers and the Howe family— Gordie, Mark, Marty and Gordie's wife Colleen, who acted as their agent. After four years in Texas, the Howes wanted out of the Houston Aeros' financially troubled management. The Boston Bruins and the Detroit Red Wings both made attempts to sign the Howes but the family turned down both overtures. It was not certain whether or not Gordie would return as an active player but he would definitely help the Whalers in their scouting and public relations departments.

Hockey lost a great competitor in mid-May. Barry Ashbee, a former Philadelphia Flyers player and assistant coach, died of leukemia at the age of 38. He had been highly regarded for the pride and determination he helped instill in the Flyers during their championship years.

1977–78

In June 1977, 43-year-old John Ziegler became the fourth president of the National Hockey League. The Detroit lawyer was elected by the governors of the NHL to replace 72-year-old Clarence Campbell. Indications were that Ziegler would operate with more jurisdiction over the teams than Campbell was able to exert in his 31 years at the helm.

There were the usual number of off-season coaching changes. Detroit Red Wings general manager Ted Lindsay demoted coach Larry Wilson to the Oklahoma City farm club and replaced him with former Winnipeg Jets' mentor Bobby Kromm. The Pittsburgh Penguins took on a new coach as well when they signed John Wilson to a three-year contract. Phil Maloney was relieved of his duties as general manager of the Vancouver Canucks. His replacement was a surprise—Jake Milford, 61, was selected by Canucks' president Bill Hughes to lead Vancouver out of the hockey wilderness. Orland Kurtenbach was named as the new coach.

The top three draft picks were Dale McCourt (Detroit), Barry Beck (Colorado) and Robert Picard (Washington). In the telephone draft of amateur players, Montreal, Toronto and the Rangers each had two first-round choices. Montreal surprised many by drafting Mark Napier of the Birmingham Bulls of the rival WHA, a 60-goal scorer the previous season. The Canadiens also grabbed Normand Dupont of Montreal. The Rangers, picking three times in the first 26 selections, took highly regarded right-winger Lucien Deblois of Sorel, Ron Duguay of Sudbury and Mike Keating of St. Catharines. Toronto, with four picks in the first two rounds, wound up with four OHA stars, John Anderson and Trevor Johansen of the Toronto Marlboros, Bob Gladney of Oshawa and high-scoring Rocky Saganiuk of Lethbridge. The Canadiens grabbed 27 amateurs in all. They astounded the other clubs by selecting seven goalkeepers.

After three days of emotional meetings in Chicago, the NHL agreed to bury the hatchet with the rival WHA. For a cool $2.9 million each, six WHA franchises—Cincinnati, Quebec, New England, Edmonton, Winnipeg and Houston—were told they could join the NHL in what John Ziegler, one of the primary architects of the merger, hoped would make hockey more competitive and exciting. The six WHA cities would be included in the 1977–78 Stanley Cup playoffs. Complete realignment was expected by 1980–81.

Then, at a subsequent meeting in New York, a contingent of NHL owners, led by Harold Ballard, voted to kill the merger plans. Five votes were necessary to defeat the proposed addition of the WHA clubs and, in the end, the Toronto Maple Leafs, Boston Bruins, Los Angeles Kings, Minnesota North Stars, Vancouver Canucks and New York Islanders registered opposition. The WHA's reaction was one of disappointment and anger. The war between the leagues was back on again.

With the merger off, the WHA decided to operate with seven or eight teams—depending on whether the Edmonton Oilers were viable—and to function with a one-division format. The teams that were ready to begin a new season included Cincinnati, Indianapolis (saved from financial ruin by Nelson Skalbania, a 39-year-old Canadian financier), Birmingham, Quebec, Winnipeg, Houston and New England. Calgary, Phoenix, San Diego and Minnesota would not be back.

Two weeks before the season opener the Oilers still hadn't indicated if they would be around for another WHA season, so two schedules were drawn up—one for an eight-team league, the other for seven teams. Oilers' co-owner Peter Pocklington was said to be trying to buy the Colorado Rockies, a move the Rockies' president Munson Campbell termed "idiotic." No sooner did Pocklington commit his team to another WHA season when defenseman Robin Sadler walked out on the club after a talk with coach Glen Sather. Two years earlier, Sadler had turned his back on a three-year $250,000 contract with the Montreal Canadiens as their number-one draft choice.

During his comeback try with the Oilers, he had complained that he "was not enjoying himself" and wanted to quit. This time he walked away from a two-year deal at $100,000 per year. He returned home to British Columbia where he became a fireman.

The WHA was pleased with the results of their exhibition games against the more established NHL. Nineteen games were scheduled and the younger league came out on top, winning 12 and losing five.

Even though Gordie Howe, now a New England Whaler, failed to score a point in exhibition play, he did agree to play another season, his 30th in professional hockey. Some players, including former Houston teammate Terry Ruskowski, thought Howe was tarnishing his image by carrying on.

The WHA was not about to let two of their Swedish scoring stars—Anders Hedberg and Ulf Nilsson—get away to the rival NHL. According to president Howard Baldwin, his league would do everything in its power to keep the pair with the Winnipeg Jets. NHL teams such as the Rangers, Chicago, Minnesota, Toronto, Detroit, Philadelphia and Vancouver had all expressed an interest in signing the pair.

The NHL lost one of its most aggressive and colorful performers with the death of St. Louis Blues' defenseman Bob Gassoff. Gassoff, 24, had been riding a trail bike on a winding road when his bike collided head-on with a car.

At the annual awards banquet Guy Lafleur of the Montreal Canadiens enhanced his hockey stock by winning the Hart Trophy as the league's most valuable player. Other winners were Montreal's Larry Robinson (Norris), the Kings' Marcel Dionne (Lady Byng) and Willi Plett of the Atlanta Flames, who captured the Calder Trophy as the outstanding rookie of the year.

The Toronto Maple Leafs wasted little time dealing with their top scorers of the 1976–77 season. Both Darryl Sittler and Lanny McDonald were rewarded with five-year contracts estimated at $150,000 per season.

On July 6, Chicago team president Bill Wirtz announced that Bob Pulford, 41, would be the Blackhawks' new general manager and coach. "This team can win, but effort comes before winning," said Pulford, who had quit the Kings in late May.

George Gund III purchased the Cleveland Barons hockey team from Mel Swig for $5.3 million. A native of Cleveland, Gund was a financier and businessman who had been closely identified with both Cleveland and hockey since his youth.

On June 15, the Minnesota North Stars announced the signing of two 26-year-old veterans from the Swedish national team, right-winger Kent-Erik Andersson and left-winger Per-Olov Brasar. "There's no question that they will help us right away," said general manager Jack Gordon.

New York Ranger general manager John Ferguson decided to concentrate solely on his duties as general manager and turn the coaching role over to Jean-Guy Talbot. The Toronto Maple Leafs said goodbye to Red Kelly, who had been relieved of his duties for medical reasons. Roger Neilson, with little experience as a pro coach but a lot of experience coaching and teaching in general, was hired to replace him. The Los Angeles Kings entered the season with a new general manager, George Maguire, and a new coach, Ron Stewart. Pat Kelly officially became the second coach of the Colorado Rockies after a summer filled with speculation about the identity of Johnny Wilson's replacement and the ultimate future of Denver's NHL club. Buffalo's general manager Punch Imlach kept everyone guessing right to the last minute, then he announced that the new Sabre head coach would be Marcel Pronovost.

The NHL agreed to a new Stanley Cup playoff format. Under the new procedure, the top two teams in each of the NHL's four divisions would qualify for post-season action. Four other teams would be admitted to the playoffs as "wild-card" entries based on their respective point standings.

There was serious concern in the camp of the New York Rangers over the plight of star right-winger Don Murdoch, who had been arrested for possession of cocaine. Murdoch, 20, was about to start his second year with the Rangers. It was the first time a member of an NHL team had been detained for drugs.

Ralston Purina Co. saved the St. Louis Blues from extinction when they bought the franchise from the Salomon family, who had indicated that if no buyer was found they would declare bankruptcy.

Many expected that 20-year-old Mike Bossy would help the New York Islanders with goal scoring. In four seasons with the Laval Nationals of the QJHL, Bossy had notched 309 goals, including 75 the previous year. Only one man had ever scored more goals in that junior loop—Guy Lafleur, who had scored five more. "I've been a big goal scorer all my life,' said Bossy. "I am confident I can help the Islanders, but sometimes things don't happen overnight."

The October 11 waiver draft, billed as an equalization draft, was a modification of the old intra-league draft that was discontinued in 1974. It was designed to allow weaker NHL teams a chance to claim some of the excess players belonging to the league's richer clubs. The rules of the draft specified that all teams would be allowed to protect a total of 18 forwards and defensemen and two goalers plus three special players who had more than two professional seasons under their belts. First-year pros were exempt and no club could lose more than three players in the draft, including a maximum of one goalkeeper. As the first pick, the Detroit Red Wings chose center Paul Woods from the Montreal Canadiens for a reported $50,000. The Washington Capitals picked left-winger Dave Forbes from the Boston Bruins for $12,500 and the New York Rangers hoped to solve their goaltending problems by selecting Wayne Thomas. The Rangers paid $12,500 to get Thomas, who had been the Leafs' number-one goaltender the season before until rookie Mike Palmateer came along and unseated him. It was the general consensus of the NHL that the 1977 waiver draft had been nothing more than a chance for teams to clean out their player lists and a waste of time and money.

Spurred by his comeback performance with Team Canada at Vienna the previous spring, Ron Ellis returned to the Toronto Maple Leafs after a two-year absence. At age 32, Ellis felt that he could still help the Leafs by filling a right-wing spot behind Lanny McDonald.

After a long absence, the Canadian Olympic Association called for Canada to get back into Olympic hockey competition. The country had not participated in the games since 1968 at Grenoble. Canada had won its last gold medal in Olympic hockey in 1952.

Rod Gilbert of the New York Rangers walked out of the Rangers' camp September 23, asking that his contract be extended to include the two option years beyond this season. He stood to earn $200,000 for the 1977–78 season. General manager John Ferguson refused and Gilbert asked to be traded. The controversy caused a shock wave throughout the NHL. Most players believed Gilbert was being treated unfairly. "There's no way I'll release him without getting compensation," insisted Ferguson. Gilbert returned to the Rangers after a 16-day walkout and attempted a reconciliation with the general manager. "I told John I'm not sorry, because it's too late for that," said

Gilbert. "I guess we've both been hard on each other."

The playing career of left-winger Stan Gilbertson came to a tragic end. The 33-year-old member of the Pittsburgh Penguins was severely injured in a road mishap and doctors were forced to amputate his mangled leg.

Chuck Lefley of the Blues, in the prime of his hockey life at age 27, stunned his employers and fans by announcing his retirement from hockey. "In the seven years I've played I've had my fill," Lefley said. "I can't see anyone doing anything for a living if he isn't happy doing it."

A landmark decision by U.S. district court judge, T. Emmett Clarke, forced the WHA to honor the contract of underaged junior Ken Linesman, signed by the Birmingham Bulls. The precedent-setting decision would profoundly affect professional hockey's amateur draft. The court declared that the WHA rule prohibiting the signing of underage players was in violation of U.S. anti-trust laws. At the time, the NHL had insisted that the decision would in no way affect their operation.

Dave "Tiger" Williams had been charged with assault following his attack on defenseman Dennis Owchar of the Pittsburgh Penguins in a game at Maple Leaf Gardens on October 20, 1976. In November a judge absolved him of any guilt, ruling that there was no satisfactory evidence that Williams had deliberately used his stick on the Penguins' player.

Phil Esposito became the third player in the history of the NHL to score 600 goals in his career while the Rangers bombed the Vancouver Canucks 5–1 on November 4. Only Gordie Howe with 786 and Bobby Hull with 604 had scored more than Espo while playing in the NHL.

One of hockey's rare and most severe penalties—a life suspension from the game—was handed down by IHL commissioner Bill Beagan when he threw the book at Willie Trognitz of the Dayton Owls for displaying excessive roughness in a game. Trognitz had heavily taped hands when he injured Gary McMonagle of Port Huron in a fight. Then he swung his stick at another player, Archie Henderson, sending him to the hospital with a severe head cut, a broken nose and a concussion.

The mid season saw many trades. The Islanders' Andre St. Laurent was shipped to Detroit for Michel Bergeron. Washington's Hartland Monahan went to Pittsburgh for the Penguins' first amateur draft choice in 1979. Pittsburgh sent Ron Schock to Buffalo in return for Brian Spencer. Two other Pens, Syl Apps and Hartland Monahan, traveled to Los Angeles for Dave Schultz and Gene Carr. Toronto's Inge Hammarstrom was dealt to St. Louis for Jerry Butler and Chicago's Pit Martin moved west to Vancouver for future considerations.

The NHL, the Canadian Major Junior League and the CAHA entered into a new agreement covering reimbursement for drafted amateur players. The agreement called for the NHL to pay junior teams $1,000 for each drafted player, $7,000 for each first-round draft signed to an NHL contract, $5,000 for each second-round player signed to an NHL contract, $4,000 for each third- or later-round draft signed to an NHL pact and $5,000 for each 40 games played by a draft choice in the NHL during the next four seasons, with a $20,000 maximum per player. Ed Chynoweth, chairman of the major leagues, said the deal was a compromise and was considerably less than the juniors had sought from the NHL.

Yvan Cournoyer of the Montreal Canadiens came close to being seriously injured when a fan hurled a whiskey bottle out of the upper regions of the Chicago Stadium at the close of a game on November 13. The bottle shattered against the plexiglass and several splinters lodged in Cournoyer's head. Three stitches were required to close the wound. Unfortunately, the stadium police were unable to locate the bottle thrower.

The Colorado Rockies displayed an aggressive, hustling brand of hockey that made them the early scourge of the Smythe Division and the surprise team in the league. Still, the Rockies failed to attract paying customers at the McNichols Sports Arena. "We had better crowds for junior games in Canada," said second year centerman Paul Gardner.

Walt McKechnie's days with the Washington Capitals appeared to be numbered. The NHL team dropped the controversial center from the active roster and told him to stop practicing with the club. Apparently McKechnie resented the trade that took him to Washington from Detroit. The 10-year veteran had been the leading scorer during his last two years with Detroit.

Under coach Bobby Kromm, the Detroit Red Wings initiated a youth movement unparalleled in the club's history. Critics were silenced when the move seemed to pay off, with seven wins and three ties in their first 15 starts. Most of the punch had been supplied by rookies Reed Larson, Dale McCourt, Paul Woods, Rob Plumb, Bob Ritchie and Rick Bowness.

The NHL introduced a new award—the Frank J. Selke Trophy—which would be awarded annually to the forward who best displayed oustanding defensive play.

The Minnesota North Stars fired Ted Harris as coach and hired his assistant Andre Beaulieu for the job. At the time the team was 5–12–2. Harris would remain with the club as a scout.

The New York Rangers completed a sweeping housecleaning on Thanksgiving Day when they "retired" Rod Gilbert, the highest scorer in the history of the New York hockey team. The Rangers then farmed right-wingers Bill Goldsworthy and Ken Hodge to New Haven.

Mike Bossy was off to a fine start in his rookie season with the New York Islanders, despite the tremendous pressure on him to succeed. "He's learned extremely well," said teammate Bryan Trottier. "He has tremendous puck sense. He always seems to know just when and where the puck is coming from."

The Philadelphia Flyers announced the signing of their first European player, 29-year-old Rudolph Tajcnar, who had defected from Czechoslovakia.

Bobby Orr, on sabbatical after a sixth knee operation, was happily involved with the Chicago Blackhawks' organization in a management capacity. "After two years of doing nothing—I played only 30 games in the last two years—I'm finally involved. Will I play again? I don't know. Not this year."

An elated Dennis Hull turned up as a member of the Detroit Red Wings. The 18-year veteran of the Chicago Blackhawks agreed to terms with the Wings after the Hawks had traded his rights to Detroit for future considerations.

Pete Mahovlich, in his ninth year with the Montreal Canadiens, was traded to the Pittsburgh Penguins on November 29 for 22-year-old Pierre Larouche. Pittsburgh also obtained minor leaguer Peter Lee, while the Canadiens were given future considerations.

Goalie Phil Myre got his wish to be traded from the Atlanta Flames, as that club included the veteran goaltender in a giant six-player swap with the St. Louis Blues. The Flames gave up Myre, defenseman Barry Gibbs and center-winger Curt Bennett to the

Blues in exchange for goaler Yves Belanger, defenseman Dick Redmond and the Blues' top scorer at the time of the deal, right-winger Bob MacMillan.

On December 12 Frank Boucher died at the age of 76 in Kemptville, Ontario. He had played for two of the Rangers' Stanley Cup winning teams (1927–28, 1930–31) and was coach of the team for the third and last time the Rangers had captured the Cup in the 1939–40 season. Boucher had won the Lady Byng Trophy seven times, so often that the league finally awarded it to him in perpetuity.

Rangers' general manager John Ferguson signed veteran defenseman Dallas Smith, 36, to a contract for the rest of the 1977–78 season. Smith, at odds with the Boston management, had "retired" from the Bruins the previous March.

The NHL's version of the Super Series, a 13-game visit from the Spartak team of the Soviet Union and two top Czech teams—Pardubice and Kladno—saw the Philadelphia Flyers and the New York Rangers earn the league a win and a tie to kick off the international series. But it took a 5–2 win by Montreal over Spartak in the final game to salvage a tie in the series (6–6–1).

In January, the Junior World Cup of Hockey was won by the Soviet Union for the second year in a row. Hockey Canada had to write off between $50,000 and $75,000 as the result of poor attendance in Quebec. Only one Canadian, center Wayne Gretzky, was chosen to the tournament All-Star team.

The Soviet Ice Hockey Federation demanded that the Toronto Maple Leafs or the Montreal Canadiens be part of the next Izvestia Cup Tournament in Moscow. The Soviets weren't happy with the kind of opposition the Winnipeg Jets and the Quebec Nordiques had provided in the previous two seasons.

Coached by Scotty Bowman and featuring seven performers from the Stanley Cup champion Canadiens, the 31st annual All-Star game at the Buffalo Memorial Auditorium shaped up as a confrontation between the Canadiens and the combined best of the Islanders and Flyers. Bowman's team from the Wales Conference edged Fred Shero's Campbell Conference All-Stars 3–2 on an overtime goal by hometown favorite Gilbert Perreault.

One of hockey's all-time great performers, Aubrey "Dit" Clapper, died at the age of 70 after a long illness. He had spent 20 brilliant years with the Boston Bruins as one of the game's outstanding defensemen and was elected to the Hockey Hall of Fame on the day he retired from the NHL. Clapper played on three Stanley Cup winning teams with the Bruins in 1929, 1939 and 1941.

Goaler Ed Giacomin, 38, was put on the voluntary retired list by the Detroit Red Wings. All the NHL clubs had waived the 18-year veteran. The Red Wings traded 31-year-old Danny Grant to the Los Angeles Kings for a third-round draft choice and future considerations. He had been one of only two 50-goal scorers in club history (retired Mickey Redmond had been the other).

In other moves, J.P. Parise and Jean Potvin were traded by the New York Islanders in exchange for Wayne Merrick and Darcy Regier of the Cleveland Barons. Eddie Johnston, the 42-year-old goaltender of the St. Louis Blues, was traded to the Chicago Blackhawks in exchange for future considerations. "Age doesn't mean anything," said Johnston. "I'll be 43 next November but I take care of myself. Johnny Bower played goal until he was 47 or 48."

Bobby Orr was named assistant coach by Bob Pulford, Chicago's general manager-coach. "When I took this job under Pully, I said I'd do anything to help him and if I can help by doing some coaching, I will," said Orr.

Veteran Jim Neilson of the Cleveland Barons reached an NHL milestone of 1,000 games on January 26 as the Barons were blanked 5–0 by Chicago. The sad part of the night for the battle-tough Neilson was that only 537 fans had turned up for the game after a snowstorm ravaged the Chicago area.

Overlooked by 14 teams in the NHL draft, rookie Mike Bossy began blasting his way to stardom. In the short span of little more than half a season, the 21-year-old proved to be the big "home-run hitter" the New York Islanders had been longing for. Bossy's statistics at the All-Star break were overwhelming. The rookie from Montreal had totalled 31 goals and 21 assists for 52 points in 42 games. Teamed with Bryan Trottier and big Clark Gillies, Bossy helped to create the most explosive new line to come along since the French Connection.

Greg Neeld, the one-eyed defenseman who had been battling the NHL and the AHL to win a chance to compete in professional hockey, won a decision against the AHL in which a federal judge awarded him $15,000 in damages and ruled that the AHL had violated his human rights by denying him the opportunity to play. "I hope it helps those handicapped people who suffer job discrimination because of their handicaps," said the 23-year-old rear guard, who was employed by Grand Rapids of the IHL.

The Minnesota North Stars, struggling with the NHL's second-worst record, installed veteran defenseman Lou Nanne as both general manager and coach. Thirty-six-year-old Nanne replaced Jackie Gordon as general manager and Andre Beaulieu as coach, becoming the North Stars' third coach of the season. The Stars were 11–35–5 when Nanne took over. The NHL continued its coaching turnover as Leo Boivin threw in the towel in sheer frustration as the St. Louis Blues continued their trip to nowhere. He was replaced by Barclay Plager.

When the Rangers' coach Jean-Guy Talbot nominated goalie Hardy Aastrom to start against the Canadiens at the Forum on February 25, nobody thought Aastrom could possibly fend off the powerful Montreal attack. Montreal hadn't lost in 28 games (23–0–5) and the Rangers hadn't beaten the Habs in Montreal since February 22, 1972. Furthermore, Aastrom hadn't played a single minute in the NHL. Despite the odds, however, the blond Swede was the key performer in the Ranger victory which ended the record Montreal streak.

Members of the NHL Players' Association voted down an owners' request which would have turned the opening round of the playoffs into a best-of-five instead of a best-of-three series.

Bobby Hull, the superstar left-winger of the Winnipeg Jets, led the eight-man group of businessmen who purchased the floundering Winnipeg team. They had one primary aim—to get into the NHL. The first piece of business was to match a lucrative offer made by the New York Rangers to Anders Hedberg and Ulf Nilsson. The Jets had to come within $20,000 of the $1.6 million offer to the Swedes.

In his more familiar role, Hull became only the second player in professional-hockey history to score 1,000 career goals when he scored his 44th of the WHA season on March 11 against the Quebec Nordiques to take his place alongside the great Gordie Howe. The Jets' brilliant left-winger had scored 299 goals in regular WHA season play, 35 in playoffs, 604 in the NHL and 62 goals in Stanley Cup playoffs.

Inge Hammarstrom, 30, of the St. Louis Blues said that he had had enough of NHL life and planned to return to his native Sweden at the close of the 1977–78 season.

The Toronto Maple Leafs swapped Errol Thompson for Detroit's Dan Maloney and a handful of draft picks dating to 1980. Thompson said that he had expected the trade because he didn't fit into coach Roger Neilson's style of play. Maloney was considered perfect for the role and the Leafs were ecstatic about getting the rugged left-winger.

Anders Hedberg of the Winnipeg Jets became pro hockey's first 60-goal scorer of the year when he banged in his 60th and 61st goals as the Jets beat Birmingham 3–1. Later, Hedberg and Ulf Nilsson each signed contracts with the New York Rangers for $2.7 million for two years. WHA president Howard Baldwin, who admitted he was disappointed but not surprised with the departure of the Swedish stars, did not feel the loss would spell the end of the WHA. The league continued its plans to enter its seventh year as a separate major league.

Frank Beaton, one of the pugnacious Birmingham Bulls, was fined $250 and sentenced to a Cincinnati jail for five days. Beaton was found guilty of punching a service-station attendant who had spilled gasoline on his shiny new automobile. The incident occurred in 1976 when he was a member of the Cincinnati Stingers.

The Bruins set an NHL record for the most 20-goal scorers on one team. Rookie Bob Miller made the record possible when he scored his 20th goal of the season on the next-to-last night of the schedule, as the Bruins beat the Leafs 3–1. He became the 11th team member to pot 20 goals as Boston eclipsed the old mark of 10 held jointly by the 1970–71 Bruins and the 1974–75 Montreal Canadiens.

Mike Bossy of the New York Islanders, who had led the NHL rookie race almost from day one, finished as the 1977–78 freshman scoring champion with a whopping 91 points. While Bossy fell short of the league-points record for rookies (which was 95, set by teammate Bryan Trottier) the young star became the NHL's first 50-goal rookie scorer, finishing with 53. Detroit's Reed Larson and Colorado's Barry Beck both closed with 60 points to lead all rookie defensemen.

The Montreal Canadiens finished 16 points ahead of Boston in the overall standings. They won 59 games, lost only 10 and tied 11 for 129 points. Guy Lafleur captured the Art Ross Trophy, finishing on top of the scoring race for the third straight time with 60 goals and 132 points.

In the WHA, the Winnipeg Jets were the only club to win as many as 50 games and the only club to top 100 points. The Jets finished with 102 points, nine ahead of the New England Whalers. Marc Tardif's league-leading point total of 154 set a new major-league regular-season record, surpassing Phil Esposito's 152 total from the 1970–71 season.

THE NHL PLAYOFFS

Preliminary Round (Best of Three)

In the preliminary round of the playoffs, Detroit took the best-of-three series against Atlanta with relative ease in two straight games. Colorado made things more difficult for Philadelphia than was expected, but, although the games were close, Philadelphia came out with back-to-back wins. The Los Angeles Kings were pathetic in losing two straight to the Toronto Maple Leafs. Eight days later, Bob Berry was introduced as the Kings' new coach replacing Ron Stewart. Berry became the eighth coach in the 11-year history of the team. At 34, he was also the youngest coach in the NHL. Buffalo played true to form by winning a pair of games at home over the Rangers by 4–1 scores and eliminating New York by two games to one.

Quarter-Finals (Best of Seven)

In round two, the Boston Bruins became the first team to reach the semi-finals with an impressive four-game sweep of the Chicago Blackhawks. Two of the games were decided in overtime. The Montreal Canadiens finally unleashed their potent offense, bombing the Detroit Red Wings 8–0 in the fourth game of their series. Back in Montreal, the Habs won game five and advanced to the semi-finals. It appeared to be a home-ice series between the Philadelphia Flyers and the Buffalo Sabres when the Flyers took the first two games in the Spectrum and the Sabres won easily back on home ice. But the Flyers bounced back with a win in game four and another in game five back at the Spectrum, where they clinched the series.

The biggest surprise of the quarter-finals occurred when the Toronto Maple Leafs forced the New York Islanders to game seven in one of the most dramatic series in Stanley Cup history. At 4:13 of overtime in the deciding game, winger Lanny McDonald took a pass from Ian Turnbull and blasted the puck past Chico Resch. The Islanders dream of the Cup in 1978 came to an abrupt end.

Semi-Finals (Best of Seven)

With the league's best offense, the Canadiens swept through the battered Leafs, winning four straight games. Boston scored a pair of victories at home to open their series against the Philadelphia Flyers. The Flyers scrambled back to win game three, then dropped games four and five. The fifth game in Boston seesawed back and forth through the first two periods with the score tied at 3–3. Boston was able to grab command in the final frame, however, and went on to win 6–3.

The Stanley Cup Finals (Best of Seven)

On May 25 at the Boston Garden, the mighty Montreal Canadiens won their 21st Stanley Cup, their third in a row. In a convincing fashion they were able to defeat a tough, gutsy Boston team 4–1 in the sixth game of the series. Don Marcotte of the Boston Bruins summed things up: "They're amazing, absolutely amazing. They skate, skate and skate for 60 minutes and have an unlimited supply of players who work and never stop working. You can't beat the Canadiens unless you play just as great…and we didn't."

While North American interest was focused on the professional-hockey playoffs, overseas the Soviet Union upset Czechoslovakia to grab the gold in the World Ice Hockey Championship. Team Canada took home the bronze medal.

In the WHA, the Winnipeg Jets were the class of the league, finishing on top with 50 victories and 102 points.

THE WHA PLAYOFFS

Preliminary Round (Best of Seven)

It was a race to the playoff wire between Birmingham and Cincinnati, both battling for sixth place and a berth in the post-season battles. The Bulls finished the season two points up on Cincinnati. The Bulls' hopes for an Avco Cup were quickly extinguished, however, by the Winnipeg Jets, who trounced them four games to one in the opening round of the playoffs. By winning, the Jets earned a bye into the finals. The Quebec Nordiques had little trouble disposing of Houston in six games. It was the earliest the Aeros had been eliminated in six years of post-season competition.

Meanwhile, New England's famous father-son combination was busy ousting Edmonton. Gordie Howe, who was 50 years old and finishing his 30th professional-hockey season with the Whalers, became a grandfather for the first time when his son Mark's wife gave birth to an eight-pound, seven-ounce boy at St. Francis Hospital in Hartford. Neither Gordie nor Mark was present for the occasion—both were in Edmonton performing in a WHA playoff game with the Whalers. Gordie celebrated with a goal and Mark had a pair of assists as the Whalers won the game. They went on to win the series 4-1.

Semi-Finals (Best of Seven)

In the follow-up series against Quebec, the Whalers' Mark Howe was brilliant, especially in game five when he produced two goals and three assists in a 6–3 triumph. That victory eliminated the Nordiques and propelled the Whalers into the finals with Winnipeg.

Avco Cup Finals (Best of Seven)

The Winnipeg Jets won their second Avco Trophy in three years by sweeping their best-of-seven series in four games against the New England Whalers. Swedish stars Anders Hedberg and Ulf Nilsson said farewell to their Winnipeg fans in an appropriate manner—by leading the Jets to the championship. The Swedes, who were signed to the NHL's New York Rangers, sparkled in the deciding game. Hedberg scored twice and Nilsson assisted on three goals in the Jets' 5–3 victory.

1978–79

In June 1978, George and Gordon Gund, owners of the Cleveland Barons, approached both Washington and Vancouver about a merger but were rebuffed. Minnesota, however, was delighted to accept. The NHL governors had never been faced with such a proposition before but they moved quickly and in two days the Gunds had folded the Barons, purchased a majority interest in the North Stars and merged the two teams. The merger gave the Stars such quality forwards as Denis Maruk, Al MacAdam, Tim Young and Per-Olov Brasar, not to mention the number-one draft choice Bobby Smith, who scored 192 points in his last year of the juniors. After grasping complete control of the 11-year-old Minnesota North Star franchise, George and Gordon Gund made it quite clear that general manager Lou Nanne would have full authority in the hockey club and that coach Harry Howell would handle the players.

The NHL rejected a proposal that would have returned overtime play to its regular-league schedule. The league also left the decision to make helmets mandatory up to a players' vote and added time-outs to the game (one 30-second time-out per team per game).

Tony McKegney, a former Kingston Canadians' scoring star, was informed he would not be signed by the Birmingham Bulls of the WHA because his asking price was too high and because some Bulls' season-ticket holders had complained that McKegney was black. The 20-year-old left-winger was shocked to encounter racism in hockey. "I never really considered color as being much of a factor in hockey," he said. "I thought all those kinds of feelings were over with years ago."

Elsewhere in the WHA, Cincinnati coach Jacques Demers turned down a contract extension from the Stingers and signed on as coach of the Quebec Nordiques. Maurice Filion, the Nordiques' general manager, had taken over the coaching reins on an interim basis after firing Marc Boileau.

The signing of former Houston Aeros' coach, Bill Dineen, was perhaps the biggest off-season plus for the New England Whalers. As the winningest coach in WHA history there was no doubt about his expertise as a hockey man. Dineen succeeded Harry Neale, who had been hired as the new Vancouver Canucks' coach and given a three-year contract from general manager Jake Milford. John Ferguson was ousted as the New York Rangers' general manager and Fred Shero replaced him in the dual role of general manager-coach.

Veteran center Andre Lacroix was obtained by the Whalers from Winnipeg "for future considerations." He was introduced as the "premier center of the WHA."

Jacques Plante, the goalie who had introduced the modern face mask to the NHL, was inducted into the Hockey Hall of Fame, along with defenseman Marcel Pronovost and right-winger Andy Bathgate. They were joined by builders Sam Pollock, Thayer Tutt and the late John Paris Bicknell.

The NHL selected 234 players in the 1978 amateur draft. It was the second-biggest plunge into the amateur player field since the draft began in 1963. Bobby Smith of the Ottawa 67s became the number-one pick of the field with Minnesota claiming the six-foot-four center, touted as Canada's best junior player of the year. Washington followed in choosing Ryan Walter from Seattle of the WCHL, St. Louis took Wayne Babych of Portland as the third pick and Vancouver chose Bill Derlago of Brandon, a prolific 89-goal scorer in the WCHL during the previous season. Players drafted in the late rounds included Paul MacLean (109th), Craig McTavish (153rd), Darryl Sutter (179th) and Chris Nilan (331st). A total of 80 collegians were taken, a sizeable increase from 51 the previous year.

The Montreal Canadiens and the New York Islanders dominated the NHL's individual awards and All-Star teams. Led by Guy Lafleur, who repeated as both the Art Ross Trophy and Hart Memorial Trophy winner, Montreal players took five of nine major awards. Larry Robinson took home the Conn Smythe Trophy as the most valuable playoff performer. Ken Dryden and Michel Larocque shared the Vezina and Bob Gainey captured the NHL's newest award—the Frank J. Selke Trophy as the best defensive forward. The Islanders' Denis Potvin captured the Norris Trophy as best defenseman, Mike Bossy received the Calder Trophy as rookie of the year and Kings' center Butch Goring was voted the Lady Byng Trophy.

The NHL dealt harshly with Don Murdoch of the New York Rangers. Murdoch was suspended for the entire 1978–79 league season and was fined $500 for actions that began on August 12, 1977, when he was arrested at the Toronto International Airport for carrying cocaine across the border. He pleaded guilty to possession of 4.8 grams of cocaine and was fined $400 by a Toronto judge. The severity of the NHL's punishment shocked both the hockey world and the New York organization. The suspension was the most startling handed to an NHL player since the 1946 season, when the league threw the book at Don Gallinger and Billy Taylor for allegedly wagering on the results of games. Neither player was allowed back to play in the league.

After wearing the Boston uniform longer than any other player—21 years—John Bucyk announced his retirement. "We've put a deal together for Bucyk," said Bruins' general manager Harry Sinden after disclosing the end of the 43-year-old Bucyk's career. "We want him to stay with the Bruins for a long time."

The Los Angeles Kings' most popular player, Rogie Vachon, signed a five-year deal with Detroit for a reported $325,000 a year. The Kings received 21-year-old center Dale McCourt as compensation. Upset with the turn of events, McCourt filed suit in a United States district court in an attempt to block his assignment to the Kings. A restraining order was granted and was expected to have far-reaching effects on the NHL's contract situation. U.S. district court judge Robert DeMascio granted the order, ruling that compensation requirements for NHL teams signing free agents were an illegal restraint of trade. The ruling would allow the 21-year-old McCourt to report to training camp and play with Detroit until the suit was heard.

Molson Breweries of Canada Ltd. agreed to pay $20 million to Carena-Bancorp Inc., outbidding John Labatt Ltd. and two other companies for the Montreal Canadiens. Molson's president Morgan McCammon said, "We have no intention of changing the management of the Canadiens." But rumors began to circulate that general manager Sam Pollock was on his way out. Pollock was a five percent shareholder of Carena-Bancorp.

The NHL board of governors announced the approval of the sale of the Colorado Rockies from Denver oilman Jack A. Vickers to New Jersey trucker Arthur E. Imperatore. It was hoped that this latest transaction would be the final obstacle in ensuring that the people of Denver would support an NHL team.

The WHA, plagued by uncertainty as to whether it would function as a major league in the coming season, intensified its rivalry with the NHL. Indianapolis Racers' owner Nelson Skalbania signed 17-year-old Wayne Gretzky, star of the Sault Ste. Marie Greyhounds and the Ontario Major Junior League's second-highest scorer, to a seven-year personal services contract for an estimated $1.7 million. Gretzky still had three years of junior eligibility remaining. The signing, which took place less than 24 hours before the start of the NHL summer meetings, drew much criticism from the rival league. According to Skalbania, he had decided to go after the much-heralded junior because of the NHL's greed in stealing away WHA free agents without compensation, such as Ulf Nilsson, Anders Hedberg and Dan Labraaten of the Winnipeg Jets.

Birmingham Bulls' owner John Bassett caused more headaches by signing seven juniors in all. Goaltender Pat Riggin, forwards Keith Crowder, Rick Vaive and Michel Goulet and defensemen Craig Hartsburg, Gaston Gingras and Rob Ramage, all reportedly agreed to one-year contracts calling for $60,000. "A kid of 18 can drink booze, fight in the army, drive a car and go to jail," said Bassett, "and I can't, for the life of me, figure out why they can't play pro hockey."

According to league president Howard Baldwin, Bassett's contracts would not be accepted by the WHA's central registry. But, in time, they were. So was the contract of Cincinnati's star rookie, Mike Gartner.

Since the unexpected loss to Toronto in the seventh game of the Stanley Cup quarter-finals, the New York Islanders had lost their president Roy Boe and had been completely reorganized under the direction of John O. Pickett and general manager Bill Torrey. The NHL accepted the Islander plan for a "relaxed payment" plan for the $6.1 million the Islanders owed individual teams. Torrey, amidst the summer's trauma, found time to sign John Tonelli, the Isles' second pick in the 1977 amateur draft. A former Toronto Marlboro, Tonelli had three years with the WHA Houston Aeros under his belt and once played on a line with Mark and Gordie Howe.

On September 18, 1978, Bobby Orr stepped onto the Chicago Stadium ice for the beginning of another comeback. Orr said there was no pressure on him from anyone to play. In fact, there was more pressure for him not to play. "If I can't help the Blackhawks be better, then I won't take a spot on the roster of somebody who could. I will hang them up and that will be it. Finished. I'll retire forever."

Many viewed the arrival in New York of the "super Swedes"—Anders Hedberg and Ulf Nilsson—along with Fred Shero, as the big bombshell of the off season. Ranger fans had been thirsting for a cup winner for the last 38 years and the excitement of seeing Hedberg and Nilsson in Ranger jerseys had been building up over the months. New Yorkers could hardly wait for the night of October 12 when they would debut in the NHL against Shero's old team, the Philadelphia Flyers. The Flyers were sporting a new look with rookie head coach Bob McCammon and talented newcomers Behn Wilson and Ken Linseman. Linseman was purchased from the Birmingham Bulls for a reported $500,000.

After 31 years in the Canadiens' organization, vice-president and general manager Sam Pollock departed. His retirement saw Irving Grundman emerge to fill the newly created post of executive vice-president and managing director. This made Grundman responsible for both the Forum and the Canadiens, the first time one man had handled both positions since Pollock succeeded Frank Selke, Sr., in 1964.

The early season saw the retirement of many veteran players. The St. Louis Blues lost captain Red Berenson, Jimmy Roberts and Claude Larose. Berenson was the first big star of the NHL's Western Division following the league's 1967 expansion and was the first modern-era player to score six goals in a game. He was named assistant coach to Bob Plager. The Pittsburgh Penguins were another club to lose more than one player to retirement with Lowell MacDonald, who had battled back from numerous knee injuries, and 23-year-old Tom Edur giving up the game for religious reasons. Three NHL goaltenders also retired: Gerry Desjardins of Buffalo, Cesare Maniago, who finished his career with Vancouver, and Eddie Johnston, who played with St. Louis and Chicago the year before. Derek Sanderson informed the Boston Bruins that he was through with the game. Sanderson, 32, said that his chronic back ailment discouraged him in his latest comeback bid.

John Ziegler, president of the NHL, stated that he was fully prepared to go all the way to the Supreme Court, if that's what it took, to ultimately resolve the litigation between

Dale McCourt and the proponents of the NHL's collective bargaining agreement.

> At issue [said Ziegler] is the effectiveness of the collective bargaining agreement set in 1975 and amended a year ago. The equalization system was agreed to by the NHL Players' Association. What we have here is a player attacking the very position his association agreed to. If he can violate his collective bargaining agreement and if it stands up in court ... we've got problems.

The falling Canadian dollar was driving the NHL Players' Association to seek remuneration for their services in U.S. currency rather than in Canadian funds. The players hoped that all league business could be conducted in U.S. dollars. Unlike major-league baseball, where all teams dealt in American currency, including Toronto and Montreal, the NHL's Canadian teams were reimbursed in Canadian dollars. The players pointed out that a $200,000 contract with the Canadiens, Leafs or Canucks would actually be worth only $170,000 due to the lower Canadian dollar.

Butch Goring, 29, had been making less than $100,000 a year with the Los Angeles Kings but this season he was starting out on a new five-year contract calling for an estimated $250,000 a year. "Edmonton of the WHA made me a great offer and I was on my way until the Kings topped it at the last minute," said Goring.

Wayne Gretzky was busy impressing his Indianapolis teammates. Defenseman Kevin Morrison said, "He's got more moves than a snake on a hot bed of coals. They said he's slow, but I don't think he is." Gretzky's teammates wasted no time in picking a nickname for their young superstar. "We call him Brinks," said Kevin Nugent. "He's got all the dough." Meanwhile, right-winger Mark Napier, left-winger Cam Connor and defenseman Rod Langway, all with WHA experience, signed with the Montreal Canadiens.

With the Rangers' exhibition season over, it was very evident that Anders Hedberg and Ulf Nilsson were everything they were cracked up to be. They were adjusting well to the style of play in the NHL and they certainly could adapt to Fred Shero's system.

On October 3, 88-year-old J. Cooper Smeaton, a trustee of the Stanley Cup since 1946 and a member of the NHL's Hall of Fame, died of a heart attack in Montreal's Royal Victoria Hospital. Smeaton was involved in officiating for more than a quarter of a century.

As the New York Islanders entered the 1978–79 season they rated just behind the Montreal Canadiens as the team with the most depth. "I would love to have some of the guys the Islanders can't use," noted a rival NHL general manager.

On the night of October 3, over 14,000 fans came to Detroit's Olympia Stadium to see Gordie Howe of the New England Whalers step on the ice for the first time since the spring of 1971. Prior to the exhibition game with the Red Wings, Howe had received a standing ovation that had lasted for over seven minutes. After the game was over and Howe had left the ice, his fans gave him a thunderous ovation that brought back memories of his Red Wing glory days. Howe, 50 years old and going into his 31st year as an active player, was beginning his seventh season of WHA play. His fantastic career, which had spanned four decades, had seen him set almost every hockey record imaginable. He was the game's all-time leading scorer and came into the 1978–79 season needing just one point to give him 2,500. He became the first player in the history of the game to reach the 1,000-goal plateau the previous December. Since that time fellow great Bobby Hull of the Winnipeg Jets had also hit that magic number.

The Washington Capitals shocked fans by firing head coach Tommy McVie two days before the hockey team's opener in Los Angeles. Owner Abe Pollin told McVie that he was a very dedicated employee, "a damn good coach," but that he wouldn't be needed anymore. McVie's replacement was Dan Belisle, 41, who was the general manager and coach of the Philadelphia Firebirds of the American Hockey League.

In the 1978 waiver draft, Washington chose defenseman Pierre Bouchard from the Montreal Canadiens for $2,500. Bouchard was later sent back to Montreal for left-winger Rod Schutt, but the trade was voided by the NHL. Bouchard then announced his retirement from hockey. He said he would rather retire than play for Washington. St. Louis had the second choice and selected centerman Larry Giroux from Detroit. After Vancouver, Colorado and Pittsburgh passed, the New York Rangers took Pierre Plante, also from Detroit. Jim Lorentz of Buffalo became the fourth player taken in the first round. Detroit acquired him for $2,500, but two days after the draft Lorentz informed the Red Wings that he was retiring.

At 17, Wayne Gretzky was making big headlines. Already he was being called "the Great Gretzky". According to Rudy Pilous, who had seen his share of young hockey players during his tenures with the Chicago Blackhawks and the Winnipeg Jets, "He's still a boy, but he's out there holding his own with men. What a bright future he has." Gretzky had been concerned about going to Indianapolis. "Let's face it," said Gretzky, "I could have fallen on my face and made a fool of myself, but I was lucky to have players who were so good to play with and who made me feel at home."

Fifteen years after the Leafs first regarded him as a franchise player, 31-year-old Walt McKechnie received what could have been the largest break of his hockey career. Unwanted by the North Stars, he was needed by the Leafs at a time when he figured his career was over. McKechnie ended up as a starting center on a contending team.

The Boston Bruins missed their defensive great Brad Park after he underwent surgery for removal of a torn cartilage in his right knee on October 14. He would be out for more than five weeks. "There's no team in the league that depends on a guy like we do Brad Park," said coach Don Cherry.

The Islanders' John Tonelli, after three years as an underage junior with the Houston Aeros of the WHA, burst upon the NHL scene this season with an impact like that of his teammate Mike Bossy. Tonelli had four goals in his first six games, including a game winner against the Canadiens. "Now I have confidence that I can play in the NHL," said the 21-year-old Tonelli.

Bobby Smith, the number-one draft choice who scored 69 goals in 62 games as a junior, typified Minnesota's bumpy start. In his first five NHL games, the six-foot-four centerman had only one goal and an assist, and those two came in a 7–2 victory over Vancouver.

The Washington Capitals dealt away a first- and a second-round draft choice in 1979 to obtain Dennis Maruk from the Minnesota North Stars and Michel Bergeron from the New York Islanders.

The Pittsburgh Penguins elected 28-year-old Orest Kindrachuk as team captain, replacing Jean Pronovost who had been traded to the Atlanta Flames. Kindrachuk had come to the Penguins during the off season from the Philadelphia Flyers, along with defenseman Tom Bladon and left-winger Ross Lonsberry. In exchange, Pittsburgh surrendered their number-one draft choice in the amateur draft.

In early November the "Golden Jet," Bobby Hull, shocked the hockey world by announcing his retirement from pro hockey. After an illustrious 22-year pro career that saw him shatter goal scoring records in both the NHL and the WHA, Hull decided to call it quits. He put to rest rumors that he would leave the Jets to be reunited with Ulf Nilsson and Anders Hedberg in New York with the Rangers.

The Edmonton Oilers dropped a bombshell on the hockey world and wound up with three players almost certain to lift the team in the WHA standings. Owner Peter Pocklington swung a deal for 17-year-old star Wayne Gretzky, rugged Peter Driscoll and promising Ed Mio from the Indianapolis Racers. The announced figure was $850,000 for the three players. Pocklington said that he had become involved in the transaction because of his commitment to provide the best possible team for Edmonton fans. Indianapolis Racer fans were furious. When news of the sale broke in Indianapolis, the Racer office was flooded with phone calls from irate fans. One season-ticket holder said that he would sue if he didn't get his money back.

In a dramatic and passionate farewell on November 8, 30-year-old Bobby Orr announced his retirement from hockey. Six knee operations had drained Orr's mobility on the ice and he was the first to admit that he felt he was taking money from the Chicago Blackhawks under false pretenses. "I had to try the knee once more. I owed it to myself," Orr commented. "And if I had to do it all again, I would do it the same way." Orr scored 264 goals and assisted on 624 others in a sensational 10-year career with the Boston Bruins. He won the Norris eight times as the NHL's best defenseman, the Hart three times as MVP and won the Ross Trophy as NHL scoring champion twice—a feat unparalleled in the history of hockey. The game would not be the same without him.

According to NHL president John Ziegler, the league was not entertaining any thought of taking in the four best WHA teams in new merger talks as had been rumoured. Ziegler stated that no discussions were occurring at any level, particularly since the Dale McCourt case had come along to upset the NHL's compensation rule for free agents. Ziegler said nothing would be done until the McCourt issue was settled.

Wilf Paiement received a 15-game suspension and was fined $500 for clubbing Dennis Polonich of Detroit in a game played on October 25. Paiement's ban ranked behind Eddie Shore's 16-game suspension in 1933 for fracturing Ace Bailey's skull, and was higher than Wayne Maki's 13-game sentence for cracking Ted Green over the head in Ottawa during a 1969 exhibition game.

Early in the new season, the Washington franchise was in trouble. Going into their ninth home date, the Caps still hadn't drawn 10,000 fans to a single game. Owner Abe Pollin had hoped for 10,000 season-ticket holders alone. Instead, he had 4,200 and the average crowd was under 7,000, down an average of 3,800 from the year before.

Harry Howell, the 45-year-old coach of the Minnesota North Stars stepped aside to allow his aide Glen Sonmor to take over the reins of the NHL club. Howell was made chief of scouting. The NHL underwent another coaching change when the Colorado Rockies dismissed Pat Kelly and brought Aldo Guidolin onto the coaching scene as his replacement. Guidolin, 46, stepped up from his post as chief scout to assume the head coaching job.

Through the first 16 games of the 1978–79 season, the Atlanta Flames were the talk of the NHL. With a 12–2–2 record the Flames were enjoying increased attendance, up some 20,000 in their first nine home games.

John Ferguson, who was replaced as general manager of the New York Rangers by Fred Shero the previous summer, signed a five-year contract as vice-president and general manager with the Winnipeg Jets of the WHA. The Buffalo Sabres went shopping for a new general manager and head coach after Punch Imlach and Marcel Pronovost were fired for failing to motivate the struggling Sabres. The Sabres brought in former Buffalo player Billy Inglis as interim coach and elevated John Andersen to the new role of director of player personnel.

The NHL sent a team of no-name players to the 1978 Izvestia Hockey tournament in Moscow on December 16–22. Predictably, the Soviet Union captured the gold medal and Czechoslovakia finished second. Team NHL's third-place finish was the surprise of the tournament.

A series of spinal tests on Montreal Canadiens' captain Yvan Cournoyer revealed what those close to the team suspected—that a second disc operation was necessary and the speedy right-winger would be finished for the season. It came at the worst possible time for coach Scotty Bowman and the Canadiens, during a month-long siege which had knocked as many as seven players out of the lineup for varying lengths of time.

The WHA tempted the NHL with a blockbuster offer of almost $5 million per team for the admission of five of its franchises to the NHL. It appeared that the offer might have finally broken the back of hard-line resistance to the WHA. "I am more optimistic than in the past about the WHA situation," said NHL president John Ziegler. "It is being viewed from a business point of view now rather than emotionally as it was in the past."

Since his arrival in Philadelphia, Ken Linseman hadn't performed like the same player who had scored 38 goals and 38 assists as a 19-year-old rookie for Birmingham. He no longer seemed like the player who was described as a Clarke-type winner and agitator, so coach Bob McCammon dropped him down to the minors. "He's a competitive kid," said McCammon. "He'll learn and he'll be back."

Before the WHA season reached the halfway mark, the Indianapolis Racers had folded. "The incentive to keep writing checks to cover the cost of playing hockey in Indianapolis seems ludicrous," stated owner Nelson Skalbania. Three thousand season-ticket holders were not going to let Skalbania off the hook. They wanted their money back. Racer fans sought more than $20 million in a lawsuit filed against Skalbania in Indianapolis county Supreme Court.

The NHL dealt with another series of stick-swinging events and abuse of officials by handing out suspensions and fines, the most spectacular being Paul Holmgren's banishment for knocking an opponent over the head. NHL executive vice-president Brian O'Neill suspended Holmgren for six games and fined him $200 for bringing his hockey stick down on Carol Vadnais of the Rangers with a two-handed motion.

Thirty games into the season the Toronto Maple Leafs were one of the NHL's biggest disappointments. Instead of challenging Boston for the Adams Division title, the Leafs were staggering along at a .500 pace. Owner Harold Ballard claimed that his team deserved pity more than criticism, that coach Neilson was by far the best man for the job and he wasn't interested in hiring Buffalo's recently fired general manager Punch Imlach.

The NHL's sizzling three-way fight for first-place honors overall continued to be a dogfight from week to week with Montreal, Boston and the New York Islanders squarely in the battle.

Wayne Gretzky and his Edmonton Oilers teammates struggled through one of the lowest stretches of the season during one week in December until Gretzky, almost single-handedly, pulled them out of the slump. The 17-year-old superstar scored three goals, his first professional hat trick, as Edmonton bumped the Cincinnati Stingers 5–2, ending a five-game losing streak.

Phil Esposito of the New York Rangers reached another scoring milestone when he counted his 650th NHL career goal the night of December 22 against Detroit. Including playoffs, the big centerman had achieved 700.

NHL president John Ziegler announced that 22-year-old right-winger Don Murdoch, who had been convicted of cocaine possession, would be eligible to play in the last 40 games of the 1978–79 season. "I've always lived by the rule that you learn by your mistakes," Murdoch said. "I don't believe that a person should be condemned his whole life for making one mistake."

In January, teenage stars Wayne Gretzky, Mike Gartner and Rob Ramage joined forces with oldtimer Gordie Howe on the WHA All-Star team. The line of Gretzky, Gordie Howe and Mark Howe was dazzling in a three-game sweep of the Soviet Union's Moscow Dynamo team.

Wayne Gretzky celebrated his 18th birthday on January 26 by signing a whopping 21-year contract, worth approximately $4 million to $5 million, with the WHA Oilers. The signing—which took place at center ice before 12,000 fans—linked Gretzky with the team through to the 1999 season and gave him the longest contract ever signed in hockey. Although the contract contained no escape clause for either party, Gretzky would be able to renegotiate the pact after 10 years. "There's more pressure on me now," said Gretzky after the signing, "because with this contract I know I'm going to have to go out and earn it."

Wayne Babych was enduring the worst part of his rookie season—he was out of action with a broken ankle. Babych, the St. Louis Blues' top draft choice for the 1978–79 season, had been spectacular. About 20 minutes before his injury, he broke the Blues' record for most goals by a rookie with his 21st goal of the season.

Rookie coach Bob McCammon of the Philadelphia Flyers did a lot of juggling in an attempt to give the Islanders a run for the Patrick Division title. But after 50 games the Flyers were in last place in their division with a record of 22–17–11. General manager Keith Allen fired McCammon and assistant coach Terry Crisp and installed 36-year-old Pat Quinn in the head coaching job.

Bill Torrey of the Islanders was chosen as the general manager of the NHL's All-Star team, which would oppose the Soviet Union in the Challenge Cup series scheduled for February 8–11 at Madison Square Garden. Cliff Fletcher of Atlanta and Harry Sinden of Boston would assist Torrey. The NHL and the Soviet Union had their best players representing their teams in the showdown. The NHL took the first game 4–2. The ecstatic NHL players seemed surprised at the ease with which they had been able to beat the Soviets. But the NHL's general manager Bill Torrey was wary. "The Russians can adjust. They're in this to be the best ... and they will adjust. You'll see." And adjust they did. The Soviets came back to defeat the NHL team 5–4 in the second game. This time the competition was fierce and the NHL was forced to a third and deciding game. In what should have been an exciting game, the Soviets badly outplayed the NHL squad, clobbering them 6–0. "We can no longer call this game ours," said Serge Savard. "For the last five or six years we have been developing goons while they have been developing good players."

The 1979 Canada Cup was abandoned because of a dispute between Hockey Canada, an umbrella group comprised of several hockey bodies, and one of those bodies, the Canadian Amateur Hockey Association (CAHA). The scrap was over which group controlled the Canadian entry in the world junior championships, Hockey Canada or the CAHA. Unfortunately, Hockey Canada was willing to cancel the Canada Cup on the principle that it controlled the international arrangements. Many NHL stars were hoping that the difficulties could be resolved so that they could have another chance against the Soviets after their embarrassing defeat at the Challenge Cup.

Phil Esposito of the New York Rangers scored his 30th career hat trick on February 18—the most ever recorded in NHL history. Bobby Hull had had 28 during his career. Late in February, another scoring ace, veteran Stan Mikita of the Chicago Blackhawks, became the sixth-highest scorer of all time. Mikita, the second-oldest player active in the NHL at 38 years of age, scored his 14th goal of the season to raise his all-time career total to 534 goals.

The Los Angeles Kings, who were looking for a left-winger to work on Marcel Dionne's line with right-winger Dave Taylor, recalled Charlie Simmer from Springfield of the American League.

The Washington Capitals signed veteran center, 35-year-old Dennis Hextall, who had been cut by Detroit, for the remainder of the season and the following year.

Mike Bossy, the electrifying young right-winger of the New York Islanders, tied the consecutive-game scoring mark at 10 and became the first player to register the quickest 100 goals in a two-year starting period. Bossy also won the distinction of being pro hockey's first 50-goal scorer of the 1978–79 season.

Despite the fact that the Colorado Rockies stood to lose close to $2 million in the 1979–80 season, club president Armand Pohan announced that the Rockies would remain in Denver.

Bernie Parent of the Philadelphia Flyers suffered a 1,000,000–1 injury when a stick blade point poked through the unprotected eye space of the goalie's mask in a game against the Rangers. The incident left him with two small conjunctival tears in his right eye. The Flyers and his fans were crossing their fingers that the great goaltender's career would not be over.

There were many rookie standouts in the 1978–79 season. Ryan Walter of the Washington Capitals commanded attention because of strong leadership qualities. Thomas Gradin amazed Vancouver fans despite a series of injuries. Wayne Babych of St. Louis was a natural scorer who keyed the club's big line. And Bobby Smith, the NHL's number-one draft choice, overcame a slow start in Minnesota to lead all rookies in scoring in March.

In a startling series of moves, Maple Leafs' owner Harold Ballard issued a "must-win" decree to his team, fired coach Roger Neilson after a 2–1 loss to Montreal and then reinstated him as coach prior to a game with Philadelphia two nights later. Neilson was given wide support by his players immediately before and after his firing, and it was pressure from them, led by captain Darryl Sittler who met with Ballard in front of all the players, which convinced the owner to rehire Neilson.

On March 13, the Atlanta Flames and the Chicago Blackhawks completed a very surprising trade. Atlanta gave up its all-time leading scorer Tom Lysiak, second-year left-winger Harold Phillipoff (a second-year player who had made a big hit the previous year with his aggressive style), two young, hard-hitting defensemen Pat Ribble and Greg Fox, and minor-league defenseman Miles Zaharko. The Hawks parted with their leading scorer, Ivan Boldirev, their best defenseman and crowd favorite, hard-hitting Phil Russell, and their fastest skater, left-winger Darcy Rota. The trade didn't sit well with the fans of either city.

Bobby Hull pulled his son, Bobby Hull, Jr., off the Lethbridge Broncos of the Western Major Hockey League because he felt that the 17-year-old right-winger wasn't learning a thing and he didn't like the attitude of the league. The elder Hull said that he wanted to put his son in a European league where he could better develop his hockey skills. He added that he was disgusted with the violence in the NHL, WHA and in the junior games. Marcel Dionne also voiced regret at the level of violence in hockey in the wake of 380 penalty minutes which were assessed in a Philadelphia–Los Angeles brawl: "If the owners don't clean up this sport I'll quit. What's the league waiting for, somebody to die out there?"

By a vote of 14–3, the NHL approved a plan for expansion which would take effect at the beginning of the 1979–80 season. The NHL would absorb the WHA's four strongest franchises—the Quebec Nordiques, the New England Whalers, the Winnipeg Jets and the Edmonton Oilers—and become a 21-team league with no major competition. For the privilege of joining the NHL, each one of the WHA teams was to pay a sum of $6 million. The remaining two WHA teams—the Cincinnati Stingers and the Birmingham Bulls—would be dissolved. After a seven-year-long war that saw the rise and fall of 30 teams and millions of dollars spent on franchise fees, player salaries and legal bills, the battle between the rival leagues was over.

Bill Dineen's one-year sojourn as coach of the New England Whalers was over as well. The Whalers fired the former two-time WHA coach of the year and replaced him with Don Blackburn.

The amazing New York Islanders were the overall point leaders for this NHL season, ending the three-year domination of the Montreal Canadiens. The Islanders were led throughout the season by Bryan Trottier (134 points), Mike Bossy (69 goals), Denis Potvin and the goaltending duo of Glenn Resch and Billy Smith.

THE NHL PLAYOFFS

Preliminary Round (Best of Three)

In the preliminary round of the Stanley Cup playoffs, the New York Rangers held the Kings' big line of Taylor, Dionne and Simmer to just one goal and swept L.A. in two straight games. Philadelphia eliminated Vancouver 2–1, Toronto pushed Atlanta aside 2–0 and Pittsburgh defeated Buffalo 2–1.

Quarter-Finals (Best of Seven)

In quarter-final play, Montreal swept past Toronto, Boston ousted Pittsburgh and the Islanders dumped Chicago. All three series were extremely one-sided, four-games-to-none matchups. In the fourth series, the Rangers outscored Philadelphia 28 goals to eight and took the series 4–1. The 28 goals were the most the Rangers had ever scored in any series in their history.

Semi-Finals (Best of Seven)

The Stanley Cup semi-finals pitted the Islanders against the Rangers and the Bruins versus the Canadiens. Home ice was a plus for both teams when the Canadiens met the Bruins. Both clubs won three times at home but the Bruins seemed to have the upper hand in game seven played at the Montreal Forum. With just 3:59 to play, Rick Middleton scored on a Boston power play pushing the Bruins into a 4–3 lead. For a minute and a half Boston had a hold on the series. But suddenly Don Cherry's Bruins were caught with too many men on the ice. The underdog Bruins were just 74 seconds away from a berth in the finals when a power-play goal by Guy Lafleur forced the game into overtime. In overtime, Yvon Lambert deflected a shot off the pads of Gilles Gilbert and into the net for a 5–4 Montreal victory.

In the other semi-final series, the Rangers took charge and outworked the Islanders to earn a surprising six-game upset. Outstanding goaltending by John Davidson was a key factor in the victory. Now only one team stood between the Rangers and their first Stanley Cup in 39 years.

The Stanley Cup Finals (Best of Seven)

In game one of the Stanley Cup finals, the Rangers shocked the Canadiens 4–1 with an amazing display of opportunistic scoring when they capitalized on mistakes by an undermanned Canadiens' defense crew. Ranger coach Fred Shero was impressed by the play of Ulf Nilsson, back in the lineup after breaking an ankle only 10 weeks prior to the game. Montreal goalie Ken Dryden, booed out of the net by the Montreal Forum crowd, was replaced by Bunny Larocque. The Canadiens rebounded with wins of 6–2 and 4–1 in games two and three and a 4–3 overtime victory in game four. Simply too strong and too determined in game five at the Forum, the Canadiens captured their eighth Stanley Cup in the past dozen years and their fourth in a row with a 4–1 knockout of New York. At the finish, Bob Gainey, hoisted onto the shoulders of his teammates, was named winner of the Conn Smythe Trophy as MVP of the playoffs.

In the WHA, the Edmonton Oilers won the most games (48), lost the least (30) and led all teams offensively with 340 goals. Goalie Dave Dryden, at 37, was the team's workhorse, winning 41 of his 63 starts. Wayne Gretzky finished third in league scoring behind Robbie Ftorek of Cincinnati and Real Cloutier of Quebec.

THE WHA PLAYOFFS

Quarter-Finals (Best of Three)

The New England Whalers captured their three-game series over Cincinnati 2–1 and ended the four-year existence of the Stingers in professional hockey.

Semi-Finals (Best of Seven)

After winning the regular-season title, the Edmonton Oilers ran into stubborn opposition in their playoff matchup with the New England Whalers, who had ousted Cincinnati. But coach Glen Sather's system, which had relied on defensive steadiness to set the stage for offensive punch, soon paid off and the Oilers claimed the series in seven games.

The other series between Quebec and Winnipeg was disastrous for the Nordiques. Although the Nordiques had split 14 games with the Jets during regular-season play, they came up empty in the post-season games, losing four straight. The Jets outscored the Nords 30–12, breaking the WHA record for most goals by one team in a playoff series.

Avco Cup Finals (Best of Seven)

The Winnipeg Jets, who came alive in the playoffs, had the distinction of winning the WHA's last championship (and the Jets' third) when they captured the Avco Trophy by defeating Edmonton in the finals. The Jets' history-making win was achieved when they upset the league-champion Oilers in six games. If any one player epitomized coach Tom McVie's concept of "total effort" it was playoff MVP Rich Preston. "I said over two months ago Rich was my most complete player," said McVie. Thousands of fans turned out to cheer the Jets during their victory parade in Winnipeg. A huge banner had Jet supporters thinking ahead to next season. It said, "1978–79 Avco Cup Champions. Next Year the Stanley Cup."

Seven turbulent seasons of WHA play ended with the Jets' victory over the Oilers. While league statistician Frank Polnazek of Hartford wondered what to do with countless volumes of team and league records, others wondered how WHA stars would adapt to NHL play in 1979–80. Would Gordie Howe, now in his fifties, be around for one more season? Would Wayne Gretzky dazzle fans in NHL cities they way he had in the WHA? What did the future hold for Bobby Hull, the Baby Bulls and so many others? In a few weeks all of these questions would be answered.

XI

A DECADE OF DYNASTIES

The Islanders and Oilers, 1979—1990

Hockey moved into the eighties with a band of scrappy amateurs grabbing the early spotlight. In one of the greatest upsets ever, the U.S. Olympic Team coached by Herb Brooks won the gold medal at the 1980 Olympic Games at Lake Placid. Gordie Howe played into the eighties, barely, then retired, ending the most remarkable career in hockey history. The 32-year veteran had played through eight White House presidents— from Truman to Reagan. Gone, too, was Bobby Orr, who had won an incredible 16 individual trophies in his dozen years in the league.

Teenager Wayne Gretzky became the game's most spectacular scoring star and throughout the decade smashed records with ridiculous ease. At age 20, Gretzky signed a $20-million 15-year contract with Edmonton Oilers' owner Peter Pocklington, making him hockey's highest-paid player. Before the decade was over, Pocklington would sip champagne from the Stanley Cup four times, survive a bizarre hostage-taking incident with a bullet wound in his arm and, in a stunning move, deal his superstar to Los Angeles in what has been called the biggest trade in the history of any sport.

As dominant as some individuals were in the eighties—Gretzky, Messier, Coffey, Trottier, Bossy, Lafleur, Dionne, Hawerchuk, Czech defector Peter Stastny and Mario Lemieux, who arrived with much fanfare and a dazzling assortment of tricks in 1984–85—it was primarily a decade of dynasties. First, the New York Islanders captured four consecutive Stanley Cups before giving way to Gretzky and the Oilers, who skated off with four of the next five Cups. By the time Montreal surprised the fans with a Stanley Cup win in 1986, the Islanders were in decline. When Calgary marched to the Cup in 1989, the Oilers, without Gretzky, Coffey and Moog, were struggling to stay up with the league leaders.

1979–80

With four new WHA teams joining the NHL—Hartford, Quebec, Edmonton and Winnipeg—a four-step expansion draft was necessary to equip the newcomers with playing rosters. The first step involved a dispersal draft to redistribute players from the defunct Birmingham and Cincinnati franchises. In all, 28 players were assigned to the four new teams joining the NHL. The 17 NHL clubs then reclaimed a total of 43 players they had originally drafted but who had gone to play with the WHA instead. All other previously drafted players not claimed were allowed to stay with their WHA clubs. Step three saw the four expansion teams protect up to two goaltenders and two skaters as priority selections. Finally, the four new teams were allowed to choose until each NHL club had lost four players, with the 17 clubs allowed to protect two goaltenders and 15 skaters. In the draft's biggest surprise, the Winnipeg Jets claimed Bobby Hull who had been reclaimed by Chicago but left unprotected. It was an obvious revenge move by the Jets' general manager John Ferguson, who was repaying the Blackhawks for reclaiming Terry Ruskowski, a player he wanted badly.

With 21 teams, the league was forced to make some division changes. Washington moved from the Norris to the Patrick Division, Hartford replaced the Caps in the Norris Division and Quebec moved into the Adams Division as the fifth team. Winnipeg and Edmonton joined the Smythe Division to swell the number to six teams.

Looking for a solution to its amateur-draft problems relating to underage players, the NHL introduced a new entry draft, with teams drafting players under the age of 20 for the first time since 1974. In lowering the age of eligibility from 20 to 19, in a sense the NHL was conducting its first ever underage draft.

According to NHL president John Ziegler, no 19-year-olds would be exempt from the entry draft. Teenage stars such as Mike Gartner, Rob Ramage, Craig Hartsburg, Rick Vaive, Michel Goulet and goaler Pat Riggin, all of whom had played as underage juniors the previous season in the WHA, would be up for grabs.

Scotty Bowman, who coached the Montreal Canadiens to five Stanley Cups, became the new general manager of the Buffalo Sabres, taking over the job left vacant when Punch Imlach was fired in December 1978. In addition, Roger Neilson tossed in the towel with Harold Ballard and the Maple Leafs and came over to join Bowman and the Sabres as an associate coach. Another surprise was the signing of Don Cherry to a multi-year contract as head coach of the previously struggling Colorado Rockies. The naming of the 45-year-old Cherry gave the Rockies' franchise instant credibility, something that had been lacking in the short history of the Denver-based franchise. General manager Ray Miron described the flamboyant Cherry as "a coach who will turn the franchise around." The Atlanta Flames' general manager, Cliff Fletcher, announced that Al MacNeil would become the third head coach in the club's eight-year history. He replaced Fred Creighton, whose contract had not been renewed after the Flames' playoff loss to the Toronto Maple Leafs. Creighton would soon move on to coach the Boston Bruins, replacing Don Cherry. Eddie Johnston, the 43-year-old former goalie, became the Chicago Blackhawks' new head coach, with Bob Pulford remaining as general manager.

For the first time in NHL history, a New York team won three individual awards in one season. Bryan Trottier, 23, of the New York Islanders became the youngest forward and second-youngest player to win the Hart Trophy as the most valuable player to his team. He also won the Art Ross Trophy as the NHL's leading scorer. Islander defenseman Denis Potvin was named winner of the James Norris Trophy as the league's most outstanding defenseman for the third time. Other award winners were Bob MacMillan of the Atlanta Flames (Lady Byng), Bobby Smith of the Minnesota North Stars (Calder), and Bob Gainey of the Montreal Canadiens (Frank Selke).

Former Bruin defense great Bobby Orr, Harry Howell of the New York Rangers, the California Seals and the Los Angeles Kings and center Henri Richard of the Montreal Canadians were named to the Hockey Hall of Fame. Gordon Juckes, former executive director of the CAHA was named to the builders' section of the hall.

The biggest sale in the history of sports was made in the off season when Jerry Buss bought the Los Angeles Kings, the Lakers, the Forum and a ranch from Jack Kent Cooke for an estimated $67.5 million.

On June 9, hockey great Fred "Cyclone" Taylor died at a private nursing home in Vancouver, two weeks short of his 94th birthday. He was one of the last 60-minute players in professional hockey and was described by many observers during his career as the greatest of all players. Days later Ivan "Ching" Johnson, the greatest defenseman in the history of the New York Rangers, died in Takoma Park, Maryland. He was 80.

Toronto Maple Leafs' owner Harold Ballard hired an old friend to guide his team back to prominence in the NHL. Punch Imlach returned to the Leafs as general manager after a 10-year absence and Floyd Smith, who had previously worked for Imlach in Buffalo, was installed as head coach.

More than 40 percent of the players chosen in the league's entry draft on August 9 were underage prospects. Seven first-round choices still had a year of junior eligibility left. Rob Ramage, the first player selected, went to Colorado. The St. Louis Blues then selected Perry Turnbull from the Portland Winter Hawks and Sudbury junior Mike Foligno was grabbed by Detroit. Brian Propp of Brandon, junior hockey's leading scorer with 94 goals and 100 assists, was ignored until the Philadelphia Flyers, drafting 14th, selected him. Glen Sather selected Mark Messier in the third round of the draft and predicted a bright future for the youngster, who had jumped from tier-two junior hockey to the WHA's Cincinnati Stingers the previous season.

Ken Dryden of the Montreal Canadiens announced his retirement after eight spectacular years of big league hockey. Dryden, 31, had played on five Stanley Cup winners with Montreal and won five Vezina Trophies as the league's best goaltender. Defenseman Bill Nyrop, 27, who had quit the Montreal Canadiens the year before and was then traded to Minnesota, announced that he would not play hockey again. Before the Montreal Canadiens officially opened their 1979–80 season, captain Yvan Cournoyer, 35, announced his retirement. After going through a second operation on his ailing back the winter before, he had wanted to give it one more try this fall. "It is almost more difficult to do this than it was to make this team, " said Cournoyer quietly before his announcement.

After retiring during the previous season, Bobby Hull returned to the Winnipeg Jets. "His return is a great bonus for the people of Canada and fans in the NHL cities who will be able to see Bobby play again," said vice-president and general manager John Ferguson. Keith Magnuson, 32, a fixture on defense for the Chicago Blackhawks since the 1969–70 season, retired from active play but remained with the club in an assistant coaching role.

The NHL established a mandatory helmet rule beginning with the 1979–80 season. The only exception to the new rule were players who had signed professional contracts prior to June 1, 1979, and who had signed a special waiver exempting them from the rule.

Bernard "Boom-Boom" Geoffrion returned home to the Montreal Canadiens after a 12-year absence. One day after Labor Day he was introduced as the new coach of the team.

The NHL signed a three-year collective bargaining agreement with the NHL Officials' Association. Among other things, the agreement provided for a salary scale rising from a minimum of $25,000 to $60,000, based on years of service in the NHL, and specific fringe benefits including insurance, pension, playoff awards and fees for international competition.

Dale McCourt of Detroit finally won his battle to stay in the Motor City. A year earlier McCourt had been awarded to the Los Angeles Kings as compensation for the Kings' signing of free-agent goaltender Rogie Vachon. McCourt spurned the Kings and their $3-million contract and claimed he would fight the NHL and its member clubs to win the right to stay in Detroit. McCourt's threat to take his case to the Supreme Court was short-circuited when the two teams agreed on alternative compensation. Andre St. Laurent, the Wings' most valuable player two seasons before, and two first-round draft choices went to the Kings instead.

The comeback bid of Detroit's Mickey Redmond ended in frustration for the once-prolific Red Wing winger. He decided that the recurring back pains from his old injury weren't worth the gamble and he looked toward broadcasting as an alternate career. Another Red Wing attempting a comeback, Frank Mahovlich, was released by the Wings in October.

The NHL hired Bobby Orr as a special assistant to president John Ziegler. "I've never wanted to coach," said Orr, "and wanted even less to manage. But I have wanted to become involved with the league and this job suits me fine."

Garry Unger of the St. Louis Blues was at odds with the team over his contract. Unger's agent announced that he would launch an anti-trust suit against the NHL and its member clubs unless Unger was traded by the Blues to another NHL team. According to the agent, the NHL was restricting Unger's freedom of movement. Unger's NHL rights were quickly purchased by the Atlanta Flames, who shipped defenseman Ed Kea and forward Don Laurence to St. Louis in exchange for Unger. Unger signed for a reported $1 million over five years. He had been seeking $165, 000 a year from St. Louis and the Blues had declined.

Scotty Bowman wasted little time in his new role as head man of the Buffalo Sabres. He promptly traded Rene Robert to Colorado for rear guard John Van Boxmeer. The swap ended the halcyon days of the famed French Connection of Robert, Perreault and Martin.

Greg Neeld, the one-eyed defenseman who could not get the NHL to bend its rules and let him play, received a reported $100,000 settlement from the league. Neeld had lost his eye while playing junior hockey in 1973. Despite the injury, the Buffalo Sabres had drafted him in 1975 and then found that they couldn't clear him to play. The settlement thus ended the legal tug-of-war that Neeld and the NHL had been waging for three years.

Early in the season, Phil Esposito became only the second player in history to attain more than 1,500 career points. The other man in the "1500 Club" was Gordie Howe. Esposito was busy off the ice as well. He became the interim president of the NHL Players' Association replacing Bobby Clarke, who had to forego the position because of his appointment as assistant coach with the Philadelphia Flyers.

Bryan Trottier of the New York Islanders joined the NHL's increasing number of instant millionaires. The Islanders signed the 23-year-old to a new seven-figure, six-year contract that would be worth as much as $2 million if he collected all his bonus money. The contract would pay the NHL's most valuable player a basic salary of $210,000.

On October 27, Toronto Maple Leafs' assistant general manager John McLellan, 51, died suddenly at his home of an apparent heart attack. Associated with hockey for more than 20 years, McLellan had succeeded Punch Imlach as coach of the Maple Leafs at the start of the 1969–70 season. He had coached for three years then became assistant general manager of the Leafs under general manager Jim Gregory in 1973.

The last time Quebec City fans were spectators to a Montreal–Quebec confrontation in the NHL had been the 1919–20 season, with the Quebec Bulldogs as local representatives. With NHL status, the Nordiques and the Canadiens began a new chapter in what would become a heated rivalry.

The New York Rangers acquired defenseman Barry Beck from the Colorado Rockies in return for three regulars: left-wing Pat Hickey, right-wing Lucien DeBlois and defenseman Mike McEwen.

After losing five straight games, the Leafs appeared to be in trouble. General manager Punch Imlach was faced with two serious contract settlements (Borje Salming and Mike Palmateer) and there were recurring rumors that Imlach was about to unload some of his unproductive Leafs in a big player trade.

Guy Lafleur stunned the Canadiens and raised some controversy in Montreal with his comments concerning assistant coach Claude Ruel. Lafleur thought Ruel was interfering too much in the operation of the team. "If Claude wants to coach, let him go behind the bench," growled Lafleur. It wasn't long before Ruel would do just that.

Jiri Crha, the Czechoslovakian goaltender who had defected from his country and signed with the Toronto Maple Leafs, was not allowed to dress for Toronto in a game against the Blues. The NHL had ruled him ineligible to play because payments to the Czech hockey federation had not been met. General manager Punch Imlach had sent a telegram to league headquarters indicating that the Leafs were ready to pay $25,000 to the Czechs for Crha's release. However, NHL executive vice-president Brian O'Neill informed the Leafs that they must also promise to pay an additional $25,000 when Crha had played 40 NHL games, an assurance Imlach refused to give. "There will be no second telegram because the first one was correct," said Imlach. "We think that $25,000 is enough to pay to allow a legally landed immigrant in Canada to earn a living." But the Leafs eventually complied with the NHL directive.

A giant step toward the reorganization of the NHL Players' Association and the possible removal of its leader, Alan Eagleson, was formally taken by the Boston Bruins. In a team vote the Boston players presented Eagleson with a two-point resolution, which ultimately would be voted upon by every member of the union. The key planks in the program dealt with the selection of a successor to Eagleson and a time limit for such a change. Mike Milbury of the Bruins claimed the operation of the Players' Association was more a function of Eagleson's whim than a parliamentary process. The defenseman felt that Eagleson had been ill-prepared for the player-owner meetings held in Nassau a few weeks earlier.

Barclay Plager resigned as coach of the St. Louis Blues because he felt he could no longer motivate the team. The team's record was 8–16–4 when Red Berenson took over at the helm. "It was probably the toughest decision of my life," Plager said, "but I was not getting the best out of the team, and when a coach believes that, it's time to get out."

Jean Pronovost of the Atlanta Flames scored his 350th career goal to move up on the all-time scoring list. Others who were making overtures at improving their lifetime marks were Gordie Howe, who had 797 NHL goals; Phil Esposito, 689; Guy Lafleur, 379; and Marcel Dionne, who at 349 was tied with retired Andy Bathgate for the 22nd spot on the list.

Boom Boom Geoffrion's stint as Montreal coach was a short one. He was replaced as coach of the Canadiens by Claude Ruel. In departing, Geoffrion blasted some of the Montreal players for not playing well. He said Serge Savard was more interested in his horses than hockey.

While the Philadelphia Flyers were busy setting a new NHL record of 29 straight games without a loss, Garry Unger's iron-man streak in the NHL ended at 914 games. "If it was causing any aggravation on the club, I'm glad it's over," the 32-year-old center said after sitting out an entire game for the first time since 1968. Late in the Atlanta–St. Louis game, with his fans shouting, "We want Unger," coach Al McNeill had grabbed the back of Unger's jersey to prevent him from jumping on the ice and prolonging the streak.

Andre Lacroix, a long-time veteran, retired from hockey to take a front-office job with the Hartford Whalers. He had been a standout over the years in the WHA with Houston and New England.

It wasn't long before Winnipeg Jets' general manager John Ferguson was disenchanted with Bobby Hull. He suspended Hull, who had injured his shoulder in October while attempting to get in shape to play for the Jets without benefit of training camp. "Hull does not fit the Jets' style and hasn't been producing," Ferguson said. The 40-year-old Hull asked the Jets to trade him to another team.

The 1979 Izvestia Hockey Tournament ended predictably. The Soviets were the class of the five-country event, rolling to a perfect 4–0 record and defeating Czechoslovakia 3–2 on the final day to capture the championship. The Canadian team, however, fell flat. A combination of nine members of the Canadian Olympic team and a dozen NHL-owned players gained only one point in the week-long event, a 0–0 tie with Finland.

Punch Imlach shook up Toronto with the biggest Leaf trade in a dozen years. Lanny McDonald, one of Toronto's most popular players, and defenseman Joel Quenneville were traded to the Colorado Rockies in exchange for left-winger Pat Hickey and right-winger Wilf Paiement. As a result, Darryl Sittler resigned as captain of the team. In his resignation statement Sittler said:

> I have had little or no contact with Mr. Imlach, and it is clear to me that he and I have different ideas about player and management communication. I am totally loyal to the Toronto Maple Leafs. I don't want to let my teammates down. But I have to be honest with myself. I will continue to fight for players' rights, but not as captain of the team.

In addition to Sittler's resignation, the trade produced shock, anger and disbelief among the Leafs and their fans.

Charlie Simmer of the Los Angeles Kings scored goals in the last five games of the previous season and a goal a game in the first six games of the new season to surpass the modern NHL record of 10 straight games with goals. The record had been shared by Andy Bathgate, Bobby Hull and Mike Bossy. But the NHL refused to recognize the record as requested by the Kings, despite the fact that it was common in other leagues to recognize two-season streaks. Simmer went on to make the controversy academic as he ran up a new string of 13 games with goals from November 24 through December 27. In these 13 games, Simmer had scored 15 goals (eight on the road) and assisted on 10. He led the NHL in game winners with six.

The Soviet Union skated off with the decision in Super Series '80 against the NHL, but it wasn't easy. The Red Army team defeated the Rangers 5–2 and the Islanders 3–2 before losing to Montreal by a 4–2 score and to Buffalo by 6–1. The other touring Soviet squad, the Moscow Dynamo, opened with a 6–2 loss to Vancouver. They then whipped Winnipeg 7–0, followed with a 4–1 victory over Edmonton and settled for a 5–5 tie with Washington. With an overall 5–3–1 advantage, the Soviets appeared to be in peak form for their next big test, the Olympic Games in Lake Placid. The Soviets were to combine the cream of the army and Dynamo teams for the Olympic Games. The next NHL–Soviet confrontation would be the Canada Cup series late in September.

The Philadelphia Flyers recorded the longest streak without a loss in North American professional-sports history. In December they went beyond the mark of 33 games established by basketball's Los Angeles Lakers with a 5–3 triumph against the New York Rangers. Their streak (25 wins, 10 ties) came to an end on January 7, however, when they were destroyed 7–1 by the Minnesota North Stars.

When Toronto general manager Punch Imlach brought 41-year-old Carl Brewer back to play on the Toronto defense, many hockey fans were questioning Imlach's sanity. After Brewer had made some progress on his comeback, Imlach decided that he would suit up 55-year-old Johnny Bower as backup goaltender when his two regulars were unfit to play.

In retaliation for the Russian intervention in Afghanistan, Canada made moves to sever its hockey relations with the Soviet Union. The government cancelled all sports exchange programs with the Soviets and there was speculation that the move would further jeopardize the proposed 1980 Canada Cup series in September. But there was no doubt that Canada would withdraw from the Izvestia Hockey Tournament in Moscow in December 1980.

Boston's Terry O'Reilly received an eight-game suspension, while Peter McNab and Mike Milbury received six-game suspensions for going into the stands after harassing fans following a game in New York on December 23. This occurred 33 days after the incident but only three days after four of the fans involved had filed a $7-million law-suit against nine Boston players, the Bruins team, the New York Rangers, Madison Square Garden, the NHL and New York City. "From this point forward," said Ziegler, "each and every player and all club personnel are on notice that any such future involvement may result in the revocation of their privilege to be employed in the NHL."

On February 15, Oiler rookie Wayne Gretzky tied Billy Taylor's 33-year-old record with seven assists in one game and set a scoring mark for first-year players in Edmonton's 8–2 rout over the Washington Capitals. The seven assists gave Gretzky 96 points for the season, surpassing Bryan Trottier's rookie scoring record. Gretzky's record of the most assists and most points in one game by a first-year NHL player would not count, however, due to NHL rules. According to NHL statistician Ron Andrews, Gretzky was not eligible for first-year records or for the Calder Trophy as rookie of the year because of his WHA experience.

Dave "Tiger" Williams, a long-time team leader for the Toronto Maple Leafs, and hard-working Jerry Butler were traded to the Vancouver Canucks in return for young centerman Bill Derlago and right-winger Rick Vaive by Toronto general manager Punch Imlach. Halfway to Vancouver, Butler turned to Williams and said, "I hope you've got this right, Tiger. Nobody yet has told me I've been traded. Only you."

The Atlanta Flames were expected to lose well over $2 million during the 1979–80 season, after losing $1.7 million in 1978–79. They were averaging only 9,800 fans per game, well below the 13,500 figure needed to break even. Rumors persisted that the Flames would be playing in another city the following year unless big things happened in the forthcoming Stanley Cup playoffs, where they had been a disastrous 1–12 since their inception.

On the afternoon of Sunday, February 24, in Lake Placid, New York, the incredible, never-say-die United States Olympic Hockey Team clinched the Olympic gold medal by beating a tough, scrappy Finnish team, 4–2. This came less than 48 hours after they had pulled off one of the most stunning upsets in sports history—beating the Soviets 4–3. Long after the players from both teams had shaken hands and headed for their respective dressing rooms, dozens of fans lingered in the arena. When they finally filtered out, many looked back over their shoulders for one last glimpse at the place where a hockey miracle had occurred. In a far corner of the arena, a small group sang "God Bless America" with tears running down their cheeks and memories that would last a lifetime.

Several members of the Olympic champion United States hockey team were being pursued by NHL teams. Star goaltender Jim Craig reported to the Atlanta Flames, while defenseman Mike Ramsey joined the Buffalo Sabres. Ramsey was the first U.S. college player ever to be picked in the first round of the NHL draft. Bill Baker joined the Montreal Canadiens, while the Minnesota North Stars counted on big things from Steve Christoff and Neal Broten. Dave Christian joined the Winnipeg Jets. He had been Winnipeg's second-round pick in the 1979 NHL entry draft. Christian became the second American-born player to put on a Jets' jersey, the other being defenseman Craig Norwich.

Two of the most impressive performers for Sweden in the Olympic hockey competition had been drafted by NHL clubs. Goaltender Pelle Lindbergh, considered by many to be the best netminder in the Olympics, had been chosen by the Philadelphia Flyers in the second round of the 1979 entry draft, while teammate Mats Naslund, a right-winger, was grabbed by the Montreal Canadiens just two players later in the same draft.

Edmonton's Wayne Gretzky, at 19 years and one month, became the youngest NHL player to score 100 points. The previous record-holder was Montreal's Pierre Larouche, who had scored his 100th point in the 1975–76 season as a member of the Pittsburgh Penguins when he was 20 years and four months old.

Bobby Hull, 41, was obtained by the Hartford Whalers from the Winnipeg Jets in return for future considerations. He soon found himself playing with 51-year-old legend Gordie Howe, as well as the Whalers' smooth center Dave Keon, who was a mere 40. With his new linemates, Howe reached another milestone of his amazing career on February 29 when he scored his 800th regular-season NHL goal before 13,622 fans at the Hartford Arena.

Former NHL president Clarence Campbell awaited sentencing after being convicted in early February of conspiracy to pay a benefit to Senator Louis Giguere to gain a lease extension for the duty-free Sky Shops Export Ltd. at Montreal's Dorval Airport. The maximum penalty for Campbell's offense was five years in prison. Campbell was fortunate; he received a one-day jail sentence and was fined $25,000. Justice Rothman of the Quebec Superior Court said the one-day symbolic sentence to the 74-year-old Campbell was given out of consideration for his failing health. He spent a total of five hours in a cell and was allowed to go home.

Bruins' rookie defenseman Raymond Bourque topped a club record for points by a first-year player on March 5 in a game against Detroit. The three-point game gave the 19-year-old 51 points on the season, erasing the club mark of 50 established by Gregg Sheppard in 1972–73.

The Edmonton Oilers made a pair of last-minute deals just before the trade deadline. First, the Oilers sacrificed captain Ron Chipperfield to get a quality goaltender, Ron Low, from the Quebec Nordiques. Coach Glen Sather then swapped tough guy Cam Connor to the New York Rangers for problem child Don Murdoch. The fast life in New York was thought to be hindering Murdoch's career.

New York Islanders' general manager Bill Torrey sent Billy Harris and Dave Lewis, two of his favorite players, to the Los Angeles Kings for Butch Goring, whom the Islanders had sought for some time.

New York Ranger Phil Esposito matched an NHL record established by Bobby Hull when he scored his 30th goal of the season in a 6–0 victory over Colorado on March 12 in Madison Square Garden. It marked the 13th consecutive year that Esposito had tallied at least 30 goals. Hull had scored 30 or more goals in 13 consecutive seasons for the Chicago Blackhawks from 1959–60 through 1971–72, before moving on to the WHA.

On March 4, Toronto Maple Leafs' coach Floyd Smith was reported to be in stable condition in hospital after surviving a car accident that left him with a broken left kneecap, cuts and bruises and internal bleeding. Smith's car had gone out of control on a highway, jumped a center median and struck an auto in the oncoming lane, killing one of the passengers. The accident occurred within a mile of the spot where former NHL defenseman Tim Horton was killed six years before while returning to Buffalo following a game in Toronto against the Leafs. After an investigation, the Ontario Provincial Police charged Smith with impaired driving and criminal negligence causing death. Assistant coach Dick Duff moved behind the bench as a temporary replacement. Later, general manager Punch Imlach took over for the rest of the season as coach (from the press box), while Joe Crozier went behind the bench.

Guy Lafleur joined the NHL's elite 400-goal scoring club when he sank his 46th goal of the season as the Montreal Canadiens defeated the Winnipeg Jets 4–3. The 28-year-old Lafleur thus became the youngest player in NHL history to score 400 goals.

A unanimous vote by the NHL board of governors ended the chances Toronto Maple Leafs' owner Harold Ballard had had of avoiding the payment of a $10,000 fine for refusing to allow two of his players—Sittler and Palmateer—to participate in the NHL's "Showdown" intermission series. Although the two players did participate in the competition, Ballard had been successful in blocking the telecast of the program in the Ontario region. Ballard planned to seek court action on the matter.

The NHL passed a motion allowing public-address announcements in Quebec's

Bill Galloway

Montreal's Rocket Richard attempts to beat Toronto's Al Rollins. The Rocket was a potent and feared sharpshooter for nearly two decades.

Ageless wonder Gordie Howe played for thirty-two years and in five decades, setting records that may never be broken.

Boom Boom Geoffrion of Montreal tests Chicago goalie Glenn Hall. Hall played in a record 502 consecutive games.

One of hockey's greatest goalies, Jacques Plante foils a Red Wing attack.

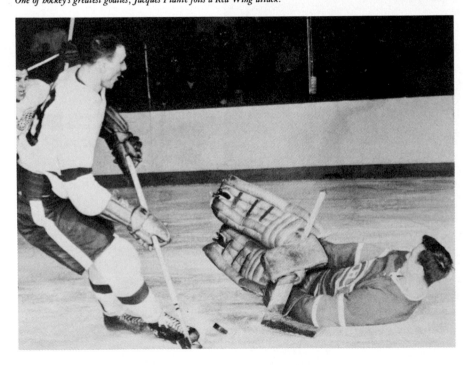

Chicago defenseman Pierre Pilote dumps a Leaf as goalie Glenn Hall covers up.

No shutout here! Goalie Terry Sawchuck holds the record for most career shutouts with 103.

The Lester Patrick Trophy is admired by Patrick's sons, Lynn and Murray, along with 1966–67 winner, Gordie Howe.

Jean Beliveau was captain and sparkplug of a Montreal Canadien dynasty that captured ten Stanley Cups. Beliveau was one of the most sought after young prospects in NHL history.

Goalie Johnny Bower didn't become a star until he was 35. After that, he played on four Cup winners and became a Hall of Famer. Here he stops Bruin record-holder Johnny Bucyk in close.

"The Golden Jet" Bobby Hull scores one of many as Phil Esposito looks on from behind the net. When Hull jumped to the Winnipeg Jets of the WHA he gave the upstart league instant credibility.

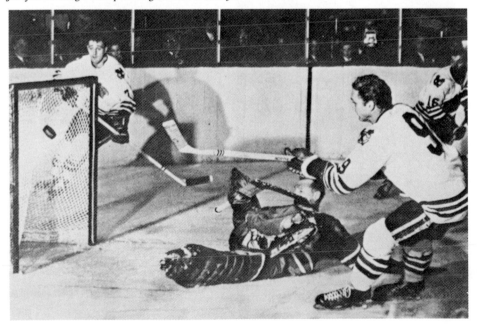

Clear the track, here comes Shack! This award-winning photo catches Buffalo's Shack leaping on the back of a startled Gerry Ehman of the California Seals.

Montreal goalie Ken Dryden is the only player to win hockey's rookie award after capturing the playoff MVP honors.

The goal of the century. Paul Henderson scores to beat the Soviets late in the final game of the historic 1972 series.

Boston's Bobby Orr is the only defenseman to lead the NHL in scoring. He accomplished the feat twice.

Center Phil Esposito scored 717 career goals playing with three different teams—Chicago, Boston and New York. Esposito and Orr were teammates in Boston during the early seventies when they led the Bruins to two Stanley Cups.

Robert Shaver

Coliseum to be made exclusively in French, with the provision that the visiting team would receive English announcements via the use of a speaker behind the bench.

In a shocking move, Boston Bruins' general manager Harry Sinden fired coach Fred Creighton. He had been the coach for eight months, during which time he had piloted them to 93 points, the fourth best in the NHL. "We had a sense that the team seemed to be floundering," said president Paul Mooney, "and part of it certainly was the coaching." Sinden named himself as Creighton's successor for the rest of the season and through the playoffs, the first time he had been behind the bench in the NHL since May 10, 1970, when he had piloted the Bruins to the Stanley Cup. Another coaching change, sudden but not unexpected, occurred when Detroit Red Wings' general manager Ted Lindsay fired coach Bobby Kromm. Lindsay then installed defensive coach Marcel Pronovost behind the bench while he assumed the dual role of manager and coach. The Wings were 24–36–11 when Kromm was fired, waging a life-and-death struggle with Washington, Vancouver, Edmonton and Quebec for the last two spots in the 16-team playoff alignment.

On March 12, for the first time in NHL history, a father and son combination formed a line when the Howes played as a unit for the Hartford Whalers against Detroit. Gordie played center for his sons Mark and Marty on the occasion of Hartford's last visit of the year to Detroit. Gordie was the only Howe to earn a point in the game, which ended in a 4–4 tie. On the final day of the schedule, Gordie scored a goal against the Wings in Hartford. It was his 801st career goal and it came in his last NHL game. Howe finished with 15 goals and 26 assists for the 1979–80 season. It brought his career totals to 1,767 games played, 801 goals, 1,049 assists and 1,850 points.

The Philadelphia Flyers coasted to first place overall, finishing with 116 points. They led the NHL with 48 wins and 20 ties, while their 12 losses were the fewest in the league. The Buffalo Sabres closed the regular season with a club record 14-game undefeated streak and won their first Vezina Trophy. The Edmonton Oilers, led by sensational 19-year-old Wayne Gretzky, finished their inaugural NHL season in dramatic fashion, posting eight wins and a tie in their final 11 games to grab the 16th and final playoff position.

Montreal center Pierre Larouche became the first player in NHL history to score 50 goals with two teams. He had had 53 goals with the Pittsburgh Penguins during the 1975–76 season. The highest scoring rookies were Brian Propp of Philadelphia with 75 points, Mike Foligno of Detroit with 71 points and Ray Bourque of Boston with 65 points. The NHL scoring leaders were Marcel Dionne of Los Angeles and Wayne Gretzky of Edmonton, both with 137 points. Guy Lafleur of Montreal finished third with 125 points and set a league record for scoring 50 goals or more in six consecutive seasons. Dionne won the Art Ross Trophy as scoring champion because he had accumulated more goals than Gretzky.

For the first time in the 63-year history of the NHL, there was a three-way tie for the league's goal-scoring lead. Charlie Simmer of Los Angeles, Danny Gare of Buffalo and Blaine Stoughton of Hartford each had 56 goals. While a record number of nine players had reached the 50-goal level in 1979–80, this was the first time in seven seasons that no player had scored at least 60 goals.

At the box office, the NHL went over the top with attendance surpassing the 11-million mark, well above the 1978–79 figure of 8 million, when the NHL had been a 17-team circuit.

THE PLAYOFFS

Preliminary Round (Best of Five)

The preliminary round involved the top 16 teams. The first-place club saw action with the last, the second club with the 15th, the third club with the 14th, etc.

The preliminary-round series of the playoffs ended as most had expected. The Philadelphia Flyers swept the Edmonton Oilers in three games. The third game ended with Ken Linseman scoring at 3:56 of the second sudden-death overtime period. The Buffalo Sabres ousted the Vancouver Canucks three games to one, while Montreal swept past the Hartford Whalers in three straight. The Islanders took Los Angeles three games to one and it required the same number of games for Minnesota to dispose of Toronto. Chicago cleaned up on St. Louis with a three-game sweep and the Rangers ousted Atlanta 3–1. Boston won its series 3–2 against the Pittsburgh Penguins. Islanders' center Bryan Trottier became the first player in NHL playoff history to ever score two short-handed goals in the same period. His goals came against Los Angeles in an 8–1 Islander victory.

Dave "Tiger" Williams proclaimed his innocence after receiving a one-game suspension for knocking Buffalo coach Scotty Bowman unconscious with an errant swing of his stick during game three of the Canucks' series against Buffalo. NHL vice-president Brian O'Neill disclosed that a videotaped replay of the fracas clearly showed that Williams had swung his stick in the direction of the Buffalo bench. According to Williams, he had taken a Buffalo player into the boards and did not know whether or not it was his stick that hit Bowman.

Quarter-Finals (Best of Seven)

The Buffalo Sabres whipped the Chicago Blackhawks four straight in their best-of-seven quarter-final series. Sabre coach Scotty Bowman became the winningest hockey coach in Stanley Cup playoff history after his team won the first two games of the series. The Philadelphia Flyers eliminated the New York Rangers and the Islanders defeated the Boston Bruins, both series going five games. In a major upset, the Minnesota North Stars defeated the Montreal Canadiens four games to three. In game seven, the North Stars' Al MacAdam scored the series winning goal with just 86 seconds remaining in regulation time, breaking a 2–2 tie. The defeat was the Canadiens' earliest exit from the playoffs since 1974 and it marked the first time in 16 years they had lost the seventh game of a series on home ice.

Semi-Finals (Best of Seven)

Just two days after they had knocked the Montreal Canadiens out of the playoffs, the North Stars roared into Philadelphia where they defeated the Flyers 6–5 to open the semi-final series. But the Flyers came back to win four straight games and advance to the finals. The Islanders took the first three games in their semi-final series against the Buffalo Sabres. Then the Sabres won two in a row. But the Isles—transformed with the acquisition of Butch Goring before the trading deadline—won game six and advanced against the Flyers.

The Stanley Cup Finals (Best of Seven)

In the Stanley Cup finals, Denis Potvin's goal in the first game at the 4:07 mark of overtime, gave the New York Islanders a 4–3 victory over the Flyers. In game two, the Flyers evened the series, defeating the Islanders 8–3. The Islanders scored five power-play goals in game three and won 6–2. They won again by 5–2 in game four, but they failed to win the Cup two nights later in Philadelphia when the Flyers rebounded with a 6–3 victory. The teams returned to the Nassau Coliseum where the Flyers had won just one game in the last five years.

Game six was marred by two disputed calls. First, there was Denis Potvin's tying goal at 11:56 of the first period. Potvin batted a waist-high pass from Mike Bossy into the Flyers' goal. Philadelphia protested that Potvin's stick was too high, but to no avail. Then, less than three minutes later rookie Duane Sutter put the Islanders in front by one goal after a blatant missed call by linesman Leon Stickle. The Islanders were obviously a foot offside on the play. After the Flyers' Brian Propp had tied the score at 2–2, the Isles jumped in front on goals by Bossy and Nystrom. But the Flyers came back again in the third period. Goals by Bob Dailey and John Paddock tied the score at 4–4 and left the teams tied 4–4 and facing overtime. At 7:11, in sudden-death overtime, everything ended. John Tonelli darted across the Flyer blue line as teammate Bob Nystrom skated full speed toward the Flyers' goal. Tonelli gave Nystrom a quick look and then hit him with a perfect pass, which Nystrom promptly converted into the game-winning goal and the Stanley Cup. During the post-game celebrations, general manager Bill Torrey said, "Nobody gave the Stanley Cup to us. We beat Boston and Buffalo and Philadelphia— three of the top four teams. Nobody can say we're not the best."

While Islander fans were overjoyed with their team's performance, fans in Atlanta were in mourning. It was announced that the Atlanta Flames had been sold to Vancouver businessman Nelson Skalbania and that the club would be transferred to Calgary. The franchise had lost money since its inception in the 1972–73 season—the losses were thought to be over $10 million.

Jacques Demers, 36, resigned as coach of the Quebec Nordiques. It was believed that Demers had been given a "resign or else" ultimatum in meetings he had had with general manager Maurice Filion. In other coaching changes, the Penguins decided not to renew the contract of Johnny Wilson and Don Cherry was fired as coach of the Colorado Rockies. Fans rallied in support of Cherry, threatening to cancel season tickets when rumors of a possible firing had first surfaced. Two days before the firing was announced, a Denver newspaper revealed the results of a poll on the Cherry situation and the response was overwhelming—3,025 to 59 in favor of retaining Cherry. Cherry said that he felt "more sadness than bitterness" over his firing. "I spent six months trying to put a team together," Cherry said, "but it's pretty tough to fly like an eagle when you're mixed up with turkeys."

1980–81

Between seasons the Chicago Blackhawks had fired popular head coach Eddie Johnston and had given his job to former defenseman and assistant coach Keith Magnuson. Johnston was quick to denounce general manager Bob Pulford. "I have no respect for that man," Johnston said. "It was my conflict with Pulford that led to my dismissal." Under Johnston, the Hawks had had an 87-point season, their best in six years. He quickly surfaced as coach of the Pittsburgh Penguins after Penguins' coach Johnny Wilson was fired.

The Quebec Nordiques' general manager Maurice Filion announced that he would be moving behind the bench for the 1980–81 season—the third time in the team's eight-year history that Filion would once again be coach. Filion named 33-year-old Michel Bergeron and Andre Boudrias as associate coaches.

Gerry Cheevers was named as the new coach of the Boston Bruins, their fourth coach in the past 14 months. "He was the most popular player among his teammates that I have ever seen in my years here," said general manager Harry Sinden. "I think Gerry will be an exciting coach. He'll be a gambler."

Billy MacMillan, a former assistant to Al Arbour with the Islanders, was named to succeed Don Cherry as coach of the Colorado Rockies. Goaltending great Glenn Hall, 49, returned to the NHL in the capacity of goaltending coach for the Rockies.

The U.S. Olympic gold-medalist goaltender, Jim Craig, was traded back to Boston by the Calgary Flames in exchange for a second-round draft choice in 1980 and a third-round pick in 1981. The Washington Capitals acquired goaltender Mike Palmateer from the Toronto Maple Leafs. In exchange, the Caps surrendered defenseman Robert Picard, the club's first-round selection (third overall) in the 1977 entry draft.

After 33 years and having played for five decades, hockey's grand old man, Gordie Howe, announced his retirement. Howe soon assumed a new role as director of player development for the Hartford Whalers.

The most penalized player in the NHL, Dave "the Hammer" Schultz, retired from hockey at the age of 31. The hard-hitting left-winger had been penalized for nearly 2,300 minutes during his eight NHL years. After the Flyers had traded him to Los Angeles in 1976, he moved on to Pittsburgh and eventually to Buffalo in 1979, where he failed to catch on with the Sabres and ended in the minors with Rochester.

The NHL's 1980 player awards were mainly characterized by new faces. Of the league's 10 major trophy recipients, only one, Bob Gainey of the Montreal Canadiens, had been there the year before. Gainey was named the Frank Selke Trophy winner as the best defensive forward for the third straight year. Wayne Gretzky became the youngest double trophy winner in the league's history at age 19, winning both the Hart and Lady Byng trophies. Defenseman Larry Robinson captured the Norris Trophy as the league's best defenseman and Raymond Bourque of the Boston Bruins, 19, won the Calder Trophy as rookie of the year. Minnesota's gritty Al MacAdam climaxed his best NHL season by winning the Bill Masterton Trophy as the league's "unsung hero." The Art Ross Trophy was won by Marcel Dionne of the Los Angeles Kings. The Vezina Trophy for the best goaltender was shared by Buffalo's Robert Sauve and Don Edwards.

In the NHL's 1980 entry draft the Montreal Canadiens had first pick and selected center Doug Wickenheiser, the WHL's scoring champion. Some fans admonished the Canadiens for not selecting local standout Denis Savard. The Winnipeg Jets had second pick and chose 19-year-old defenseman David Babych, the younger brother of Wayne Babych of St. Louis. The Chicago Blackhawks then selected playmaking wizard Denis Savard from the Montreal Juniors.

The NHL introduced eight rule changes for the 1980–81 season and half of them were aimed at cutting down on fisticuffs, bench-clearing brawls and abuse of game officials.

The Kings' Marcel Dionne became the highest-paid player in the history of the NHL when he signed a multi-year contract, reported to be worth $3.6 million over the next six years.

After requesting to be traded, 34-year-old Rogie Vachon had his wish granted on July 23, when Detroit sent him to Boston for goaltender Gilles Gilbert, 31.

In October it was announced that two of the famous Stastny brothers had signed with the Quebec Nordiques after defecting from Czechoslovakia. Peter Stastny, 23, and Anton Stastny, 21, had been standout players on the Czechoslovakian National Team. For three years Peter and Anton, as well as their older brother and linemate Marian, had been avidly sought by the Quebec Nordiques. The effort to get the Stastnys to Canada had involved secret meetings, huge financial payments, cloak-and-dagger intrigue and midnight car rides through the Austrian Alps.

Punch Imlach's future with the Toronto Maple Leafs was uncertain. Imlach suffered a serious heart attack in late August and his role as the Leafs' boss was being filled by a committee of three—coach Joe Crozier and assistants Dick Duff and Floyd Smith.

One of hockey's most renowned stick-swinging cases of the mid-1970s was settled out of court five years after it occurred. Henry Boucha, who had played in the NHL with Detroit, Minnesota and Colorado from 1971–77, reached a settlement in the $3.5-million lawsuit he had filed against Dave Forbes, then a member of the Boston Bruins, for allegedly striking him in the eye with his stick during an NHL game on January 4, 1975. The amount of the settlement was not disclosed. The decision to settle out of court came three years after Boucha had retired from playing, insisting that his NHL career was never the same after the eye injury.

Darryl Sittler started the Leafs' season with the captain's *C* back on his jersey after a meeting with Toronto owner Harold Ballard.

The NHL's Players' Association voted against the implementation of overtime during the 1980–81 regular season. According to Sam Simpson, the director of operations for the NHLPA, "More than 85 percent of the players were against overtime, mainly because they didn't like the idea of a team not getting any points at all if they were tied after 60 minutes of regulation play and then lost it in overtime."

After a dismal pre-season record of seven losses and two ties in nine exhibitions, the winless Vancouver Canucks decided to make changes. They moved several new faces into the lineup including Rick Lanz, their top 1980 choice, Brent Ashton, Curt Fraser and Gerry Minor.

The NHL's waiver draft, designed to provide the "have-not" teams with more talent at the start of the season, was not very productive. Only five players were selected and none of the 12 goalies available was claimed. The biggest news was the pre-draft move pulled off by the Quebec Nordiques, who picked right-winger Danny Geoffrion from the Montreal Canadiens for a mere $100 and then peddled him to the Winnipeg Jets for $50,000.

Brad Marsh, 22, of the Atlanta Flames became the youngest captain in the league, replacing Brian Sutter of St. Louis, who was chosen the year before at age 23.

Borje Salming, 29, and the Toronto Maple Leafs finally reached an agreement over a new contract. Salming sat down with Leafs' owner Harold Ballard and signed an 11-year contract that would net the Swedish star approximately $2 million. It was a six-year pact with a five-year option.

On November 18, Conn Smythe, the man who had built Maple Leaf Gardens, established the Toronto Maple Leafs and was a major reason why the NHL had become a success, died at the age of 85. Smythe was responsible for assembling the New York Rangers for their entry into the NHL before returning to Toronto and purchasing the St. Patricks, which he renamed the Maple Leafs. In 1931, in the height of the Great Depression, he opened Maple Leaf Gardens, one of the world's most famous buildings and over the next 30 years built the Maple Leafs into an NHL powerhouse with shrewd trades and astute scouting. Smythe had led the Leafs to seven Stanley Cup victories during his tenure as manager. Outside of hockey he had been a much-decorated soldier who had fought in both world wars, a great philanthropist, who had turned over large sums of money to charities and had been an untiring fundraiser for good causes. Smythe was also a loud opponent of the NHL's rapid expansion in the late sixties:

> I'm for perfection in everything and we had the best players in the world split among six teams. Our hockey was worth the money. But what's happened to the NHL is no different than what's happened to most other things in the world. Everybody is after the fast buck and no one thinks about quality.

Just 18 games after Bryan Watson started as the Edmonton Oiler bench coach, he was fired by general manager Glen Sather. The Oilers had won only one game in 10 at home. Glen Sather then stepped in as coach.

After Fred Shero resigned as coach of the New York Rangers, admitting that he had a drinking problem that was "now under control," American-born Craig Patrick, the Rangers' director of operations, replaced him. Patrick's grandfather, Lester Patrick, had coached the Rangers from 1926 to 1939 and his father Lynn and his uncle Muzz had also been Ranger coaches.

Darryl Sittler of the Toronto Maple Leafs clicked for his 800th NHL point to move up to 28th place on the all-time point list, past former Boston Bruin and New York Ranger Ken Hodge.

Marcel Dionne of the Los Angeles Kings reached the 400-goal plateau on December 4 when he scored his 20th goal of the season, in a game in which the Kings defeated the Vancouver Canucks 3–1. He joined his teammate Garry Unger, who had recorded his 400th goal a week earlier. The two also moved into a tie for 14th place on the NHL's all-time goal-scoring list behind Guy Lafleur of the Montreal Canadiens, who was in 12th spot with 415 career goals, and Rod Gilbert, who had retired after scoring 406 goals. Another NHL milestone occurred when Boston's Brad Park became only the second defenseman in NHL history to record 500 assists when he set up a goal against Detroit. Bobby Orr had retired as the leader with 645 assists.

Tommy McVie of the Winnipeg Jets became the fourth coach of the season to be dismissed from his job. Under McVie, the Jets had gone for 25 straight games without a win—two shy of the existing NHL record of 27 set by the Kansas City Scouts in 1976. General manager John Ferguson selected assistant Bill Sutherland as McVie's replacement.

Goaltender Michel Dion of the Quebec Nordiques stormed off the ice during a game and disappeared in protest over the way the Quebec fans had continually harassed and booed him. Nordiques' coach Michel Bergeron was emphatic on what should be done to Dion for walking out on the team: "Enough is enough. If it were up to me alone, Dion would never again wear a Nordique uniform."

Mike O'Connell, a defenseman who was born in Chicago but played his hockey in Canada with the Kingston Canadians, was swapped by the Chicago Blackhawks to the Boston Bruins for left-winger Al Secord.

Hot scoring Wayne Gretzky continued to stash away the individual awards. The Oiler superstar was chosen as Canada's male athlete of the year by the Canadian Press. In the annual CP year-end poll, Gretzky was an overwhelming choice over Terry Puhl, the Melville, Saskatchewan, native who starred for the Houston Aeros, and Marathon of Hope runner Terry Fox.

The Winnipeg Jets announced that Mike Smith, 35, had been appointed associate coach with the team. He would be in charge of the Jets' specialty units and defense.

Mark Howe of the Whalers was seriously injured in a freak accident involving a goal net. Checked into the net by John Tonelli of the Islanders, Howe knocked the net off its moorings. The net tilted, the metal puck deflector jutted straight up and Howe slammed into it, impaling himself on the sharp point. The metal penetrated his buttock to a depth of five and a half inches, a wound that came within half an inch of his spine. Doctors said the Whaler star was half an inch away from becoming an invalid. Howe made an astonishing recovery and returned to action in early February.

Phil Esposito of the Rangers came to a sudden decision in mid-season. He would retire from the game. After four seasons with Chicago, eight in Boston and six in New York, he quit with a career record of goals (717) and points (1,590) second only to Gordie Howe. One of his fondest memories was his record season of 76 goals and 152 points in 1970–71.

In February, Mike Bossy of the Islanders scored twice against Quebec to become only the second player to score 50 goals in 50 games. His 50th came with only 1:29 remaining on the clock. Maurice Richard was the first, scoring 50 in a 50-game season in 1944–45.

Charlie Simmer of the Kings almost matched Bossy's feat. He scored his 49th goal eight seconds from the end of game number 50. He had entered the game with 46. Afterwards, during a game in Toronto, Simmer broke his right leg and was out for the rest of the season.

The Los Angeles Kings did a first-rate job in handling the annual All-Star game. The sellout crowd of 16,005 watched the Campbell Conference win their first All-Star tilt in six starts. The fans were treated to one of the finest individual efforts in All-Star history by Mike Liut of the Blues, who sparkled in goal and was named the game's first star. The pre-game dinner entertainment was handled by George Burns, Harvey Korman, Tim Conway, Gordon Lightfoot and recently retired Phil Esposito, who ripped into a version of the "Hockey Sock Rock" while surrounded by leggy showgirls.

The Edmonton Oilers dispatched Dave Semenko to their Wichita farm club for two weeks to work on fundamental things like stick handling, slap shooting and even body checking. "In practice, Dave does a lot of good things, but in games he's nervous and he tightens up," said coach Glen Sather. "He's got to get over that."

Dan Bouchard was traded to the Quebec Nordiques by the Calgary Flames in return for Jamie Hislop. In another trade involving a goaltender, Gary Edwards, 33, of the Minnesota North Stars was traded to the Edmonton Oilers in return for a third-round draft choice in 1982.

Real Cloutier accused Peter Stastny of not wanting to play with him. The Nordiques right-winger made the astounding accusation following a 4–3 loss to the Winnipeg Jets. Cloutier was quoted as saying, "It's easy to see. Peter wants to play with his brother

Anton and he refuses to pass the puck to Marc [Tardif] and me." As for Stastny, he was badly shaken by Cloutier's remarks. "I'm surprised and saddened over Real's statements. My job is to carry the puck and pass it to my wingers. I don't start checking which of my teammates is there."

Don Blackburn of the Hartford Whalers became the sixth coaching casualty of the 1980–81 NHL season as the downtrodden Whalers relieved him of his duties and turned the team over to assistant Larry Pleau for the rest of the season. The club had managed only two victories in 25 games.

Defenseman Rick Chartraw, 26, of the Montreal Canadiens was traded to the Los Angeles Kings. Despite nearly six seasons with the team after being chosen in the first round of the amateur draft in 1974, Chartraw had played only sporadically and had been used mainly in spot roles. In two other NHL trades, the Quebec Nordiques recalled goalie Michel Dion from Indianapolis of the CHL and dealt him to the Winnipeg Jets for a future draft pick. The Boston Bruins sent center Bob Miller to the Colorado Rockies in exchange for left-winger Mike Gillis.

On February 19, Nick Fotiu of the Rangers led his teammates in a charge into the stands in Detroit's Joe Louis Arena after being doused with beer thrown by a jeering fan. Fotiu was hit with an eight-game suspension, Don Maloney sat out two games for flinging his glove at a tormentor and five teammates were assessed fines.

> The league's policy has been firm and clear [said Ziegler]. The spectator area is out of bounds to players regardless of the provocation. It must also be noted that we will not accept abuse of our players. A person alleged to have thrown debris at the players in Detroit has been arrested and charged. We expect this policy to be followed in all our arenas.

Eleven days after the first incident, Minnesota coach Glen Sonmor battled a fan in Boston after a game between the Bruins and the North Stars. Sonmor, upset that his team's record at the Boston Garden had been a dismal 0–27–8 since the Minnesota franchise was awarded, was caught by a photographer holding the fan with one hand while preparing to wallop him with the other.

One of hockey's all-time great goaltenders, Cecil "Tiny" Thompson, died at the age of 76. The former NHL player had played for the Boston Bruins and the Detroit Red Wings and had won the Vezina Trophy four times during his 10 years with the Bruins.

The Philadelphia Flyers shattered their own infamous penalty-minutes record (1,980 minutes set in 1975–76) when they pushed their 1980–81 total to 2,092 minutes after a penalty-filled game with the Vancouver Canucks.

By mid-February, the St. Louis Blues, whose 34–12–12 record added up to 80 points, sat atop the NHL for the first time since the inception of their franchise 14 years before.

On March 4, Guy Lafleur of the Montreal Canadiens became the fastest 1,000-point scorer in the history of the NHL. The 29-year-old, 10-year veteran scored two goals and added an assist in Montreal's 9–3 romp over the Winnipeg Jets in Montreal to reach the NHL scoring plateau in his 720th career game.

The Islanders' Glenn Resch, one of the most popular players on the team, and Steve Tambellini were shipped to the Colorado Rockies for Mike McEwen and Jari Kaarela. Fans flooded the Islanders switchboard in protest. Even coach Al Arbour, who did not always get along with Resch, said: "How could I not feel bad? We had seven years together and that's a long time." Defenseman Bill Baker of Montreal was sent to Colorado for a third-round draft choice in 1983. Montreal also traded goaltender Michel Larocque and an eighth-round draft choice for defenseman Robert Picard of the Toronto Maple Leafs. The Los Angeles Kings obtained left-winger Rick Martin and center Don Luce from Buffalo for a first-round 1981 draft pick. They also obtained goalie Jim Rutherford from Toronto for a low draft pick in 1981 and secured a second-low draft pick from Edmonton in exchange for veteran center Garry Unger.

The Buffalo Sabres went on a record-setting spree in a 14–4 blast of the Toronto Maple Leafs. The Sabres overwhelmed the Leafs with a nine-goal barrage in the second period, the most goals ever scored by an NHL team in one period. The old mark was eight, set by Detroit in 1944 and since matched by four other teams. The 12-goal total of the second period was also a new mark for the most goals scored by two teams in a single period. The previous record was 10, set by the old New York Americans in 1939 and matched on two other occasions. In addition, the two teams rifled seven goals into the net in three minutes and 39 seconds, the fastest scoring ever achieved by two league clubs. The 14 goals which the Sabres scored on the embarrassed Leafs also amounted to the worst loss ever inflicted on a Maple Leaf hockey team.

Edmonton's Wayne Gretzky set another NHL record when he collected his 90th assist of the season in a March 21 game against Los Angeles. Thus he replaced Bobby Clarke's name in the record book as the NHL center who had recorded the most assists in one season. Clarke had done it in 1975–76. Gretzky's five-point night had raised his season count to 145 points, just seven behind Phil Esposito's single-season record. Espo had set the mark in 1970–71 while with the Boston Bruins.

Ted Lindsay, former coach and general manager of the Detroit Red Wings, sued the NHL team for $700,000 which he claimed the Wings owed him in back wages and severance pay.

Guy Lafleur of the Montreal Canadiens had a close brush with death on the morning of March 24 when he fell asleep at the wheel of his car and rammed a fence while heading to his home on Montreal's West Island. A metal fencepost had jabbed through the windshield, slicing off the top part of his ear and he required plastic surgery that morning. Had Lafleur's head been a quarter of an inch to the right, the career of one of hockey's greats would have suddenly ended.

Wayne Gretzky continued to make hockey history. The 20-year-old Oiler whiz kid ended his pursuit of Phil Esposito's single-season record of 152 points when he collected three assists in the Oilers' 5–2 victory over the Pittsburgh Penguins. At the same time Gretzky earned his 102nd assist of the year, tying the NHL record set by Bobby Orr in 1970–71 when he was with the Boston Bruins. Gretzky finished the season with the highest points-per-game average for a season at 2.05. The previous best was 1.97, set in 1943–44 by Bill Cowley, who had played 36 games for the Boston Bruins.

Gretzky also recorded the most assists in one season, including playoffs. In the 1970–71 playoffs, Bobby Orr had added seven assists to his total to bring his assists to 109. Gretzky had 109 before the 1980–81 playoffs began and was assured of breaking the record in the playoffs.

The Detroit Red Wings finished 20th overall in the standings (only Winnipeg had a worse record), with only one victory in their final 21 games and a nine-game winless streak. Their record was 19–43–18—the second smallest Detroit victory total in 40 years. The Wings decided to make several off-season changes but coach Wayne

Maxner's job appeared to be safe. "I don't regret anything I did," said Maxner. "To progress, you have to go through the turmoil. Every coach would like to stand behind the Montreal bench or the New York Islander bench. But being here is a great experience."

Howard Baldwin, the Hartford Whalers' managing general partner, fired general manager Jack Kelley and promoted Larry Pleau, the current head coach, to assume Kelley's duties. Afterwards Kelley said, "I'll keep most of my thoughts to myself. Over the years I've been man enough to dish it out; I've got to be man enough now to take it."

Ray Miron stepped down as general manager of the woeful Colorado Rockies. Miron said his effectiveness as general manager had been compromised by a withdrawal of support from both the fans and the media. The Rockies finished in 19th place in the final NHL standings, with a dismal 22–45–13 record.

With the revitalized St. Louis Blues providing the biggest gain, the NHL's box office rocketed to another record season. League attendance went over the 11-million mark for the second straight year as the 21 teams attracted a new high of 11,328,001 fans for the 840-game 1980–81 schedule.

The Blues' hopes for a first place finish were scuttled by the Islanders, who enjoyed a late-season 13-game unbeaten streak and finished with 110 points, three more than St. Louis. Montreal was the only other club to surpass 100 points, finishing with 103. The Winnipeg Jets had a disastrous season, winning only nine games.

When Wayne Gretzky scored his last point of the season he forced another revision of the record book. The final point was Gretzky's 301st in 159 games covering two NHL seasons. It brought him to the 300-point mark faster than any player in history. Gretzky set five other NHL records, including establishing a new mark for points in a season with 164.

THE NHL PLAYOFFS

Preliminary Round (Best of Five)

In preliminary-round action of the 1981 Stanley Cup playoffs, upsets prevailed. In the biggest surprise of the playoffs, the 14th-place Edmonton Oilers won their best-of-five series against the third-place Montreal Canadiens in three straight games. "I guess the pesky Oilers have come of age," chortled 19-year-old defenseman Paul Coffey after the series. "Beating the Montreal Canadiens in three straight playoff games...well, that's make-believe." Claude Ruel resigned as coach of the Montreal Canadiens four days after their stunning upset at the hands of the Oilers. "I'll never coach again," said Ruel.

It was no surprise when the New York Islanders, who finished in first place overall, eliminated the Toronto Maple Leafs with relative ease in three straight games. Minnesota also bested the Bruins in three games, as did Buffalo over Vancouver and Calgary over Chicago. The New York Rangers took out the Los Angeles Kings 3–1 while the St. Louis Blues (second-place overall finishers) won their best-of-five series against the Pittsburgh Penguins 3–2 and Philadelphia eliminated Quebec by the same margin.

During the playoff battle between Quebec and Philadelphia, the Nordiques' goaltender Dan Bouchard found himself in the embrace of the Flyers' little troublemaker Ken Linseman. Bouchard fought to disengage himself from Linseman's grasp, but as he pulled one arm free he felt a sharp pain. "He bit me on the hand," said Bouchard. "Now I know why they call him the Rat!"

Quarter-Finals (Best of Seven)

The Edmonton Oilers, with four 20-year-old forwards, a 19-year-old defenseman and a 21-year-old goalie, who had never played more than three NHL games in a row until the playoffs, carried the New York Islanders to six games before bowing out in the quarter-finals. The New York Rangers outplayed the St. Louis Blues and defeated them 4–2, Minnesota eliminated Buffalo 4–1 and Calgary upset the Philadelphia Flyers, ending it all for the Flyers in game seven.

Semi-Finals (Best of Seven)

In the Stanley Cup semi-finals, the New York Islanders swept the New York Rangers in four straight games. "I think you'd have to say we're a great team," said Denis Potvin after the series. "I don't think there's any doubt about that." At the same time, the ninth-place Minnesota North Stars completed their third upset of the playoffs by defeating the seventh-place Calgary Flames four games to two. The win put the North Stars into the Stanley Cup final against the New York Islanders, the NHL's regular-season champions.

The Stanley Cup Finals (Best of Seven)

In the Stanley Cup finals, the Islanders came on strong, winning the first three games by scores of 6–3, 6–3 and 7–5. The Minnesota North Stars came up with their biggest game of the series when they absolutely had to, winning game four by 4–2, staving off elimination and forcing a fifth game back in Long Island. In what proved to be the final game of the 1981 playoffs, the Islanders ran in three quick goals in the first 10 minutes of play and coasted to a 5–1 victory and a 4–1 Stanley Cup series victory. Ribbons of confetti showered the ice when the final siren wailed and the players circled the Stanley Cup, slapping and hugging it. It was their second consecutive Stanley Cup.

The Islanders were led by Smythe Trophy winner Butch Goring and his 10 playoff goals. "We need a little more experience and consistency to go all the way," said Minnesota left-winger Steve Payne, who scored an amazing 17 goals in the playoffs. "And that will come. The playoffs this year will give us that."

In post-season coaching developments, the resignation of the L.A. Kings' coach Bob Berry, over a contract dispute, caught everyone by surprise. But owner Jerry Buss wasted little time installing assistant coach Parker MacDonald to replace Berry for the 1981–82 season. Tom Watt was appointed as the head coach of the Winnipeg Jets by general manager John Ferguson. Watt had made his pro-coaching debut the season before as an assistant to the Vancouver Canucks' coach Harry Neale.

1981–82

The Kings' Charlie Simmer was walking much sooner than expected after he had broken his leg and his teammates waited for invitations to his July wedding to lovely Terri Welles. But Charlie fooled them. He and Terri decided not to wait. They grabbed a flight to Las Vegas and got married in the We've Only Just Begun Wedding Chapel.

Winnipeg Jets' general manager John Ferguson was looking forward to a long-term relationship with junior star Dale Hawerchuk. He opened the 1981 June draft proceedings by drafting Hawerchuk from Cornwall of the QMJHL. "I've been waiting for Dale for two years," admitted Ferguson. "When I saw him as a 16-year-old in Brandon, I was sold on him then." The Los Angeles Kings, who drafted second, took another center, Doug Smith of the Ottawa 67s. Next, the Washington Capitals chose Bob Carpenter, who was considered the greatest hockey prospect to come out of the eastern seaboard in years. The Hartford Whalers then picked center Ron Francis of the Sault Ste. Marie Greyhounds of the Ontario League. Goaltenders were a big attraction at the draft with 25 young netminders selected by the 21 teams. Grant Fuhr of the Victoria Cougars was snapped up by Edmonton, drafting eighth. Fuhr became the first goaltender drafted in the first round since 1975.

Herb Brooks, the coach who led the U.S. Olympic team to a gold medal at Lake Placid, was given the coaching duties of the New York Rangers. In other moves, the Montreal Canadiens announced that Bob Berry would be their new mentor. The announcement came less than two weeks after Berry had left the Los Angeles Kings.

A third Stastny brother joined the Quebec Nordiques after defecting with his family from Czechoslovakia via Austria in August. He was 28-year-old right-winger Marian Stastny, who had spent six years with the Czechoslovakian National Team before being suspended by the Czech federation in 1980, in reprisal for the earlier defection of brothers Peter and Anton.

Wayne Gretzky, 20, who had won the 1980–81 NHL point-scoring championship, walked away with two trophies—the Ross, as scoring champion, and the Hart, as the league's most valuable player. The only other trophy winner to make a return appearance was Bob Gainey of the Montreal Canadiens, who won the Frank J. Selke Trophy for the NHL's best defensive forward. It marked the fourth year in succession that Gainey had won the award since it was first presented in 1978. Peter Stastny of the Quebec Nordiques was named rookie of the year, winning the Calder Trophy. Randy Carlyle of the Pittsburgh Penguins capped his best NHL season ever by winning the Norris Trophy as the best defenseman in the league. Rick Kehoe of the Penguins won the Lady Byng Trophy for the player who best combined sportsmanship and hockey skills. The New York Islanders' Butch Goring captured the Smythe Trophy as the best player in the playoffs. Blake Dunlop of the St. Louis Blues won the Masterton Trophy as the NHL's "unsung hero." Red Berenson, also of the Blues was named coach of the year and received the Jack Adams Award. The Canadiens' goaltending team of Richard Sevigny, Denis Herron and Bunny Larocque combined to win the Vezina Trophy with the best goals-against average, despite the fact that Larocque was traded and finished the final eight games of the season with Toronto. It was the first time in NHL history that three goalies had had their names on the Vezina in the same year.

The Detroit Red Wings made some changes. The biggest transaction was a trade with Minnesota which brought veterans Don Murdoch and Greg Smith to Detroit, along with the North Stars' top draft choice in 1982, in exchange for the Wings' top pick in the same draft. Rick MacLeish was traded from Philadelphia to Hartford in a multi-player deal which included Hartford's number-one draft pick in 1982.

Serge Savard, who had spent 14 years with the Montreal Canadiens, officially retired from hockey in August. Savard played on eight Stanley Cup-winning teams with Montreal and was a member of Team Canada in the 1972 showdown series against the Soviet Union. He played in the 1976 Canada Cup and the 1979 Challenge Cup international hockey series. In 1969, Savard was awarded the Conn Smythe Trophy and in 1979 captured both the Bill Masterton Memorial Trophy and an All-Star team berth. "The last two years have been sad for me," said Savard, referring as much to catcalls from disgruntled fans as his diminished output. "I didn't like the way things went in the last two years."

Bill Jennings of the New York Rangers was elected to the Hockey Hall of Fame as a builder. Players inducted included Frank Mahovlich, John Bucyk and Allan Stanley. John Ashley was named to the referees' section.

The 1981 Canada Cup Tournament would long be remembered as the tournament most North Americans would like to forget as the Soviet Union crushed Team Canada 8–1 in the final game. The game was characterized by an awesome goaltending performance from Vladislav Tretiak. Tempers flared when the Soviets attempted to take the Canada Cup with them as they left the Montreal Forum after their triumph. Al Eagleson won a wrestling match for the trophy and told the Soviets that the cup must remain in Canada no matter who wins it.

Nick Fotiu signed a contract that he and his lawyer felt would assure him of spending the rest of his playing career as a New York Ranger. "It's great to be back," said Fotiu, who rejoined the Rangers from Hartford.

There were changes in the NHL with all four divisions realigned, an unbalanced 80-game schedule devised and a distinctive new playoff format for the 16 teams that would make it to the Stanley Cup playoffs in the spring of 1982.

In the Adams Division, Boston, Buffalo and Quebec remained where they were the previous season, with Hartford and Montreal moving over from the Norris to the Adams Division. The Patrick Division was barely changed, with only Calgary moving out and Pittsburgh shifting in from the Norris Division. Calgary transferred to the Smythe Division, joining Colorado, Edmonton and Vancouver. Los Angeles left the Norris Division to take a spot in the Smythe Division as well. The new divisional structure virtually wiped out the Norris Division of the previous year. There were five new teams in the Norris including Chicago, St. Louis and Winnipeg from the Smythe Division and Minnesota and Toronto from the Adams. Only Detroit remained intact in the Norris Division.

In the previous season the Norris and Adams divisions had made up the Wales Conference. The new Wales Conference was comprised of the Patrick and Adams divisions. The Norris and Smythe divisions would be aligned with the Campbell Conference.

Mike Rogers, who had been the leading scorer on the Hartford Whalers was traded to the New York Rangers. The Rangers gave up three players: defenseman Chris Kotsopolous, left-winger Doug Sulliman and defenseman Gerry McDonald. The Whalers also secured right-winger Garry Howatt, an eight-year performer, from the New York Islanders in return for future considerations and purchased the contract of veteran defenseman Paul Shmyr from Minnesota.

Even before the new NHL season had started, suspensions were being handed out.

Goaltender Billy Smith of the Islanders and defenseman Barry Beck of the Rangers were each assessed a three-game suspension for their part in a bench-clearing brawl during an exhibition game between the two teams. Beck was suspended for being the first player off the bench and Smith was penalized for incurring three major penalties in a single game. Earlier, the NHL had suspended Ron Zanussi of the Toronto Maple Leafs for three games as well, after Zanussi led the charge of the Leafs off the bench in a penalty-filled game with the Quebec Nordiques.

The Nordiques announced that they had filed a contract with the NHL for Czechoslovakian Miroslav Frycer. Frycer was one of four players permitted to come to the NHL under the terms of an agreement between the league and the Czechoslovakian Ice Hockey Federation, whereby veteran members of the Czech national team would be made available for a draft by NHL clubs. The Vancouver Canucks sabotaged the Czech draft by signing two veteran Czech stars, Ivan Hlinka and Jiri Bubla. The Canucks were praised by the media for jumping in and signing the imports while other clubs sat around watching and waiting.

The Soviet Union, winners of the 1981 Canada Cup tournament, finally received their own Canada Cup trophy, even if it wasn't the real thing. George Smith, a Winnipeg trucker, hockey fan and self-proclaimed nationalist, and his friends collected $2,600 to have a replica made and he and Manitoba Lieutenant-Governor Bud Jobin presented the cup to a member of the Soviet Union's Canadian embassy in what Smith said had amounted to a victory for hockey over bureaucracy.

In the most productive waiver draft held in recent years, the NHL shifted 12 active players and one retired player around the league. In the most surprising move, the Winnipeg Jets drafted retired Montreal defenseman Serge Savard ninth for the minimum $2,500 price, thinking that they could persuade the nearly 36-year-old Savard to abandon his retirement plans and join them.

New head coaches for the 1981–82 season included Scotty Bowman at Buffalo, Parker MacDonald at Los Angeles, Bob Berry joining Montreal, Herb Brooks with the Rangers, Tom Watt at Winnipeg and Bert Marshall with Colorado.

Millionaire sportsman Nelson Skalbania officially gave up his remaining interest in the NHL Calgary Flames. The move by Skalbania left the team ownership in the hands of six prominent Calgary businessmen.

Mike Bossy of the New York Islanders and Wayne Gretzky of the Edmonton Oilers both locked up their hockey futures with new lucrative contracts. Gretzky reached a verbal agreement on a renogotiated contract under which he would earn $1 million annually by 1984. Bossy signed a pact with the Islanders that would make him one of the highest-paid players in the league. The 24-year-old Bossy would receive $4.5 million over a seven-year period.

Harry Neale, coach of the Vancouver Canucks, claimed that the media had fingered his European players for the Canucks' slow start this season and he was ripping mad.

> Everyone's blaming our Europeans and that's a lot of bull [charged Neale].
> It's an unfair diagnosis of what's wrong with the team. It's an easy way out,
> strictly a matter of the media. It seems to be something for them to write
> about. To me, it's a form of racism, that's what it is.

The Minnesota North Stars inked general manager Lou Nanne to a new six-year contract that would keep him in the team's employ until the 1987–88 season.

Abe Pollin, owner of the Washington Capitals, fired general manager Max McNab, coach Gary Green and assistant coach Bill Mahoney after the team tallied a 1–12 record. Roger Crozier, the assistant general manager under McNab was named to replace all three, at least for a few days. Later, Bryan Murray, the coach of the Capitals' Hershey farm club, was promoted to the position of head coach.

The New York Rangers and Bobby Hull had decided against the Golden Jet coming back to hockey. Hull announced that he was retiring for good.

Disgruntled Toronto defenseman Ian Turnbull and his $185,000-a-year contract were sent to the Los Angeles Kings for right-winger Billy Harris and defenseman John Gibson.

In November, the Minnesota North Stars blasted the Winnipeg Jets 15–2, setting a club record for single-game scoring and tying the NHL's second-highest score. The Stars' eight goals in one period also set a team mark and again tied the second best in NHL history.

In a flurry of trade activity, the Calgary Flames swapped left-winger Eric Vail to Detroit for right-winger Gary McAdam. Then they sent their team captain and defenseman Brad Marsh to the Philadelphia Flyers for former Flyer captain, center Mel Bridgman. As if that weren't enough, Calgary Flames' general manager Cliff Fletcher shipped right-winger Randy Holt and minor leaguer Bobby Gould to Washington in return for defenseman Pat Ribble. Later Fletcher traded left-winger Don Lever and right-winger Bob MacMillan to the Colorado Rockies in return for veteran right-winger Lanny McDonald and the Rockies' fourth-round draft pick in 1982.

Philadelphia defenseman Behn Wilson received a four-game suspension from the NHL after his stick caught Rangers' defenseman Reijo Ruotsalainen in the face, just missing his right eye. Chris Nilan of the Montreal Canadiens was suspended for three games by the NHL for throwing a puck at Pittsburgh Penguins' defenseman Paul Baxter. Nilan wanted to fight with Baxter but the Pittsburgh defenseman wanted no part of it. After they were in the penalty box Baxter yelled something at Nilan, who then picked up a puck and fired a strike which hit Baxter on the head.

The New York Islanders announced that 1981 Smythe Trophy winner Butch Goring, 32, had been named as an assistant coach to Al Arbour. Goring would continue in his active playing role but would also be an assistant in directing the team on and off the ice.

A blockbuster trade occurred when Buffalo Sabres general manager Scotty Bowman unloaded goaltender Bob Sauve, defenseman Jim Schoenfeld, center Derek Smith and right-winger Danny Gare to the Detroit Red Wings. In return the Sabres received three of Detroit's former number-one draft choices—forwards Dale McCourt, Mike Foligno and Brent Peterson—plus future considerations. The reaction to the swap was primarily one of disbelief. Many of the Buffalo players were bitter. "The part that really hurts is that one man [Bowman] can be so powerful," said Danny Gare, the team's top goal scorer in the previous season. "I had no communication whatsoever with him. I just can't understand why he is the way he is. That's the reason I'm glad I'm getting out of here. I'm going with the heart and soul of the Sabres."

The lowly Colorado Rockies, who had been having their troubles winning this season, decided that they had nothing to lose by allowing assistant general manager Marshall Johnston and head coach Bert Marshall to switch jobs in an attempt to stimulate the team.

On December 12, Rick Martin of the Los Angeles Kings and formerly of the Buffalo Sabres, announced his retirement from hockey at the age of 30. If he had played any longer on his right knee, which he had injured 14 months earlier, he might have become a cripple.

To everyone's surprise, Serge Savard, the veteran defenseman who sparked the Montreal Canadiens to seven Stanley Cups, agreed to terms on a two-year contract with the Winnipeg Jets. "I really thought I was done with hockey after the last playoffs," said Savard after his short-lived retirement. Savard planned to get himself into condition before playing regularly with the Jets on defense. The team declared that they would make him the team captain when he was ready to play.

Alan Eagleson was recommending that most of his clients play their hockey in the United States rather than Canada. He was reacting to the November 12 Canadian fiscal budget, which had ended income-averaging annuities for athletes. He added that he hoped college players would be persuaded to remain in Canada. At the time Eagleson was the agent for Brian Bellows, the young Kitchener star who was rated as Canada's finest amateur-hockey player and the junior who was expected to be the number-one choice in the 1982 NHL entry draft. He said that under no circumstances would he allow Bellows to sign with a Canadian team, even if he were drafted by one of the seven Canadian NHL clubs.

The Hartford Whalers obtained 26-year-old center Pierre Larouche from the Montreal Canadiens for future considerations. "So far I love it here," said Larouche, who showed four goals and two assists in his first four games with Hartford. "I'm not sorry that I left Montreal because I wasn't playing there." In a second major deal, the Whalers swapped Rick MacLeish to the Pittsburgh Penguins for defenseman Russ Anderson and future considerations.

When Marian Stastny got off to a fast start for the Nordiques there was talk that he would succeed his brother Peter as the NHL rookie of the year. The same critics who had howled that Peter was not a bona fide rookie because he'd played international hockey for several years, now declared that Marian was not a proper candidate for the same reasons.

The NHL continued to crack down on stick swingers. Left-winger Wayne Cashman of the Boston Bruins was suspended by the NHL for four games for deliberately trying to injure another player when he speared Dean Hopkins of the L.A. Kings.

At mid-season, Mario Lemieux, 16, was the talk of hockey. The youngster had led the Laval Voisins in scoring with 48 points in his first 34 games and he had been a big factor in Laval's continuing fight to keep in the race for a QHL playoff berth.

Parker MacDonald, head coach of the Los Angeles Kings, moved from behind the bench to become assistant general manager. According to owner Jerry Buss, MacDonald was not removed as coach because he'd done a poor job, but because the Kings needed an assistant for general manager George Maguire. Don Perry, a career minor-league coach who was directing the Kings' farm team in New Haven, became the new coach.

After an incident that resulted in the loss of the Penguins' leading scorer Paul Gardner for at least six weeks, Pittsburgh coach Eddie Johnston called it, "the most vicious thing I've seen in all my years in hockey." Gardner's jaw was broken in two places when Winnipeg Jet right-wing Jimmy Mann sucker-punched him during a stoppage in play late in the second period of a January 13 game. The punch was apparently in retaliation for a cross check Gardner had given the Jets' Doug Smail a few minutes earlier. As a result of the incident, the NHL gave Jimmy Mann a 10-game suspension. Gardner felt cheated by the NHL suspension. "I'm going to miss 25 to 30 games, and he's only going to miss 10," said Gardner.

Darryl Sittler of the Toronto Maple Leafs was traded to Philadelphia in exchange for Providence College freshman Rich Costello, a 1982 second-round draft choice, and future considerations. The trade brought to a close Sittler's career as a Leaf, during which he had set club records for goals (389), assists (527), points (916), as well as the most 30-goal seasons (eight), and the most 40-goal seasons (four), not to mention some of his outstanding single-game feats, such as six goals and 10 points in a game and five goals in a playoff game.

Wayne Gretzky of the Edmonton Oilers agreed to terms on a new contract worth $20 million over the next 15 years. It made Gretzky the highest-paid player in the NHL, surpassing the former high of $600,000 per year being paid to Marcel Dionne by the Los Angeles Kings. Making good on his contract, Gretzky became the fastest 50-goal scorer in NHL history during a frigid December night in Edmonton. On December 27, Gretzky struck for five goals against Philadelphia in a 7–5 Oiler win, to reach the 50-goal plateau in a mere 39 games. His fifth goal was into an empty net with three seconds left on the clock.

Emile Francis, president, governor and general manager of the St. Louis Blues, was named the recipient of the 1982 Lester Patrick Trophy "for outstanding service to hockey in the United States."

There was growing concern in the NHL over the rash of eye injuries suffered in this 1981–82 season. The league lost two of its bright young hockey stars when Ron Francis of the Hartford Whalers and Buffalo's Ric Seiling were both sidelined after being clipped in the eye by high sticks. Other NHL players, including Terry Martin, Rene Robert and Glen Sharpley, all received eye injuries during the season.

In the NHL's 32nd annual All-Star game in Washington, the Wales Conference defeated the Campbell Conference All-Stars 4–2 on a pair of goals by New York Islander sharp-shooter Mike Bossy. The feat brought Bossy the award as the game's most valuable player as well as a $16,000 sports car and a silver tray. It was the sixth win in seven years for the Wales against the Campbells. During the All-Star festivities, the players were invited to the White House where they lunched with Ronald Reagan. "Nice lunch," said Mark Messier. "The plates had so much gold in them I could hardly lift them."

Vancouver's Thomas Gradin and Ivan Hlinka both scored on penalty shots against Detroit's netminder Gilles Gilbert to establish a first for the NHL—never before had the NHL experienced two penalty-shot goals in a single game.

Serge Savard was upset with the Montreal Canadiens when Jeff Brubaker inherited his old sweater, number 18. "For my whole career I've spoken out against violence," he said, "then they give my sweater to a guy who established an NHL record by fighting three times in his first 40 seconds on the ice against Philadelphia."

The New York Islanders broke the NHL's longest-winning streak when they defeated the Colorado Rockies on February 20, giving them a 15-game winning streak. The previous NHL record of 14 straight victories was set in 1929–30 by the Boston Bruins. John Tonelli's goal at 19:13 of the third period kept the streak alive. The Islanders' streak ended the following night, however, when the Pittsburgh Penguins upset them 4–3.

General manager Bob Pulford took over as coach of the Chicago Blackhawks after

Keith Magnuson resigned. "I told the players I would not return," said the 34-year-old Magnuson. "We have a young club. It needs an experienced coach and I can't offer that."

Wayne Gretzky tied Phil Esposito's record of 76 goals in a single NHL season, but he did so in 15 fewer games. He scored his record-tying goal with less than four minutes to play against the Detroit Red Wings on February 21 while 20,270 fans in the Joe Louis Arena cheered him on. On February 24, in a game against Buffalo, he went on to break Esposito's record, by scoring three goals. The brilliant Oiler had also established a new NHL single-season points record two nights earlier in Edmonton, as the Oilers defeated Hartford 7–4. Gretzky scored three times and assisted on two more to eclipse his own mark of 164 points.

Former NHL player Herbie Cain died at the age of 68. Cain had set an NHL points record (82) when he won the NHL scoring championship in 1943–44. He had helped the Montreal Maroons in 1935 and the Boston Bruins in 1941 to win the Stanley Cup. Cain had ended his NHL career in 1946, having scored 206 goals and picking up 194 assists.

After a season of alternating great and sputtering play, the Minnesota North Stars embarked on the longest unbeaten streak in the history of the franchise—11 games (eight wins and three ties).

The Quebec Nordiques sent Miroslav Frycer and a late draft choice to Toronto for Wilf Paiement. The rugged left-winger had been the third-highest scorer with the Leafs at the time of the trade, with 18 goals and 40 assists.

Wayne Maxner, head coach of the Detroit Red Wings, was fired and replaced by his assistant Billy Dea for the final 11 games of the season. The Wings, in last place in the Norris Division, were 12 points behind fourth-place Chicago when the change took place.

The Pittsburgh Penguins traded center Mark Johnson, the leading scorer on the 1980 gold medal-winning U.S. Olympic team, to the Minnesota North Stars for a second-round draft pick in the 1982 entry draft.

Pat Quinn, coach of the Philadelphia Flyers, was fired and the man whom he had succeeded three years before, Bob McCammon, replaced him.

The Quebec City police investigated an incident during a March 20 game after Vancouver Canucks' coach Harry Neale and some of his players went into the stands after a fan. Neale reportedly began trading punches with a fan, who Neale maintained had slugged Tiger Williams of the Canucks. Several Canucks then followed Neale into the stands and a brawl broke out. The police had to be called to restore order, but no arrests were made. NHL president John Ziegler, however, suspended Neale for 10 games. The stiff suspension meant that Neale would miss the final five games of the regular schedule and the first five games of the playoffs. He was replaced behind the bench by assistant coach Roger Neilson.

Right-winger Dave Taylor of the Los Angeles Kings signed a new seven-year contract that would put him in the top three or four money earners in the NHL. It was believed that Taylor had agreed to a figure of $3.2 million.

NHL attendance hit a record high of 11,375,554 for the 1981–82 season—the third straight year the league had surpassed the 11-million mark at the box office.

At the season's end, Wayne Gretzky had rewritten many pages in the NHL record book. His accomplishments included a record number of goals (92), assists (120) and points (212), a margin of 65 points more than runner-up Mike Bossy of the Islanders, a record 1.5 assists per game, a record 2.65 points-per-game average and a record 10 games in which he had scored at least three goals.

While Gretzky dominated the season, there were many other highlights. The Pittsburgh Penguins scored a record 99 power-play goals while the Edmonton Oilers registered 417 goals, another record. For the first time in history, 10 players scored 50 goals or more and 13 players topped 100 points. Winnipeg's Dale Hawerchuk became the first rookie to score over 40 goals and 100 points in the same season. He finished with 45–58–103.

For the second consecutive year, the Islanders finished in first place overall with 118 points, seven points ahead of the Edmonton Oilers. Winnipeg, coached by Tom Watt, made the most dramatic improvement, soaring to 33 wins and 80 points, good enough for second place in the Norris Division. This followed a dismal season of nine wins and 51 points in 1980–81.

THE NHL PLAYOFFS

A new playoff format was introduced this season. All the emphasis would be on standings within the four divisions with the top four teams in each division qualifying for post-season play. The former overall-standings system was abandoned. When the playoffs got underway, there was widespread criticism of the new format, especially when upsets occurred in half of the eight first-round best-of-five series.

Smythe Division

Hockey fans rubbed their eyes in disbelief when the lowly Los Angeles Kings (17th place) eliminated the mighty Edmonton Oilers (second place) in the first round of the Stanley Cup playoffs. The teams set a playoff record with 18 goals in the opener, which was won by the Kings 10–8, who then went on to a 3–2 series victory. In regular-season play, the Kings had won only 24 games to the Oilers' 48. The Oilers' sudden demise brought much criticism from the media. One critic, *Edmonton Journal* columnist Terry Jones, had some harsh words about the team. "From today until they've won a playoff series again, they are weak-kneed wimps who thought they were God's gift to the NHL but found out they were nothing but adolescent, front-running goodtime Charlies who couldn't handle any adversity," wrote Jones in his daily sports column.

In the other Smythe matchup, the Vancouver Canucks sent the Calgary Flames packing with a three-game sweep. In the division finals, the Canucks enjoyed their greatest success in the 12-year history of the franchise by advancing to the conference final after ousting the Los Angeles Kings 4–1.

Norris Division

Minnesota finished 22 points ahead of Chicago in the Norris Dvision standings but the Hawks emerged from their playoff matchup as 3–1 victors. Elsewhere, Brian Sutter, Bernie Federko and Brian Mullen led the St. Louis Blues to a 3–1 series win over the Winnipeg Jets. In the division finals, the Hawks hurdled the Blues four games to two and advanced to the Campbell Conference finals against Vancouver. It would be a battle of regular-season losers. The Hawks had finished eight games below .500, the Canucks three games below .500.

Patrick Division

John Tonelli emerged as the early playoff hero for the Islanders after he scored the game-tying goal with less than three minutes to play in game five and then sank the overtime winner in a dramatic win over the Penguins. The Isles' victory earned them a berth in the division finals against the Rangers, who had won their series over the Philadelphia Flyers by 3–1. In the finals, the Rangers pushed the Isles to the wall before bowing out in six games.

Adams Division

It was another year of disappointment for Buffalo fans, who saw their Sabres lose to the Boston Bruins in four games. In Quebec, Dale Hunter's goal after 22 seconds of overtime in game five won the Battle of Quebec for the Nordiques over the Montreal Canadiens. The Habs had been expected to sweep the series with three straight games. The Nordiques went on to outlast the Bruins in a rugged seven-game series that was decided on Boston ice. It was simply a case of too many Stastnys for the Bruins, as Marian, Peter and Anton sparkled.

Campbell Conference Finals

The Vancouver Canucks polished off the Chicago Blackhawks 4–1 in their best-of-seven Campbell Conference final to win the right to advance to the Stanley Cup finals against the Islanders. During their lone loss to the Hawks, coach Roger Neilson and his players on the bench waved white towels in mock surrender when referee Bob Myers disallowed a Canuck goal. Their antics resulted in $11,000 in fines to the club. If one person had spearheaded the Vancouver Canucks into their first-ever Stanley Cup final, it had to be hot goaltender Richard Brodeur. Brodeur, 29, who broke the Hawks' backs in the series with his brilliant goaltending, was one of the outstanding figures of the 1982 playoffs.

Wales Conference Finals

The New York Islanders proved to be too strong for the Quebec Nordiques, eliminating them 4–0 in the best-of-seven series and capturing the Wales Conference championship. It looked like an easy road to the Cup for the Isles, who would now face Vancouver. In the regular season, the Isles had finished in first place overall with 54 wins and 118 points. The Canucks had only won 30 games and had finished 11th overall with 77 points.

The Stanley Cup Finals

In the Stanley Cup finals, the Canucks looked to Richard Brodeur for one more miracle. But even Brodeur's goaltending heroics could not stem the surging Islander tide. On Sunday, May 16, the New York Islanders ended the 1981–82 hockey season by sweeping the Vancouver Canucks to become the first United States team to ever win the Stanley Cup in three consecutive years. The heavily favored Islanders had maintained their superiority throughout the final series, winning the deciding game 3–1 after blanking the Canucks 3–0 in game three. Coupled with their two victories in New York, in which they won game one 6–5 and game two 6–4, the Islanders outscored the Canucks 18–10 in the series and finished with an imposing 15–4 playoff record. Mike Bossy won the Conn Smythe Trophy as the most valuable player of the playoffs. Bossy's 17 post-season goals had matched his output for the preceding year and he was the only regular on either side who had completed the playoffs without a penalty. "This is a team with tremendous desire," Bossy said. "If we keep that desire, we'll never lose the Cup."

During the playoffs, the Edmonton Oilers' millionaire owner, Peter Pocklington, emerged from a bizarre 12-hour hostage-taking drama in his home with a bullet wound in his arm. An unemployed 29-year-old Edmonton man had held him hostage and demanded $1 million in ransom money. The police ended the affair when they stormed his house, firing shots which hit both Pocklington and his abductor.

The 1982 World Hockey Championships held in Tampere, Finland, were a big disappointment for Team Canada. The controversial 0–0 tie in the wind-up game between the gold-medal winning Soviets and the Czechoslovakians pulled the latter into a second-place tie with Canada. But the Czechs captured the silver medal because they had outscored Canada 8–6 in two meetings between the clubs. "I won't say the fix was in, but I know if it had been the other way around, we'd have sweated for the Russians and they didn't sweat for us," Team Canada chairman Alan Eagleson said. Wayne Gretzky won the scoring championship with 14 points in 10 games.

1982–83

The Boston Bruins and the Minnesota North Stars made a surprise arrangement prior to the 1982 entry draft. After Kitchener junior star Brian Bellows became the most publicized player in the draft, Bruins' general manager Harry Sinden, drafting first, agreed to pass up Bellows so that Minnesota could claim him. The North Stars paid for the favor by shipping left-winger Brad Palmer, 21, and center Dave Donnelly, 20, to Boston. Sinden then selected defenseman Gord Kluzak, a choice he defended by saying, "I would have taken Kluzak even if I hadn't made the deal with Minnesota." The drafting of Kluzak enabled Sinden to deal Brad McCrimmon, an unhappy defenseman who had achieved free-agent status, to Philadelphia for goalie Pete Peeters.

The Minnesota North Stars, picking second, snatched up the celebrated Bellows. "It might be the best move we've ever made," said North Star general manager Lou Nanne. "We need some character and leadership and those are exactly the qualities Bellows has." Drafted third overall was defenseman Gary Nylund, who was chosen by the Toronto Maple Leafs. Philadelphia, drafting fourth, picked Ron Sutter, whose twin brother Rich was taken later in the first round (number 10) by Pittsburgh. Defenseman Scott Stevens was claimed by Washington and Buffalo's Scotty Bowman, drafting sixth overall, claimed Phil Housley, an 18-year-old high-school player from

St. Paul, Minnesota. "He's the closest thing to Orr I've ever seen," said Bowman.

The New Jersey Devils were so anxious to draft Bryan Trottier's brother Rocky, that they sent Rob Ramage to St. Louis in return for the Blues' first draft choices in 1982 and 1983. After getting Trottier (number 8), the Devils selected Ken Daneyko and Pat Verbeek in later rounds. And the Rangers looked to the future when they drafted 18-year-old Tony Granato from Northwood High School in New York, who was the 120th player chosen. The L.A. Kings made history at the draft table when they claimed a 27-year-old Soviet player, Victor Nechaev. Nechaev had met and married a University Yale student, Cheryl Haigler, when she was touring the Soviet Union. Nechaev was allowed to leave his homeland and he became a U.S. resident.

A half-century of tradition had ended in Detroit. The Red Wings' franchise and two farm teams were sold to Mike Ilitch, ending 50 years of Norris family ownership. The purchase price was believed to be about $9 million. Ilitch chose Jimmy Devellano, formerly with the Islanders, to restructure the NHL franchise. "As long as I'm general manager of the Detroit Red Wings, I will not trade a draft choice," said Devellano, 39, formerly assistant general manager of the New York Islanders. "Not a first round, not a third round, not a fifth round, not a 10th round. You can write it down. That's a commitment."

The NHL approved the sale of the Colorado Rockies to a New Jersey-based syndicate headed by John McMullen, part-owner of baseball's National League Houston Astros, for an estimated $30 million, including transfer fees and indemnities to be paid to the New York Rangers, New York Islanders and Philadelphia Flyers for invading their territories. The team, to be called the Devils, would be placed in the Patrick Division, where they would join the Rangers, Islanders, Philadelphia, Washington and Pittsburgh. The Winnipeg Jets agreed to a transfer from the Norris Division to the Smythe Division, replacing the Rockies.

At the league's summer meetings in Montreal, Wayne Gretzky captured the Ross and Hart trophies. He was a unanimous choice for the Hart; never before had every ballot gone to one player. Boston's Steve Kasper edged Montreal's Bob Gainey for the Selke Award. Other winners included Chicago's Doug Wilson (Norris), Winnipeg's Dale Hawerchuk (Calder), Boston's Rick Middleton (Lady Byng) and the Islanders' Billy Smith (Vezina).

Larry Pleau, who had replaced Don Blackburn as interim head coach for the Hartford Whalers on February 20, 1981, and then replaced Jack Kelley as the club's general manager 39 days later, turned over his coaching duties to Larry Kish. The Chicago Blackhawks hired Orval Tessier as their new head coach, while Washington Capitals' owner Abe Pollin announced that general manager Roger Crozier would be relieved of his duties. David Poile, the Calgary Flames' youthful assistant general manager, was chosen to replace Crozier. The new coach of the Detroit Red Wings was Nick Polano, 41, a veteran of 15 minor-league seasons. He became Detroit's 16th coach in the previous 15 seasons. Buffalo general manager Scotty Bowman added Red Berenson to his staff in the capacity of assistant coach. Berenson had been the NHL's coach of the year in 1981 with St. Louis.

The NHL suspended Boston Bruin Terry O'Reilly for 10 games to start the 1982–83 season and fined him the maximum $500 for hitting referee Andy van Hellemond with two seconds left in the Bruins' playoff season.

Bobby Smith signed a seven-year contract with the Minnesota North Stars that

206

would escalate his salary up from about $300,000 toward a total package worth about $2.6 million.

NHL owners and representatives of the Players' Association reached agreement on a five-year collective bargaining contract that satisfied both sides with a new formula for free-agent compensation.

The Philadelphia Flyers obtained defenseman Mark Howe from the Hartford Whalers in exchange for center Ken Linseman, left-winger Greg Adams and their first-round draft pick in 1983. Hartford then dealt Linseman along with center-winger Don Nachbaur to Edmonton for defenseman Risto Siltanen and another left-winger, 18-year-old Brent Loney. Philadelphia wanted Howe badly. They reportedly gave him a $100,000 bonus to sign, upped his yearly contract (roughly $175,000) by $50,000 a year, and offered to buy his house in Connecticut if he was unable to sell it in 90 days.

The NHL's first civil lawsuit resulting from an on-ice incident ended in August with Dennis Polonich, the plaintiff, receiving an $850,000 award from a U.S. Federal Court jury. Polonich, a former Detroit Red Wing, had sued for damages for an injury he suffered in an NHL game on October 25, 1978, at Olympia Stadium when he was struck in the face with a stick wielded by Wilf Paiement, then playing for the Colorado Rockies. Paiement and the Rockies were defendants in the landmark case, only the third of its kind in major-league sports.

The NHL board of governors passed a rule that called for an automatic 20-game suspension to any player guilty of roughing up a referee or linesman.

The Calgary Flames obtained center left-winger Doug Risebrough, 28, from the Montreal Canadiens for a third-round draft pick and a switch of second-round picks in 1983. Risebrough had asked the Canadiens to trade him. Montreal also sent defensemen Brian Engblom and Rod Langway along with center Doug Jarvis and winger Craig Laughlin to the Washington Capitals. They got back an aggressive, scoring winger in Ryan Walter and a steady but unspectacular defenseman in Rick Green. No one could understand how the Canadiens' Irving Grundman could give up one of the best defensive pairs in the NHL and only receive a left-winger and a defenseman who hadn't come close to an All-Star berth. "How are we going to get the puck out of our end?" goaltender Rick Wamsley asked.

An historical era in Canadian broadcasting ended when Bill Hewitt, son of hockey-broadcast pioneer Foster Hewitt, announced that he was retiring. The 53-year-old Hewitt, a broadcast partner of this author for 17 years, had been ill throughout the previous season.

The annual NHL Hall of Fame induction ceremonies in Toronto were highlighted by the inclusion of four new members into the hockey shrine: Norm Ullman, Yvan Cournoyer, Rod Gilbert and Emile Francis. Gordie Howe was honored as the first recipient of a milestone award that paid tribute to past performers who had scored 1,000 points, 400 goals, 600 assists as well as had played in more than 1,000 games.

A total of nine players changed hands in the NHL's 1982 waiver draft, with the New Jersey Devils leading the way by grabbing three defensemen—Carol Vadnais, Dave Hutchison and Murray Brumwell. The New York Rangers drafted rear guard Bill Baker from St. Louis and left another defenseman, Tim Bothwell, off their list. The Blues promptly claimed Bothwell, then drafted center Jack Carlson from Minnesota. Pittsburgh ended the round by grabbing center Doug Lecuyer from Winnipeg. The Rangers claimed Graeme Nicolson after New Jersey left him open. Edmonton then drafted defenseman Bob Hoffmeyer from Philadelphia.

Ken Linseman didn't waste any time making his mark with his newest NHL team, the Edmonton Oilers. He was handed a four-game suspension by the league for poking Toronto forward Russ Adam with his stick during an exhibition game.

Philadelphia's Jim Watson, 30, announced that his hockey days were over. A degenerating disc in his lower back had left him with no other option.

Hartford right-winger Blaine Stoughton missed the first eight games of the 1982–83 season after receiving a stiff suspension for cross-checking Pittsburgh defenseman Paul Baxter.

The Boston Bruins handed Olympic goaltending hero Jim Craig his unconditional release at the conclusion of training camp by buying out the option year of his contract. Craig, who had a no-cut contract, had a stormy career with the Bruins after refusing demotion to the minors. Injuries had plagued him since his dramatic Olympic Games performance in the 1980 upset win over the Soviet Union. Ever since then it had been downhill for Craig. During training camp, Craig was cleared of any blame in the May 29 auto accident that had killed one woman and injured two others.

When Mark Johnson and the Hartford Whalers squared off against the Calgary Flames in Alberta, it marked the first time in the 66-year history of the NHL that a son had played against a team coached by his father. Mark's father, Bob, was chosen coach of the Flames in June after a long and successful college career at the University of Wisconsin. "We talk all the time," said Mark. "He keeps asking me for our secrets, but I never tell him anything."

A rookie's career ended tragically in Vancouver one night early in the season. Boston Bruin forward Normand Leveille, 19, one of the bright young stars in the NHL, had to fight for his life after suffering a brain hemorrhage between the first and second periods of a game against the Vancouver Canucks on October 23. "It didn't result from a check or a hard hit in the game," said Canuck team doctor Ross Davidson, who made the initial examination in the dressing room. "It could have happened if he'd sneezed going down the street. It's a risky thing to say that he'll never play again, but the risk of further damage would be too great to play hockey." Dr. Davidson said that there was a grave risk that Leveille had already suffered permanent damage.

There appeared to be an increase in the number of wild stick-swinging incidents in the NHL, despite new legislation to curb rowdiness. Dave "Tiger" Williams of the Vancouver Canucks was handed a seven-game suspension for engaging goalie Billy Smith of the Islanders in a stick duel in Vancouver. Willi Plett of Minnesota received an eight-game suspension for clubbing goalie Greg Stefan of Detroit. Also, Jerry Korab of Los Angeles was set down for six games after he connected on Dale Hunter of Quebec.

The first Soviet player ever to perform in the NHL, center Victor Nechaev of the Los Angeles Kings, was released by the team. After Nechaev had said that he didn't want to return to the minors for more seasoning, the Kings decided not to offer him a contract and promptly released him. Nechaev did manage to score a goal during his brief stint in the NHL.

Fred Arthur, Philadelphia's 21-year-old defenseman, found himself torn between two careers. The six-foot-five-inch rear guard said he wasn't getting much satisfaction out of hockey and might quit the game to follow a medical career.

Defenseman Mark Howe of the Philadelphia Flyers had filed a $5-million lawsuit seeking damages for an accident that had happened two years before while he was a member of the Hartford Whalers. He was suing Jayfro Corp., of Waterford, Connecticut (a hockey-equipment manufacturer), the city of Hartford and the Hartford Civic Center and Coliseum Authority. During a Whaler–Islander game in Hartford on December 27, 1980, Howe had slid into the net feet first, hitting the pointed centerpiece and puncturing his rectum. At that time it was feared the injury would end his NHL career.

Wayne Gretzky of the Edmonton Oilers added yet another record to his already mounting collection. By scoring one goal and adding four assists against the Los Angeles Kings on December 5, it marked the 29th straight game in which he had garnered at least one scoring point. Gretzky had removed the name of Guy Lafleur from the record book; Lafleur had set the original mark of 28 straight games with at least one point in 1976–77. Gretzky's streak ended at 30 on December 9 in a game against the Kings. Gretzky now held 22 NHL scoring records.

Normand Leveille of the Bruins amazed doctors at the Montreal Neurological Hospital with his determination to overcome the massive brain hemorrhage that had threatened his life in October. After being in a coma, the young winger was now conscious and alert. He did, however, suffer from a paralysis of his right side and was unable to speak. "Normand was going to be good, he was going to be great," said teammate Terry O'Reilly. "He was going to be a bigger star than Cournoyer."

On December 14, Marcel Dionne of the Los Angeles Kings became the ninth player in NHL history to score 500 career goals. The Kings' center, playing his 12th NHL season, joined Gordie Howe, Bobby Hull, Maurice Richard, Jean Beliveau, Phil Esposito, Johnny Bucyk, Stan Mikita and Frank Mahovlich as 500-goal scorers.

Philadelphia's Bobby Clarke passed the 1,100-point plateau with four points in the Flyers' 7–2 romp over Detroit.

The Washington Capitals extended their club-record undefeated streak to 13 games, after they beat the Philadelphia Flyers 3–1 on December 19 in the Spectrum. The Caps' streak came to an abrupt end on December 27 when the Flyers defeated them 6–3. They had won nine and tied five in a 14-game stretch that had made them the hottest team in the league.

Bruce Gamble, a former NHL netminder, died at the age of 43, an apparent victim of a heart attack. Gamble, who had played for the Toronto Maple Leafs and Philadelphia Flyers, was forced to quit pro hockey in 1972 after suffering a heart attack during a game in Vancouver.

The Chicago Blackhawks acquired Curt Fraser, a left-winger from the Vancouver Canucks. To get him, Chicago had to give up 19-year-old right-winger Tony Tanti, their first choice in the 1981 NHL entry draft. Tanti had scored 81 goals for Oshawa to break Wayne Gretzky's Ontario Hockey League rookie goal-scoring record.

Don Murdoch, once a New York Ranger superstar, was put on waivers by the Detroit Red Wings for the purpose of giving him his release. Murdoch had tried to bounce back with the Edmonton Oilers and came to the Red Wings via the Minnesota North Stars. Murdoch not only couldn't make it with the parent club, but he had failed in his bid to stick with Adirondack of the AHL.

Glen Sonmor, head coach of the Minnesota North Stars, resigned in January because he said he had lost enthusiasm for his job. Murray Oliver became interim head coach while J.P. Parise handled the defense. Both had been assistants to Sonmor. Sonmor was reported to be taking treatment for an alcohol problem.

Winnipeg's coach Tom Watt was fined $2,500 by the NHL for his remarks about referee Bob Myers after a 6–4 loss to Vancouver on January 16. Watt was quoted as saying that Myers had cheated the Jets.

The St. Louis Blues traded backup goalie Glen Hanlon and reserve center Vaclav Nedomansky to the New York Rangers in exchange for defenseman Andre Dore and future considerations.

Ralston Purina, the company that had purchased the Blues in 1977 as a civic gesture when the team appeared about to fold, had an offer from Edmonton promoter Bill Hunter. Hunter proposed to purchase the Blues and move them to Saskatoon where "I'll have a $43-million 18,000-seat arena ready for play within six months." The team owners voted 15–3 to reject the proposed sale, which prompted Ralston Purina to launch a $60-million suit against the NHL, alleging that the governors' meeting was "conducted in an unfair and improper manner." The NHL filed a counter suit accusing Ralston Purina of "a breach of trust with the citizens of St. Louis."

There was a hockey first in Hartford on January 15. A blizzard had prevented referee Ron Fournier and linesman Dan Marouelli from getting there in time for the first period of the Whalers' game against the Devils. So linesman Ron Foyt recruited Garry Howatt of the Devils and Mickey Volcan of the Whalers to assist him while he refereed the game. Both were on the injury list and said it had been a once-in-a-lifetime experience. Luckily, Fournier and Marouelli arrived in time to start the second period.

Darryl Sittler of the Philadelphia Flyers became the NHL's 17th 1,000-point scorer when he notched his 30th goal in a 5–2 win over Calgary on January 20. It also marked the 10th straight year that Sittler had scored 30 goals in a season. Gilbert Perreault of the Buffalo Sabres also grabbed some of the scoring limelight when he became the league's 14th highest all-time point scorer after he connected for his 1,047th career point.

In one of the most unusual hockey trades ever recorded, the Seattle Breakers of the Western Hockey League swapped the rights to left-winger Tom Martin in exchange for a used bus from the Victoria Cougars. "Actually, it was just the down payment," said the Breakers' owner John Hamilton. "It might have been the best deal I ever made. Our old bus blew its engine on a road trip last month. Victoria had a bus they couldn't use and we had a player we couldn't use. Bingo."

After 49 games as head coach of the Hartford Whalers and a record of 12–32–5, Larry Kish resigned. The club's director of hockey operations, Larry Pleau, assumed coaching duties for the remainder of the season.

Jamie Macoun, one of the top prizes in the U.S. college free-agent market, agreed to contract terms with the Calgary Flames. He was expected to be in the lineup before the season's end.

Boston's Wayne Cashman, who at 37 was the club's only surviving player from the 1970 and 1972 Stanley Cup victories, played in his 1,000th regular-season game with the Bruins on February 3.

Goalie John Garrett of the Canucks made some splendid saves for the Campbell Conference All-Stars in the annual game against the Wales Conference played on Long Island. Garrett was the odds-on favorite to win MVP honors and a new car, when Wayne Gretzky suddenly caught fire. Gretzky scored four goals in the third period—an All-Star first—to take the car away from Garrett and help win the game for the Campbells.

Mark Pavelich of the New York Rangers became the first American-born NHL player to score five goals in one game, during a 11–3 romp of the Hartford Whalers.

Pittsburgh Penguin owner Edward DeBartolo said his NHL team was staying in Pittsburgh and the jobs of coach Eddie Johnston and general manager Baz Bastien were secure, at least until the end of the season. "We're not thinking of moving, period," DeBartolo said in reference to rumors that the struggling Penguins would be moved or sold. "This year we'll lose $3.4 million on the Penguins. That's a lot of money. But that doesn't make any difference to us."

Mike Bossy of the New York Islanders was approaching the playoffs in fine shape. He scored his 49th and 50th goals against the Washington Capitals, matching Guy Lafleur's NHL record of six consecutive 50-goal seasons and six overall. Bossy also became the first NHL player to score 50 or more goals in each of his first six seasons.

Larry Pleau, the Hartford Whalers' general manager who was also coach for 18 games after the dismissal of Larry Kish, relinquished the coaching reins to John Cunniff. Under Pleau, the team was 4–13–1.

Defenseman Ed Kea, a 10-year veteran who had been demoted to Salt Lake by the parent St. Louis Blues, suffered a cerebral contusion on March 7, when he crashed into the boards during a Central Hockey League game after colliding with rookie George McPhee of the Tulsa Oilers. Kea sustained a broken nose and severe head injuries and lapsed into a coma. Doctors performed four hours of surgery but he remained in critical condition. Kea would recover, but not fully, and he would never play hockey again. Kea's accident, which occurred while he was not wearing a helmet, caused considerable concern among his fellow NHL players. Two staunch non-helmet wearers, Bill Barber of Philadelphia and Willi Plett of Minnesota, promptly put on helmets for the first time after learning of Kea's tragic injury.

Penguin general manager Aldege "Baz" Bastien, whose name was synonymous with hockey in Pittsburgh for five decades, died on March 15 from injuries he had received in an automobile accident. He was 62.

Willy Lindstrom, 32, a Winnipeg player for eight years, was traded to the Edmonton Oilers for Laurie Boschman. "I've always liked Edmonton's style," said Lindstrom. "They play like a European team with good skating and passing. They're always sweet to watch."

The NHL sweetened the pot for the 1983 playoffs, guaranteeing Stanley Cup-winning team members $20,000 per man, an increase of $5,000 in bonus money. The losers would receive $15,000. The NHL also revealed that a playoff pool of $2,549,400 would be divided among the competing clubs. In addition, each player on a regular-season division-champion team would receive $4,000 and the runner-up club would collect $2,000 per player.

Thirty-one-year-old Marcel Dionne of the Los Angeles Kings scored his 50th goal for the sixth time in his career to tie an NHL record held jointly by Guy Lafleur and Mike Bossy. Dionne also became the sixth-leading point scorer in NHL history when he collected three points in a 4–3 win over the Winnipeg Jets on March 15. It enabled Dionne to raise his lifetime total to 1,270 points.

A week later, Dionne became the first player to reach the 100-point plateau in seven straight seasons. Dionne's assist in a 9–3 loss to Edmonton on March 26 was the vital point that enabled him to break the record previously shared by Bobby Orr, Phil Esposito and Guy Lafleur.

Olympic gold-medal hero Jim Craig was given another chance at the NHL when the Minnesota North Stars announced that they had signed the former goaltending hero to a one-year contract. "A lot of people have given up on Craig," said general manager Lou Nanne. "But we obviously think he can still play."

Wayne Gretzky won the NHL scoring championship for the third straight year. He ended the season with 196 points, scoring 71 goals and picking up a record 125 assists in 80 games. In another scoring feat, Mike Bossy of the New York Islanders scored his 60th goal of the season to become the first player in NHL history to register 60 goals in three consecutive years.

The Boston Bruins, winners of 50 games, finished on top of the NHL overall standings with 110 points, four more than the Philadelphia Flyers. The Edmonton Oilers registered 106 points and a record 424 goals. Chicago showed an improvement of 32 points over the previous season, finishing fourth with 104.

THE NHL PLAYOFFS

Smythe Division

In the Smythe Division, the Edmonton Oilers had little trouble defeating the Winnipeg Jets in three straight games, while the Calgary Flames were winning their series 3–1 over Vancouver. When the Flames and the Oilers met for the division title, Wayne Gretzky and his teammates combined to tie or set several playoff records. While demolishing the Calgary Flames 10–2 in the third game of their best-of-seven series, Gretzky attained a record seven points to break the old mark of six. The Oilers, in winning the series 4–1 in games, scored 34 goals to set a record for most goals in a five-, six- or seven-game series. Gretzky also tied a playoff record with his third shorthanded goal and his four-goal outburst in game three equaled another playoff mark for most games with three or more goals.

Norris Division

In the semi-finals of the Norris Division, the Chicago Blackhawks eliminated the St. Louis Blues 3–1, while the Minnesota North Stars were busy ousting the Toronto Maple Leafs, also in four games. Then the Blackhawks, with three of their oldest players leading the way, expelled the North Stars from further playoff competition in five games. Tony Esposito, Tom Lysiak and Rich Preston were the Hawk veterans who played starring roles.

Patrick Division

The New York Rangers ousted the Flyers in the first round for the second consecutive year with a stunning three-game sweep. In the other Patrick Division match-up, the New York Islanders defeated the Washington Capitals 3–1. The New York Islanders captured the Patrick Division title as they defeated the injury-riddled Rangers in six games.

Adams Division

The Buffalo Sabres fashioned one of the major upsets of the playoffs when they swept past Montreal in three games, two of them shutouts by Bob Sauve. In the other Adams Division battle, the Boston Bruins defeated the Quebec Nordiques by 3–1, with Pete Peeters providing the goaltending edge. In the division final, the Boston Bruins became the champions as they defeated the Buffalo Sabres 4–3 in the best-of-seven series. Brad Park scored in overtime in game seven to send the Bruins to the conference final against the Islanders.

Campbell Conference Finals

In the conference finals, the Edmonton Oilers were too much for the Chicago Blackhawks to handle. The Oilers breezed past the Hawks 4–0 to become the Campbell Conference champions. As a result, everyone anticipated a thrilling Stanley Cup final, as both Edmonton and the Islanders (the Wales Conference champions) had demonstrated that they had the depth and talent to go all the way.

Wales Conference Finals

The defending Cup-champion New York Islanders went on to dispose of the Boston Bruins in six games, capturing the Wales Conference championship. Mike Bossy, frustrated by the close checking of the Bruins, broke loose for four goals as the Islanders scored an 8–4 victory in game six to clinch the conference title.

The Stanley Cup Finals

Nobody expected the Islanders to do what they did in the spring of 1983—beat Edmonton in four straight games to capture their fourth consecutive Stanley Cup. In game one, it was truly a case of the defense beating the offense, as the Islanders blanked the Oilers 2–0. A three-goal assault in the first period of game two forced the Oilers into a catch-up situation and while they managed to close the gap to 3–2, they couldn't overtake the Islanders who won 6–3. The pendulum continued to swing with the Islanders as they chalked up their third straight victory over Edmonton, winning with ease, 5–1. The Islanders wasted little time laying claim to their fourth consecutive Cup as they scored three times in the space of one minute and 37 seconds midway in the first period of game four. Even though the Oilers battled back to narrow the New York lead to 3–2, they never scored again, as Billy Smith held them off in the third period with some miraculous saves. The Islanders became the first U.S. team to win four consecutive Cups. One more and they would match the record of the Montreal Canadiens, who had won five times from 1956 to 1960. Billy Smith emerged as the playoff hero for the Islanders. He had won all four games and had held the Oilers to seven goals (none by Gretzky) to come up with the Conn Smythe Trophy as the MVP of the playoffs, the first goalie to win the award since Bernie Parent of Philadelphia had done it in 1975.

There were some interesting off-ice developments just four days after the Canadiens' third consecutive first-round exit from the Stanley Cup playoffs. The team's top three front-office members were fired. Bob Berry, appointed coach of the Canadiens on June 2, 1981, was relieved of his duties, but was expected to remain in the organization as a scout. Ronald Caron, director of player recruitment, was told his services would no longer be needed after the NHL's entry draft in June. Irving Grundman, 54, who had inherited the managing director's job in September 1979, was told that his contract would not be renewed.

Serge Savard was hired by the Montreal Canadiens as their new managing director. Savard had had a year remaining on his contract with the Jets, but the Canadiens had pried him loose by surrendering a draft pick and a fair sum of cash. Thirty-eight days after Bob Berry was relieved of his coaching duties with the Montreal Canadiens he was reappointed and given a two-year contract.

Emile Francis, 56, was named the new president of the Hartford Whalers. Francis promptly proclaimed, "The holy grail, to me, is the Stanley Cup. I've never won one, not in 36 years. I've come close, but close only counts in horseshoes and hand grenades. Before I quit, I'll win one in Hartford."

1983–84

The 1983 NHL entry draft was to be remembered as "the year of the Yankee"—the year that five American-born players were selected in the first round. Of the 242 players taken in the draft, 63 were Americans, compared to 35 Europeans and 144 Canadians.

The highlight of the draft occurred when 18-year-old Brian Lawton of Cumberland, Rhode Island, pulled a Minnesota North Star jersey over his head to become the first American to be chosen number one overall in the entry draft. Moments later Lawton was joined by Pat LaFontaine from suburban Detroit, who went third overall to the New York Islanders. Tom Barrasso, a netminder from Acton-Boxboro High School near Boston, went fifth overall to the Buffalo Sabres. "I guess we all owe something to Bobby Carpenter and Phil Housley," said Lawton. "They were both drafted high in the first round and both of them proved that a U.S. player could star in the league."

The Hartford Whalers, picking second, were expected to take Pat LaFontaine. But Emile Francis, the team's new president and general manager, ignored LaFontaine and chose another center, Sylvain Turgeon, who had totalled 54 goals and 163 points with the Hull Olympics the previous season. That left LaFontaine available to the Islanders, who picked third, and general manager Bill Torrey grabbed the 18-year-old Detroit native.

While the top three picks got most of the attention, the Detroit Red Wings, selecting fourth, were confident that Steve Yzerman, a baby-faced center plucked from the Peterborough juniors, would shine as brightly as any of the others.

The St. Louis Blues were conspicuous by their absence at the draft table. They claimed no players and suffered the consequences in the years ahead. A few days after the draft, the NHL assumed control of the franchise, since Ralston Purina had indicated that it would no longer acknowledge the Blues' existence, except, of course, in any future lawsuits.

At 38, Wayne Cashman was gone from the game. Cashman had claimed the distinction of being the last survivor of the old six-team league to play in the NHL. He played his last game for the Boston Bruins on April 24, in the seventh game of the

Boston–Buffalo playoff series, won by Brad Park's overtime goal. Two other surviving players of the six-team era had played their final games only a couple of weeks earlier—Carol Vadnais of the New Jersey Devils, on April 3, and Serge Savard for the Winnipeg Jets, on April 9.

After more than two months of performing the duties of general manager of the Pittsburgh Penguins, without the actual title, Eddie Johnston was officially awarded the job and title in June. Johnston had coached the Penguins to a last-place finish in the National Hockey League the previous season, the worst season in the franchise's 16-year history. In September, 45-year-old Lou Angotti was given the unenviable task of coaching the Pittsburg team. Angotti had been handling the Penguins' Baltimore Skipjack farm team in the American Hockey League.

There were the usual number of player moves. The Quebec Nordiques traded disgruntled forward Real Cloutier and their first-round draft pick, 11th overall, to Buffalo for three players and a third-round draft pick. Coming to Quebec were left-winger Tony McKegney and centers Andre Savard and Jean-Francois Sauve. McKegney had been the second-highest scorer with the Sabres the previous year, with 36 goals and 37 assists. Detroit general manager Jimmy Devellano traded big Willie Huber and forwards Mike Blaisdell and Mark Osborne to the New York Rangers for goalie Ed Mio and forwards Ron Duguay and Eddie Johnstone. Winnipeg's Dave Christian was traded to Washington for the Capitals first-round draft pick in 1983.

Inducted into the Hockey Hall of Fame were Ken Dryden, Bobby Hull, Stan Mikita and Harry Sinden.

Overtime was in and long pants were out following a board of governors' meeting. Overtime had been part of the game until 1942, when travel restrictions imposed by World War II had led to its being dropped until it was proposed again in 1980. The Philadelphia Flyers, who had introduced full-length pants two seasons before would be back in the conventional short pants. The board switched back to the old style because it sought uniformity between its 21 teams.

Harry Ornest, the fast-talking Beverly Hills promoter, bought the St. Louis Blues for the bargain-basement price of $3 million. Pittsburgh governor Paul Martha said that Ornest had bought the team with mirrors and would be back in mid season looking for a handout.

On July 21, Arthur M. Wirtz, chairman of the board of the Chicago Blackhawks and the Chicago Stadium Corp., died at the age of 82 of complications from diabetes. "The sport of hockey and the National Hockey League have lost a great friend and one of their greatest contributors," said NHL president John Ziegler. "I'm certain his name will live forever in the city of Chicago and the sport of hockey."

Barely nine months after doctors had cut a hole in his skull to save his life, and seven-and-a-half months after he had come out of a coma, Normand Leveille was able to leave a rehabilitation hospital in Montreal to be the guest of honor at the Normand Leveille Golf Tournament. The 20-year-old left-winger had been struck down by a cerebral hemorrhage in Vancouver the previous October 23. He was still partially paralyzed on his right side and had to use a wheelchair, but the big Leveille grin was still readily apparent.

Brad Park, 35, signed a two-year contract with the Detroit Red Wings and touched off quite a controversy in the process. The Boston Bruins, Park's team for nearly eight seasons, claimed he still had contractual obligations to them and that they would go to court to prove it. The Wings and Park saw things differently. "According to the NHL, I'm a free agent with no compensation," Park said at a press conference during which he was introduced as a Red Wing. "I haven't signed anything with Boston since my contract expired June 1."

The NHL started the 1983–84 season with only four new faces in its coaching ranks, the lowest number in nearly a decade at the outset of a season. With some 160 coaches having been dismissed in a 10-year period, the NHL had had one of the worst records in pro sports. Newcomers to the NHL coaching club included Lou Angotti in Pittsburgh, Bill Mahoney in Minnesota, Jack Evans in Hartford and Jacques Demers in St. Louis. It appeared that the NHL was recovering from its worst turnover at the coaching level since it had come into existence 66 years before. Sixty-three coaches had been dismissed since the 1979–80 season. There were 11 coaching changes in the 1982-83 season, 10 the year before, 16 in 1980–81 and a whopping 22 coaches dismissed in 1979-80.

In September Rejean Houle called it quits with the Montreal Canadiens and new Whaler boss Emile Francis let Pierre Larouche and Russ Anderson go for nothing. Anderson then signed his most lucrative contract ever with the L.A. Kings and Larouche was picked up by the Rangers. Also in September, Jimmy Devellano, Detroit's general manager, gave Don Murdoch another chance after a cocaine conviction and a half-season suspension, signing him to a 25-game pro-tryout contract.

On October 5, 32-year-old Marcel Dionne rocketed past Maurice Richard on the National Hockey League's all-time goals list. "All summer I thought about it," Dionne commented after scoring his 546th goal.

On October 15, after three years of trying to squeeze 7,243 people into the 6,492-seat Stampede Corral, the Calgary Flames moved into their new home, the Saddledome. Although it was completed one year later than anticipated and was way over budget, the new facility, built for the 1988 Winter Olympics, finally put the Flames' franchise on an even financial keel. President, governor and general manager Cliff Fletcher estimated that the team had lost more than $5 million in its first three years in Calgary. He predicted a reasonable profit in 1983–84.

On October 18, the Los Angeles Kings dealt defenseman Larry Murphy, once untouchable, to the Washington Capitals in exchange for defenseman Brian Engblom and right-winger Ken Houston.

NHL president John Ziegler announced a controversial one-year suspension for Ric Nattress of the Montreal Canadiens, after Nattress had been caught with three grams of marijuana and one gram of hashish two summers before.

In Buffalo, Scotty Bowman was unhappy with the play of Dale McCourt so he terminated McCourt's contract, which had another season to run. According to the league agreement, the Sabres would pay one-third of McCourt's salary for double the number of years remaining on his contract. At $300,000 a year he was believed to have been one of the most highly paid NHL players. McCourt then moved on to Toronto and signed with the Leafs.

Montreal native Mario Lemieux, 18, showed more than just potential as he rocketed through the hottest takeoff in major junior hockey with 59 points in 15 games. He had the hockey world buzzing.

The North Stars' Bobby Smith was traded to the Montreal Canadiens for Keith Acton and Mark Napier. Smith was elated with the move. "I am pleased to be able to play in Montreal. It's the best place in the NHL to play."

On November 7, Winnipeg's Tom Watt became the 65th coach in five years to lose his NHL job. He was succeeded by the man who had fired him, general manager John Ferguson. Watt had been named the NHL's coach of the year in 1982 after the Winnipeg Jets had shown a 48-point improvement, the most dynamic turnabout in league history. Six games after the coaching change and numbed by his own lack of success behind the bench (2–4–0), John Ferguson excused himself as coach of the Winnipeg Jets. He turned the reins over to assistant coach Barry Long.

When Kirk McKaskill was a student at the University of Vermont, he had gained the attention of both the California Angels baseball team and the Winnipeg Jets. Both teams had selected him in the fourth round of their sport's draft of amateur players. After finishing a season of rookie baseball in 1982, McKaskill began to think about pursuing his opportunity with pro hockey. While Winnipeg could offer a guaranteed contract, the Angels had less flexibility. Eventually McKaskill decided to sign with Winnipeg even though the Angels threatened a lawsuit.

Tom Lysiak of the Chicago Blackhawks was automatically suspended for 20 games when referee Dave Newell found him in violation of category one of rule 67, for tripping linesman Ron Foyt during an October 30 game against Hartford in Chicago. Lysiak was bitter and didn't feel that his crime warranted the severe punishment he received. "I stole a loaf of bread," he said. "Should I get life imprisonment?"

On November 19, Wayne Gretzky, in the wake of a 13–4 thrashing of the New Jersey Devils, ripped into the NHL's weakest team. "It's not funny, it's disappointing," said Gretzky of the debacle. "These guys [the Devils' management] better get their act together. It's ruining hockey. They are putting a Mickey Mouse operation on the ice." Later Gretzky issued an apology for his statements.

On November 19, 47-year-old Bruce Hood became the first NHL referee to officiate 1,000 games. He had worked his first NHL game in February 1965.

Attention shifted briefly to the Laval Voisins where center Mario Lemieux became the first Quebec League player to score 50 goals in 27 games. He took time out from his scoring exploits to say that he wouldn't play for Canada's junior team at the world championships because he didn't like the treatment that last year's coach, Dave King, had given him and he wasn't too keen on what he had heard from this year's coach, Brian Kilrea. He also expressed his disappointment at being snubbed by the Canadian Olympic team.

When the New Jersey Devils lost 18 of their first 20 games, owner John McMullen fired Bill MacMillan as general manager-coach. McMullen installed Tommy McVie as the new head coach-assistant general manager and Max McNab as the new general manager.

Vladimir Krutov, 23, considered by many Soviet hockey experts to be their top player, took some pot shots at Wayne Gretzky and the NHL in an interview released by the Novosti Press Agency. "He isn't very fast, but he handles the stick perfectly," said Krutov. "However, his physique leaves much to be desired. On the whole, he's a good player, but I don't think he'd perform as well in our league as in the NHL."

"That's his opinion," responded Gretzky, coming off his best-ever month in the NHL, a 49-point November.

Glen Sather, coach-general manager of the Edmonton Oilers wasn't quite as diplomatic when he issued this challenge: "Any time they have the courage to play our team again, we'd be glad to accommodate them. In fact, we'd even go over there, kick the snot out of them and take their money."

Guy Lafleur joined the National Hockey League's 500-goal club when he scored his 14th goal of the season in a 6–0 win by the Canadiens against the Devils on December 20.

NHL Hall of Famer Max Bentley died on January 19 at the age of 63. Known as the Dipsy-Doodle Dandy from Delisle, Saskatchewan, Bentley had played 12 seasons in the NHL and in 646 career games he had totalled 245 goals and 299 assists. He had begun his career in Chicago, where he played with his brother Doug and Bill Mosienko on the Pony Line. In the 1947–48 season he was dealt to Toronto, along with minor-leaguer Cy Thomas, for Gaye Stewart, Bud Poile, Gus Bodnar, Bob Goldham and Ernie Dickens. Leaf's owner Conn Smythe had promised that his team would win the Stanley Cup with Bentley, and Toronto had gone on to win it for three of the next four years.

When asked how he planned to approach the NHL's 36th annual All-Star game in New Jersey on January 31, Don Maloney of the Rangers said, "You just go out, do your best and shoot for the car." After he had scored a goal and three assists to lead the Wales Conference to a 7–6 victory over the Campbell Conference and had earned MVP honors, Maloney drove away in a fancy new sports car.

Thanks to an agreement between Carling O'Keefe Breweries and the 14 U.S.-based NHL teams and the Quebec Nordiques, hockey fans in Canada would be able to see at least 20 more games on national television in the 1984–85 season. The controversial deal stripped Molson Breweries of its exclusive association with nationally televised NHL games in Canada, something it had had for more than 50 years. The plan was to show a "Game of the Week" (either on Sunday or mid-week) during the NHL regular season of 26 weeks. The games would originate in the U.S. and feature either two American teams or one American and one Canadian team.

Many wondered about the possible union of goaltender Vladislav Tretiak of the Soviet Union and the Montreal Canadiens. Managing director Serge Savard had drafted Tretiak the previous summer and a contract offer had been presented to him at the Olympics in Sarajevo. Soviet officials would get $500,000 if the 32-year-old goaltender decided to join Montreal. Soviet officials insisted that Tretiak was free to make his own decision, but for some reason he decided to pass on the Montreal offer.

Barry Shenkarow threatened to sell his Winnipeg Jets hockey team in what many believed was an attempt to shock the city into giving his team a better lease arrangement. Winnipeg responded by offering the Jets their arena rent-free for the next 10 years. In return, the Jets agreed to pay a penalty of $7 million to the city if the team should cease operations in Winnipeg.

In March, the Jets traded their number-one pick in the 1984 NHL entry draft and future considerations to the Pittsburgh Penguins in exchange for former Norris Trophy-winning defenseman Randy Carlyle.

In Montreal, Serge Savard dismissed Bob Berry as coach 63 games into the NHL season. Savard said Berry had 99 percent of the press against him. Berry was replaced by former Canadien star Jacques Lemaire.

New Jersey Devils' president Bob Butera infuriated the Pittsburgh Penguins when he implied that the Pens might be more interested in securing the number-one pick in June's entry draft (Mario Lemieux?) rather than winning hockey games. "What he [Butera] said was shocking and an insult to our organization," said the furious

Pittsburgh general manager Eddie Johnston. "To say something like that, to even think it, is unbelievable." The Penguins lost eight of their last 10 games to finish three points back of New Jersey. The Devils, however, managed only one win in their final 10 matches.

Former NHL defenseman Steve Durbano, who was serving a seven-year sentence for drug smuggling, claimed that 20 to 25 percent of NHL players used drugs, ranging from marijuana to cocaine to speed. "I think he's mad at the world," said former teammate Ron Delorme. "I don't believe that figure he gave. How could he know? How could he say that, especially from where he is now?"

Tony Esposito of the Chicago Blackhawks, who had not played in a game since a 4–3 loss to the Hartford Whalers on February 5, consented to play in the Hawks' final game of the season and then reneged a day before the game. The 41-year-old Esposito had been openly critical of Hawks management and said "under the present circumstances it's completely impossible" that he would be back with the team for the next season.

At the conclusion of the 80-game schedule, the Edmonton Oilers found themselves far in front of the pack with 57 wins and 119 points. The Islanders and the Bruins finished in a second-place tie in the overall standings with 104 points.

Overshadowed by Wayne Gretzky's remarkable season with 87 goals, 118 assists and 205 points were Paul Coffey's totals—40 goals, 86 assists and 126 points. Coffey finished second in scoring and broke Bobby Orr's record for most points by a defenseman. Orr had registered 120 points in 1969–70.

THE NHL PLAYOFFS

Smythe Division

When Edmonton won game three in the best-of-five series against the Winnipeg Jets, it became Winnipeg's 15th straight defeat to the Oilers. The Calgary Flames won their best-of-five series against Vancouver 3–1. In game seven of the division finals, the Edmonton Oilers crushed the Calgary Flames 7–4, capturing the Smythe Division championship 4–3 in games.

Norris Division

The St. Louis Blues eliminated Detroit in three games. St. Louis forward Jorgen Pettersson scored three goals in game three, including the winner at 2:42 of sudden-death overtime. Minnesota, after losing to Chicago in the playoffs for the last two seasons, finally beat its Norris Division rival. The decisive blow was a 4–1 win in the fifth game at the Met Center, which gave the Stars a 3–2 win in their best-of-five series. In the Norris Division final, the Minnesota North Stars were 4–3 victors over the St. Louis Blues in a series that went for the full seven games.

Adams Division

Thirteen years after Ken Dryden backstopped Montreal to a surprise upset over Boston in the quarter-finals, history repeated itself as rookie goalie Steve Penney starred in a three-game sweep of the Bruins. Penney had appeared in only four games for the Canadiens in the regular season. The Quebec Nordiques had owned the Buffalo Sabres in the regular season with six wins and a tie in eight games. It was no different in the playoffs as the Nords pushed the Sabres aside in three straight games. In the Adams Division final, the Montreal Canadiens overpowered the Quebec Nordiques 5–3 in game six—one of the most fight-filled games ever seen in Stanley Cup playoff history. The Nordiques had a two-goal lead before mass fighting broke out when the teams were leaving the ice at the conclusion of the second period. After a 40-minute delay while officials sorted out the penalties, a total of 12 players were thrown out of the game with misconduct penalties. Referee Bruce Hood and the linesmen had their hands full trying to keep tempers in line as the result of the bad blood that had built up between the teams in the series. Montreal won the turbulent best-of-seven series 4–2 and advanced to the Wales Conference finals against the New York Islanders.

Patrick Division

The Washington Capitals swept past the Flyers in three games, while the New York Islanders won their preliminary series against the crosstown Rangers in the fifth and deciding game at the Nassau Coliseum. Ken Morrow scored the winning goal at 8:56 of the first overtime period to give the Isles a thrilling 3–2 win. The game was described as one of the best in playoff history. Driving for their fifth straight Stanley Cup championship, the seasoned Islanders had too much of everything for the inexperienced Washington Capitals in the Patrick Division finals. They outscored the Caps 20–13 and won the series 4–1.

Wales Conference Finals

The remarkable New York Islanders advanced to the Cup finals for the fifth consecutive season by eliminating the Montreal Canadiens. It was another amazing playoff comeback for the defending champions. After falling behind by two games, the determined Islanders put it all together to sweep the next four games and win the series 4–2. "The Islanders are the best team in North America," said Montreal coach Jacques Lemaire after the game. "I think they'll win the Cup."

Campbell Conference Finals

When the injury-ridden Minnesota North Stars lost 3–1 in game four to the Edmonton Oilers, it gave the Oilers a four-game sweep in the series. It was the first time in North Star history that they'd been wiped out 4–0 in a seven-game playoff series.

The Stanley Cup Finals

In 1979, Edmonton Oiler owner Peter Pocklington had made a prediction: "Within five years Edmonton will have the Stanley Cup." The response he got was mainly laughter. But Pocklington's prediction came true when Dave Lumley slid the puck 160 feet dead center into an empty New York Islander net with 13 seconds remaining in the game, capping a 5–2 Oilers' victory and a four-games-to-one triumph in the best-of-seven series.

The Oiler domination of the Islanders was awesome. In game one, a 1–0 Oiler win

220

on Long Island, netminder Grant Fuhr was outstanding. In games three and four, Messier, using his blazing speed and strength to advantage, was the dominant individual player. In games four and five, Gretzky was magnificent. Meanwhile, players such as Kevin Lowe, Paul Coffey, Kevin McClelland, Pat Hughes, Ken Linseman and Dave Semenko consistently got the job done. Again Pocklington minced no words. He figured that this could be the start of a dynasty. "No question. I can see we're going to keep this Cup in Edmonton. It's going to be awfully tough to get it out of here. We're going to have our ups and downs, but it will be here."

1984–85

Two enthusiastic young men were given important coaching positions in the summer of 1984. Harry Neale hired Bill LaForge to be the eighth coach of the Vancouver Canucks. LaForge had just four years of coaching experience in junior hockey in Regina and Oshawa. In March 1981, LaForge had made headlines for a pre-game scuffle with Peterborough coach Dave Dryden after players from both teams had begun fighting on the ice. Then, when he was leaving the ice, LaForge was struck on the head by a stick wielded by Peterborough's Doug Evans. LaForge threw the player to the ice and was subsequently suspended for 50 games by the league commissioner.

The Toronto Maple Leaf coaching choice as successor to Mike Nykoluk was 33-year-old Dan Maloney. Maloney's lack of experience did not concern general manager Gerry McNamara, for the former hard-rock winger had been the Leafs' assistant coach for the previous season. His new posting to head coach made him the second-youngest head coach in the league, the youngest being 32-year-old LaForge.

General manager Rogie Vachon announced that the Philadelphia Flyers' coach, Pat Quinn, would be the new head coach of the Los Angeles Kings. On May 30 the 41-year-old Quinn signed a multi-year contract.

Bobby Clarke, after 15 distinguished seasons and three Hart Trophies, accepted the job as general manager of the Philadelphia Flyers. The 34-year-old's retirement from playing hockey caught everybody by surprise. Bob McCammon had been the original choice for the position as general manager, but he had walked out on the Flyers when told he could only be general manager and not coach the team. Clarke's first act as general manager was the hiring of Mike Keenan to fill the void left by McCammon's departure. Keenan, a Toronto native, had coached the University of Toronto to a national title in 1983–84.

Two teams that had finished well back the year before looked for new help. The Pittsburgh Penguins, who had finished last overall for the second year in a row, replaced first-year man Lou Angotti with Bob Berry, who had been fired by the Montreal Canadiens. The New Jersey Devils, who had finished second last overall, hired Doug Carpenter, who had coached minor-league teams for the Toronto Maple Leafs for four years. Carpenter succeeded Tommie McVie.

In Montreal, a familiar voice was gone from the Canadiens' telecasts. Danny Gallivan, 67, the man who had made "cannonading shots" and "spinnerama moves" household words, retired from the broadcast booth.

The Hockey Hall of Fame selection committee announced that John "Jake" Milford, 67, and George "Punch" Imlach, 64, would be inducted as builders. They joined former players Phil Esposito, Jacques Lemaire and Bernie Parent as members.

Pittsburgh's Mario Lemieux arrived on the pro-hockey scene in the summer of 1984. Said one scout, "In terms of natural ability, he's the closest thing I've seen to Wayne Gretzky. He has unbelievable moves. It will be interesting to see what kind of player he turns out to be." Lemieux's attitude was thought to be a potential problem. He had avoided the Penguins' brass at the draft meetings and had talked about playing in Europe or going back to junior hockey when contract negotiations did not go smoothly.

After the Penguins had selected Lemieux first overall, the Devils took Kirk Muller, the Blackhawks grabbed hometown boy Ed Olczyk, the Leafs selected defenseman Al Iafrate and Montreal surprised everyone by drafting an 18-year-old defenseman from Czechoslovakia, Petr Svoboda, as their number-one choice and fifth overall. Serge Savard believed that Svoboda may have been the best player in the draft. "Time will tell," Savard said. "I wanted to make sure that he was here, otherwise I would not have taken him." Svoboda had arrived in Montreal at 4:00 P.M. the day before the entry draft and was hidden in a downtown hotel away from those attending the annual NHL congress. The Canadiens were worried that the New Jersey Devils, who were selecting second overall, might choose Svoboda instead of Muller.

On June 4 at the NHL awards banquet, Wayne Gretzky took home the Art Ross Trophy as the league's leading scorer and the Hart Trophy as the league's most valuable player. Washington Capital defenseman Rod Langway captured his second consecutive Norris Trophy for the league's top defenseman, beating out Oiler defenseman Paul Coffey, who had broken the 100-point barrier. Buffalo's rookie goalie Tom Barrasso, who edged Detroit's Steve Yzerman by 39 points in the Calder Cup race, also won the Vezina Trophy as the top netminder in the league. Mike Bossy of the New York Islanders took home the Lady Byng Trophy for the second consecutive season, while veteran center Doug Jarvis of the Washington Capitals won the Selke Trophy as the top defensive player. Bryan Murray, who guided the Capitals to a second-place finish in the Patrick Division after they were winless in their first seven games of the season, was named coach of the year.

On June 24, Rhodes scholar, soldier, lawyer, hockey referee and president of the NHL for 31 years, Clarence Campbell, died of pneumonia in a Montreal hospital after a lengthy illness. His tenure as NHL president had been stormy at times. His most famous moment came after he had suspended Montreal Canadiens' scoring ace Maurice "Rocket" Richard for the remainder of the season and the playoffs in 1955, prompting death threats and triggering an ugly riot at the Montreal Forum. In 1977, Campbell gave up his presidency to John Ziegler, but continued to work out of the league office as an advisor until poor health forced him to retire.

The 1984 Canada Cup Tournament was an exciting and controversial pre-season event. Team USA's roster was impressive. It included Norris Trophy winner defenseman Rod Langway, Vezina Trophy winner Tom Barrasso, proven playmakers at center and several immensely talented first- and second-year pros, among them Pat Lafontaine, Brian Lawton and Ed Olczyk. There was also a surprise addition to the U.S. squad. Bryan Trottier, the New York Islanders' center who was considered by some to be the best all-round player in the NHL, suited up with Team USA. Trottier's special status as a North American Indian gave him the opportunity to play for the U.S. "Nothing against Canada, but I'd like to play for the U.S. and do something for the country that has been good to me," said Trottier. Despite his explanation, he was unjustly jeered and heckled by Canadian fans throughout the Canada Cup series.

Glen Sather headed up the 1984 version of Team Canada and was criticized when eight of the 31 players invited to camp came from his defending Stanley Cup champion team. Scott Stevens, the Washington Capitals' tough young defenseman, was one of the victims when Sather elected to retain all eight Edmonton players (four defensemen) on Team Canada's roster. Stevens felt that he had not received a fair chance to make the team. "It was a difficult thing to take," said Stevens. "It's been a long time since I was cut from a team. I can't even remember the last time I was cut, maybe when I was nine or 10."

Sather was very upset with Canadian hockey fans and the media and blasted them for what he called "a very negative attitude" towards the club. He was particularly disturbed by published comments from Alberta native Louis Sutter, the father of Team Canada's Brent Sutter, and five other NHL players who said the problem with the team was that "there are too many Oilers on it." Canadian criticism mounted against the Canada Cup tournament format in the media and among the public. Games not involving Canada versus the Soviet Union were said to be "merely window dressing and quite unnecessary." Attendance was disappointing, perhaps due to the $27 price tag for the best seats. In the semi-finals of the Canada Cup, Canada beat the Soviets 3–2 in a thrilling overtime game, silencing some of the criticism. For the winning goal, Coffey had taken a pass from John Tonelli and wristed a shot towards goal. Then, after knocking Myshkin's goal stick out of his hands, Mike Bossy had redirected Coffey's shot into the net.

That sent Team Canada into the finals against Sweden, the tournament's surprise team. Sweden had stunned Team USA 9–2 in the other semi-final game. Team Canada lacked some of the emotion it showed against the Soviets, but won the crown with 5–2 and 6–5 victories over the Swedes in the best-of-three finals. John Tonelli was named as the tournament's most valuable player. The win was sweet revenge for the disappointment of 1981, the year that Canada had lost the championship in a sudden-death final to the Soviet Union. "We've heard for four years about that last game," said Gretzky. "Now we win 3–2 against them. Does that mean we're better? We're a great hockey country, they're a great hockey country. It's about time everyone realizes that."

The Toronto Maple Leafs believed that they had found a perfect assistant coach when they hired John Brophy. Brophy, a veteran minor-league defenseman who had coached in the WHA with the Birmingham Bulls and more recently with the Nova Scotia Voyageurs of the American League, was hired by Gerry McNamara to assist head coach Dan Maloney. Gerry Meehan, the former captain of the Buffalo Sabres, was hired to assist Scotty Bowman in his role as general manager and director of hockey operations. Meehan became the first former Buffalo player to move into the team's front office. Doug Carpenter, 41, was hired as head coach for the New Jersey Devils.

After tough contract negotiations, the Pittsburgh Penguins and Mario Lemieux signed a two-year agreement, plus an option, for about $700,000. "I think if the fans of Pittsburgh give us maybe two or three years we'll be successful," said Lemieux.

Boston Bruins' general manager Harry Sinden sent center left-winger Mike Krushelnyski to the Edmonton Oilers in exchange for Ken Linseman, a trade which pleased Sinden. Linseman had inexplicably slipped to the number-four center spot on the Oilers but he had scored 10 goals in the playoffs, including the Stanley Cup winner against the Islanders. Other player transactions included Charlie Simmer, the Kings leading scorer for the previous season with 44 goals and 92 points, who demanded to be traded. Eventually the Kings dealt him to Boston for a first-round draft choice. Dave "Tiger" Williams, the combative left-winger who had begun his career in 1974 with Toronto and was traded to Vancouver in 1980, moved eastward again. Williams was traded to the Detroit Red Wings for winger Rob McClanahan.

Harold "Baldy" Cotton, the hockey scout who had discovered Bobby Orr, died on September 9 at 81. Cotton had spent 52 years in the NHL as a player and scout. In 1933, he was involved in a bizarre incident with his Toronto roommate Charlie Conacher. Cotton was known for his fear of heights. After getting into an argument with him, Conacher grabbed Cotton, pushed him out a window and held him by the ankles 20 floors above the ground until he cooled off. In 1962, when he was working for the Boston Bruins, Cotton spotted Orr playing bantam hockey in a midget tournament in Unionville, Ontario.

The Chicago Blackhawks announced that Tony Esposito would not be invited to training camp on September 18, thus ending a bitter relationship. Coach Orval Tessier had used Esposito infrequently during the previous season, and that bothered the veteran, who at age 41 was the oldest player in the league.

Referee Andy van Hellemond became the first NHL official to wear a helmet. He donned the helmet for an exhibition match between Toronto and Edmonton.

Bobby Clarke made a controversial move by trading future Hall of Fame center Darryl Sittler to the Detroit Red Wings for two young but unproven left-wingers, Joe Paterson and Murray Craven. The night before the deal Sittler had been told he would be the Flyers' new captain.

On October 13, Mark Pavelich of the New York Rangers broke his leg and was expected to be out for at least 10 weeks. Three nights later, Ken Linseman, the feisty center of the Boston Bruins, bit former Oiler teammate Lee Fogolin at a game in Edmonton. As a result, Fogolin had to have a tetanus shot and Linseman drew a triple minor.

Less than 24 hours after the Buffalo Sabres had suffered a humiliating 7–3 loss to the Detroit Red Wings, general manager and coach Scotty Bowman demoted goalie Tom Barrasso to Rochester of the American League. Barrasso had not been playing up to his Vezina Trophy form.

On November 9 the Edmonton Oilers replaced the 1943–44 Montreal Canadiens in the record book by winning their 15th game from the start of the season without a loss (12–0–3). The Philadelphia Flyers snapped the Oiler streak in the next game, however, beating them 7–5.

The Los Angeles Kings acquired left-winger Steve Shutt from the Montreal Canadiens on November 18. Shutt, 32, held the record for most goals by a left-winger with 60.

On November 15 at the Spectrum, the Philadelphia Flyers retired Bobby Clarke's number 16. Ed Snider, the club's owner, spoke for the fans when he said that Clarke was "the hardest working athlete we've ever seen. The Flyers are a team of character and tradition, largely because of Bobby Clarke. He showed us how to win."

After a mere 20 games, the Vancouver Canucks' general manager, Harry Neale, fired coach Bill LaForge. "I made a mistake thinking his coaching style was right for our club," he said. Neale took over as coach, just as he had done only nine months before after Roger Neilson had been fired.

Thirteen was proving to be an unlucky number for the Rangers. On November 13, left-winger Don Maloney broke his leg. A month earlier, on October 13, Mark Pavelich had gone down with a similar injury.

Suddenly and quite unexpectedly, 33-year-old Guy Lafleur decided that it was time to step out of the limelight. On November 26, Lafleur announced that he was retiring from the NHL. The "Demon Blond" had been the most exciting player of the seventies, playing the game with a distinctive flair. Even when it appeared that much of his magic was deserting him, the fans still chanted "Guy, Guy, Guy," whenever he led the rush. In 961 games, Lafleur had scored 518 goals, just 26 shy of the team record of 544 goals set by Maurice Richard.

On December 4, hockey lost another fine player when Darcy Rota retired from the Vancouver Canucks. The 31-year-old, 11-year veteran of the NHL took the advice of three doctors who said he would risk permanent damage to his neck if he were to play again.

Jake Milford, the Vancouver Canucks' senior vice-president and a recent inductee into the Hockey Hall of Fame, died of cancer on December 24 at the age of 68.

Veteran defenseman Brad Maxwell and Brent Ashton of the Minnesota North Stars were traded to the Quebec Nordiques for Tony McKegney and Bo Berglund.

On December 19, Scotty Bowman set an NHL record for most wins by a coach when the Buffalo Sabres beat the Chicago Blackhawks 6–3. Bowman refuted the record, saying that he had not broken the record set by former Canadiens' coach Dick Irvin, Sr., because he was wrongly given credit for victories in which he was not the official coach.

Wayne Gretzky became the 18th member of one of the NHL's most exclusive groups—the 1,000-point club. Number 99 became the fastest player to achieve this goal—after a mere 423 career games.

Harold Ballard, the majority owner of the Toronto Maple Leafs, Maple Leaf Gardens and the Hamilton Tiger-Cats was offered $40 million for the entire package by a group headed by Canadian singer Anne Murray. Ballard snorted, "I'll never sell to anybody. If I got outta here, what the hell would I do? What would [King] Clancy do?" Clancy, the Leafs' 81-year-old executive vice-president, responded, "I'd die. That's what I'd do."

New York Rangers' coach Herb Brooks was fired by general manager Craig Patrick, who had been Brooks' assistant when the two had guided the United States to a gold medal at the 1980 Winter Olympics in Lake Placid, New York. Patrick took over the coaching duties on an interim basis, with Robbie Ftorek as his playing assistant.

Edmonton Oilers' center, Mark Messier, drew a 10-game suspension for cracking the cheekbone of Calgary's Jamie Macoun with a crushing blow on December 26. New York Islanders' goalie Billy Smith was suspended for six games after he slashed Chicago's Curt Fraser and broke his cheekbone in a game on Long Island on January 13.

Marcel Dionne, veteran center of the Los Angeles Kings and a future Hall of Famer, tied Bobby Hull for third place on the NHL's all-time goal-scoring list. The achievement occurred on January 16 when he scored a goal in a 4–3 loss to Toronto.

Paul Stewart, 29, who once received an eight-game suspension for hitting a referee and had logged more than 1,200 penalty minutes in fewer than five seasons of pro hockey, became one of seven referees in the NHL training program.

In February, the controversial and outspoken coach of the Chicago Blackhawks,

Orval Tessier, was fired by general manager Bob Pulford. The Hawks had just endured their fourth consecutive loss, leaving them eight points behind the Blues in the Norris Division. "It's probably an unfair situation," said general manager Pulford, who took over as coach. "The coach takes the brunt of the blame. But you can't fire 20 players."

Jimmy Devellano, the Detroit Red Wings' general manager, was having a rough year. None of his off-season moves had produced results. The Tiger Williams and Darryl Sittler trades had proved fruitless. Czech imports Frank Cernik and Milan Chalupa had not worked out and Shawn Burr, the Wings' number-one draft pick, wasn't ready to step in and contribute as Steve Yzerman had done a year before.

Guy Lafleur became the fifth Montreal player to have his number retired. As he made his appearance on the ice, over 18,100 hockey fans gave him a five-minute standing ovation. Tears glistened in Lafleur's eyes as Canadiens' president Ronald Corey presented him with the game jersey he had worn in his final game against the Detroit Red Wings.

Gerry Cheevers was fired as coach of the Boston Bruins and six days later was replaced by general manager Harry Sinden. "I didn't realize my record (204–126–46) was so good until I got fired," quipped Cheevers. "When I looked at it, I think I should have got a raise".

On February 28, the International Olympic Committee (IOC) cleared the way for National Hockey League players to be eligible for the 1988 Olympics. However, according to IOC president Juan Antonio Samaranch, the age limit for players would be under 23. Because the Olympics occurred during the season, it was unlikely that the pro teams would allow their players, young or old, to participate.

Hall of Famer Eddie Shore, one of the most controversial men to ever be associated with the game of hockey, died on March 16 at the age of 82. Shore had played for 13 years for the Boston Bruins, scoring 108 goals and adding 179 assists. He had been on two Stanley Cup-winning teams, in 1928–29 and 1938–39. An outstanding defenseman, Shore was the only one to win the Hart Trophy as the NHL's most valuable player four times—in 1932–33, 1934–35, 1935–36 and 1937–38.

On March 16 the Toronto Maple Leafs were destroyed by the Philadelphia Flyers 6–1, resulting in a new Toronto club record for most losses in a season at 46.

A freak accident ended the season for Doug Wickenheiser of the St. Louis Blues, just when the 23-year-old center was playing the best hockey of his career. Wickenheiser was hit by a car on a street in Eureka, Missouri, a small town on the outskirts of St. Louis. He suffered a severe knee injury and required four hours of reconstructive surgery the following day. Wickenheiser's recovery time would be nine to 12 months.

On March 12, 31-year-old left-winger Dave "Tiger" Williams, the all-time NHL penalty king, was traded to Los Angeles from Detroit in exchange for future considerations.

Bob Carpenter became the first American to reach the 50-goal plateau. After previous seasons with 32, 32 and 28 goals, Carpenter said, "I just hope this gives a boost to the kids in the States and gives them some incentive to stay in hockey longer."

The young Philadelphia Flyer team of 1985 did what no other previous team had done—win 11 consecutive games, the longest winning streak in the 18-year history of the franchise. The record win over the Canadiens put the Flyers eight points up in their division and ahead of the defending Stanley Cup champion Edmonton Oilers in total points. During the streak, the Flyers picked up 20 points on the Oilers, a team had they trailed by 19 points as late as February 9. The list of accomplishments amassed by the youthful Flyer team was impressive: first place in the Patrick Division, a club record with 11 consecutive wins, only four losses over the season at the Spectrum and the best overall record in the NHL. All of this was done with a rookie coach, Mike Keenan, a first-year general manager, Bob Clarke, and four rookies highlighting the youngest team in the club's 18-year history.

During the final week of the season, Vancouver Canucks' general manager Harry Neale was told by the owners, Frank and Arthur Griffith, that he was no longer wanted by the club and was free to pursue employment elsewhere.

Many rookies played key roles. Pittsburgh's Mario Lemieux had an outstanding season, scoring 43 goals and 57 assists in 73 games. The 19-year-old was chosen as the MVP in the NHL's All-Star game in Calgary. Other rookies who turned in strong performances included Lemieux's linemate Warren Young, the NHL's oldest rookie at 29 who scored 40 goals; Carey Wilson, the 22-year-old Calgary Flames' center who had 24 goals and 48 assists in 74 games; fast-skating Chris Chelios, the 23-year-old Montreal Canadien who had 64 points; Peter Zezel, 20, who had 15 goals and 46 assists as a Philadelphia Flyer; and Steve Penney, the 24-year-old goaltender who recorded a 3.08 goals-against average in 54 games with the Montreal Canadiens.

THE NHL PLAYOFFS

Preliminary round playoffs were best-of-five series. All others were best-of-seven.

Smythe Division

It was experience that made the difference when the Edmonton Oilers disposed of the Los Angeles Kings in the quickest manner possible during the best-of-five series. The victory enabled the Oilers to erase the memory of the Kings' stunning five-game upset three years before. The Winnipeg Jets won their first-ever series in Stanley Cup playoff competition, eliminating the Calgary Flames in four games to advance to the division finals. In the Smythe Division finals, Edmonton's Wayne Gretzky went on a spree in game four with a record-tying seven-point night. Gretzky's three goals and four assists equalled the Stanley Cup playoff standard had he established on April 17, 1983, in Calgary—four goals and three assists. Edmonton eliminated the Jets in four games.

Norris Division

The Detroit Red Wings were devastated after being swept out of the NHL playoffs by the Chicago Blackhawks in just three games. Five days after the the defeat, Detroit veteran Brad Park, seven-time All-Star defenseman, announced his retirement saying, "Seventeen years is enough."

Three consecutive outstanding performances led the Minnesota North Stars to victory over the St. Louis Blues. The shining star of the series was 34-year-old goaltender Gilles Meloche. But the on-ice action ended for Minnesota with their defeat to the Chicago Blackhawks in the Norris Division finals. The Hawks won four games to two.

Patrick Division

Philadelphia's Tim Kerr set two playoff records and tied a third, with a four-goal performance in game three as the Flyers swept the Rangers aside. Kerr set NHL individual playoff records with four goals in one period and three power-play goals in one period. He also tied the league record for power-play goals in one playoff game. With New York sidelined, Ranger star Anders Hedberg announced his retirement from hockey. The New York Islanders became the first team in NHL history to win a best-of-five series after losing the first two games, when they defeated the Washington Capitals 2–1 in the deciding game. But the Islanders were unable to pull off the same feat against the Philadelphia Flyers in the Patrick Division finals. The Flyers won the first three games of their best-of-seven series against the Islanders, dropped the fourth game, then wrapped it up with a 1–0 victory in game five at the Spectrum. "Do me a favour," Bob Nystrom of New York told reporters after the final game. "Tell those guys [the Flyers] to beat Edmonton for us. I mean that with a passion."

Adams Division

The Montreal Canadiens were forced to a fifth and deciding game against the Boston Bruins in their best-of-five series. The series was particularly exciting for Montreal's Steve Rooney, the Providence College graduate who was married just hours before game five. Rooney had planned the wedding a year before and had never expected to be with the Canadiens at this time. Fortunately the Habs' arrival in Boston coincided with his wedding day. Immediately after the service he was whisked off to the Garden with a police escort and went out to score his first playoff goal in the Habs' 4–2 victory.

The Quebec Nordiques eliminated the Buffalo Sabres in the first round of the playoffs for the second consecutive season. In the fifth and deciding game in Quebec City, the Sabres were less than 10 minutes away from a series victory with a comfortable 5–3 lead, but the Sabres were unable to hold on, giving up three goals in the final minutes of the game. In the Adams Division final, the Montreal Canadiens, who had finished first in the Division, were defeated by their arch rivals, the Quebec Nordiques, in overtime in game seven.

Campbell Conference Finals

For the third time in four years, the Chicago Blackhawks reached the Campbell Conference finals. But the Hawks couldn't cope with the speed and depth of the Edmonton Oilers and were eliminated from the playoffs in game six.

Wales Conference Finals

The Philadelphia Flyers' center, Dave Poulin, scored a dramatic goal while his team was playing two men short, to break the spirit of the Quebec Nordiques in the sixth and final game of the Wales Conference finals. The Flyers won the game 3–0 and the series 4–2 to advance to the Cup finals against Edmonton. Poulin, hampered by a rib injury and a strained knee, stole a pass from Mario Marois while Quebec had a five-on-three advantage in the game that ended the series. He raced in and launched a perfect shot over the glove of goalie Mario Gosselin for a 2–0 Flyer lead.

The Stanley Cup Finals

On May 30, at the Northlands Coliseum in Edmonton, the Oilers bounced the Flyers 8–3 in game five of hockey's biggest series to win a second consecutive Stanley Cup. "It's sweeter this time," said defenseman Paul Coffey in the winners' dressing room. "When you're the biggest team on the block, people want to beat you." Philadelphia was at a disadvantage with a rash of injuries. They were forced to play the entire series without top defensemen Brad McCrimmon, who had a separated shoulder, the final three games without leading scorer Tim Kerr, out with a strained knee, and the final game without their regular-season MVP Pelle Lindbergh, sidelined with a torn knee ligament. In addition, captain Dave Poulin was suffering with a cracked rib and Ilkka Sinislao was nursing a bruised shoulder. "We haven't won four or five in a row, but I would think we have the start of a dynasty," said Coffey. "If we continue to be dedicated, with the players and organization we have there's no reason why we can't be a dynasty."

During the playoffs on April 21, Foster Hewitt, the dean of hockey broadcasting who probably touched more fans' lives than any other individual, died in Toronto at 83. Hewitt was a member of the Hockey Hall of Fame, the Canada Sports Hall of Fame and he had received an Order of Canada medal of service. Esteemed hockey broadcaster Dan Kelly put it best when he said, "Foster Hewitt was to broadcasting what Gordie Howe was to hockey."

Two well-known players left the game at the end of the season. Steve Shutt decided to retire after the Los Angeles Kings returned him to the Montreal Canadiens. Shutt, a three-time All-Star, had helped the Canadiens win five Stanley Cups in the 1970s. And after 891 games with the Boston Bruins, Terry O'Reilly also called it quits. O'Reilly finished his career with 204 goals, 402 assists and a team record of 2,095 penalty minutes.

1985-86

Toronto and Pittsburgh had high hopes for the new season after plucking two of hockey's brightest young players out of the entry draft in June. The Leafs made tough and talented Wendel Clark the number-one choice overall and were faced with the decision of playing him on the blue line or as a forward. Michigan State center Craig Simpson, rated as the top eligible player by NHL central scouting, was the second player chosen. He went to Pittsburgh. "When the Leafs took Clark, I knew where I was headed," Simpson said.

There was a murmur throughout the room when Buffalo's Scotty Bowman selected Keith Gretzky in the third round of the draft. But onlookers just shrugged when Calgary picked Cornell University center Joe Nieuwendyk in the second round.

Following the draft, teams went scrambling after the free agents that were available. Detroit gambled on Adam Oates, a two-time All American from RPI by making him the richest rookie in NHL history. Oates was given a four-year contract calling for $1.1 million. A few days later, the Wings made another collegian even richer. They signed Ray Staszak, 22, a right-winger from little-known Illinois-Chicago University.

Staszak's deal was even sweeter than Oates'—a $1.3 million pact over five years. A total of 18 NHL clubs made serious bids for Staszak. Most of them were impressed with his toughness, on and off the ice. He once took on three Chicago thugs who were trying to steal his car and beat them until they fled.

The Wings went after free agents with a vengeance. They also signed 29-year-old Warren Young, a 40-goal scorer as a Pittsburgh rookie, Harold Snepts from Minnesota, Mike McEwan of Washington and collegians Dale Krentz, Chris Cichocki and Tim Friday. The spending spree left other clubs seething. "There are 20 owners in this league who are totally teed off by what's happened," said Pittsburgh general manager Ed Johnston. "The Wings have put the NHL salary structure completely out of whack."

In July, 92-year-old Frank Selke, Sr., died at his home in Rigaud, Quebec. One of hockey's great builders and the managing director of the Montreal Canadiens in their glory years of the late 1950s, Selke was also instrumental in the building of Maple Leaf Gardens. "He was tough but he did things in a very nice way," recalled Montreal's Jean Beliveau. "In French we have a phrase for such men—A hand of steel in a velour glove."

In the off season, Pat Verbeek of the New Jersey Devils severed his left thumb in a corn-planting machine on his farm near Forest, Ontario. The thumb was found by Verbeek's father in a bag of fertilizer. Surgeons reattached the thumb but didn't give much hope of success. "You put it back on and I'll make sure it stays on," said Verbeek. By training camp his thumb looked remarkably healthy. "I think it's even grown a bit," he quipped. "Probably because of all that fertilizer it fell in."

In mid-summer the Canadiens announced a coaching change, their fifth since 1979. Jacques Lemaire, who said he'd had enough of the pressure-filled job, stepped down and was replaced by Jean Perron. Perron had a degree in physical education, a masters degree and a level-6 coaching certificate. It was enough to make old-time coaches like Toe Blake and Punch Imlach shake their heads in wonder. While many fans said they'd miss Lemaire, others accused him of forcing aging superstar Guy Lafleur into retirement during the previous season.

Rookie coach Lorne Henning brought to Minnesota four years of experience as an assistant to Al Arbour and one year as head coach of the Springfield Indians of the AHL. Tom Watt, a former NHL coach of the year in Winnipeg, signed a three-year contract as coach of the Canucks, a team that had finished 20 points out of the playoffs the previous spring. Former Vancouver coach Harry Neale signed a two-year pact to coach the Red Wings, bringing 18 years of coaching experience and a reputation for funny one-liners with him. To fill their vacant head-coach position, the Rangers hired a magna cum laude college grad who had been assisting Mike Keenan in Philadelphia. Ranger general manager Craig Patrick said, "I know Ted Sator will be the most successful coach in the quickest time." Scotty Bowman decided to stick to managing in Buffalo and hired former Sabre defenseman Jim Schoenfeld to coach the club, while in Boston Harry Sinden dropped Gerry Cheevers and turned to Butch Goring.

In September, the once-happy marriage between Guy Lafleur and the Montreal Canadiens ended in divorce. Even though the Canadiens were paying Lafleur the $400,000 he was due on the final year of his contract and had agreed to pay him an additional $100,000 annually as a goodwill ambassador, Lafleur said he did not want to be paid "like a simple clerk." Ron Corey, the Canadiens' president, said, "I will not be blackmailed. Guy is free to pursue whatever he wishes. Good luck to him in the future."

Todd Bergen of the Flyers said he was quitting hockey to pursue a career as a golf pro. Asked if he'd trade Bergen, general manager Bobby Clarke replied, "Who am I gonna trade him for—Lee Trevino?" Meanwhile, Quebec's Michel Goulet, said he was prepared to sit out the entire season if monetary clauses in his contract were not changed. The Nordiques quickly came to terms with Goulet. The team began the season with seven straight wins, one game shy of the league record.

One of the game's most popular players stepped aside prior to the new season. Darryl Sittler, who had spent many turbulent years in Toronto before moving on to Philadelphia and Detroit, bowed out after 15 seasons. He ended his career just 16 goals shy of the 500-goal plateau. Although he was an All-Star only once, Sittler left his mark as the only man to score 10 points in a game. He had also scored the winning goal in overtime against Czechoslovakia in the 1976 Canada Cup. Another player who left the game behind was Bill Barber, whose damaged knee forced him into retirement. One of the most versatile players in the game, Barber had helped lead Philadelphia to two Stanley Cups, in 1974 and 1975.

The *Hockey News* revealed that Wayne Gretzky was hockey's highest-paid player, with on-ice earnings of $1.2 million (Cdn.) or slightly more than $800,000 (U.S.). Trailing Gretzky in the salary sweepstakes were Mike Bossy of the Islanders ($610,000), Kings' center Marcel Dionne ($475,000), Islanders' center Bryan Trottier ($475,000), Kings' winger Dave Taylor ($450,000), Bruins' defenseman Ray Bourque ($435,000) and Hartford's goalie Mike Liut ($435,000).

Wayne Gretzky and Paul Coffey were critical of the league vote which eliminated four-on-four situations during coincidental penalties. Seventeen of the 21 clubs voted for the measure which had become known as the "Oilers' rule." Coffey said, "I know which teams voted for it. All the slowpoke teams with the big lugs."

In September Bert Olmstead was inducted into the Hockey Hall of Fame along with Gerry Cheevers and Jean Ratelle. At first Olmstead was reluctant to accept the honor. "You might think I'm an egomaniac," he said, "but my first reaction was to tell them to stick it. Finally I figured I'm a bigger man than that. It's all political, you know. I knew a few people had to die before I'd get in."

On August 18, Petr Klima, one of the top players on Czechoslovakia's 1985 national team, slipped away from the team's training camp in West Germany and, with the help of his agent, defected to North America and the Detroit Red Wings. The 20-year-old left-winger was given an excellent chance of emerging as an NHL superstar. One scout labeled Klima "a brilliant, brilliant player."

In September, Craig MacTavish, a former Boston Bruin, began the long road back to the NHL when he signed with the Edmonton Oilers as a free agent. MacTavish had just been released from a Massachusetts correctional institution after pleading guilty to a charge of vehicular homicide in 1984. Coach Glen Sather of the Oilers said, "He made a mistake and he has paid for his error. But I want him because he's a whale of a hockey player."

There was heartache in Philadelphia on the morning of November 10. Flyer goalie Pelle Lindbergh, 26, was driving his ultra-customized sports car with two passengers aboard and slammed into a retaining wall at high speed. The passengers were seriously injured and Lindbergh died later in hospital. The night before, Lindbergh and his teammates had celebrated the Flyers' 10th-straight win. His death was said to be alcohol related. "We had talked to Pelle about his fast driving," said general manager

Bobby Clarke, "but when you are that young, and that strong, you just feel invincible." Through the darkness of the Lindbergh tragedy, the Flyers never faltered on the ice. For a 32-day stretch, from October 17 to November 19, they didn't lose a game, winning 13 in all. Their bid to match the NHL record of 15 straight wins was halted, however, by the Islanders at the Nassau County Coliseum.

Early in the season the Islanders' Denis Potvin tied Bobby Orr's record for most points earned by a defenseman, with 915. Potvin's 915 points consisted of 265 goals and 650 assists in 877 games. Orr had totalled 270 goals and 645 assists for 915 points in 657 games.

In Winnipeg, John Ferguson shocked Jet fans by trading David Babych to Hartford in return for right-winger Ray Neufeld. When Ferguson made Babych the second overall selection in the 1980 draft he called him "our franchise."

The Minnesota North Stars felt that they could lure center Todd Bergen away from the golf course and back to the arena. They gave tough guy Dave Richter and Swedish forward Bo Berglund to Philadelphia for the missing Bergen and defenseman Ed Hospodar.

On December 14, referee Ron Wicks established a league record for the most regular-season games worked by a referee when he called his 1,034th game. The previous record holder was Bruce Hood. In January, referees and linesmen were summoned to Toronto to attend seminars aimed at reaffirming a message which had been delivered before the season—to treat both restraining and stick fouls with more severity. An alarming number of eye injuries, including Ryan Walter of Montreal and Charlie Simmer and Michael Thelvin of the Bruins served to point out the potential dangers of carelessness with sticks.

Also in January, the Soviet Union won the gold medal at the 1986 World Junior Championships. Canada captured the silver after a 4–1 loss to the Soviets.

Detroit suffered through a disastrous first half with only eight victories in 35 games. Coach Harry Neale was released and Brad Park, 37, replaced him, also becoming the director of player personnel. The dual role gave him complete control of the Wings' fortunes. This move occurred only eight months after Park had ended his 17-year illustrious playing career.

On December 31, Bruce Norris, former owner of the Red Wings, died of liver failure at age 61. Norris had taken control of the Wings when he was 31 and in his first season in 1954–55 his team had rolled to the Stanley Cup. Norris had sold the club to the current owner, Mike Ilitch, in 1982, severing a half-century of family ownership.

Early in the new year, the Toronto Maple Leafs unveiled a second Ihnacak after they helped Peter's brother Miroslav defect from Czechoslovakia. General manager Gerry MacNamara was so confident the younger Ihnacak would be a star that he dusted off number 27 for him—a jersey made famous by former Leaf greats Frank Mahovlich and Darryl Sittler.

The Penguins were busy opening the coffers for Mario Lemieux, the 20-year-old superstar. He signed a new five-year contract which he believed would make him the second-highest paid player, behind Wayne Gretzky. Lemieux's new pact was worth an estimated $650,000 per season.

Hot scorer Pierre Larouche returned to the New York Rangers late in January. Larouche and several other Rangers had been shuffled to the minors by rookie coach Ted Sator during the final weeks of training camp. Larouche became the fifth of the seven players that Sator had been forced to recall.

In February, Buffalo's Dave Andreychuk became the first player in team history to score five goals in a game, when he collected six points in an 8–6 victory over the Boston Bruins. He failed to match the modern-day record of six goals in a game shared by Red Berenson and Darryl Sittler, despite several good scoring chances. In 1920, Joe Malone of the Quebec Bulldogs had set the all-time record of seven goals in a game.

Goalie Grant Fuhr was named the most valuable player in the All-Star game played in Hartford. The Islanders' Bryan Trottier scored in overtime to give the Wales Conference a 4–3 victory.

At the All-Star game, Marcel Aubut, president of the Nordiques, announced a plan called Rendez-Vous '87, a two-game series between the Soviet Union and the NHL All-Stars. According to Aubut, it would be the Super Bowl of hockey and would take place during Quebec City's winter carnival. Some NHL players were not enthusiastic about another confrontation with the Soviets, especially at mid-season. Wayne Gretzky said, "It will be all work and all business playing the Soviets. Personally, I think the players need a break."

Late in February, the Boston Bruins were hit hard by injuries—four regular defensemen were out of the lineup. Assistant coach Mike Milbury was forced to turn in his clipboard and suit up again.

Leaf captain Rick Vaive, like other Leaf captains before him, found himself in trouble with team owner Harold Ballard late in February. Vaive had overslept and missed an early morning practice and the Leaf owner stripped the captaincy from him. "I'm very saddened and disappointed," said Vaive. "On the other hand, what I did was irresponsible and I have to take full responsibility and pay the consequences."

Dave Hunter of the Edmonton Oilers was in more serious trouble. He was sentenced to 28 days in jail after he was convicted of impaired driving for the third time. The Hunter incident followed the arrest of teammate Mark Messier, who was charged after ramming his sports car into some parked automobiles.

The death of 57-year-old Jacques Plante in a Swiss hospital shocked his many fans and friends. He had died of stomach cancer. Plante had spent the last few weeks of his life as a goalie instructor with the St. Louis Blues. He had been a member of six Stanley Cup teams with the Canadiens and had won the Vezina Trophy seven times. Plante had revolutionized the art of goaltending. He had been the first to skate out of his net and get involved in the play, the first to signal when an icing call was imminent and the first to yell instructions to his teammates during the play. While he had not been the first goalie to wear a face mask, he was the first to make facial protection standard equipment among goalkeepers.

There were a number of mid season trades. The Calgary Flames, looking for scoring punch, acquired Joey Mullen from the Blues in a February deal involving six players. The Blues sent Mullen and defensemen Terry Johnson and Rik Wilson to the Flames in return for forwards Ed Beers and Gino Cavallini, plus defenseman Charlie Bourgeois. But Mullen was the key. The previous season he had scored 40 goals and 52 assists. Buffalo general manager Scotty Bowman dealt seven-year veteran defenseman Larry Playfair, right-winger Sean McKenna and the rights to 1985 unsigned draftee Ken Baumgartner to Los Angeles for defenseman Brian Engblom and center Doug Smith. Defenseman Reed Larson went from Detroit to Boston in return for rear guard Mike O'Connell. Quebec obtained speedy Risto Siltanen from Hartford in exchange for winger John Anderson, and later swapped veteran forward Wilf Paiement to the

Rangers for defenseman Steve Patrick. Washington gave up defenseman Darren Veitch to get two Detroit defenders, Greg Smith and John Barrett. Hours before the trading deadline, the Flames swung another major deal, trading left-winger Richard Kromm and defenseman Steve Konroyd to the Islanders in return for left-winger John Tonelli, the MVP in the 1984 Canada Cup.

On March 9, Gilbert Perreault became the 12th player in NHL history to reach goal number 500, ending his frustratingly long bid to reach that plateau. A few days later, Paul Coffey of the Oilers tied a scoring mark for defensemen with two goals, six assists and eight points in a game.

In mid-March, veteran center Mark Pavelich of the Rangers was missing from a New York practice session. Later in the week, Pavelich confirmed that he was retiring from the game, citing conflicts with coach Ted Sator as the reason. "They [the coaching staff] don't know what they're doing," said Pavelich bitterly. "That's their problem. I don't understand their thinking at all. And that's why I'm quitting."

Another unhappy player was rookie Kirk McCaskill of the Jets. He quit the game to try his luck as a pitcher in professional baseball. McCaskill described conditions in Sherbrooke, Quebec, where he'd been dispatched by the Jets as miserable. "The town was terrible, the rink was terrible, the hockey was terrible. And the coaching was non-existent." McCaskill jumped at a chance to sign a lucrative contract with the California Angels of the American League. "He should be a natural as a pitcher," quipped Jet coach Barry Long. "With us he showed he liked to play once every four days."

The race for the rookie award attracted a lot of interest. One of the contenders, Kjell Dahlin of Montreal, told reporters that he rated the Leafs' Wendel Clark no better than fourth in the race. Fourth, that is, behind himself, Calgary defenseman Gary Suter and New York Rangers' center Mike Ridley. "I find it difficult to understand a guy like Wendel getting much consideration for rookie of the year. He has only 10 assists," said the 23-year-old from Sweden.

Mario Lemieux's 28-game scoring streak ended when Washington held him without a point in a 5–3 Caps' victory. The streak tied those compiled by Oilers' defenseman Paul Coffey and former Montreal right-wing Guy Lafleur for the fourth longest streak in NHL history. The record for the three longest streaks—51, 39 and 30 games—belonged to Wayne Gretzky.

Late in the season, Marcel Dionne passed Phil Esposito and took over sole possession of second place on the NHL's all-time points list. After collecting 1,591 points, he hinted at retirement. "It's been a tough, frustrating year," said Dionne, who was leading the Kings in scoring with 34 goals and 52 assists in 72 games. "Another season like this...I don't know...I may just pack it in."

Another league graybeard, Larry Robinson, played his 1,000th game in Winnipeg on March 19, becoming only the third Canadien to reach that plateau. Robinson recalled his first day at the Canadiens' training camp. As a rookie he was last in line when the equipment was handed out. "I got Maurice Richard's old shin pads," he recalled. "They were too small for me but I was too shy to ask for a larger pair."

Minnesota's Neal Broten, the five-foot-eight-inch native of Roseau, Minnesota, became the first American-born player to reach 100 points, with two assists in a 6–1 victory in Toronto on March 26.

Tom Watt, coach of the Canucks, blew his cool over referee Don Koharski's delay-of-game penalty called during a game against Calgary. "Koharski is a dirty, no-good vindictive [expletive deleted] who deliberately cheated us out of two points," fumed Watt. His vivid verbal description of the official earned him a $5,000 fine from league headquarters. Another Smythe Division coach, Barry Long of the Jets, found himself out of a job after 65 games. "My fault is I'm too nice a guy," said Long after Jets' general manager John Ferguson fired him and decided to coach the team himself.

For Wayne Gretzky and Paul Coffey of the Oilers the season produced personal records. Gretzky collected 215 points, breaking his own single-season points record. His 163 assists represented more points than any other NHL player had ever scored in a season. Coffey had been in hot pursuit of Bobby Orr's goal-scoring standard for defensemen, once thought to be unreachable. Coffey slammed in his 47th goal on April 2 against the Canucks, breaking Orr's illustrious mark by one. Two nights later he scored number 48. But Coffey, with 138 points, missed equalling Orr's single-season standard for defensemen by one point. A third Oiler, Jari Kurri, succeeded Gretzky as the league's top sniper, becoming the first European player to win the goal-scoring title. Kurri finished the season with 68 goals.

Once again the Edmonton Oilers were the class of the league, registering 56 wins and 119 points. Only two other clubs, Patrick Division rivals Philadelphia and Washington, topped 100 points. For the first time in his career, Scotty Bowman found himself out of the playoffs, even though the 80 points totaled by his Sabres would have assured them a playoff spot in any division but the Adams.

THE NHL PLAYOFFS

Smythe Division

The Smythe Division champion Edmonton Oilers breezed to a three-game victory over the fourth-place Vancouver Canucks. The defending Stanley Cup champions surrendered a mere five goals in the process of capturing their ninth-straight playoff series. The Calgary Flames, led by old-timers Doug Risebrough, John Tonelli and Lanny McDonald, squashed the Winnipeg Jets, who set some kind of record by employing four goalies in the short series. In an exciting Smythe Division final series, the Flames emerged victorious, ending the Oiler bid for another Cup. In game seven, the Oilers had rallied from a 2–0 deficit in the second period to pull even on a Mark Messier goal. But in the third, rookie defenseman Steve Smith had banked the puck off Grant Fuhr's leg into his own net. The unexpected goal snapped a 2–2 tie and enabled the Flames to escape with a 3–2 victory and the division title.

Norris Division

The Chicago Blackhawks, first-place finishers in their division, were stunned by the fourth-place Toronto Maple Leafs in the opening round. The Leafs swept the series behind the excellent goaltending of Ken Wregget. The Minnesota North Star season ended with a loss to St. Louis in game five. The Blues' coach Jacques Demers admitted that he coined a few illegal time-outs in ousting the Minnesota North Stars. Demers threw pennies onto the ice during stoppages in play to give his players an extra breather. The Norris Division finals went to seven games before the Blues were able to eliminate the Leafs. The Leafs, with the second-worst regular-season record in the NHL, lost the final game 2–1, but their six playoff wins were a half-dozen more than anyone expected.

Patrick Division

The New York Rangers registered the biggest upset of the playoffs by stealing their opening round match up from the division champion Philadelphia Flyers. The Rangers brought the Flyers' season to a stunning halt by defeating them 5–2 in the fifth and deciding game. Washington swept past the Islanders, who managed only four goals against steady Pete Peeters in the three games played. In the Patrick Division finals, the underdog Rangers eliminated the Capitals on home ice in game six, winning 2–1.

Adams Division

Despite injury problems, many thought the Boston Bruins would eliminate the Montreal Canadiens in the opening round. The Canadiens had stumbled into the playoffs and appeared to be weak in goal. Nobody expected rookie Patrick Roy to give up a mere six goals in a three-game Montreal sweep and maintain a Montreal playoff-series winning streak over Boston dating back to 1943.

The Hartford Whalers upset the Quebec Nordiques in straight games. Only in game one, which Sylvain Turgeon had ended with an overtime goal, were the Whalers seriously challenged. In the division finals, the Whalers forced the Canadiens into a seventh game and an extra period before succumbing to them. Despite their loss, there was a feeling of achievement amongst the Whalers, who were led by the goaltending of Mike Liut and the spunky goal scoring of Kevin Dineen.

Wales Conference Finals

The makeup of the final four was a total surprise, with the top five regular-season clubs all eliminated. Calgary, number six overall, and Montreal, number seven, were the highest ranking of the teams still in contention. St. Louis finished 12th and the Rangers 14th. With a combination of weathered veterans like Larry Robinson and Bob Gainey, and the fuzzy-cheeked kiddie corps that included goaltender Patrick Roy and Claude Lemieux, the Montreal Canadiens found themselves in a position to capture their 23rd Stanley Cup. The Canadiens eased past the spent Rangers in five games to earn a berth in the Stanley Cup finals. New York never did reach the level of intensity they had achieved in upsetting Philadelphia and Washington.

Campbell Conference Finals

The Calgary Flames defeated the St. Louis Blues 4–3 in the best-of-seven series. Unheralded Steve Bozek gave the Flames skating strength and joined others such as

Hakan Loob in shutting down the Blues' inept power play. The Blues' coach Jacques Demers forced a few more illegal time outs for his team by throwing pennies on the ice again. "Do you know how many coaches in the NHL do it?" asked Demers, who was warned to stop throwing his money around. Demers had no comment when asked if he had learned the trick from Mike Keenan of Philadelphia. Keenan had coached against Demers in the American League during the early eighties and commented, "I don't make that much money that I can throw it away. Jacques recently signed a healthy new contract so maybe he can afford to do it."

The Stanley Cup Finals

Seven years following their 22nd Stanley Cup championship, the Montreal Canadiens brought their 23rd Cup home to set a professional-sports record for the most playoff titles. Calgary was a convincing 5–2 winner in game one of the finals. Montreal won game two 3–2 in overtime. Brian Skrudland, thought to be too slow for the NHL, set a record for the fastest overtime goal in NHL history, scoring at nine seconds of sudden death. It was his first-ever Cup goal. The series then shifted to Montreal where the Canadiens found home ice to their liking. They won games three and four by 5–3 and 1–0. Game four featured two of the most prominent rookies of the playoffs. Claude Lemieux, who had displayed a consistent knack for scoring big goals in his first Stanley Cup playoff year, got the only goal at 11:30 of the third period. Patrick Roy, who would go on to win the Conn Smythe Trophy as the top playoff performer, recorded his first-ever NHL shutout and the first by a rookie goaltender in 31 years. Game five was full of heart-stopping action at the Saddledome in Calgary. Montreal hung on to beat Calgary 4–3, thanks to a great toe save by Roy on Jamie Macoun with 14 seconds left in regulation time.

While the Canadiens were celebrating in Calgary, their victory triggered a riot thousands of miles away. Montrealers took to the streets and the victory party soon turned ugly. People overturned cars, broke windows and looted stores. They lit a bonfire in downtown Montreal and when a fire truck arrived, they attacked it. A riot squad eventually cleared the streets.

On May 5, the New York Rangers lost a piece of their franchise when Bill Cook passed away at the age of 89. From 1926–27 until his retirement following the 1936–37 season, the right-winger had twice won the Art Ross Trophy as the NHL's leading scorer and had earned berths on the first All-Star team three times and on the second team once. He had joined his brother Bun Cook and playmaking center Frank Boucher on one of the most famous lines in league history. The Brantford, Ontario, native scored the Rangers' first-ever goal and was the team's first captain. Hockey also mourned the loss of Johnny Gottselig, a star forward for Chicago from 1928 to 1944, who passed away at age 80. Gottselig had coached the Blackhawks from 1945 to 1948.

1986-87

Prior to the 1986–87 season, Islanders' fans were surprised when Al Arbour announced his decision to step down as coach of the four-time Stanley Cup champions. Upon leaving the bench for a front-office job, Arbour said, "I've had a helluva run at it.

Now it's time for somebody else to handle the reins." That somebody turned out to be Terry Simpson of Prince Albert, Saskatchewan, a junior coach with no previous big-league experience. Simpson, 42, had coached the Prince Albert Raiders to a Memorial Cup in 1985 and had guided the Canadian National junior team to a gold medal in the 1984 World Championships.

There was another coaching change in Detroit. After just 45 games behind the bench, Brad Park was fired. After he lost the battle for control of the Red Wings to Jimmy Devellano, Park said, "Everybody seems to be worried about the mistakes I made in three months and not all the mistakes Devellano has made in four years." The NHL's worst team then lured Jacques Demers, one of hockey's best coaches, away from St. Louis with a five-year $1.1-million contract. Demers became Detroit's 17th coach in 18 years. Along with Demers, the Wings counted heavily on Joe Murphy, a nifty center from Michigan State, to move them up in the standings. Murphy became the first college player selected number one overall in the entry draft.

Seven Americans were chosen in the first round of the draft, besting the previous mark of five set in 1983. Tops among the young Americans was Detroit's Jimmy Carson (70–83–153) from Verdun, who was drafted number two by Los Angeles. The Rangers felt they had a "blue chipper" in Brian Leetch and the Whalers felt the same way about Scott Young.

Due to his size, six-foot-three-inch winger George Pelawa, was the hit of the draft. The 235-pound native of Bemidji, Minnesota, drafted by Calgary, was the single most scouted player in Flames' history. Two months after being drafted, the husky teenager died in a two-car collision near Bemidji.

On June 2, Hall of Famer Aurel Joliat died of a heart attack in Ottawa. He was 85. Known as "the Little Giant," Joliat had joined the Montreal Canadiens in 1922 and had remained with them for 16 years, scoring a total of 270 goals and winning the Hart Trophy in 1930. Despite his age, he was still skating regularly and prior to his death he had played a major role in a movie about the Canadiens.

Also in June, Dan Maloney rejected a one-year contract offer of $75,000 from Leaf owner Harold Ballard. On his way out of Maple Leaf Gardens, Maloney called John Ferguson in Winnipeg and 72 hours later was signed as coach of the Jets.

Meanwhile, the St. Louis Blues were busy looking for a replacement for Jacques Demers. They finally settled on Jacques Martin, who had guided the Guelph Platers to a Memorial Cup in his first season as a head coach.

In July, Phil Esposito became the New York Rangers' new general manager, succeeding Craig Patrick. Esposito became the fourth straight Rangers' general manager to be hired with no previous experience. He said, "My experience is playing this game for 19 years. It's studying the game since I was four years old. Frankly, I've got more experience than any general manager that's been around—when they first went in."

The Minnesota North Stars and the Washington Capitals were busy tracking down two Czech defectors. Center Michal Pivonka, 20, and his fianceé had defected during a vacation in Yugoslavia and were flown to Washington by Caps' general manager David Poile. At about the same time, 21-year-old defenseman Frantisek Musil arrived in Minnesota having also defected via Yugoslavia.

John Brophy brought his tough-guy reputation to Toronto as the new coach of the Leafs. Brophy would have to get along without defenseman Gary Nylund, 22, who was swayed by a lucrative Chicago contract. The injury-hobbled Nyland said it was "strictly a financial decision." An arbitrator awarded the Leafs Ken Yaremchuk and Jerome Dupont as compensation. The Leafs were hoping to get Ed Olcyk.

Toronto's veteran defenseman Borje Salming was suspended for eight regular-season games and four pre-season games after he had admitted that he'd experimented with cocaine several years earlier.

A former Leaf, Gordon Drillon, died at the age of 71 in Moncton, New Brunswick. Drillon, a member of the Hall of Fame, had been the last Toronto player to win the NHL scoring crown, back in 1937–38.

Barry Beck, former Rangers' captain, announced that he would retire from hockey rather than play for coach Ted Sator. Beck cited "philosophical differences" between the two, but would not elaborate. Sator said he was "surprised and disappointed" at Beck's decision.

Harry Ornest, credited with saving hockey in St. Louis, sold the franchise on October 1 for $19 million. Three years earlier he had bought the club, which had been left for dead, for $3 million.

Mario Tremblay decided to retire from the Canadiens after 12 seasons. Tremblay told reporters, "If my shoulder would be all right, I would be out on the ice right now. It's tough to retire at 30."

The International Ice Hockey Federation announced that professionals would be allowed to participate in the 1988 Olympic Games at Calgary. But in the minds of many NHL officials this would not be feasible for most of the league's top stars. "We simply can't shut down our season for two or three weeks," said John Ziegler. Citing the U.S. gold medal-winning performance at Lake Placid in 1980, U.S. team manager Art Berglund said that the decision would have no effect on his organization. "The Olympics provide an excellent outlet for amateur players," he explained. "We feel our amateur approach works."

Early in the new season, Wayne Gretzky scored a hat trick against the Bruins, the 38th of his career and an NHL record. With his 874th point, Gretzky moved into fourth place on the all-time scoring list, one ahead of Phil Esposito.

With each game played by the New Jersey Devils, a remarkable comeback story became ever more incredible. Pat Verbeek, whose left thumb had been sheared off in a farming accident the previous summer, set a Devils' club record by scoring goals in six consecutive games.

In November, Butch Goring was sacked as coach of the Bruins. He was replaced by former Bruin Terry O'Reilly, who moved from the broadcast booth to the bench. "O'Reilly will coach for at least the rest of the season," stated general manager Harry Sinden. O'Reilly's reaction was less than enthusiastic. "If I made a list of 100 possible occupations, coaching would be at the bottom of the list," he said.

In Buffalo, Scotty Bowman gave up his dual role as general manager and coach. He appointed Craig Ramsay his successor as coach. Bowman left with a record number of coaching wins—739.

Early in the new season, Gilbert Perreault, the original Sabre, called it quits and went home. By taking himself out of the lineup, Perreault had forfeited a considerable amount of money. Best estimates were that his contract called for slightly more than $400,000. It's believed that Perreault gave up three-quarters of that amount and, because he did not play in 40 games to qualify for a one-time pension bonus as mandated by the new collective-bargaining agreement, he sacrificed another $250,000.

The flashy centerman retired with 512 goals, six fewer than Guy Lafleur, another great French-Canadian scorer.

Loveable King Clancy, one of the game's most colorful characters, died in Toronto on November 10 at the age of 83. Clancy had been famous as a player, coach, referee and assistant general manager. Years ealier, Harold Ballard had named him "vice-president for life" of the Toronto franchise. Clancy once played every position in a Stanley Cup game, including goaltender.

After failing to impress his bosses, rookie Joe Murphy of Detroit was sent to the Wings' AHL affiliate in Adirondack, New York. "He has not worked hard in practice and he has not worked hard in games," growled Jacques Demers. "I'm very disappointed in him."

When Mike Bossy of the Islanders scored his 10th goal of the season he moved into sixth place on the league's all-time goal-scoring list, one ahead of the legendary Maurice Richard, who had retired with 544 goals.

Pittsburgh center Mike Bullard was traded to Calgary for center Dan Quinn, just one day after being thrown out of practice and stripped of his captaincy by coach Bob Berry. "He wasn't putting out," said Berry.

Ranger coach Ted Sator treated his friends in the press to dinner one night and joked about it being "the last supper." The next day Sator was fired. Phil Esposito went behind the bench for a few games, then signed Tom Webster as the Rangers' 22nd coach. Esposito had selected Webster over Terry Crisp, another strong candidate. "It was so close between the two," said Esposito. "It was incredible. I think Tom was a little hungrier, maybe he wanted the job more."

Wayne Gretzky made more headlines on November 22. He reached the lofty plateau of 500 goals in just 575 games, easily beating the NHL's previous best—Mike Bossy's 500 goals in 689 games.

Fighting appeared to be on the decline in the NHL. Through the first quarter of the season, there were 54 fewer fights than in a similar span a year earlier. The major reason for the reduction was attributed to the introduction of an extra penalty for those who instigated fights.

Early in December, Scotty Bowman's term in Buffalo came to an end. Bowman was dismissed as general manager and director of hockey operations. He was replaced by assistant general manager and former Sabre captain Gerry Meehan. Despite past coaching successes in Montreal and St. Louis, Bowman's efforts over seven years to get his Buffalo team into the Stanley Cup finals had been unsuccessful. One of Meehan's first moves as general manager was to fire Craig Ramsay and hand the coaching job to Ted Sator, former Ranger skipper.

In December, Boston mayor Raymond Flynn issued a warning to all pro athletes playing in Boston sports facilities: "Arrests will be made if violence continues." The mayor was disturbed by a November bench-clearing brawl between the Habs and the Bruins. "I wish I had been at that game," said Flynn. "I would have instructed my police commissioner to go on the ice with the police department and have the players taken off in handcuffs and arrested."

Late in December, the league's iron-man title went to diminutive Doug Jarvis of the Hartford Whalers. When Jarvis played in his 915th consecutive game on Decmber 26 he surpassed the previous standard of 914 established by Garry Unger.

On December 30, a volunteer driver at the wheel of a 1969 bus carrying the junior-A

Swift Current Broncos hockey team lost control while crossing a railway overpass. The team bus plowed into an embankment, flipped over and crashed on its side. Four young players were killed and several others were injured. One of the victims was Brent Ruff, brother of Buffalo's Lindy Ruff.

The Philadelphia Flyers began the new year by trading disgruntled goalie Bob Froese to the Rangers for defenseman Kjell Samuelson. Flyer fans were shocked to see general manager Bobby Clarke make a deal with his arch-rivals from New York. Froese wasn't the only NHL player anxious for a change of scene. In Washington, Bobby Carpenter made no bones about his disdain for coach Bryan Murray. Carpenter was told to sit at home until a deal could be made for him. Carpenter protested: "Murray cut my ice time and told me he was going to show me how to play hockey. I'm glad I didn't listen to him or I wouldn't be half the player I am now." On New Year's Day, Carpenter, along with a second-round draft choice, was traded to the Rangers in return for Mike Ridley, Kelly Miller and Bob Crawford.

International hockey suffered what may have been its blackest day early in 1987 when the final game between the Soviet Union and Canada was called during the World Junior Championships in Czechoslovakia. Canada, assured of a medal but needing a victory margin of at least five goals, was comfortably ahead 4–2 when a bench-clearing brawl erupted at 13:53 of the second period. Incredibly, tournament officials turned off the arena lights in an attempt to restore order, while the referee and linesmen retreated to their dressing room, leaving others to solve the problem. The IIFH directors met for 35 minutes, then decided to expel both teams from further play.

Pat Quinn found himself in hot water on January 9. In an unprecedented announcement, NHL president John Ziegler ordered the expulsion of Quinn from the league, "pending a complete investigation regarding Quinn's signing a contract to become general manager of the Vancouver Canucks for the 1987–88 season, and for accepting money from Vancouver while acting as coach of the Kings." A shocked Rogie Vachon, the Kings' general manager, named assistant coach Mike Murphy to replace Quinn until the matter was resolved.

Following a salary survey of its 1986–87 membership, the National Hockey League Players' Association released figures that revealed that the median salary of the 455 players surveyed was $135,000. The average base salary for Canadian players was $163,727 and for those playing in the U.S. it was $155,513.

In mid-season, Detroit and Quebec were involved in a major six-player swap. The Wings acquired much sought after Brent Ashton, along with defenseman Gilbert Delorme and winger Mark Kumpel. They gave up John Ogodnik, a one-time 50 goal scorer, Doug Shedden and Basil McRae, all wingers.

In Florida, Brian Spencer, a former NHL player with the Leafs, the Islanders and the Sabres, was charged with first-degree murder and kidnapping, five years after the West Palm Beach slaying of Michael James Dalfo.

On February 1, Wayne Gretzky moved ahead of ex-Blackhawks' star Stan Mikita into fourth place on the NHL's all-time scoring list. Gretzky's second assist in a game against Chicago was his 1,468th point.

John Ziegler made his findings public in the Pat Quinn affair. The mid-season soap opera saw the Kings' coach accept a $100,000 signing bonus to become president and general manager of the Vancouver Canucks in 1987–88. Quinn was barred from coaching until the 1990–91 season. The Canucks were fined $310,000 and the Kings $130,000, the stiffest fines permissible under NHL bylaws. Ziegler commented, "It is clear that at some point everyone forgot the essential and crucial element of the professional-sport business … the integrity of competition."

In February, Marcel Aubut, boss of the Quebec Nordiques convinced the NHL owners to replace the annual All-Star game with an event called Rendez-Vous '87. It was to be a two-game series between the NHL's best players and the Soviet national team, the first major meeting of the two hockey powers since the Challenge Cup of 1979. Rendez-Vous '87 produced two sparkling performances, a 4–3 Team NHL win on February 11 at Le Colisee and a 5–3 Soviet triumph two nights later on the 13th. "We're disappointed in not winning both games," said Wayne Gretzky, "but we're proud to split with them. I think we all would have loved a third game." Gretzky was named Team NHL's most valuable player and received a new car, his 10th. Valery Kemensky, a rising star in Soviet hockey at 20, was chosen as the top visiting player in the tournament.

There were fireworks at Maple Leaf Gardens in February. Frustrated at not being able to gain access to the Leafs' dressing room after games—a ban ordered by crusty Leaf owner Harold Ballard—the Toronto chapter of the Professional Hockey Writers Association voted to invade the dressing room en masse to "see what happens." Scott Morrison of the *Toronto Sun* beefed, "There are 119 major pro-sports teams in North America and 118 allow reporters in the dressing room following games." When Ballard caught the reporters pushing their way into the dressing room following a Leafs' game, he exploded with a string of obscenities.

"Just what the [expletive deleted] do you think you're doing?" he screamed.

"We're doing our job, or trying to," answered soft-spoken Bill Houston of *The Globe*.

"Get out of here, you [expletive deleted] and don't ever come in here again," Ballard shouted back.

After the stormy confrontation, which included Ballard striking the flash unit attached to a camera, he took the ban a step further. In future, he decreed, all interviews would take place in the team weight room across the hall from the dressing room.

While Ballard was blasting members of the media, the Islanders' Bryan Trottier was lashing out at NHL officials. Trottier said:

Some nights I think the refereeing in the NHL is worse than at any time since I joined the league in 1975. There's just so much interference in the game today and the refs aren't calling it. By not cracking down, they are helping to slow the game down from where it was two years ago. Who's the best ref? They're all bad. Kerry Fraser's the best and even he has some bad nights.

The league slapped a $1,000 fine on Trottier for his remarks. Boston Bruins' general manager Harry Sinden obviously didn't share Trottier's opinion of referee Fraser. Sinden was fined $2,000 for suggesting that Fraser was either a liar or a cheat following a Boston–Montreal game.

Prior to the March trading deadline, there was a major deal between the Kings and the Rangers. Marcel Dionne, the second-leading scorer in NHL history with 689 goals, went to New York in return for center Bobby Carpenter and defenseman Tom Laidlaw. The Rangers also received minor-league center Jeff Crossman and a third-round pick in the 1989 draft. Dionne, who had asked to be traded, was described by Kings' general manager Rogie Vachon as "someone special, a legend. He's like Kareem. You expect him to be around forever." Phil Esposito, accused by his critics of trading away the Rangers' future, said, "I totally disagree. I honestly believe Marcel can play three or four more years as well as he has in the past."

Mervyn "Red" Dutton, a former player who went on to become league president, died in Calgary at age 89. Dutton, a defenseman in the NHL for ten years, had then coached and managed the New York Americans. He had served as league president for two years following the death of Frank Calder in 1943. After he passed the presidency over to Clarence Campbell in 1945, Dutton had turned his back on the league, refusing to enter an NHL rink for 35 years and declining to answer questions about the calibre of play in the league.

The NHL's fourth president, John Ziegler, a 55-year-old native of Grosse Pointe, Michigan, was elected to the builders' section of the Hockey Hall of Fame, along with Matt Pavelich, 54, who was a linesman for 21 years. Three players were also elected: Bobby Clarke, Ed Giacomin and Jacques Laperriere.

With six games remaining in the regular season, Mike Bossy's quest for another 50-goal season came to a painful end. With 38 goals in 74 games, Bossy's aching back forced him to the sidelines. For the first time in his 10-year career, he had failed to top 50 goals.

The Minnesota North Stars, in a desperate effort to avoid missing the playoffs for the first time since 1979, made a coaching change with two games left in the schedule. Lorne Henning was fired and Glen Sonmor replaced him on an interim basis. Player reaction was harsh. Craig Hartsburg said, "There've been some stupid things done in my eight years here but this ranks with the stupidest. The people in the front office haven't done their job. At one time we had a bunch of guys who really cared and now it's all gone." The Stars, with only two wins in their final 17 games, watched helplessly as the Toronto Maple Leafs stole the final playoff berth in the Norris Division.

Bob Berry was sacked as coach when the Penguins missed the playoffs for the fifth straight year. Injuries that had kept Mario Lemieux out for nearly a quarter of the season had contributed to the team's poor showing. With Mario sidelined, Wayne Gretzky was an easy winner of the NHL scoring title with 183 points. He captured his seventh straight Art Ross Trophy.

Three rookies had made big impressions. Goalie Ron Hextall of Philadelphia played the most games (66), had the most wins (37) and the best save percentage (.902). The Kings' Luc Robitaille finished with 42 goals and 77 points in 73 games. His teammate Jimmy Carson (a Detroit native passed over in the draft by the Red Wings in favor of Joe Murphy) collected 33 goals and 71 points.

The Edmonton Oilers, the Smythe Division champions, finished in first place overall with 106 points. The only other club to reach the 100-point plateau was the Philadelphia Flyers, the Patrick Division winners, with an even 100. Hartford surprised everyone by capturing the Adams Division crown, while St. Louis finished atop the Norris Division.

THE NHL PLAYOFFS

Smythe Division

In round one, the Oilers lost their opening playoff game to the Kings, then settled down and captured four straight. In game two, Gretzky had a goal and six assists as the Oilers won 13–3, establishing a league record for goals in a playoff game. The Winnipeg Jets' tight checking and hard hitting surprised the Flames and Calgary bowed out in six games. Injuries to key big men hurt the Flames in the series. In the Smythe Division finals, the Oilers swept the Jets aside in four straight games. Despite the rout, Winnipeg general manager John Ferguson insisted that his team was good enough to win the Stanley Cup.

Norris Division

After the Toronto Maple Leafs had upset the St. Louis Blues in six games, coach John Brophy said, "Tell the man in Detroit [Demers] the miracle just happened." Earlier, Demers had allegedly said, "It would take a miracle for the Leafs to make the playoffs." Demers, meanwhile, was celebrating his team's sweep of the Chicago Blackhawks. A glum Hawks' president Bill Wirtz told the press his team would have "a whole new coaching staff by next season."

In the Norris Division finals, the Red Wings were desperate for a miracle of their own when they fell behind Toronto three games to one. That's when goalie Glen Hanlon turned miracle maker with some spectacular puck stopping. He blanked the Leafs twice in five days. The Wings came back from the brink and, by winning in seven games, advanced to the Campbell Conference finals against the Oilers.

Patrick Division

In the Patrick Division, the Islanders and the Capitals played a memorable seven-game series. Fans will long remember the final game which ended at 1:55 A.M. on Easter Sunday. The Islanders' Pat Lafontaine banked a slapshot off the left goal post and into Bob Mason's net at 8:47 of the seventh overtime period, ending the longest NHL game in 44 years. By winning three straight games and the series, the Isles became one of a handful of teams in NHL history to rally from a 3–1 deficit. In the division's other match up, the Philadelphia Flyers ousted the Rangers in six games and moved on to the division finals against the Islanders. It took seven games to declare a champion. Flyer captain Dave Poulin, playing in a flak jacket to protect his cracked ribs, gave the Flyers the lift they needed to win game seven.

Adams Division

For the fourth straight year, Montreal met Boston in the Adams Division semi-finals and for the fourth straight year the Bruins were eliminated. The Bruins failed to win a game and grew weary of reporters reminding them of Montreal's mastery over them in post-season play—18 consecutive series wins. In the Hartford–Quebec series, there was gloom in Quebec City after the Hartford Whalers, first-place finishers in the Adams Division, dumped the Nordiques in the first two games of their semi-final series. But Nords' goalie Mario Gosselin was undismayed. He publicly advised the fans to "bet the farm" on the club that finished 21 points back of the Whalers. "We'll take them in six games," promised the brash 23-year-old puckstopper. Then Gosselin stopped 57 of 59 shots in games three and four as Quebec stormed back with two wins. Prior to game five, Michel Goulet had received three threatening phone calls in his Hartford hotel room. Each time the caller had said, "You will be killed tonight." But Goulet and his teammates ended the Whalers' Stanley Cup hopes with a third straight win. Perhaps it was the thought of returning to Hartford that had inspired the Nordiques to end the series in six games as Gosselin had brazenly predicted. Peter Stastny scored the winning goal in overtime to propel Quebec into the division finals against arch-rival Montreal.

The Battle of Quebec for the Adams title was bitterly contested and when it ended Michel Bergeron said he would never accept the outcome. "It was our series, not Montreal's, but some individuals decided otherwise," he told reporters. Bergeron was referring to referee Kerry Fraser, who disallowed a goal in game five, one that cost Quebec the game and probably the series. At 17:17 of the third period, Quebec's Paul Gillis became entangled with Montreal's Mats Maslund and goalie Brian Hayward. While Hayward was off balance, Alain Cote scored what appeared certain to be the winning goal. But Gillis and Naslund drew penalties on the play and referee Fraser ruled that it was not a goal. Bergeron was livid, especially when Montreal roared back to score the winner 17 seconds later. He accused the NHL of being anti-Nordique. Team president Marcel Aubut said, "We can't let one man ruin careers and make a team lose millions of dollars simply by blowing a call on the ice. And with millions of people watching such a disgrace on television."

Campbell Conference Finals

Montreal met Philadelphia in the Wales Conference finals, while the Detroit Red Wings were underdogs in their Campbell Conference match up with Edmonton. The Wings won the series opener against Edmonton and, while the Oilers responded with four straight victories of their own, it was never easy. At home, the Oilers won the decisive fifth game 6–3 on a pair of goals by Mark Messier. The Wings were eliminated but, revived by Jacques Demers, in one season they had moved from last place overall to the final four. "We gave it our best shot," said Demers, destined to be named coach of the year.

Wales Conference Finals

Montreal fans were shocked when the Canadiens, always strong on home ice, lost three playoff games to Philadelphia at the Montreal Forum. After splitting the first two games in Philadelphia, the Canadiens stumbled badly back at the Forum, losing twice. Then they rallied briefly for a second win at the Spectrum. Game six will long be remembered for an astonishing pre-game brawl. Two Flyers, tough guy Ed Hospodar and backup goalie Chico Resch, tried to stop the Habs' pre-game ritual of shooting a puck in the opponent's empty net at the conclusion of the warm-up period. When Montreal rookie Shane Corson teamed up with Claude Lemieux for the empty-net shot, Hospodar raced over and hooked Corson while Resch threw his goal stick at the puck. Then Hospodar attacked Lemieux. In seconds, players from both clubs were back on the ice involved in a skirmish which lasted 10 minutes. In the game that followed, Montreal was unable to hold a 3–1 lead and the Flyers rallied to capture the Campbell Conference crown. By winning, they had stymied Montreal's bid for a 24th Stanley Cup. Following the series, NHL executive vice-president Brian O'Neill assessed fines totalling $24,500 to players involved in the brawl. In addition, Flyer Ed Hospodar was suspended for the balance of the playoffs.

The Stanley Cup Finals

When the Flyers advanced against the Oilers they didn't miss Hospodar. But they longed for big Tim Kerr, their leading scorer. Kerr had missed the entire semi-final series with a shoulder injury and was through for the season. The Oilers, meanwhile, were concerned that their number-one shooter, Wayne Gretzky, hadn't scored a goal since the Oilers had eliminated the Jets and had just scored two others against Los Angeles. So, with something to prove, Gretzky scored the opening goal in game one, set up the winner by Paul Coffey and engineered a series of dazzling plays. The Oilers won 4–2. Gretzky began the scoring in game two and set up the overtime game winner by Kurri in a 3–2 win. After the Flyers had snatched a 5–3 win on home ice, Gretzky came right back in game four, collecting 3 assists in a 4–1 Oiler victory. It was in this game that goalie Ron Hextall slashed Kent Nilsson across the legs with his goal stick, an infraction that eventually cost him an eight-game suspension. The Flyers captured the fifth game 4–3, behind Hextall's brilliant goaltending and Rick Tochett's third-period game winner. They were strong again in game six, winning 3–2 after rallying from a 2–1 deficit. In game seven, the Flyers opened the scoring when Murray Craven beat Grant Fuhr in the opening moments of play. But that's all the Flyers got. The Oilers peppered Ron Hextall with 43 shots and scored a goal a period to capture the Stanley Cup, their third in four years. Jari Kurri scored the Cup-winning goal and Wayne Gretzky led all playoff scorers with 34 points.

Hextall was a near-unanimous choice for the Conn Smythe Trophy as the MVP of the playoffs. He became the seventh goalie, the third rookie and the fourth member of a Cup-losing team to capture the award. After watching Hextall and Fuhr wage a magnificent goaltending battle in the final game, Wayne Gretzky said, "Hextall may be the best goaltender I've ever faced. But then, I've never had to play against Grant." Nearly a month after the incident, Hextall was given an eight-game suspension to be served at the beginning of the 1987–88 season. Incredibly, the Flyers might have won the Stanley Cup with a player who, it was later ruled, shouldn't even have been allowed to play.

1987–88

In the summer of 1987, the Detroit Red Wings reached an out-of-court settlement with the St. Louis Blues over the Wings' signing of coach Jacques Demers following the

1985–86 season. The Blues claimed that Demers was under contract to them and had agreed to an extension, while the Wings and Demers claimed he never signed a contract with the Blues. Under the terms of the settlement, the two teams would play three exhibition games over a four-year period. It was believed that the Blues would get the proceeds, which would likely be around $150,000 per game.

Gilbert Perreault, Buffalo's all-time leading scorer and a member of the NHL's exclusive 500-goal club, said that he and the club were unable to agree on an appropriate post-career position. "They talked to me about P.R.," Perreault said, "but I'm a hockey man, not a sweet talker. If I wanted a P.R. job I would have practiced P.R. all my life. I didn't do that. I practiced hockey." Less than a week after the Buffalo Sabres had signed the number-one overall draft choice, Pierre Turgeon, on July 31, Perreault announced that he was returning home to Quebec.

The Montreal Canadiens' all-star defenseman, Larry Robinson, turned down an offer to play in the Canada Cup, preferring the spirited competition of his favorite summertime sport, polo. During a polo match, he fractured his right tibia just below the knee and required at least a three-month recovery period.

Viktor Tikhonov, coach of the Soviet Union's national team, indicated that it may not be long before Soviet players would be permitted to play in the NHL But he denied a report that said the Soviet's five best players—forwards Igor Larionov, Vladimir Krutov and Sergei Makarov plus defensemen Viacheslav Festisov and Alexei Kasatonov—would be in the NHL for the 1988-89 season.

A disturbing incident occurred at a Team Canada practice session in St. John's, Newfoundland, on August 10. Sylvain Turgeon maintained that Ron Hextall had broken his arm. "He nailed me with a two-hander and I'm very angry," Turgeon said. "There was no reason for it. I won't forget it." Team Canada officials declared the incident an accident and took no disciplinary action against the Flyers' goaltender.

The Toronto Maple Leafs traded right-winger Rick Vaive, left-winger Steve Thomas and defenseman Bob McGill to the Chicago Blackhawks for tough left-winger Al Secord and center winger Ed Olczyk. Vaive was relieved to escape the turmoil he had experienced in Toronto. Brad McCrimmon of the Philadelphia Flyers was traded to the Calgary Flames for first- and third-round draft choices in 1988 and 1989. Duane "Dog" Sutter joined the Chicago Blackhawks after eight "great years" with the New York Islanders. The 27-year-old right-winger, known for his dogged determination, was traded early in September for future considerations. In another move, the Vancouver Canucks traded Patrik Sundstrom, a solid producer at center, to the New Jersey Devils. In return they got Greg Adams, a talented young forward and Kirk McLean, a fine goaltending prospect.

The Pittsburgh Penguins acquired Charlie Simmer, 32, from the Boston Bruins for $2,500 in the NHL waiver draft. Simmer's best years had been as a member of the Los Angeles Kings' "Triple Crown Line" with right-winger Dave Taylor and center Marcel Dionne. In both 1979–80 and 1980–81, he had scored 56 goals.

Brendan Shanahan, only 18, was expected to play the role of saviour for the New Jersey Devils. While management downplayed Shanahan's signing, for $600,000 plus bonuses over three years plus an option term, the New Jersey fans were soon calling the six-foot-three-inch centerman a "franchise" player.

The Canada Cup, won in dramatic fashion by Team Canada, had its share of controversy. Andrei Lomakin of the Soviet Union required about 20 stitches around his eye as a result of a two-handed slash from Gary Suter, playing for Team USA. "He is crazy," defenseman Igor Kravchuk said of Suter, who had attacked Lomakin during the Soviet Union's 5–1 win on September 4. Suter did not escape National Hockey League justice. He was suspended for 10 games, including the first four games of the 1987–88 NHL season, as a result of the incident.

Team Canada captured the Canada Cup after forcing the Soviet Union into a third and deciding game. The victory was one for the history books, like the eighth game in Moscow in 1979 and Canada's 3–2 overtime victory in the 1984 Canada Cup. The finale in Hamilton was rated as one of the finest games ever played between the world's top two hockey-playing nations. "It was like a marathon," said Gretzky, whose five assists led the Canadian effort. The game ended when Mario Lemieux rifled in his tournament-record 11th goal with 1:24 left to play in the third period. The final score was Team Canada 6, the Soviets 5. Gretzky, who assisted on nine of Lemieux's goals, scored a record 18 assists and 21 points in the tournament. Lemieux said that scoring the last two game-winning goals were "my greatest thrill ever."

Since the last NHL expansion in 1979–80, it had been determined that an average of eight coaches had been unable to hold their jobs from the start of one season to the next. An average of nearly five didn't even last a full season. So it was no surprise when signings and pink slips preceded this new season. Michel Bergeron signed a five-year deal with the New York Rangers, believed to be worth nearly $1 million. In a hockey first, the Rangers gave up a first-round draft choice and $100,000 to Quebec in order to land Bergeron. Former Ranger coach Herb Brooks signed a two-year deal with the Minnesota North Stars for about $160,000 a season. Terry Crisp took over in Calgary while Andre Savard moved behind the bench in Quebec. Bob McCammon accepted the coaching position with Vancouver while Bob Murdoch, previously an assistant in Calgary, became the new coach of the Chicago Blackhawks. In Pittsburgh, Pierre Creamer stepped in for the fired Bob Berry.

In an attempt to make bench-clearing brawls a thing of the past, the National Hockey League introduced measures that would impose a 10-game suspension on the first player to leave his bench and join a fight. In addition, the tough new measures would include a five-game suspension for the offending player's coach and a $10,000 fine for the team. Any teams caught paying their players' and coaches' fines would be hit with fines of $100,000.

The future looked bleak for New York Islanders' Mike Bossy, who was suffering from a bad back. Since his back troubles had begun a year before, Bossy had seen eight doctors, a chiropractor and an acupuncturist, as well as receiving many calls and letters from faith healers. His ailing back had contributed to Bossy missing 50 goals for the first time in his 10-year career. Still, he scored 38 goals in 63 games.

On September 25, New York Islander defenseman Denis Potvin announced that he would retire after this, his 15th NHL season. Potvin, who was approaching 34, said, "I want to be a contributor right to the end and a solid one. And then I want to walk out without feeling I stayed too long."

Dissatisfied with his role as backup to Grant Fuhr, Andy Moog became a free agent over the summer. But NHL compensation requirements scared off potential bidders— he would cost any team signing him at least a first-round draft choice. When Oiler coach-general manager Glen Sather didn't trade him, Moog opted for the Canadian Olympic team. And while he wouldn't be collecting on a big contract with the Olympic team, his earnings would be supplemented by a deal with the IGA grocery-store chain, for whom he would be acting as a company spokesman.

The top seven choices in the 1987 entry draft were making spirited bids for NHL lineups in their first year of eligibility. The 18-year-olds who stood good chances of making the leap from junior to professional hockey included Pierre Turgeon (Buffalo), Brendan Shanahan (New Jersey), Glen Wesley (Boston), Wayne McBean (Los Angeles), Chris Joseph (Pittsburgh), Dave Archibald (Minnesota) and Luke Richardson (Toronto).

The Canadian and Soviet hockey players who had been suspended for 18 months for their bench-clearing brawl at the World Junior Championships in Czechoslovakia in January, were reinstated. They would be eligible to participate again in international hockey on December 1.

Jacques Demers, coach of the Detroit Red Wings, spoke boldly when considering his team's prospects. "No way we're going to ir prove 38 points," he said, referring to the remarkable rise to 78 points from the 40 points Detroit had achieved in 1985–86, the season before Demers' arrival. "And we're not going to win the Stanley Cup this year. If we do, it would be another miracle on ice."

The Edmonton Oilers were the choice of 16 out of 22 hockey writers to win the Stanley Cup, while the Philadelphia Flyers received four votes and the Montreal Canadiens got two.

Doug Jarvis of the Hartford Whalers saw his all-time NHL consecutive-game streak of 964—a streak that had spanned 12 seasons and two games—come to an end early in the season. In Boston on October 11, Jarvis quietly sat down after Jack Evans told him that Brent Peterson would replace him for the game. When the Whalers' play-by-play TV announcer, Rick Peckham, learned that the streak was about to end, he asked the 32-year-old veteran if he would be his guest in the press box between periods. "Sure," said Jarvis. "But where's the press box?"

On October 15, Toronto Maple Leafs' defenseman Borje Salming was sent home from Bloomington, Minnesota, after he and three teammates had been evicted from the Marriott Hotel for making excessive noise at about three o'clock that morning.

In less than an hour on October 16, a Palm Beach, Florida, circuit-court jury found former NHL player Brian Spencer not guilty of first-degree murder in the shooting death of restaurateur Michael Dalfo. Had Spencer been found guilty by the seven-man, six-woman jury, he could have faced 25 years in prison with no chance of parole or possibly the electric chair.

Mario Lemieux was rapidly becoming the most popular athlete in Pittsburgh. For the first time in years it appeared that someone could give Gretzky a real run for his money in the NHL scoring race.

After the Hartford Whalers stumbled from the gate at 0–4–0, they purchased the contract of left-winger Dave "Tiger" Williams from the Los Angeles Kings. Williams said he was "happier than a pig in slop" after learning of the trade.

Boston Bruins' defenseman, Gord Kluzak, who five months earlier had been contemplating a future outside hockey, was playing regularly again for the first time since April 12, 1986. After undergoing four surgical procedures on his ailing left knee, Kluzak exceeded the Bruins' expectations with his comeback.

A moment of silence was held in Winnipeg before the Jets' October 23 game against

Los Angeles, in memory of 43-year-old Lars-Erik Sjoberg, who had died of cancer three days before in Uppsala, Sweden. Sjoberg had joined the Jets for the 1974–75 season and had retired after Winnipeg completed its first season in the NHL in 1980.

Edmonton Oiler Paul Coffey, his agent and Oiler owner Peter Pocklington met on October 26 to try to resolve differences which had appeared irreconcilable after Pocklington had questioned the defenseman's courage. Coffey, the 26-year-old, two-time Norris Trophy winner said, "It's impossible for me to go back and put that hockey sweater on again." Coffey's agent, Gus Badali, claimed that Pocklington had accused Coffey of having "no guts." Pocklington countered, "I didn't say that. What I said was he played like that a couple of times last year and it was upsetting to us all."

Left-winger Wendel Clark of the Toronto Maple Leafs had a disappointing early season. After two-and-a-half weeks of accomplishing little while playing with a sore shoulder and back, it was decided that Clark should sit out until he returned to full strength.

Dave Brown of the Philadelphia Flyers was suspended for 15 games, effective November 2, for striking New York Rangers' right-winger Tomas Sandstrom in a game October 26 at Madison Square Garden. In announcing the suspension, NHL executive vice-president Brian O'Neill said, "This was a deliberate action by Brown in which he severely cross-checked Sandstrom in the facial area." Madison Square Garden and the New York Rangers expressed their dissatisfaction in a joint release: "The penalty is a travesty given the gravity of the offense. Madison Square Garden and the Rangers are outraged by the length of this suspension and feel that it is not severe enough."

British Columbia Supreme Court justice Patrick Dohm reduced the fine NHL president John Ziegler had assessed the Vancouver Canucks for hiring Pat Quinn as general manager while he was still under contract to the Los Angeles Kings, from $310,000 to $10,000. However, Dohm did uphold the NHL's suspension of Quinn from coaching in the league until 1990.

The Philadelphia Flyers missed goalie Ron Hextall, who had been suspended for the first eight games of the season for slashing Kent Nilsson in the Stanley Cup finals in May. The Flyers won only five of their first 19 games and hit rock bottom on November 14 when the Toronto Maple Leafs buried them 6–0 at the Spectrum. "We're a disgrace to our uniforms," said Hextall, after compiling a 1–5–2 record upon his return.

New Jersey Devils' rookie Brendan Shanahan, after scoring his first National Hockey League goal, planted a kiss on teammate Claude Loiselle. "I knew I was going to kiss the guy who assisted me on my first goal," said Shanahan. "I don't know if Claudie noticed it, but I gave him a big wet one right on the cheek."

Boston Bruin Reed Larson returned to the club after a traumatic summer. On June 22 Reed had been in a serious car accident resulting in four hours of surgery and nine days in hospital. His left arm could only approach 70 percent of its former strength. Larson, 31, began therapy on August 1 and returned to action with the Bruins on November 9 in a game against the Quebec Nordiques.

George Hayes, a former linesman and one of the most colorful personalities in NHL history, died at his home in Beachville, Ontario, on November 19. He was 67. Hayes had worked 1,549 NHL regular-season, playoff and all-star games between 1946 and 1965 before being suspended by league president Clarence Campbell for refusing to take an eye examination. Hayes had said that he didn't need an eye test because he took one every night reading the labels of whiskey bottles. Both the firing and the fact that he was never elected to the Hockey Hall of Fame had left him a bitter man.

Pittsburgh traded for an All-Star defenseman on November 24, but it cost Penguin general manager Eddie Johnston a substantial chunk of his team's future. Promising forward Craig Simpson, 20, and defenseman Chris Joseph, 18, went to the Oilers in return for the immediate assistance Johnston thought Paul Coffey could provide.

Minnesota North Star right-winger Dino Ciccarelli faced a $700 fine or 90 days in jail after being arrested for indecent exposure at his Eden Prairie, Minnesota, home on November 25. Ciccarelli was arrested following police surveillance, prompted by a formal complaint filed by a nearby resident.

During the off-season NHL officials had been instructed to be more vigilant in calling holding, hooking and interference penalties, restraining fouls widely blamed for slowing down the game and giving lesser-skilled players an advantage. There were 379 more holding, hooking and interference penalties called through 210 games this season than during the same period the previous year, representing an increase of 38 percent.

December 4 was "Phil Esposito Night" in Boston. Espo's number seven was hoisted to the rafters to join those of other Bruin immortals. Midway through the ceremonies, Ray Bourque, wearing his customary number seven, skated out to meet the guest of honor. He shook hands with Esposito and then, with a flourish, pulled the number-seven sweater off and handed it to Esposito. Underneath was a sweater bearing number 77, Bourque's new number.

Andre Savard was fired as the coach of the Quebec Nordiques, just 24 games into the season. "I've never seen a guy stabbed in the back so often and by so many people," said right-winger Alain Cote, one of the few Nordique players to offer a comment after the firing. Savard was replaced by 38-year-old Ron Lapointe.

Darcy Wakaluk, whose nickname was "Lotsa Luck," became the first American League goaltender to score a goal. The Rochester player shot the puck into an empty Utica Devils' net with one second left in Rochester's 5–2 win on December 5.

George "Punch" Imlach, the man mostly responsible for Toronto's glorious hockey empire of the 1960s, lost a lengthy battle with heart disease and died on December 1. He was 69 years old. In his 20 years as a general manager and coach with Toronto and Buffalo, his teams had appeared in the Stanley Cup finals seven times and had won four championships. Imlach had displayed a great affinity for veteran players but never quite related to the younger ones. That inability had led to his demise in Toronto.

The Los Angeles Kings fired coach Mike Murphy on December 5. The Kings were 0–4–1 in Murphy's final five games and in last place in the NHL's overall standings with a 7–16–4 record. They had also given up 133 goals, the highest in the league. Robbie Ftorek, 35, previously the head coach of the Los Angeles's American League affiliate New Haven Nighthawks, was hired as head coach of the Kings.

Ron Hextall made NHL history on December 8 by becoming the first NHL goalie to score a legitimate goal. He picked up Gordie Kluzak's dump-in and whipped it 170 feet into the empty Boston Bruin net, making the feat look easy. "It's really surprising when you think about it, that nobody has ever done it before," said Hextall.

On December 19, the Canadian Olympic team was elated. They had upset the Soviet national team 3–2 and went on to win the Izvestia Tournament in Moscow. The game marked Canada's first win in the Soviet Union since the 1972 summit series and its first-ever win over the Russians in this tournament. Two third-period goals by Ken

Berry and Sean Burke's brilliant goaltending made the difference for Canada.

The new year brought changes for both the Calgary Flames and the Hartford Whalers. On January 3, the Flames sent center Carey Wilson, defenseman Neil Sheehy and the rights to U.S. Olympic team left-winger Lane MacDonald to the Whalers for defenseman Dana Murzyn and right-winger Shane Churla. Calgary general manager Cliff Fletcher had lots of praise for Murzyn. "When I say he could be a cornerstone defenseman for 10 years, I'm probably understating the fact," said Fletcher.

Dino Ciccarelli of the Minnesota North Stars may have anticipated the 10-game suspension he received from NHL officials as a result of his clubbing Toronto Maple Leaf defenseman Luke Richardson in the head with his stick. What he didn't anticipate was a warrant for his arrest from Toronto police on charges of common assault. According to the police, the warrant was issued because a weapon had been used.

The Chicago Blackhawks lost their best defenseman, veteran Doug Wilson, who had major surgery on his left shoulder and would be out for the rest of the season. Wilson was having one of his best offensive years, with eight goals and 32 points in 27 games. He was tied with Montreal's Chris Chelios as the NHL's highest-scoring defenseman.

Hockey operations director Brian Burke of the Vancouver Canucks announced, upon returning from Moscow, that the Canucks would like to train there in the fall of 1988. It seemed hard to believe that a team that travels 80,000 miles a season would want to travel through 11 time zones and set itself up for 10 to 12 days of bad food for the privilege of training under Soviet guidance. Many surmised that this had something to do with the Canucks' drafting of Soviet national stars Vladimir Krutov (12th round, 1986), Igor Larionov (11th round, 1985) and Viktor Tuminev (8th round, 1987).

On January 11, Edmonton Oiler superstar Wayne Gretzky announced his engagement to actress Janet Jones. The couple planned to be married in Edmonton in the summer.

Jerry Buss, the majority owner of the Los Angeles Kings (51 percent), negotiated to sell out to minority owner and president Bruce McNall. "This will free me to actively pursue the acquisition of another sports entity," said Buss in a prepared statement. "It has been no secret that I have had an interest in other professional sports, namely baseball and football."

The Toronto Maple Leafs established a club futility record for the most games without a victory on January 23, when they lost to Chicago 3–2 at the Gardens. It was the 14th straight game (0–10–4) that Toronto had failed to win. The streak went to 15 games when the Leafs were destroyed by Calgary 11–3 and ended two days later when they beat the Kings 5–2.

A prominent agent stated that he wouldn't recommend any of his clients for either the Toronto Maple Leafs' coaching or general manager jobs, should either become available in the future. "It's a disaster working for Harold Ballard," the agent said.

Ballard fired his general manager, 54-year-old Gerry McNamara, on February 7. During his term, McNamara tried to have coach John Brophy fired twice but had been overruled by Ballard. He said that had been the beginning of his troubles.

Minnesota North Star right-winger Dino Ciccarelli pleaded guilty to one misdemeanor count of indecent exposure on January 20. Judge David Duffy placed Ciccarelli, 27, on probation for one year and ordered him to complete counseling. Ciccarelli's attorney said that his client had entered the plea to put the situation behind him and to avoid further public embarrassment. A week later, Lou Nanne, general manager of the

North Stars, announced his resignation. He said that the mental and physical stress of a managerial career, which began in glory but was ending with a team skimming the bottom of the NHL standings, was just too much for him to continue.

In Montreal, Chris Nilan's feud with coach Jean Perron finally led to the inevitable trade. Nilan, the Boston-born right-winger, was traded to the New York Rangers on January 27.

Fifty games into his fourth season, New Jersey Devils' coach Doug Carpenter was fired. The dismissal followed a five-game losing streak. General manager Lou Lamoriello offered former Buffalo defenseman and coach Jim Schoenfeld the job as Carpenter's replacement.

Wayne Gretzky missed 13 games with a sprained knee. Gretzky's injury occurred when Philadelphia defenseman Kjell Samuelsson tumbled on his leg just as Gretzky had scored a goal, one that pulled him even with Mike Bossy for fifth place on the career list with 573.

On February 6, 46-year-old Barclay Plager lost his 39-month battle against inoperable brain tumors. Plager had come to St. Louis from the New York Rangers during the Blues' inaugural 1967–68 season. He had served the team as head coach, assistant coach and scout until his death.

Jack Evans, coach of the Hartford Whalers, was relieved of his duties early in February. Larry Pleau was named as Evans' replacement. Pleau had been general manager-coach of the Whalers in 1981 but then was exiled to Binghamton of the American League for more than four years.

On February 9, Mario Lemieux gave a stunning performance at the NHL All-Star game in St. Louis, where he earned six points, a second MVP award, a truck and additional respect for his enormous skills.

Marcel Dionne of the New York Rangers overtook Phil Esposito for second place on the NHL's all-time goal-scoring list. Dionne scored goal number 718 on February 14, leaving Gordie Howe's 801 as the only target remaining. "Determination, confidence and consistency…that's how I got to 718," said Dionne.

"It now appears obvious," said the NHL Players' Association executive director Alan Eagleson, "that the Soviet Union will release players to play in the NHL for the first time. You can be almost assured that there will be Soviet players playing for some NHL clubs during the 1988–89 season." Only one Soviet-trained player, Viktor Nechaev, had ever played for an NHL team. He had skated briefly with the Los Angeles Kings in 1982–83.

Emile Francis did not hide his displeasure with NHL president John Ziegler regarding what he perceived as the inequities of the playoff system. "This spring," said Francis, "there could be two Patrick Division teams, each with more than 80 points, missing the playoffs while the second-place team in the Norris Division could make the playoffs with 20 points fewer." Although many clubs, particulary in the Patrick and Adams divisions, favored Francis' "wild-card" playoff system, Emile was convinced that he'd never get enough votes to support it.

Wayne Gretzky didn't hesitate to express his opinion of the playoff format. "Sometimes the league hurts itself—instead of making the game better, they make it worse," he said, referring to a formula that would eliminate two of its top four teams prior to the midway point of the Stanley Cup tournament. "There are 21 teams in the league and I think, for everyone's sake, it would be more beneficial for people to see different teams, one versus eight, two versus seven, and so on," continued Gretzky.

"The whole thing just doesn't make sense the way it is right now. The logical thing is to cross over. It would be better for the game."

The Soviets didn't dominate the 1988 Olympic Winter tournament, they ruled it. Only on the final day, February 28, did they lose their first Olympic hockey game since 1980. Finland, needing a tie or a win to get the silver medal, beat them 2–1. That gave the Finns a 3–1–1 mark for the silver and left Sweden (2–1–2) with the bronze. The Soviets were 4–0–1. Canada finished fourth with a 2–2–1 record. The Soviets' cumulative Olympic record since entering hockey in the 1956 games stood at 53–5–2.

When the Calgary Flames dealt right-winger Brett Hull and left-winger Steve Bozek to St. Louis for defenseman Rob Ramage and goaltender Rick Wamsley, they made it clear they were shooting for nothing less than the Stanley Cup. In the deal made on March 7, a day before the NHL trading deadline, the Flames sacrificed some of their future to add depth and talent for the present.

On March 1, Wayne Gretzky recorded his milestone 1,050th NHL assist, surpassing the legendary Gordie Howe's 1,049 assists. And Gretzky had done it in his 681st game — 1,086 fewer than was required by Howe.

Steve Yzerman of the Detroit Red Wings sustained ligament damage to his right knee, requiring exploratory arthroscopic surgery and eight to 10 weeks of rehabilitation. The 22-year-old captain's 50th goal had come 14 minutes and 35 seconds before he was injured late in the second period of a 4–0 win over Buffalo on March 1. "I can't believe it," Yzerman said. "I went from the happiest point of my career to the saddest, so fast."

A number of Olympians joined the NHL following the Olympic Games in Calgary. Defenseman Jeff Norton and right-winger Todd Okerlund, from the U.S. Olympic team, signed with the New York Islanders. Team Canada goaltender Sean Burke went to the Devils while Serge Boisvert joined the Canadiens and Bob Joyce lined up with the Bruins. The Vancouver Canucks signed Ken Berry of the Canadian team, Minnesota grabbed Wally Schreiber and Chicago picked up Trent Yawney. The Flames aroused some interest when they signed Czech star Jiri Hrdina. Randy Gregg and Andy Moog returned to the Oilers, Tim Watters to Winnipeg and Ken Yaremchuk to Toronto.

Early in March, Vancouver Canucks' goalie Richard Brodeur was traded to the Hartford Whalers in return for goalie Steve Weeks. Another goalie, disgruntled Oiler Andy Moog went to the Boston Bruins in exchange for left-winger Geoff Courtnall and goalie Bill Ranford. Harry Sinden had once considered Ranford to be Boston's "goalie of the future."

The night of March 10 belonged to Mike Bossy. For 25 minutes prior to the Quebec Nordiques–New York Islanders matchup at the Nassau Coliseum, 14,388 fans stood up and cheered the Islander star on "Mike Bossy Night." Bossy's recurring back problems would soon force him to announce his retirement.

By beating Chicago's Darren Pang on a breakaway during the Los Angeles Kings' 9–5 victory on March 26, Jimmy Carson became the second-youngest player and only the second American in league history to reach the 50-goal plateau. Gretzky had been 19 years, two months old when he scored 51 goals in 1979–80, his first NHL season. Carson was six months older. He joined teammate Bobby Carpenter as the second American to score 50. Carpenter had had 53 goals in 1984–85 with the Washington Capitals.

In April, former Chicago goalie Tony Esposito was given the newly created job of director of hockey operations for the Pittsburgh Penguins. Esposito would determine the futures of all employees of the Penguins, including general manager Eddie Johnston and coach Pierre Creamer. He would also be faced with renegotiating a mammoth contract for Mario Lemieux, a first-time winner of the Art Ross Trophy. Lemieux scored a career high 70 goals and 98 assists for 168 points, 19 more than Wayne Gretzky. Despite Lemieux's heroics, and Pittsburgh's above .500 record, the Penguins missed the playoffs for the sixth straight season. The Penguins finished with 81 points, 29 more than the Leafs who were playoff bound in the Norris Division.

The Calgary Flames, led by 100-point men Hakan Loob and Mike Bullard and assisted by rookie Joe Nieuwendyk's 51-goal season, captured first place overall with 105 points, two more than the Montreal Canadiens.

THE PLAYOFFS

Smythe Division

In the Smythe Division, the defending Stanley Cup champion Edmonton Oilers and regular-season champion Calgary Flames advanced through the first round with relative ease, both winning their series in five games. Edmonton eliminated Winnipeg, while Calgary defeated the Los Angeles Kings. The big shock came in the division finals when the Flames lost to the Oilers in four straight games. The Flames' four 40-goal scorers took much of the heat for the sweep. Against the champions, Hakan Loob, Joe Nieuwendyk, Mike Bullard and Joe Mullen scored a mere three goals while their counterparts, Wayne Gretzky, Mark Messier and Jari Kurri were dominant figures for the winners.

Norris Division

In the Norris Division, the Detroit Red Wings sidelined the Toronto Maple Leafs in six games. Game six was played before the first non-sellout playoff crowd at Maple Leaf Gardens in decades. Leaf coach John Brophy found himself hit with a barrage of criticism after the series. Leafs' player Mirko Frycer said of Brophy, "Everybody hates him and nobody wants to play for him."

Brophy spat back, "Every time he [Frycer] came back on the ice this year, he fell down and got injured. He's the last guy who should say anything...they can't dig up enough plastercast in Toronto to keep him together."

The St. Louis Blues eliminated the Chicago Blackhawks 4–1. It was no surprise. The Hawks had finished the last eight games of the regular season with a record of 0–7–1. In the division final, the Detroit Red Wings moved into the final four with a five-game victory over the St. Louis Blues. The Wings' nifty centerman Steve Yzerman added $50,000 to his bank account when owner Mike Illitch rewarded him with a bonus for his 50-goal season.

Patrick Division

Despite the fact they had won only one of their last nine regular-season games, the Washington Capitals were ready for the Philadelphia Flyers in their semi-final series. Washington became only the fifth team to rebound from a 3–1 deficit in winning the series 4–3. Dale Hunter's goal in game seven at 5:57 of overtime completed one of the most remarkable comebacks in playoff history.

New Jersey, coming of age in only the second playoff series of the franchise's 14-year history, toppled the New York Islanders 4–2 in the division's other best-of-seven series. In game four, the Islanders won in overtime on Brent Sutter's shorthanded goal. The win upped the Islanders' record to an incredible 24–7 in playoff overtime games, the best in history. But it was the Devils who advanced against the Caps. The Capitals fell to the Devils four games to three in the division finals. Patrik Sundstrom's record eight-point performance (three goals and five assists) in game three was a highlight of the series.

Adams Division

In the Adams Division the Montreal Canadiens led Hartford 3–0, then lost two in a row before squeezing out a 2–1 victory in game six to move into the finals. The Boston Bruins, in a grueling series with the Buffalo Sabres, also advanced with a 4–2 victory in games. The Bruins would face the Canadiens for the 19th time in 45 years, and without a series win to show for all those confrontations.

In the division final, the favored Canadiens surrendered in five games to the Bruins, who could hardly believe that the long jinx was finally broken. Injuries had hurt the Habs, especially the broken thumb of 50-goal scorer Stephane Richer, as did their impotent power play, which was zero for 20 in the first four games.

Campbell Conference Finals

After the Edmonton Oilers took a 2–0 lead over Detroit, Steve Yzerman made a dramatic return to the Red Wing lineup and led his team to their first and only victory. Yzerman, out since March 1 with a knee injury, assisted on the game's opening goal by Brent Ashton. Detroit won 5–2, narrowing the Oilers' advantage to 2–1. But the Oilers had too much firepower and required only five games to dispose of the Wings. Detroit coach Jacques Demers was furious when he discovered that six Red Wings had broken curfew the night before the final game. Bob Probert, John Chabot, Darren Veitch, Joey Kocur, Darren Elliot and Petr Klima had all been spotted at a nightclub. It turned out to be a costly night on the town for the players. Red Wing owner Mike Ilitch had planned to double each Red Wing's playoff bonus of $16,000. All but the curfew breakers received the additional cash.

Wales Conference Finals

The Boston Bruins became the Prince of Wales champions when they defeated the New Jersey Devils 4–3 in the best-of-seven series. After game three, the NHL suspended New Jersey Devils' coach Jim Schoenfeld for derogatory remarks made to referee Don Koharski after game three on May 5. In an unprecedented move to block the suspension, the Devils served the NHL with a restraining order granted by a New Jersey superior court judge, allowing Schoenfeld to coach the team in game four. The move triggered an angry protest by officials assigned to the game. Referee Dave Newell, president of the NHL Officials' Association, and his linesmen Gord Broseker and Ray Scapinello, staged a wildcat strike to protest what they felt were unsafe working conditions. The game began more than one hour late, with three amateur substitute officials, whose experience was extremely limited. To Schoenfeld's delight, the Devils evened the series with the Bruins at two games each with a 3–1 victory. But after seven games it was the Bruins who advanced to the Stanley Cup finals.

The Stanley Cup Finals

The Edmonton Oilers surrendered just nine goals as they swept the Boston Bruins in four games to win their fourth Stanley Cup in five years. In three of the four games, the Bruins had managed fewer than 20 shots. It didn't help that Edmonton got an extra home game, after a power failure at the Boston Garden forced the cancellation of game four. "As far as I'm concerned," said Bruins' coach Terry O'Reilly, "that's a great team that beat us. We weren't at our best. We weren't playing the hockey that got us to the final but I'd have to say a large part of that is due to the way they checked us." Wayne Gretzky was the winner of the Conn Smythe Trophy. He had collected points in the final 16 games of the playoffs, plus the blackout game of May 22 at the Boston Garden. Along the way, he had earned 12 goals and 31 assists to eclipse by one his own NHL record for a single playoff season. "He's the best," said Terry O'Reilly, referring to Gretzky. "There should be a league rule that he has to be passed around from team to team every year."

While the playoffs were ongoing, Gord Stellick was appointed general manager of the Toronto Maple Leafs. At age 30, Stellick became the youngest general manager in NHL history. He first joined the Maple Leaf organization as a press-box runner at the age of 17. "Gord has top authority," said owner Harold Ballard. "It's his team to run, and he reports only to me."

Lou Nanne, general manager of the Minnesota North Stars was appointed as the club's president. Nanne, 46, would be in charge of business and marketing for the team and the Met Center.

After months of speculation and rumors, the Philadelphia Flyers fired Mike Keenan, despite his record as one of the most successful coaches in the NHL. On May 16, Jean Perron announced his resignation as the coach of the Montreal Canadiens, citing "pressures from within the organization, including player criticism" as the reasons for his departure. Pat Burns, a 36-year-old former detective in the Gatineau, Quebec, police force, took over as the 20th coach of the Montreal Canadiens on June 1. Burns was recommended by Wayne Gretzky for a job in the NHL, as he had coached Gretzky's junior team, the Hull Olympiques, for four years. The day after Burns was hired, the St. Louis Blues fired coach Jacques Martin, despite the Blues' second-place finish in the Norris Division, 17 points behind the Detroit Red Wings.

Coach Jacques Demers of the Wings, nominated for his second straight Jack Adams Award as NHL coach of the year, was given a two-year contract extension on May 18.

His deal included a raise from an estimated $50,000 to $250,000 annually, which general manager Jimmy Devellano said made Demers the highest-paid coach in the NHL. The deal came just one day after the Quebec Nordiques phoned the Wings seeking permission to speak with Demers about the vacant Nordique general manager's position in Quebec.

1988–89

Although his friends had urged him to leave Florida and return to Canada to start a new life, Brian Spencer wouldn't listen. As a result, he paid with his life. The former NHL player, who was acquitted of murder months earlier, was gunned down at Riviera Beach at midnight on June 2, shot through the heart while in the act of buying crack cocaine. According to a witness, a man in a white car had pulled up to Spencer's vehicle, demanded money, then shot Spencer in the chest. Later, a grand jury would indict two men arrested in connection with the murder.

In Philadelphia, Bobby Clarke selected Paul Holmgren, a former teammate, as the new coach of the Flyers, replacing Mike Keenan. Keenan, fired in mid-May, quickly surfaced with the Chicago Blackhawks, who had dismissed Bob Murdoch. Keenan rehired the unemployed Jacques Martin as one of his assistant coaches. The Blues retired captain Brian Sutter and then rehired him as coach. Pittsburgh dropped Pierre Creamer and signed Gene Ubriaco. Minnesota dismissed Herb Brooks and brought in Jack Ferreira as general manager. Ferreira, the former New York Rangers' director of development, had found empty team offices in Minnesota. Club owners Gordon and George Gund had not only fired Brooks, they had fired the rest of the staff—assistant coaches, scouts and trainers. Ferreira hired former Calgary assistant coach Pierre Page as the Stars' sixth coach in six years and the 15th in 21 seasons.

The purge in Minnesota occurred right after the North Stars had selected Mike Modano as the number-one player in the entry draft, a slick six-foot-two-inch center from the Prince Albert Raiders of the WHL. The Westland, Michigan, native, became only the second American chosen number-one overall. The first, Brian Lawton, had been a North Star selection in 1983. Vancouver, with second choice, grabbed Trevor Linden, a member of the Memorial Cup champion Medicine Hat Tigers, and Quebec, drafting third, passed up francophone star Martin Gelinas in order to select Curtis Leschyshyn, a defenseman with the Saskatoon Blades. Gelinas was drafted number seven by Los Angeles and within weeks would figure prominently in the biggest trade in hockey history. Chicago, drafting eighth, took Jeremy Roenick, a U.S. high-school player and St. Louis, with ninth choice, selected Rod Brind'Amour of Notre Dame. The latter two were labeled "can't miss." When the North Stars selected Link Gaetz, a six-foot-three-inch, 207-pound defenseman, in the second round they felt that they owned the best player in Modano and the toughest in Link. Link had earned 313 penalty minutes with Spokane in junior hockey and had appeared at the draft meetings with two black eyes, acquired in a bar brawl a few days earlier.

Mario Lemieux was the overwhelming choice as 1987–88's MVP, winning the Hart Trophy and ending Wayne Gretzky's eight-year run as hockey's top player. Edmonton goalie Grant Fuhr won the Vezina Trophy. Montreal center Guy Carbonneau captured the Frank Selke Trophy as the best defensive forward. His teammate, Mats Naslund, took home the Lady Byng. Calgary rookie Joe Nieuwendyk, who had scored

51 goals, two short of Mike Bossy's rookie record, was an easy winner of the Calder Trophy. Boston's Ray Bourque won the Norris Trophy for the second straight year, the Flames' Lanny McDonald was the recipient of the new King Clancy Trophy for his leadership qualities and contributions to his community. Detroit's garrulous Jacques Demers was a repeat winner of the Jack Adams Trophy as coach of the year.

On his 85th birthday, Harold Ballard was in hospital undergoing quintuple heart-bypass surgery. The Leafs' owner was counting on new general manager, 31-year-old Gord Stellick, to turn things around for the team, which had finished 20th overall in 1987–88.

The Islanders lost two of their biggest stars, Denis Potvin and Mike Bossy. Bossy's recurring back problems forced him into retirement while Potvin had simply had enough. It wasn't long before three other stars followed suit; Terry Ruskowski, Dennis Maruk and Craig Hartsburg, all with Minnesota, retired as well.

After becoming little more than excess baggage behind Bob Sauve and Sean Burke, goalie Alain Chevrier was traded to Winnipeg for winger Steve Rooney. The Boston Bruins bought out the final year of 34-year-old Rick Middleton's contract, paying him two-thirds of a salary estimated to be $350,000. That made him a free agent without compensation at the June 30 deadline. Lanny McDonald signed with Calgary for his 16th NHL season. By returning, McDonald could attain two personal milestones—he was 11 goals short of 500 career goals and 12 points short of 1,000 points. Larry Robinson, the 16-year veteran defenseman with the Montreal Canadiens, announced his decision to play out his option during the 1988–89 NHL season and become a free agent without compensation.

On June 28, a group of investors headed by Donald G. Conrad and Richard H. Gordon purchased full control of the Hartford Whalers for an NHL record of $31 million. The last two teams to be sold, the Los Angeles Kings and the St. Louis Blues had commanded $20 million and $19 million respectively

The game's greatest player, Wayne Gretzky, did it in style when he took Hollywood actress Janet Jones for his bride in Edmonton on July 16. Thousands of well-wishers lined the streets outside St. Joseph's Basilica, the scene of the ceremony. Among the 650 invited guests was Soviet Union goaltender Vladislav Tretiak. Gretzky's wedding gift to Janet was a $250,000 Rolls-Royce.

On August 9, 1988, word of the greatest trade in history rocked the hockey world. The Edmonton Oilers traded center Wayne Gretzky, left-winger Mike Krushelnyksi, defenseman-winger Marty McSorley and minor-league defenseman John Miner to the Los Angeles Kings. In return, the Kings sent the Oilers approximately $15 million (U.S.), center Jimmy Carson, left-winger Martin Gelinas (L.A.'s first-round pick, seventh overall in the 1988 entry draft), three first-round draft picks (1989, 1991, 1993) and the rights to minor-league defenseman Craig Redmond. Gretzky told the fans, "After spending some time with [Kings' owner Bruce McNall], I decided that for the benefit of myself, my new wife and our expected child in the new year, it would be beneficial for everyone involved to let me play for the Los Angeles Kings."

Paul Coffey, Gretzky's ex-teammate and a close friend said, "I'm surprised at all the crap that's coming out. There's no bloody way he wanted to go there [L.A.]. I don't think the people in Edmonton who know Wayne should believe that. He's a small-town guy. I don't care if he married the Queen of England."

Criticism of Gretzky's new wife Janet hit hard. She was called everything from

Jezebel to the Yoko Ono of professional hockey. Eddie Mio, Gretzky's best man at the wedding, came to her rescue, stating publicly that she did not deserve to be persecuted. Mio said that Gretzky did not want to be traded at first and was devastated at the thought of not playing in Edmonton. Mio suggested that only after the papers were drawn up did Gretzky decide that he'd had enough of Peter Pocklington. It was then that Gretzky had requested the trade to L.A. Coffey backed up Mio's statement and so did former Oiler Dave Lumley. Gretzky, however, chose not to comment. The Gretzky trade was not only the biggest in hockey history, but in all of sports. Followers of other major sports agree that there has never been a deal to match the impact of his trade to Los Angeles.

New York Ranger general manager Phil Esposito felt his team had nothing to lose by giving former Montreal star Guy Lafleur a tryout. Lafleur flew to New York on August 18 and agreed to a tentative two-year contract, contingent upon Guy making the team. "I don't think the odds of Lafleur making it back are very good but I'll be very, very happy if he does," said Esposito.

Detroit Red Wings' general manager Jim Devellano and coach Jacques Demers had well-publicized problems with players Petr Klima and Bob Probert. Devellano insisted that both players were alcoholics who needed help. The Wings had hoped that each would seek treatment during the summer and had tried to persuade Probert to enter the Betty Ford Center in California for what would be his fifth stay at a treatment center in two years. Instead, Probert bought a boat and Klima bought a motorcycle. In August, Probert admitted he was drinking again and claimed that the Wings had a private detective following him. He said he wouldn't be surprised if he was traded. "I've been having a few drinks here and there," he told the press, "but that's my business. In my opinion, I don't think I have a problem." Klima and Probert were assigned to Adirondack, Detroit's top minor-league affiliate, after Probert had missed a team flight from Chicago to Detroit and Klima had been an hour late for practice. During training camp they were suspended without pay after they skipped a morning practice, missed a flight and failed to report by Demers' 11:00 P.M. deadline.

Probert's playing career would suddenly end later in the season when a package containing 14.3 grams of cocaine fell out of his underwear during a search by U.S. Customs on the U.S. side of the Detroit–Windsor tunnel. If convicted, Probert could face a prison sentence of up to 20 years and a fine of up to $1 million. NHL president John Ziegler promptly expelled Probert from hockey and the Red Wings announced that they were writing him off their roster.

Frank Zamboni, inventor of the ice-resurfacing machine which bears his name, died during the summer in California at the age of 87. He had invented the machine in 1947, using a Jeep engine and the front ends of two cars. Zambonis are used in 33 countries today.

On August 24, North Star right-winger Dino Ciccarelli made news when a provincial court judge in Toronto convicted him of assaulting Toronto defenseman Luke Richardson and sentenced him to a day in jail and a $1,000 fine. Ciccarelli became the first NHL player to receive a jail term in Canada for an on-ice attack. Judge Sidney Harris said that the courts would no longer tolerate such violence. Ciccarelli was convicted of hitting Richardson over the head with a stick and punching him in the mouth during a game in Toronto. Cicarelli called his two-hour stay in jail "a little scary," although he spent most of his time there signing autographs.

For $51 million, more than double the $24 million that ESPN had paid, Sportschannel America obtained the rights to televise the NHL on cable television over the next three years.

In a ceremony in Toronto on September 7, former hockey greats Brad Park, Tony Esposito, Guy Lafleur and Buddy O'Connor, along with a colorful linesman, the late George Hayes, were inducted into the Hockey Hall of Fame.

The Calgary Flames gave up their second-leading scorer, Mike Bullard, in a controversial seven-player trade that ranked as the second-biggest blockbuster of the summer. In a deal with St. Louis, the Flames received center Doug Gilmour, right-winger Mark Hunter, left-winger Steve Bozek and defenseman Michael Dark. In return, the Blues received Bullard, right-winger Craig Coxe and the rights to college defenseman Tim Corkery of Ferris State. Bozek was later traded to the Vancouver Canucks.

The Quebec Nordiques shipped two disgruntled players to the New York Rangers. Defenseman Normand Rochefort and center Jason Lafreniere were traded for center left-winger Walt Poddubny, defensemen Jari Gronstrand and Bruce Bell and the Rangers' fourth-round pick at the 1989 entry draft. Brent Ashton had thought that he would be staying in Detroit for at least a while, when he was traded once again—this time to the Winnipeg Jets. Ashton arrived in Winnipeg to begin his 10th NHL season and play for his seventh NHL team. Later, Montreal sent strongman right-winger John Kordic and a sixth-round draft choice in 1989 to the Toronto Maple Leafs in return for speedy Russ Courtnall. Courtnall became an overnight favorite with Montreal fans while Kordic struggled in Toronto. Tony Esposito, general manager of the Penguins, sent two promising young players – defenseman Doug Bodger, 22, and left-winger Darrin Shannon, 18—to Buffalo for goalie Tom Barrasso and a third-round draft pick in 1990. "Unfortunately, to get something of quality, you have to give up a lot," said Esposito.

In a Canadian Gallup poll, 48 percent of respondents said that Wayne Gretzky had been the top NHL player over the last 50 years. Former Montreal Canadiens' right-winger Maurice Richard was favored by 15 percent, followed by Gordie Howe (10 percent), Bobby Orr (seven percent), Guy Lafleur (four percent), Bobby Hull and Jean Beliveau (at three percent each) and Phil Esposito (with one percent). Also, 71 percent of respondents said criminal charges should be laid for violence on the ice.

Early in October, Calgary Flame center Doug Gilmour and his wife Robyne filed a $4-million lawsuit in St. Louis county court, charging a St. Louis couple with slander and libel after Gilmour had been accused of having abused their teenage daughter. When the case came to trial, the St. Louis county grand jury ruled that there was insufficient evidence to proceed against Gilmour. "Any time you go before a grand jury, you don't know what to expect," said Gilmour. "It was tough, but everything went well. I just want to get on with my hockey and on with my life."

The NHL pledged to crack down on illegal use of the stick and in October it made good on that promise. Throughout 54 games of the 1988–89 season, from October 6 to 16, players were ejected for stick-related infractions nine times. One player, Montreal Canadiens' defenseman Petr Svoboda, was nailed twice and given an automatic one-game suspension.

On October 15, Mario Lemieux scored eight points in a game. NHL players had scored eight or more points in a game only 10 previous times in NHL history. Lemieux tallied two goals and six assists in a 9–2 Pittsburgh victory over St. Louis. He was off to a torrid start with 18 goals and 23 assists in his first 12 games

John Ferguson, the only general manager that the Winnipeg Jets had ever had in the NHL, was fired on October 30.

> I was shocked. It came right out of left field [said Ferguson]. I had no idea it was coming. I'm not very happy about it. I can justify my draft choices, my scouting staff. Hell, we've made the playoffs every year for the last seven years.

A few days later, Mike Smith was named to replace Ferguson. Other clubs also made coaching changes. Terry Simpson of the New York Islanders was fired after his team had suffered through a long losing streak. It had been almost 16 years since general manager Bill Torrey had fired a head coach, but he dismissed Simpson and replaced him with the team's leader of past Stanley Cups, Al Arbour. John Brophy was axed in Toronto and replaced by 58-year-old George Armstrong. Coach Ron Lapointe of the Quebec Nordiques was forced to resign due to a malignant tumor on his right kidney. Within a week the eight-inch, four pound tumor was successfully removed. It had been the second crisis of the season for the Nords, who were nearly bought by an unidentified group until team president Marcel Aubut formed a group of investors which purchased the team on November 29. The day after Lapointe's resignation, assistant general manager Jean Perron was named as his replacement.

Hockey writers stated that L.A. Kings' coach Robbie Ftorek's indifferent and hostile attitude toward the media was negating the Kings' positive image created by the Gretzky deal. Ftorek was said to be turning off a lot of people who came out to write about the Kings.

From Christmas until the March trading deadline, several deals were completed. The Chicago Blackhawks sent right-winger Rick Vaive to Buffalo for center Adam Creighton. The Rangers traded Brian Lawton, defenseman Norm Maciver and left-winger Don Maloney to Hartford for center Carey Wilson and the Whalers' fifth-round draft choice in 1990. Bobby Carpenter, the much-traveled center left-winger was traded by the L.A. Kings to the Boston Bruins for center Steve Kasper. Goalie Alain Chevrier became the Chicago Blackhawks' latest acquisition, obtained from the Winnipeg Jets for a fourth-round draft pick in 1989. The Kings got the goalie they were looking for when they traded two promising youngsters, goalie Mark Fitzpatrick and defenseman Wayne McBean to the Islanders for 28-year-old Kelly Hrudey. The Sabres dealt with Washington for goalie Clint Malarchuk and defenseman Grant Ledyard, giving up defenseman Calle Johansson and a draft choice. Washington sent 10-year veteran Mike Gartner, the most popular player in the history of the franchise, along with Larry Murphy to Minnesota in return for Dino Cicarelli and Bob Rouse. And the Canucks confused everyone by acquiring Greg Adams from Edmonton, even though they already had another Greg Adams on their roster.

The Quebec Nordiques, after sliding into last place in the Adams Division, were miffed when a local radio station began playing a song which labeled the club "a bunch of turkeys." The station ran a full-page ad in the city's largest newspaper, *Le Soleil*, to promote the song. As a result, Nordique players refused to speak to the media.

Wayne Gretzky moved in front of Marcel Dionne to second place on the all-time scoring list on January 21. The Kings' center had one a goal and three assists in a 5–4 loss in Hartford to give him 1,771 points, one more than Dionne and 79 fewer than the all-time leader Gordie Howe. With an assist against the Edmonton Oilers early in the new year, Gretzky increased his career-point total for regular-season and playoff scoring to 2,011, surpassing Gordie Howe's career combined total of 2,010. Gretzky said his next goal was to surpass Howe's regular-season career record of 1,850 points before the 1988–89 season ended. (He would fall short by 14 points.)

Mario Lemieux also held a hot stick. He scored his 50th goal of the season in his 44th game. Only Gretzky—who had scored 50 in 39, 42, and 49 games—had done it faster. Maurice Richard and Mike Bossy were the only other players in league history to score 50 goals in as few as 50 games. Guy Lafleur, however, wasn't on a 50-goal pace. He would finish with 18, but the two he enjoyed most were scored against Montreal when he returned to the Forum for the first time as a player on February 4. An adoring crowd of 17,897 fans greeted him with a two-minute standing ovation and shouts of "Guy, Guy, Guy!"

Meanwhile, the third-leading scorer in NHL history, Marcel Dionne, was demoted to the minors for the first time in his 18-year career. Ranger coach Michel Bergeron was not happy with the February decision that sent Dionne to Denver of the IHL for 14 days of conditioning, even though general manager Phil Esposito apparently approved the move. "It's really a sad situation because Marcel is going to be a Hall Of Famer," Bergeron said. "It's like Wayne Gretzky playing for New Haven."

Pittsburgh coach Gene Ubriaco urged his players to use a wide-open offensive style in Philadelphia for a game on February 2 and it paid off in a Penguin victory, their first at the Spectrum since January 1974—a span of 42 games.

Dan Kelly, the St. Louis Blues' play-by-play announcer for 21 years and a recipient of the 1989 Lester Patrick Trophy, died of cancer on February 10 in St. Louis at the age of 52. On January 6, Ziegler had presented Kelly with the Patrick Trophy in Kelly's hospital room in St. Louis. Kelly had also received notice that he had been selected by the NHL Broadcasters' Association to the media section of the Hockey Hall of Fame. "I don't know of anything I would rather have been doing for the last 25 years than broadcasting hockey," Kelly said.

The 40th annual NHL All-Star game brought Wayne Gretzky back to Edmonton on February 4. The L.A. Kings' center got one goal and two assists to lead the Campbell Conference to a 9–5 win over the Wales Conference before 17,503 fans at the Northlands Coliseum.

The Blackhawks announced the retirement of numbers one and 35, the uniform numbers of goaltenders Glenn Hall and Tony Esposito respectively. Esposito, general manager of the Pittsburgh Penguins, had had 74 shutouts in his 16-year career with the Hawks. His 15 shutouts in 1969–70 were the most for one season in modern NHL history. Hall, a goaltending consultant with the Calgary Flames, held the NHL record for 502 consecutive games played by a goaltender, from 1955–56 to 1962–63. Fifty-year-old Bobby Hull returned to Winnipeg and shed tears as the Winnipeg Jets honored him before a game by retiring his WHA sweater number nine. And in New York, former Ranger goalie Eddie Giacomin had his sweater retired in a ceremony at Madison Square Garden. Giacomin was so moved he told reporters, "If I could, I would put those 17,500 fans on the ice and I would sit in the stands and cheer them."

Two more coaches were dismissed late in the season. Winnipeg Jets' general manager Mike Smith fired coach Dan Maloney and brought in Rick Bowness, coach and general manager of the Moncton Hawks, Winnipeg's American League affiliate, to replace him. The Jets angered TV commentator Don Cherry by signing a European coach, Alpo Suhonen, to take over in Moncton. "There are lots of good coaches in the minors who'd like that job," said Cherry. "Besides, Alpo sounds like dog food." In another surprise move, Ranger general manager Phil Esposito fired coach Michel Bergeron on the final weekend of the regular season. A large portion of the Madison Square Garden faithful shouted insults when Esposito appeared behind the Ranger bench for the final two games and the playoffs. Bergeron resurfaced in Quebec City only 13 days after his dismissal and signed a multi-year contract to coach his old club, the Nordiques. For the second year in a row, Jean Perron resigned from a big-league coaching job, this time to make room for Bergeron.

The future of Boston defenseman Gord Kluzak appeared to be in jeopardy when he underwent yet another knee operation, his second of the season and the ninth of his career. He had already missed two full seasons recuperating from knee operations.

A movement to dump Al Eagleson as the NHL Players' Association executive director was organized by agents Ron Salcer and Rich Winter, who had met with several NHL clubs. Eagleson, vacationing in Florida and with four years remaining on his contract, didn't appear to be concerned about the plot to overthrow him.

Bernie Nicholls of the Kings set an unusual record. He fashioned the most dramatic single-season improvement in NHL history. In 1987–88 Nicholls had scored 78 points in 65 games. In the 1988–89 season he zoomed to 150 points, representing an increase of 72 points, nine more than the previous high of 63 set by Guy Lafleur in 1974–75. In another scoring feat, Lanny McDonald's countless fans were delighted to see him reel off seven goals in seven games (after scoring just four in the first 66 games), to become the 14th player in history to reach the 500-goal plateau. Two weeks earlier, McDonald had achieved his 1,000th point. Joe Nieuwendyk, McDonald's teammate, became only the third player in league history to score 50 goals in each of his first two seasons. Wayne Gretzky and Mike Bossy were the others.

Buffalo's Clint Malarchuk suffered a frightening neck injury on March 22 against the St. Louis Blues. A skate blade slashed the goalie's neck and severed his jugular vein. The scene was so gruesome that several spectators fainted and the Sabres' telecast team refused to show replays of the incident. Malarchuk made a speedy recovery.

Right-winger Joey Mullen of the Flames set a single-season scoring record for an American-born player when he finished with 110 points, three more than Jimmy Carson had collected in 1987–88. Mullen also became the third American-born player to reach the 50-goal mark.

Mario Lemieux scored or assisted on 199 of the Pens' 347 goals, 57.3 percent of them. He broke Wayne Gretzky's unofficial record of 51.8 percent set in 1984–85. Lemieux also scored a record 13 shorthanded goals while the Pens set league marks for power-play goals (119) and penalty minutes (2,670).

It was a season of comebacks. Tim Kerr of the Flyers, with three goals in eight games of the previous season, scored 48 goals in 69 games for this year. He recuperated from five shoulder operations to regain his position as one of hockey's top snipers. Thirty-seven-year old Guy Lafleur, despite a 15-game slump without a goal to close out his season, collected 18 goals and 27 assists for 45 points in 67 games. Paul Reinhart, nursing a chronic back injury, was traded by Calgary to Vancouver in September.

With the Canucks he responded with seven goals and 50 assists in 64 games, to finish third in team scoring. Jamie Macoun of the Flames completed a remarkable recovery from nerve damage to his arm and shoulder which he had suffered in a car accident two years earlier.

John Ziegler said the NHL was prepared to expand once the league's expansion committee had identified the best markets out of the 30 that had applied for franchises. Speculation followed that the 21-team league would add three teams in time for the 1991–92 season.

Throughout the season, fans had been intrigued by a battle between two strong-willed men for control of the Hartford Whalers. Richard Gordon and Donald Conrad had made headlines the previous summer, when they purchased the team for an NHL record of $31 million. A compromise was reached between the two in March, with Gordon emerging with his 37.5 percent of the team's ownership intact and with full decision-making power. Conrad relinquished day-to-day control of the team in return for several million dollars to be paid over the coming months.

On March 29, the first Soviet national-team player to perform in the NHL lined up with the Calgary Flames. Sergei Priakin, a 25-year-old left-winger from the Soviet Wings, was signed to a two-year contract by general manager Cliff Fletcher. It was a major coup for Fletcher and the Flames. It was thought that Vancouver and New Jersey had had the inside track to land the first Soviet player. A Soviet spokesman said negotiations for other Soviet players sought by NHL clubs would begin following the world championships in Stockholm.

The builders' section of the Hockey Hall of Fame opened its doors to Alan Eagleson and the late Father David Bauer, former Canadian Olympic hockey coach. They were joined by players Darryl Sittler, Vladislav Tretiak, the first Soviet player to be included, and 84-year-old Herbie Lewis, a member of Detroit's first Stanley Cup winning team in 1936.

Joey Mullen of Calgary not only reached the 50-goal plateau for the first time, but he set a single-season record for the most points by an American-born player when he finished with 110. Mullen, Hakan Loob, Joe Nieuwendyk and Doug Gilmour provided most of the scoring punch as the Flames soared from 13th to first place overall, finishing with 117 points and 54 wins. The Montreal Canadiens under rookie coach Pat Burns, and without a single player amongst the league's top 25 scorers, finished two points back of the Flames. The Los Angeles Kings not only led the league in goals scored with 376, but zoomed from 18th place to fourth overall, one point behind Washington. The Quebec Nordiques finished last overall but with Michel Bergeron back in command, and with young stars like Joe Sakic, Curtis Leschyshyn and Bryan Fogarty maturing quickly, the future looked bright.

THE NHL PLAYOFFS

Smythe Division

The Calgary Flames got the surprise of their lives in their opening-round battle with the Vancouver Canucks. It took seven games, a period of overtime and some spectacular goaltending by Mike Vernon before the the Flames could contemplate a second playoff series. Joel Otto's goal at 19:21 of extra play won the deciding game for the Flames 4–3 as Vernon turned away 42 shots, 11 of them in overtime. Meanwhile, the Los Angeles Kings became only the sixth team in playoff history to overcome a 3–1 series deficit when they eliminated the defending champion Edmonton Oilers in seven games. Wayne Gretzky scored a playoff record 86th goal in the series. The Oilers, who had slipped to seventh place in the overall standings, simply weren't good enough to defend their title. In the division finals, the Flames ousted the Kings in four straight games, outshooting them 155–95 and outscoring them 22–11.

Norris Division

The Chicago Blackhawks, who had slipped into the playoffs ahead of Toronto on the final night of the regular season, stunned Detroit with a six-game victory in the opening round. The goaltending of Alain Chevrier made the difference. The St. Louis Blues, paced by the goal scoring of Peter Zezel (with six) and Brett Hull (with four), eliminated the Minnesota North Stars in five games. In the division finals, Chicago's Jeremy Roenick, a 19-year-old rookie center who had played just 20 regular-season games, scored the winning goal in the series-clinching fifth game. The Hawks, who finished 16th overall with 66 points, moved on to challenge Calgary, who finished first overall with 117 points.

Patrick Division

The New York Rangers had lost 16 of their last 19 games, including four straight to Pittsburgh, in the first round of the playoffs, leaving Rangers' fans wondering about the future of general manager Phil Esposito. Penguins' goalie Tom Barrasso played brilliantly in the Pittsburgh sweep, the Penguins' first playoff-series victory since 1979. Goaltending was also a major factor in the other semi-final series between Philadelphia and Washington, with the Flyers' Ron Hextall outperforming the Capitals' Pete Peeters. In game five, Hextall thrilled Flyer fans with a 180-foot shot into an empty Washington net to become the first NHL goalie to ever score a playoff goal. The Flyers captured the series in six games.

A sprained knee kept Hextall on the sidelines for game six of the division finals against Pittsburgh, but Ken Wregget, an ex-Leaf, emerged as the hero in Philadelphia's series-clinching victory. Wregget had played only one full game since being acquired (for two first-round draft choices) from Toronto. In game five of the series, Mario Lemieux tied an NHL playoff record with five goals and three assists for eight points in a 10–7 Penguin victory.

Adams Division

In a clutch and grab series, the Montreal Canadiens swept past Hartford in four straight games. The Whalers lost each of the final three games of the series by one goal, the last two in overtime. The Boston Bruins, who hadn't beaten Buffalo all season and had compiled an 0–5–3 record, bounced the Sabres aside in five games in the division's other semi-final series. Two of the Sabres, Mike Foligno and Larry Playfair, pointed

266

the finger at coach Ted Sator when it was over. "We were outcoached," said Foligno. "A lot of players can't play for him," added Playfair.

In the finals, Boston faced the Canadiens, another team they hadn't beaten all season. Against Montreal they were 0–7–1. Montreal captured the series 4–1 in games, but all contests were decided by a single goal. Boston coach Terry O'Reilly resigned immediately after the series, stating that he had never intended to be a career coach and wanted to spend more time with his family.

Campbell Conference Finals

The Calgary Flames reached the Stanley Cup finals for the second time in four years by shutting down the Chicago Blackhawks' offense and beating the Norris Division representatives 4–1. The Chicago power play was a woeful three for 31 in the series. For the eighth consecutive year, a Smythe Division team would represent the Campbell Conference in the finals.

Wales Conference Finals

The Montreal Canadiens managed to win their series with the Philadelphia Flyers in six games, sweeping all three games played at the Spectrum. The Flyers' power play, tops in the NHL throughout the regular season, vanished against the Habs and was 0–24. In game one, the Flyers' Brian Propp was checked heavily against the glass by Montreal's Chris Chelios, suffering a concussion which caused him to miss game two. In game six, with 1:37 left to play in the third period and Montreal leading by two goals, goalie Ron Hextall dashed out of his net and attacked Chelios. He smashed his stick and flailed his blocker pad against Chelios. Hextall drew a match penalty and was later suspended for 12 games. The incident tainted a well-played series.

The Stanley Cup Finals

At the Saddledome in Calgary, Theoren Fleury, a former altar boy and the NHL's smallest player at five feet, three inches, scored the winning goal for the Calgary Flames in their opening-game 3–2 win over the Montreal Canadiens. But in game two, the Flames' power play failed them—they were one for eight—and Montreal tied the series with a 4–2 victory. Chris Chelios figured in all but one of the Montreal goals. When Montreal winger Claude Lemieux sat out game two for disregarding coach Pat Burns' orders to stop taking dives on the ice, Montreal journalist Rejean Tremblay touched off a storm of controversy by suggesting that Burns was anti-francophone. Burns and Serge Savard reacted angrily and Tremblay was booted off the Canadiens' charter flight back to Montreal. Game three in Montreal went into the second overtime period before Ryan Walter won it 4–3 at 18:18 with a shot fired from just outside the crease. Larry Robinson appeared in his 200th playoff game, an NHL record. The Flames were right back in the hunt after a 4–2 victory in game four to tie the series. Calgary held a 35–19 edge in shots on goal.

In game five at Calgary, the Flames opened up a 3–1 lead in the first period, allowed one goal in the second but turned the Habs away with strong defensive play in the third period and won 3–2. The sixth game was played at the Forum in Montreal where no visiting team had ever won the Stanley Cup. The oldest Flame, Lanny McDonald, was inserted into the Calgary lineup and responded with his first goal of the playoffs, as the Flames ended a storybook season with a 4–2 decision over the Habs. McDonald was able to sip champagne from the Cup for the first time in his brilliant 16-year career. The Flames' coach Terry Crisp became the 12th person in NHL history to win the Cup both as a player (with the Philadelphia Flyers) and as a coach. Flames' defenseman Al MacInnis, who led all playoff scorers with 30 points, was named the winner of the Conn Smythe Trophy as MVP of the playoffs.

At the World Hockey Championships in Stockholm, Brian Bellows was named the tournament's best forward as Team Canada finished second to the Soviets and captured a silver medal. Team Canada players were peeved at themselves for losing 5–3 to the Soviets. Had they won, they would have been in a position to bring back Canada's first gold medal since 1961. Immediately after the tournament, on May 4, 20-year-old Alexandr Mogilny became the first Soviet national-team player to defect. He slipped away from his hotel room in Stockholm and met secretly with Buffalo Sabres' general manager Gerry Meehan and Don Luce, the director of player development. After negotiations, the group flew to Buffalo where the defection was revealed at a press conference. Soviet coach Viktor Tikhonov called the defection "disgusting." Other Soviet officials said it might seriously jeopardize Soviet relations with the NHL.

In a front-office surprise, Phil Esposito was fired as general manager of the Rangers. The Boston Bruins named Mike Milbury to succeed Terry O'Reilly as coach. The Hartford Whalers gave Larry Pleau his walking papers a week after Eddie Johnston had been named as the team's general manager. Pleau had been the first player signed by the franchise in 1972 when it had been the New England Whalers in the WHA. Former Whaler Rick Ley was offered the coaching job. The Winnipeg Jets signed former Chicago coach Bob Murdoch to a three-year contract. Murdoch replaced Rick Bowness who returned to Moncton to manage and coach the Jets' farm team. Tom Webster took over the coaching reins in Los Angeles, Rick Dudley replaced Ted Sator as coach of the Sabres and Glen Sather turned over the Edmonton bench job to long-time assistant John Muckler.

Wayne Gretzky captured the Hart Trophy for the ninth time in 10 years, outpolling Mario Lemieux and Steve Yzerman. Montreal's Chris Chelios won the Norris Trophy as top defenseman, Guy Carbonneau took the Selke Trophy for best defensive forward, the Canadiens' Patrick Roy was chosen as top goalie and rookie coach Pat Burns won coach-of-the-year honors. New York Rangers' defenseman Brian Leetch won the Calder Trophy as best rookie, Joe Mullen of Calgary won the Lady Byng for being the most gentlemanly player and the Islanders' Bryan Trottier was awarded the King Clancy Trophy as the player who best exemplified leadership qualities on and off the ice.

1989—90

The 1989-90 NHL season will forever be remembered as the Year of the Soviet. There were Sergei Priakin and Sergei Makarov in Calgary, Igor Larionov and Vladimir Krutov in Vancouver, Viacheslav Fetisov and Sergei Starikov in New Jersey, goalie Sergei Mylnikov in Quebec, oldtimer Helmut Balderis in Minnesota and defector Alexandr Mogilny in Buffalo. Closer ties with Soviet hockey were established during a training camp Friendship Tour of the Soviet Union by the Washington Capitals and the Calgary Flames.

On June 17, at the Met Center in Bloomington, Minnesota, Mats Sundin, an 18-year-old Swedish star, became the first European player to be chosen number one in the NHL entry draft. The Quebec Nordiques drafted Sundin despite the fact he would not be available for NHL play until the 1991-92 season, at the earliest, because of a two-year contract he signed with Djurgardens of the Swedish Elite league. Dave Chyzowski, a left-winger from Kamloops, was picked second overall by the Islanders. The Toronto Maple Leafs, drafting third, took Belleville's Scott Thornton, then grabbed two of his teammates, Steve Bancroft and Rob Pearson with their other two first-round choices.

Eighteen Soviet players were snapped up in the draft, including 36-year-old Balderis, the oldest player ever drafted. A draft oddity: 10 players named Jason were selected, four of them in the first round.

The biggest of the off-season trades was a six-player swap between Winnipeg and Pittsburgh. The Pens shipped Randy Cunneyworth, Dave McIlwain and goalie Rick Tabaracci to the Jets in return for 37-goal scorer Andrew McBain, defenseman Jim Kyte and center Randy Gilhen. The Devils and the Whalers swapped former 40-goal scorers when Pat Verbeek went to Hartford for Sylvain Turgeon. The Devils also acquired center Walt Poddubny from Quebec in return for defenseman Joe Cirella and center Claude Loiselle. Gone from Calgary was veteran Rob Ramage, who went to the Leafs for a second-round draft pick. Gone from Montreal were three popular veterans: Bob Gainey accepted a coaching job in France; Larry Robinson, a free agent without compensation, jumped to the Los Angeles Kings; and Rick Green retired. The Flames' Hakan Loob went back to Sweden and signed with Farjestads, his former club, while Lanny McDonald, scorer of 500 NHL goals and holder of a Stanley Cup ring, retired from the Flames. Next stop — the Hockey Hall of Fame.

A Hall of Famer still active, 38-year-old Guy Lafleur, returned to the city of his glory days as a junior. The Flower signed with Quebec for one year with an unlimited number of option years. After Lafleur's signing was announced, the Nordiques began selling 100 season's tickets per day.

The Montreal Forum, scene of many of Lafleur's greatest games, faced demolition after 65 years as a hockey mecca. A new Forum was planned with a 20,000-seat capacity and 100 luxury boxes, on a site to be determined, and opening scheduled for 1995.

Edmonton goalie Grant Fuhr said he was retiring from hockey. Fuhr, who was the target of criticism from coach Glen Sather during the season, said he would sell cars for a living. "I don't need this crap [hockey] anymore," he said. Later, Fuhr would reconsider, once he accepted a league rule that prevented him from placing Pepsi-Cola ads on his goal pads.

One of the game's most popular figures, NHL director of officiating John McCauley, died in hospital in Georgetown, Ontario following surgery to remove an infected gall bladder. He was 44.

Former Sabre Rick Dudley became Buffalo's 12th coach in the team's 19-year history when he replaced Ted Sator. Rick Ley replaced Larry Pleau behind the Hartford bench. The Jets hired Bob Murdoch as their new coach. Glen Sather stepped aside as coach of the Oilers and handed the job to longtime assistant John Muckler. The

Kings hired Tom Webster to succeed Robbie Ftorek as coach, and the Rangers signed Neil Smith as their new general manager. Smith considered several candidates for the Ranger coaching job before settling on Roger Neilson, who'd been fired by four other NHL clubs during his career. Gold Stellick resigned as Toronto general manager and joined the Rangers as assistant GM a few days later. George Armstrong was dismissed as Leaf's coach and replaced by Doug Carpenter, while Floyd Smith, the Leafs' chief scout for years, was named interim general manager of the club. In Boston, rookie coach Mike Milbury, who replaced Terry O'Reilly, looked for greater team speed and more scoring from his Bruins.

The St. Louis Blues won a bidding war for free agent goaltender Curtis Joseph. They signed the former University of Wisconsin star to a $1.1-million contract over four years. Joseph's contract was puny compared to the package the Penguins worked out for superstar Mario Lemieux. The mega-deal, largest in the history of Pittsburgh sports, made Lemieux hockey's second $2-million-a-year player, behind Wayne Gretzky.

Philadelphia goalie Ron Hextall was suspended for 12 games for his attack on Montreal's Chris Chelios during the last game of the Wales Conference finals.

Duncan MacPherson, a New York Islander first-round draft choice in 1984, went missing without a trace in Europe. The 23-year-old from Saskatoon was visiting friends in Germany and was en route to a coaching job in Scotland when he disappeared. While foul play was suspected, police also speculated MacPherson may have fallen into a mountain crevasse while skiing.

In Florida, one of two men accused of killing former NHL player Brian Spencer pleaded guilty to second-degree murder. Lump Daniels, 35, was sentenced to 18 years in prison.

Detroit's Bob Probert faced a year in jail and deportation from the United States after pleading guilty to importing cocaine. "I realize I was wrong in what I did," said Probert. The threat of a long-term jail sentence — he faced up to 20 years in prison and a $1-million fine before his plea bargain — scared him straight, Probert said.

While NHL scouts doubted that many 18-year-olds would crack NHL lineups, there were few reservations about 16-year-old star Eric Lindros. "I think he could play on any team right now," Flyers' general manager Bobby Clarke said of the six-foot-four, 217-pound junior phenomenon from Toronto.

Wayne Gretsky replaced Dave Taylor as captain of the Kings while Rob Ramage was named the Leafs' first captain in three seasons. In Montreal, Guy Carbonneau and Chris Chelios were named co-captains of the Canadiens.

On September 28, the Philadelphia Flyers and the Winnipeg Jets were involved in a controversial deal. The Flyers sent goalie Pete Peeters and forward Keith Acton to Winnipeg in return for future considerations. On October 3, one day after the waiver draft, Peeters and Acton were shipped back to Philadelphia. President John Zeigler decided to investigate when it was suggested league by-laws had been violated.

Two days before the season opened, Marcel Dionne was cut by the New York Rangers. Dionne, 38, scored 731 goals and 1,040 assists in 1,328 games. In 19 years, Dionne never played in a semi-final playoff game.

On October 15, Wayne Gretzky surpassed Gordie Howe as hockey's greatest scorer. He did it in his customary dramatic style, scoring the tying goal on Bill Ranford of the Oilers with 53 seconds remaining in the third period, for point number 1,851. An assist early in the game had tied Howe's mark of 1,850. After Gretzky's record-setting goal, the red carpet was rolled out at the Northlands Coliseum and the Great One was presented with gifts and lauded in speeches by Gordie Howe, John Zeigler and others. Gretzky said, "This is the greatest feeling in the world. It will be the highlight of my life." He praised the Oilers, his teammates and Bruce McNall. He kissed his wife Janet and the game continued. In overtime, to no one's surprise, Gretzky slipped the winning goal past Ranford for point number 1,852 as the Kings edged the Oilers 5–4.

The Oilers suffered another loss that week. Jimmy Carson announced he was retiring from hockey because he "couldn't get mentally up for the games." General manager Glen Sather immediately suspended the troubled player.

Four times in NHL history a team has scored two goals in four seconds of play. When the Calgary Flames became the fourth club to do it, against Quebec on October 17, they added a twist. Doug Gilmour and Paul Ranheim scored two goals in four seconds while playing shorthanded. It was an NHL first.

On October 19, goalie Ron Hextall of the Philadelphia Flyers ended a 42-day holdout. Hextall's agent, Rich Winter, had declared the goalie's contract with the Flyers invalid.

On the same day, Chris Chelios became the highest-paid Montreal player in history when he inked a new five-year contract calling for $575,000 per year plus a reported $200,000 a year in deferred payments. A less fortunate defenseman, Gord Kluzak of the Bruins, recuperating from his 10th knee operation, said he was ready to start skating with his team. Kluzak played in only three games in 1988-89. But after two days of full workouts, Kluzak complained of fluid in the knee saying, "This is no fun. I probably bit off more than I can chew."

Quebec's Peter Stastny recorded his 1,000th career point on October 19 against Chicago. Stastny required the third fewest games (682) to reach the milestone. Only Wayne Gretzky (424) and Mike Bossy (656) did it faster. Stastny, who was the second most prolific NHL scorer (Gretzky was number one) in the 1980s, got a late start in pro hockey. He was 24 when he defected from Czechoslovakia to join the Nordiques. Guy Lafleur called Stastny "the best center I've played with since Jacques Lemaire."

Not since Stastny won the Calder Trophy as a 24-year-old rookie was there so much early season discussion about a current Calder candidate. Calgary winger Sergie Makarov, a 31-year-old veteran of international play and three-time player of the year in the Soviet Union, jumped into the lead among rookie scorers. NHL vice-president Brian O'Neill spoke for most fans when he said, "It's not really fair that a Mike Modano or a player like that has to compete for the rookie award against an elite player from the Soviet Union with ten years' experience."

Igor Larionov of the Vancouver Canucks claimed in his book *The Front Line Rebels* that Soviet hockey players received injections and conspired with laboratory workers to deceive drug testers at the 1986 World Hockey Championships in Moscow. Larionov accused his fo.mer coach, Viktor Tikhonov, of ordering players to take drug injections even though the contents of the shots were not known to the players.

On November 2, the Detroit Red Wings paid a steep price for Edmonton's disgruntled Jimmy Carson, a 100-point scorer in 1988-89. The Red Wings sent Joe Murphy (the player they chose instead of Carson in the 1986 entry draft), Adam Graves and Petr Klima, all left-wingers, and defenseman Jeff Sharples to the Oilers in exchange for Carson and right-winger Kevin McLelland. Carson had angered a lot of people when he'd walked out on the Oilers two weeks earlier. "He was like a little kid," said Petr Klima. "He quit and changed the lives of a lot of people."

In Calgary, popular team captain Jim Peplinski also quit, but without any ulterior motives. He simply made a surprise early-season decision to retire at age 29. Peplinski ended his nine-year career as the Flames' all-time leader in games played (705) and playoff games played (99). He was in the second year of a four-year contract, and his decision to retire probably cost him half a million dollars.

Just 14 games into the season, Jim Schoenfeld was fired as head coach of the New Jersey Devils despite his team's .500 record. Assistant coach John Cuniff replaced Schoenfeld, who said the coaching change was "very, very premature."

The Quebec Nordiques, despite the fine play of Guy Lafleur, sank quickly to the bottom of the NHL standings. In November, Lafleur scored goal number 544 to tie Rocket Richard for eighth place on the all-time scoring list.

Under Mike Keenan, the Chicago Blackhawks, with a 14–6–1 mark, soared to first place overall.

A study by University of Ohio exercise physiologist Frederick Hagerman determined hockey to be the most difficult sport to play of 11 professional sports analyzed. In another study, hockey was found to be a poor cousin of four other pro sports. While pro football teams received an average of $17 million per season from TV revenues, baseball teams received $14 million and basketball teams $5.6 million, NHL hockey teams received slightly more than $800,000 per season.

Early in November, NHL president John Zeigler met with convicted drug smuggler Bob Probert, who was serving a 90-day sentence in a federal prison. Zeigler said he was impressed with Probert's commitment to rehabilitation, and hinted that Probert could be back playing for the Red Wings as early as March 5, the one-year anniversary of his expulsion from the NHL.

Four unnamed Toronto Maple Leafs ripped into teammates Gary Leeman and Ed Olczyk in a November *Globe and Mail* story for putting themselves before the team. "We've got to get rid of one of the two," said one teammate. "They're making more money than anybody else and they think they're better than anyone else. Quite a few of the Leafs are upset with their attitude."

Blackhawk goalie Alain Chevrier was startled during a game when Calgary forward Theoren Fleury called him a "sawed-off little runt." Chevrier, at five-foot-eight, stands two inches taller than Fleury.

The floundering Quebec Nordiques were looking for help in December. They picked up Brian Lawton for the $12,500 waiver price from Hartford, and dealt with Detroit for veteran Tony McKegney, a former Nordique.

In St. Louis, red-hot Adam Oates was making the Blues' general manager Ron Caron look good. Caron traded Bernie Federko and Tony McKegney to Detroit in the off-season for Oates and Paul McLean. The trade was called one of the most one-sided imaginable. And with Brett Hull, acquired from Calgary in March 1988, on a 60- or 70-goal pace, Caron was hailed as hockey's shrewdest dealer.

The Islanders were pleased with a trade they completed with the Kings. Bruising defenseman Ken Baumgartner and Hubie McDonough provided quick relief to the struggling Islanders while Mikko Makela, who joined the Kings, discovered a slump isn't always cured by a change of scenery.

Goalie Olaf Kolzig, a first-round draft choice of the Washington Capitals, made Western League history by scoring a goal for the Tri-City Americans against the Seattle Thunderbirds. Kolzig, who started the season with Washington, scored on a rink-length shot through a maze of players into an empty net. It was the first goal by a goalie in Western Hockey League play.

Following a meeting of the NHL board of governors in Florida in December, NHL president John Zeigler announced the league's plans for the coming decade. He said the board agreed in principle to expand by one or more teams to begin play no sooner than the 1992-93 season, with the entry cost per team to be no less than $50 million (U.S.). By the turn of the century, the league would include 28 teams. "It's a big day in the history of the league," said Marcel Aubut, owner of the Quebec Nordiques. "There is hope for many cities now. Even if we choose one, two or three teams to join us in 1992-93, there will still be four more spots available."

One man who had desperately sought a franchise, Peter Karamanos of Detroit, said he wouldn't shell out $50 million for an expansion franchise. "It's crazy," he said, "I don't know how the NHL arrived at that $50 million figure. There may be people willing to pay it, but I don't see how anybody who does can ever make any money."

Zeigler also announced plans for a $20-million extravaganza to celebrate the 75th anniversary of the NHL during the 1991-92 season and the 100th anniversary of the Stanley Cup in 1992-93. A novel idea was to have the original six teams play each other on opening day in 1991, wearing replicas of 75-year-old uniforms. In other business, the board approved a suggestion to move the goal lines out, from 10 to 11 feet, with the extra two feet taken from the neutral zone. Broadcaster John Davidson took a tape measure to the Civic Arena in Pittsburgh and discovered the distance there was already 11 feet.

The famous Patrick name was back in hockey on December 5. Craig Patrick left a comfortable job as athletic director at the University of Denver to take over as general manager and interim coach of the Pittsburgh Penguins. He replaced both Tony Esposito and Gene Ubriaco, who were sent packing. Players and fans were delighted with the coaching change. One reporter wrote: "The Penguins were split on their reaction to Patrick's arrival. Some were ecstatic, others merely delirious with joy." Ubriaco delivered a parting shot at superstar Mario Lemieux. "Trying to coach Lemieux," he said, "was like trying to teach a shark table manners."

In pre-Christmas deals, the St. Louis Blues sent veteran goaltender Greg Millen and forward Tony Hrkac to Quebec in return for defenseman Jeff Brown. Brown and Nordiques coach Michel Bergeron had been at loggerheads. Dave Christian moved from Washington to Boston in exchange for Bob Joyce. The Whalers sent Paul MacDermid to Winnipeg and received Randy Cunneyworth. In January, Vancouver's Tony Tanti, Barry Pederson and Rod Buskas were traded to Pittsburgh for Andrew McBain, Dan Quinn and Dave Capuano.

Junior star Eric Lindros, 16, was traded from Sault Ste. Marie to the Oshawa Generals despite a petition asking Soo general manager Sherry Bassin not to make the deal. "Let him rot in Detroit," said one unhappy fan. Lindros had refused to report to the Soo and played the first half of the season with Detroit Compuware.

After just 10 days on the job as the director of hockey operations for the Tri-City

Americans, Bill LaForge faced a mutiny. Twenty of the Americans went on strike, forcing cancellation of a game with the Portland Winter Hawks. "He came in a took over the practices," said goalie Olaf Kolzig. "He didn't even introduce himself. He just started swearing at us. He turned everybody off." Team owner Ron Dixon assigned LaForge to a scouting position with the organization.

Highly-touted Czech center Vladimir Ruzicka, 26, signed a four-year contract with the Edmonton Oilers. Ruzicka's rights were obtained from Toronto in the off-season. "This is the first time a Czech player in his prime has been released," said Glen Sather. "And it's the first time a player has been given permission to leave during the season." The New Jersey Devils received a Christmas present when Soviet star Alexei Kasatonov — billed as the best defenseman in the world — was signed and sent to Utica for conditioning.

On December 26, Doug Harvey, the leader of the great Montreal teams that swept to five straight Stanley Cups from 1956-60, died after a lengthy illness. He was 65. Harvey was a seven-time winner of the Norris Trophy as the NHL's best defenseman. He was an NHL all-star 11 times and played on six Cup winners. His ability to head-man the puck changed the face of hockey. Considered by many to be the greatest defenseman who ever played, Harvey was elected to the Hockey Hall of Fame in 1973. He passed up the induction dinner in favor of a fishing trip.

On December 28, the Chicago Blackhawks and the Minnesota North Stars engaged in a lively pre-game brawl that netted each club $25,000 in automatic fines. The Hawks accused North Stars' players Basil McRae and Shane Churla with coming over the red line in the warmup and jabbing Hawks' players with their sticks.

As the year ended, Oiler goalie Grant Fuhr underwent his second shoulder operation. He was expected to be out of the Edmonton lineup for 12 weeks. Washington defenseman Rod Langway underwent arthroscopic surgery on both knees.

Nearing the halfway mark of the season, the Calgary Flames — picked by 18 of 22 experts to win the Stanley Cup — were in third place in the Smythe Division. The Flames and the Kings were tied with 42 points, five points fewer than Edmonton. The Quebec Nordiques were struggling through one of their worst seasons ever, and were said to be eyeing Peterborough junior star Mike Ricci for the number one draft pick that comes with a last-place finish.

Leafs' owner Harold Ballard, 86, was in critical condition in a Miami hospital on January 8. The club's board of directors took over the day-to-day operation of the team for the first time in Ballard's 18-year stewardship.

At the World Junior Championships in Helsinki, Finland, goalie Stephane Fiset, a 19-year-old Quebec Nordique netminder of the future, led Canada to a 5–1–1 record and a gold medal. "Stephane was unbelievable," said Canadian coach Guy Charron. The U.S. finished 1–6–0, including an embarrassing 6–5 defeat to Norway. Only Poland (0–7–0) had a worse record.

Veteran Nordique right-winger Guy Lafleur scored his 545th career goal against Toronto on January 3. The goal moved him ahead of Rocket Richard and into eighth place on the career goal-scoring list.

The long search for a successor to NHLPA president Alan Eagleson ended in January when Bob Goodenow, a 37-year-old lawyer from Dearborn, Michigan was named to the position. Eagleson said Goodenow would take a lead role in negotiations between the NHLPA and team owners regarding a new collective bargaining agreement.

Mario Lemieux turned in a spectacular show at the annual All-Star game in Pittsburgh. He scored four goals in a 12–7 Wales Conference victory over the Campbell Conference to tie a Wayne Gretzky record. He also won his third straight All-Star MVP — another record. In the skills competition on the day before the All-Star game, Al Iafrate of the Leafs displayed the fastest shot at 96 miles per hour, Mike Gartner of the North Stars the greatest skating speed at 28.1 miles per hour and Ray Bourque of the Bruins the greatest accuracy, hitting four targets in seven shots. Kirk McLean of the Canucks stopped 11 of 12 breakaways and 12 of 15 rapid-fire shots, and was named top goaltender.

Mid-season trades saw Flyer captain Dave Poulin go to Boston in return for Ken Linseman. Bernie Nicholls was traded from L.A. to New York in exchange for Tony Granato and Tomas Sandstrom. Nicholls told his former GM Rogie Vachon: "You got the raw end of the deal."

In Washington, one brother replaced another behind the Caps' bench. Bryan Murray was fired as coach after his team lost seven games in a row, and his brother Terry succeeded him. Bryan Murray left the Caps as the seventh most successful coach in league history based on winning percentage (343–246–83, .572). In Quebec, general manager Martin Madden was sacked by president Marcel Aubut and replaced on an interim basis by Maurice Filion. During Madden's tenure, the club earned record was a woeful 36–82–13.

On February 1, the Global Hockey League, co-founded by Michael Gobuty and Dennis Murphy, surfaced publicly for the first time when Albany, New York was awarded the initial franchise. The GHL, which promised to begin operations in November with divisions in North America and Europe, became the first professional league to rival the NHL since the NHL absorbed four WHA teams in 1979. No sooner had the GHL announced its plans to open in November than plans for a second rival pro league were made public. Gordon Stenback, a 56-year-old native of Thunder Bay who lives in Cleveland, said he was heading up a six-team league, as yet unnamed, to play in North America. Tentative sites named included Cleveland, Atlanta, Hamilton and Tampa Bay.

Salary disclosure was a hot topic in 1989–90, but when base salaries were published, there was quite a letdown. They ranged from accurate to totally erroneous. No provision was made for income from other sources, for example, which meant that significant payments to certain players were ignored. Income in the form of bonuses didn't show up, nor did performance bonuses. According to the figures, the Los Angeles Kings paid the highest average salary, $374,250, while the St. Louis Blues paid the lowest, $156,250. The average for all NHL players was $222,017.

Kings' owner Bruce McNall, who annoyed other owners with his generosity toward employees, reworked Wayne Gretzky's contract, extending it through 1997–98 at $2-million per season. Gretzky will receive deferred payments of $1-million for seven years when the contract expires. The package totalled $31.32-million. McNall said he was rewarding Gretzky for turning around the team's financial fortunes.

Less happy about their team's financial situation were the Gund brothers, owners of the Minnesota North Stars. The Gunds threatened to move their team to Oakland unless $15-million in renovations were made to the Metropolitan Sports Center in Bloomington. Even if the Metropolitan Sports Facilities Commission met their demands (which it didn't), the Gunds said they would still move unless there was a demonstrated show of community support for the North Stars. "Minnesota without hockey would be like Montreal without hockey," groaned North Stars coach Pierre Page.

Pittsburgh's team physician gave Mario Lemieux the bad news: a herniated disk might require off-season surgery. Doctor Charles Burke said the operation had a 95 percent success rate. Meanwhile, the Penguins' star goalie, Tom Barasso, was given a leave of absence on February 9 to join his family in Los Angeles, where his two-year-old daughter Ashley was being treated for cancer. The child was in a program for poor prognosis patients.

In Buffalo, the Sabres were seeking a psychologist for Soviet defector Alexandr Mogilny. When Mogilny failed to show up for a two-game road trip, it was revealed that he had a fear of flying. His terror was such that he told a teammate he would quit hockey and find an off-ice job if necessary.

On February 10, Brett Hull scored his 50th goal of the season, a game winner over Toronto. Father Bobby witnessed the goal that made him and Brett the only father-son combination to score 50 in the NHL. Three days later, Bryan Trottier of the Islanders scored his 500th career goal at home against the Calgary Flames. At 33, Trottier became the 15th player to reach the 500-goal plateau.

Clarence (Hap) Day, who played and coached a total of 23 seasons with the Toronto Maple Leafs, died in St. Thomas, Ontario on February 17. He was 88. Day coached the Leafs to five Stanley Cups, including a memorable comeback win over Detroit in 1942. Down three games to none in the series, Day made lineup changes and the Leafs stormed back to win four straight games, a feat that has never been duplicated in a final series.

Mario Lemieux's back problems forced him to give up his pursuit of Wayne Gretzky's consecutive-game scoring record of 51. Lemieux was forced to the sidelines for at least a month of rehabilitation when his streak reached 46 games, the second-longest in NHL history. He was leading the league in scoring with 121 points in 58 games when he was scratched from the Pens' lineup.

At age 36, retired Soviet goaltender Vladislav Tretiak was said to be considering a comeback with the Detroit Red Wings, five years after he last played competitive hockey. Three weeks of intense talks ended when the NHL informed the Wings that signing Tretiak would violate league by-laws. In order for a team to sign a European player like Tretiak, he must have been drafted twice and released twice. Tretiak was drafted only once, by Montreal in 1983. He was released in 1986.

Brett Hull became the 13th player to score 60 goals in a season when he clicked for three goals against Montreal on February 25. Hull also surpassed the single-season high of his father Bobby, who scored 58 goals during the 1968–69 season.

A brawl between the Los Angeles Kings and the Edmonton Oilers at the Great Western Forum on February 28 resulted in a record 86 penalties for 356 minutes. The Oilers were assessed a league record of 45 penalties for 199 minutes, the Kings a club record of 41 penalties for 157 minutes.

Hall of Fame defenseman Brad Park was back in the news the same day. He was named head coach and general manager of the New England Clippers of the proposed Global Hockey League. The Clippers were expected to play out of the Providence

Civic Center. Mike Eruzione, captain of the U.S. gold-medal Olympic team in 1980, was signed to an executive position with the club.

Suffering through a dismal season with 10 players over 30 years old, the Flyers traded 11-year veteran Brian Propp to Boston for a second-round draft choice. The Blackhawks dealt with Quebec, acquiring Michel Goulet and Greg Millen in return for Everett Sanipass, Dan Vincelette and Mario Doyon. Quebec also disposed of longtime star Peter Stastny, 33, trading him to New Jersey for defenseman Craig Wolanin and future considerations. Stastny cried when told of the trade. "This is harder for me than when I left my native Bratislava," he said. The Rangers acquired Mike Gartner, 30, from Minnesota for Ulf Dahlen, 23, and a fourth-round draft choice.

Wayne Gretzky was leading the league in scoring with 141 points in 72 games when he was sidelined with a groin injury. It was hoped Gretzky would be back for the playoffs. The Oilers lost goalie Grant Fuhr with another shoulder injury, and the Jets' steady defenseman Randy Carlyle went down with torn knee ligaments. Within a span of three days, Trevor Linden (Canucks) and Brian Leetch (Rangers), last year's two leading rookies, ended frustrating sophomore seasons with injuries. Linden suffered a separated shoulder and Leetch a broken ankle.

Bob Probert made a successful return to the Detroit lineup on March 22 after a year-long suspension for a drug conviction. Probert scored a goal in each of his first three games back and was involved in three fights. He said he was taking the remainder of the season as he was his life — one day at a time.

In late March, women's hockey held the spotlight in Ottawa. Clad in controversial pink-and-white uniforms, Team Canada overwhelmed Team U.S.A. 5-2 in the championship game. Close to 9,000 fans, the largest crowd ever to watch women's hockey, were there at the finish. "These championships should get us into the Olympics," said Canada's Dawn McGuire, "And maybe there'll be a pro league for women someday."

With the playoffs approaching, a Gallup Canada poll revealed that Calgary was the choice of 15 percent of hockey fans to retain the Stanley Cup. Boston was picked by 14 percent, Montreal by 12 percent, Edmonton by seven percent, Toronto by six percent and Los Angeles by two percent. Gallup also asked who was the better player, Wayne Gretzky or Mario Lemieux? Gretzky was named by 50 percent while 27 percent named Lemieux. Twenty-three percent were not sure.

Brett Hull scored two goals in the final game of the season for a total of 72 — a record for right-wingers. Steve Larmer of Chicago played in every game for the eighth straight season, bringing his consecutive game streak to 640. The Penguins set a franchise attendance record by attracting 640,700 fans, and the Flyers set a franchise record for losses with 39. The Nordiques set team records for losses (61) and fewest wins (12).

On the day before his beloved Leafs were eliminated from the playoff race, Harold Ballard died peacefully in a Toronto hospital. With the 86-year-old owner in control, the Leafs had skated from one disastrous season to the next. In the 1980s, they never finished above .500, and they missed the playoffs in four of those years. Prior to his death, Ballard's feud with family members and his relationship with Yolanda Ballard (not his wife) made daily headlines in papers across Canada.

THE NHL PLAYOFFS

Smythe Division

For the second time in three years, the Calgary Flames lost a playoff series in which they were heavily favored. After finishing with 18 points fewer than they earned in 1988–89, the Flames were eliminated by the Los Angeles Kings four games to two in the first round of the playoffs. Kings' goalie Kelly Hrudey played superbly, starting in all six games and finishing with a 4–1 record. His prior record against Calgary was 1–10–3. The Kings established the second-highest goal total ever in a playoff game when they walloped the Flames 12–4 in game two. The Edmonton Oilers, down 3–1 in games to the upstart Winnipeg Jets, roared back with three consecutive victories and moved on to the division finals against Los Angeles. The Oilers found the injury-plagued Kings much easier competition than the Jets and ousted them in four games.

Norris Division

The St. Louis Blues lost seven of eight games to the Toronto Maple Leafs during regular season play and were outscored 42–21. But in the playoffs, the Blues got timely scoring from Brett Hull (five goals and 10 assists) and bounced the Leafs aside in five games. Chicago Blackhawks' coach Mike Keenan started goalie Greg Millen in the first six games of the series with Minnesota and pulled him in three games. Keenan also benched newcomer Michel Goulet for games two, three and four. The Blackhawks won the series in seven games. Keenan continued to look for goaltending excellence in the division finals, scratching Millen in games four and six against St. Louis, and relying on rookie Ed Belfour and Jacques Cloutier. The Hawks won the series four games to three, humiliating the Blues 8–2 in the deciding game.

Patrick Division

The New York Rangers and the New York Islanders engaged in a turbulent series to open the playoffs, with the Rangers winning in five games. After Islanders' star Pat Lafontaine was knocked unconscious in game one by the Rangers' James Patrick, the Islanders looked for vengeance with two seconds left to play. The predictable brawl, said to be instigated by Islanders' coach Al Arbour, resulted in a $25,000 fine to the Islanders and a $5,000 fine to Arbour. Washington forward John Druce had eight goals in 45 games during the regular season. In six games against New Jersey, he produced three goals, two of them game-winners as the Capitals ousted the Devils four games to two. Druce continued his red-hot play in the division finals against the Rangers, scoring nine more goals as the Caps won four games to one. Defenseman Rod Langway, who had gone 92 games without a goal, scored the game-winner in overtime in game five.

Adams Division

The Hartford Whalers' pathetic power play cost them dearly in their opening-round series with the first-place Boston Bruins. The Whalers finished the seven-game series, won by the Bruins 4–3, with only three goals in 34-man advantage situations. Coach Rick Ley called his players "spoiled and pampered" when the series was over. Montreal fans didn't expect much from the Canadiens in their series with Buffalo, with Chris Chelios sidelined with injuries, but the Habs raised their game a notch and ousted the Sabres in six games. In the 1990 division final, the Bruins defeated the Canadiens for the second time in the past three meetings. Prior to 1988, the Bruins had lost 18 consecutive playoff series to Montreal. Woeful was the word for the Montreal power play in the playoffs: two for 51. Boston won in five games, and Bruins' general manager Harry Sinden had the last word about the chippy series: "The Canadiens miss the class of leaders like Larry Robinson and Bob Gainey."

Campbell Conference Finals

When Denis Savard scored six points in games two and three of the Blackhawks series with the Oilers, and the Blackhawks took a 2–1 series lead, Oilers' coach John Muckler called on Esa Tikkanen to shadow the pesky center. "He's a helluva player," said Tikkanen, "he skates unbelievable." While Tikkanen's blanket frustrated Savard, the Oiler "kid line" of Adam Graves, 22, Martin Gelinas, 19, and Joe Murphy, 22, excelled throughout the series, and the Oilers swept the final three games to advance to the Stanley Cup finals.

Wales Conference Finals

The Boston Bruins were clearly the better team in their series with the Washington Capitals, who finished the regular season with 78 points to the Bruins' 102. The Bruins and Andy Moog allowed only six goals in the four-game sweep by Mike Milbury's club. Washington general manager David Poile saw a bright future for his team despite the outcome. John Druce was a major surprise, scoring 14 goals in 15 playoff games after scoring just 16 times in 93 previous regular-season games.

The Stanley Cup Finals

Just 21 months after Peter Pocklington sold Wayne Gretzky, a move that was supposed to leave his team in tatters, the Edmonton Oilers found themselves on top of the hockey world again, clutching and kissing the Stanley Cup. It was their fifth Cup win in seven years, and it followed a comparatively easy four-games-to-one triumph over the Boston Bruins. The Oilers were much faster than the Bruins and they excelled offensively, defensively and in goal. They had no fear of the Bruins' power play, but in fact held Boston snipers to one goal in 20-man advantage situations.

There were many who had said the Oilers couldn't reach the top without Gretzky. "Yeah, we demoralized all the critics," said winger Glenn Anderson. "Nobody can say we're not the greatest hockey team in the world today." During the post-game celebration in the Boston Garden, Oiler leader Mark Messier looked into the cameras and said, "This one's for you, Gretz."

Goalie Bill Ranford, who was loudly criticized after the opening game of the playoffs when he played poorly in a loss to Winnipeg, was the hero of the final series and was named winner of the Conn Smythe Trophy as the playoff MVP. He held the

Bruins to eight goals in five games. "It's something I'll never forget," said Ranford. "A player doesn't get too many opportunities to go through this. Hopefully, I've got a lot of years left. But winning this won't sink in until the summer."

Kevin Lowe said that as he and roommate Mark Messier relaxed on their beds prior to game five, Messier looked over and said, "Let's win this one for the G-man [Gretzky]." Lowe added, "Wayne was so great. We were able to follow on his coattails for years. He showed us how to win and took a lot of pressure off us. In our hearts, he's still part of this."

The 1989–90 season saw the Soviet national team win a record-setting 22nd World Championship, defeating Czechoslovakia 5–0 in the gold-medal game. Team Canada finished fourth, behind second-place Sweden and third-place Czechoslovakia. It marked the final NHL season for Mats Maslund of Montreal, whose hockey future was in Switzerland, and for Borje Salming of Detroit, who signed with a Swedish team.

Bobby Clarke was fired as general manager of the Philadelphia Flyers and was replaced by Russ Farwell. Pierre Page left the North Stars to accept the general manager's job with the last-place Nordiques. Page promptly antagonized some Quebec fans by hiring a unilingual coach, 50-year-old Dave Chambers. Guy Lafleur promised to grace the Nordiques' lineup again in 1990-91 but added, "It will be my final season." Terry Crisp, despite an outstanding record (144–63–33) behind the bench, was fired as coach of the Calgary Flames and replaced by Doug Risebrough. Tom Watt, a Crisp supporter and assistant coach of the Flames, was dismissed, and surfaced as an assistant coach with the Leafs. Scotty Bowman and Bob Johnson joined the Pittsburgh Penguins, Bowman in the role of a "super scout" and Johnson as coach.

The Global Hockey League announced franchises for Miami and the European cities of Lyon, Milan, Rotterdam, Prague and East Berlin. Other North American cities said to be in the league include Providence, Rhode Island; Albany, New York; Hamilton, Ontario; Saskatoon, Saskatchewan; Cleveland, Ohio; and Los Angeles, California. Early in June, a league spokesman said the GHL would not open as planned November 1990, but would be ready for play the following year.

The reading of Harold Ballard's will and testament revealed that his real estate and hockey team, valued at $125-million, would be placed in a foundation and directed to several non-profit organizations. Yolanda Ballard, his longtime companion, was left $50,000 a year until her death or marriage. She was expected to contest the will in court.

After 16 hours of deliberation, the NHL board of governors approved the sale of the Minnesota North Stars by George and Gordon Gund to a group headed by Morris Belzberg and Howard Baldwin for $30-million plus $1-million in assumed liabilities and the assignment of expansion fees (to the Gund brothers) from the next three teams that come into the league. The Gunds agreed to pay $50-million for an expansion franchise in the Bay area of California, getting the team one year ahead of the NHL's announced expansion plans. With the $38.1-million they received for selling the North Stars, the Gunds were happy to be tapping into the California market for less than $12-million. San José was said to be their eventual destination because of a planned $100-million arena there. The Gunds said their new team would begin play in 1991-92 at the San Francisco Cow Palace. When Belzberg and Baldwin were unable to complete the financing of the purchase of the North Stars from the Gunds, Norman Green, one of six co-owners of the Calgary Flames, stepped forward and rescued the sale

In 1974 and 1975 the "Broad Street Bullies" of Philadelphia fought their way to two consecutive Stanley Cups. Here they square off against Montreal.

Bobby Clarke was the heart and soul of the Flyers for fifteen years, winning the Hart Trophy as the NHL's MVP three times.

Bernie Parent won the Conn Smythe Trophy as the outstanding playoff player in each of the two years Philadelphia won the Cup.

Robert Shaver

Bruce Bennett

When the Canadiens swept to four straight Stanley Cups from 1976–79, Guy Lafleur was their ace scorer, winning three scoring titles in a row.

Robert Shaver

Buffalo's "French Connection" of Gilbert Perreault, Rene Robert and Richard Martin led the Sabres in the seventies.

Robert Shaver

Gordie Howe came out of retirement to play with his sons, Marty (left) and Mark. Playing hockey with his two sons was his "biggest thrill" and a hockey first.

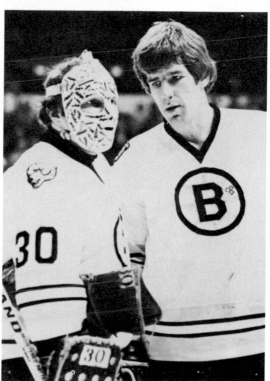

Boston teammate, Terry O'Reilly, checks out goalie Gerry Cheever's unusual mask marked by "stitches" that might have been required if the mask hadn't protected his face.

Darryl Sittler's overtime goal against Czechoslovakia was the Canada Cup winner in 1976.

Bob Nystrom scores an overtime goal in 1980 to win New York Islanders' first of four consecutive Stanley Cups.

All-Star Bryan Trottier was a key to the Islander Stanley Cup dominance in the early eighties.

Mike Bossy of the Islanders scored fifty or more goals a year for nine straight years. Back problems forced him to retire in 1988.

Islander star defenseman Dennis Potvin scored 310 goals and 1052 points during his career. Both are records for defensemen.

Mark Messier and Wayne Gretzky celebrate their fourth Stanley Cup victory in five years. The following summer saw Gretzky traded to the Los Angeles Kings in what has been called the "biggest trade in sports history."

Grant Fuhr, the first black goaltender in NHL history, played a major role in the Oiler Stanley Cup wins.

After seventeen seasons and five Stanley Cups with Montreal, Larry Robinson decided to finish his career with the Kings.

Popular Lanny McDonald scored his five hundredth goal and captained the Calgary Flames to a Stanley Cup championship in 1989.

Bruce Bennett

Wayne Gretzky, the dominant star of the eighties, enters the nineties as a King.

Pittsburgh's Mario Lemieux. The 1988–89 season saw him capture his second consecutive scoring title and establish himself as one of the best in the world.

by purchasing 51 percent of the Minnesota franchise.

In the closest vote for the Hart Trophy in NHL history, Edmonton's Mark Messier nosed out Boston's Ray Bourque by 227 to 225. Incredibly, Wayne Gretzky, who had captured nine of the past 10 Hart Trophy awards, received a single vote and finished 14th in the balloting. Gretzky took home the Art Ross Trophy as the league's scoring champion, Bourque won the Norris Trophy as top defenseman and 31-year-old Soviet rookie Sergei Makarov won the Calder Trophy. Winnipeg coach Bob Murdoch, who led the Jets to a surprising 85-point season, was named coach of the year. The Blues' Brett Hull won the Lady Byng Trophy for his gentlemanly play, and promptly signed a three-year contract with a year's option that will pay him between $5-million and $6-million. Montreal goalie Patrick Roy won his second consecutive Vezina Trophy as the league's best goaltender and 36-year-old Blues' forward Rick Meagher edged out Montreal's Guy Carbonneau as best defensive forward. Edmonton's Kevin Lowe was awarded the King Clancy Memorial Trophy for his off-ice contributions, and Gord Kluzak of the Bruins won the Masterton Trophy for his "perseverance, sportsmanship and dedication to hockey."

Gilbert Perreault, Bill Barber and Fernie Flaman were selcted for induction into the Hockey Hall of Fame. Perreault scored 512 goals in a 17-year career with Buffalo, and ranks eighth on the NHL career scoring list with 1,326 points. Barber scored 420 goals during his 12 years with Philadelphia, and Flaman was a star defenseman for Toronto and Boston during a 17-year career that began in 1944. Retired IHL president Norman (Bud) Poile was selected for the Builders' Division.

During the June draft meetings in Vancouver, Winnipeg's Dale Hawerchuk was traded to the Buffalo Sabres for defenseman Phil Housley and forwards Scott Arniel and Jeff Parker. Veteran Calgary Flame forward Joe Mullen went to Pittsburgh for a second-round draft pick. The Quebec Nordiques made Owen Nolan, a Cornwall junior, the number one player in the draft. Petr Nedved of Seattle was taken as number two by Vancouver. Detroit, with third choice, selected Keith Primeau from Niagara Falls before Philadelphia grabbed Mike Ricci of Peterborough.

XII

DAYS AHEAD

The Future of Hockey

Hockey has changed dramatically in a hundred years. Gone forever are seven-man rosters, 60-minute men, straight-bladed sticks and raccoon-coated goal judges standing on the ice waving handkerchiefs to signal a score. Gone are the days when dingy arenas, with boards a mere 12 inches high, hosted championship games played on natural ice covered in pools of water. Gone is the era when NHL teams traveled exclusively by train, and when the seventh-best goalie in the world played in the minors because a six-team league required only one netminder per team.

Hockey's turbulent, ever-changing past is an indicator that change will figure prominently in its future. On the immediate horizon is an expanded NHL. Hockey returns to the Bay Area in California in 1991, 15 years after Charlie Finley's white-skated Seals floundered in Oakland. The population explosion of the Bay Area to 5.5 million and Wayne Gretzky's impact on the state have people talking hockey again. Art Savage, president of the new franchise granted to the Gund brothers, says of the market:

> Fifteen years ago, baseball was attracting a mere 6 or 7 hundred thousand fans a year in the Bay Area. Last season the A's and the Giants drew 5 million between them. Things have changed in the past decade. The Bay Area is now the number five television market in the U.S.

A 1989 survey by the *The Hockey News* revealed that 73 percent of fans favor further expansion. NHL president John Zeigler has stated that all potential expansion sites will be thoroughly analyzed on everything from market demographics to the city's identification with hockey to television potential:

282

The atmosphere is conducive to expansion exploration [Zeigler says]. Why? Because we've had 10 straight years of attendance increases, 10 straight years of gross revenue increases for both the product on the ice and the product on TV. We've never been in a better position to look at growth. Any city that has expressed interest in the past few years will be looked at.

Ten groups of the 53 that expressed interest in expansion franchises showed up in New York prior to the August 15, 1990 deadline. Each plunked down a fee of $100,000 along with their applications for NHL membership. Three bids were from Florida — Miami, St. Petersburg and Tampa. Two were from San Diego and the others came from Milwaukee, Houston, Seattle, Hamilton and Ottawa. All agreed to pay the rest of the required $50-million 10 months before their team would begin play. The NHL envisions six new teams in place before the end of the century.

One high-profile businessman who has long desired a franchise, Peter Karmanos of Detroit Compuware Corporation grumbled to *The Hockey News* about paying $50-million:

> If an expansion franchise is worth $50-million, then all the existing ones are, too. Are the Minnesota North Stars, who lost more than $6-million a year ago, worth that kind of money? No way.

Among the growing pains and problems associated with expansion, Karmanos lists:
• A recession. "If there's a recession in the 1990s, and economists are predicting one, the worth of a franchise may drop considerably."
• Free agency and higher salaries. "There's going to be more free agency and salaries will escalate. With a new man [Bob Goodenow] heading the Players' Association, the league may have more labor difficulties than at any time in the past."
• Lack of competition. "I've been told there are only about 30 players outside the NHL in minor pro hockey who are ready for NHL play. If the NHL adds three teams by 1992, there won't be enough good players to go around and the teams will not be competitive for a number of years."
• A rival league. "Someone will certainly start one, and when they do, even if they're unsuccessful in the long run, they will drive up the cost of doing business."

Karmanos says the odds of running a profitable NHL franchise, considering the aforementioned factors and the $50-million fee, are all but insurmountable. Despite his reservations, Karmanos is backing the St. Petersburg bid.

The NHL won't procrastinate on expansion, not when the threat of a rival league or leagues remains a strong possibility. Former NHL Players' Association boss Alan Eagleson thinks a new league makes sense. When the entry fee for an NHL franchise was a predicted $30-million — not the $50-million later dictated by Zeigler — Eagleson said:

> Why spend $30-million to buy into the NHL when you can spend $3-million to join a new league with six solid owners? You can lose $3-million a year for six years and you'll still have $12-million left to build up your franchise.

A new league would attempt to offer fans something unique; different rules, perhaps, such as no fighting, the elimination of the red line and a different form of overtime. The Global Hockey League announced grandiose plans to bring a new look to hockey, including several European franchises, but it stumbled badly in the formative stages and few hockey experts give it much chance for long-term success. The International Ice Hockey Federation has not yet sanctioned the league, and the Swedish Ice Hockey Federation has threatened a three year suspension for any Swedish player signing with a Global team.

A new league, to gain credibility, must go after superstars like Mario Lemieux and Brett Hull, and stars-to-be like junior sensation Eric Lindros. The WHA once enticed Brett Hull's famous father Bobby with pro hockey's first million-dollar contract; in the nineties, it might take more than $10-million to get Brett to jump leagues.

It will not be surprising if a professional league is organized for women players. Women are registering for hockey in record numbers, and the highly successful eight-nation World Championships for women, held in Ottawa in March 1990, produced entertaining, highly-skilled competition. Can the Olympics, or a pro league, be far behind?

Wayne Gretzky believes the growth of hockey will be limited until the fighting issue is tackled. In 1989 he spoke out against fighting for the first time in his 10-year career. Gretzky believes potential fans in the U.S. are turned off by brawling on the ice. Mario Lemieux agrees:

> Our game is a speed-and-finesse game. Fighting should not be allowed. Any time there is a fight in other big-league sports, there is a big suspension that goes with it. It should be the same in hockey.

Despite these sentiments, a majority of fans — and many of the players — aren't bothered by fisticuffs. Sixty-six percent of fans participating in *The Hockey News* survey voted against automatic ejection from a game for fighting.

Superstars of the nineties will rise from a galaxy of teenage stars, including: Quebec's Owen Nolan, right-winger from the Cornwall Royals; Keith Primeau, a six-foot-five, 220-pound center from the Niagara Falls Thunder, now with Detroit; Mike Ricci of the Flyers, former center with the Peterborough Petes; Vancouver's Petr Nedved, drafted from the Seattle Thunderbirds. In 1991, Oshawa Generals' star Eric Lindros, a six-foot-four, 210-pound center from Toronto who attracted all the scouts while playing for St. Michael's College in Junior B hockey, will be eligible for the draft.

A century ago, players often resembled jockeys in height and weight. A big team was one that averaged 150 pounds. Today's NHLers are almost six inches taller and 50 pounds heavier, on average, than their turn-of-the-century counterparts. Arena ice surfaces may have to be enlarged to give these brawny individuals room to display their abundant skills.

The NHL will continue to attract the greatest players in the world. In the 1989 entry draft, 18 Soviet players were taken, an indicator that Soviet names would soon be commonplace on NHL rosters. Forty-eight players were drafted from U.S. colleges and 47 from U.S. high schools. A quarter of a century ago, NHL scouts seldom looked at college players and totally ignored high schoolers.

Once the NHL grows to 24 or 28 teams, the expansion that follows may be global in nature, with a European division joining the league. The NHL has already found a lucrative television market in Europe. Joel Nixon, the league's vice-president in charge of broadcasting, predicts $5-million in gross sales from the overseas market by 1995. "And by the year 2000," Nixon says, "the NHL will reach 80 million European homes via television. Overseas broadcasts could be our largest potential area of growth."

It is conceivable that by the 21st century Stanley Cup games will be played in Moscow, London, Prague and Stockholm. Throughout the years ahead, just as it has in the past, NHL hockey will remain one of the most exciting team games, a rousing spectacle of skill on skates wherever it is played.

A STATISTICAL RECORD

THE STANLEY CUP

Awarded annually to the team winning the National Hockey League's best-of-seven final playoff round. It is symbolic of the World's Professional Hockey Championship.

The first four teams in each division at the end of the regular schedule advance to the playoffs. In each division, the first-place team opposes the fourth-place club while the second- and third-place teams meet, all in best-of-five division semi-finals. The winners oppose the other winners in each division in best-of-seven division-final series. The division winners then play the opposite winners in each of the two conferences in best-of-seven conference championships. The Prince of Wales Conference champions then meet the Clarence Campbell Conference champions in the best-of-seven Stanley Cup championship series.

The Stanley Cup, the oldest trophy competed for by professional athletes in North America, was donated by Frederick Arthur, Lord Stanley of Preston and son of the Earl of Derby, in 1893. Lord Stanley purchased the trophy for 10 guineas ($50 at that time) for presentation to the amateur-hockey champions of Canada. Since 1910, when the National Hockey Association took possession of the Stanley Cup, the trophy has been the symbol of professional hockey supremacy. It has been competed for only by NHL teams since 1926 and has been under the exclusive control of the NHL since 1946.

STANLEY CUP WINNERS AND FINALISTS

SEASON	CHAMPION	FINALIST	GP IN FINAL
1989–90	Edmonton Oilers	Boston Bruins	5
1988–89	Calgary Flames	Montreal Canadiens	6
1987–88	Edmonton Oilers	Boston Bruins	4
1986–87	Edmonton Oilers	Philadelphia Flyers	7
1985–86	Montreal Canadiens	Calgary Flames	5
1984–85	Edmonton Oilers	Philadelphia Flyers	5
1983–84	Edmonton Oilers	New York Islanders	5

SEASON	CHAMPION	FINALIST	GP IN FINAL
1982–83	New York Islanders	Edmonton Oilers	4
1981–82	New York Islanders	Vancouver Canucks	4
1980–81	New York Islanders	Minnesota North Stars	5
1979–80	New York Islanders	Philadelphia Flyers	6
1978–79	Montreal Canadiens	New York Rangers	5
1977–78	Montreal Canadiens	Boston Bruins	6
1976–77	Montreal Canadiens	Boston Bruins	4
1975–76	Montreal Canadiens	Philadelphia Flyers	4
1974–75	Philadelphia Flyers	Buffalo Sabres	6
1973–74	Philadelphia Flyers	Boston Bruins	6
1972–73	Montreal Canadiens	Chicago Blackhawks	6
1971–72	Boston Bruins	New York Rangers	6
1970–71	Montreal Canadiens	Chicago Blackhawks	7
1969–70	Boston Bruins	St. Louis Blues	4
1968–69	Montreal Canadiens	St. Louis Blues	4
1967–68	Montreal Canadiens	St. Louis Blues	4
1966–67	Toronto Maple Leafs	Montreal Canadiens	6
1965–66	Montreal Canadiens	Detroit Red Wings	6
1964–65	Montreal Canadiens	Chicago Blackhawks	7
1963–64	Toronto Maple Leafs	Detroit Red Wings	7
1962–63	Toronto Maple Leafs	Detroit Red Wings	5
1961–62	Toronto Maple Leafs	Chicago Blackhawks	6
1960–61	Chicago Blackhawks	Detroit Red Wings	6
1959–60	Montreal Canadiens	Toronto Maple Leafs	4
1958–59	Montreal Canadiens	Toronto Maple Leafs	5
1957–58	Montreal Canadiens	Boston Bruins	6
1956–57	Montreal Canadiens	Boston Bruins	5
1955–56	Montreal Canadiens	Detroit Red Wings	5
1954–55	Detroit Red Wings	Montreal Canadiens	7
1953–54	Detroit Red Wings	Montreal Canadiens	7
1952–53	Montreal Canadiens	Boston Bruins	5
1951–52	Detroit Red Wings	Detroit Red Wings	4
1950–51	Toronto Maple Leafs	Montreal Canadiens	5
1949–50	Detroit Red Wings	New York Rangers	7
1948–49	Toronto Maple Leafs	Detroit Red Wings	4
1947–48	Toronto Maple Leafs	Detroit Red Wings	4
1946–47	Toronto Maple Leafs	Montreal Canadiens	6
1945–46	Montreal Canadiens	Boston Bruins	5
1944–45	Toronto Maple Leafs	Detroit Red Wings	7
1943–44	Montreal Canadiens	Chicago Blackhawks	4
1942–43	Detroit Red Wings	Boston Bruins	4
1941–42	Toronto Maple Leafs	Detroit Red Wings	7
1940–41	Boston Bruins	Detroit Red Wings	4
1939–40	New York Rangers	Toronto Maple Leafs	6
1938–39	Boston Bruins	Toronto Maple Leafs	5
1937–38	Chicago Blackhawks	Toronto Maple Leafs	4
1936–37	Detroit Red Wings	New York Rangers	5
1935–36	Detroit Red Wings	Toronto Maple Leafs	4
1934–35	Montreal Maroons	Toronto Maple Leafs	3
1933–34	Chicago Blackhawks	Detroit Red Wings	4
1932–33	New York Rangers	Toronto Maple Leafs	4
1931–32	Toronto Maple Leafs	New York Rangers	3
1930–31	Montreal Canadiens	Chicago Blackhawks	5
1929–30	Montreal Canadiens	Boston Bruins	2

1928–29	Boston Bruins	New York Rangers	2
1927–28	New York Rangers	Montreal Canadiens	5
1926–27	Ottawa Senators	Boston Bruins	4
1925–26	Montreal Maroons	Victoria Cougars	4
1924–25	Victoria Cougars	Montreal Canadiens	4
1923–24	Montreal Canadiens	Vancouver, Calgary	2,2
1922–23	Ottawa Senators	Vancouver, Edmonton	3,2
1921–22	Toronto St. Pats	Vancouver Millionaires	5
1920–21	Ottawa Senators	Vancouver Millionaires	5
1919–20	Ottawa Senators	Seattle Metropolitans	5
1918–19	No decision*	No decision*	5
1917–18	Toronto Arenas	Vancouver Millionaires	5

*In the spring of 1919 the Montreal Canadiens traveled to Seattle to meet Seattle, PCHL champions. After five games had been played—teams were tied at two wins and one tie—the series was called off by the local department of health because of the influenza epidemic and the death from influenza of Joe Hall.

STANLEY CUP WINNERS PRIOR TO FORMATION OF NHL IN 1917

SEASON	CHAMPIONS	SEASON	CHAMPIONS
1916–17	Seattle Metropolitans	1903–04	Ottawa Silver Seven
1915–16	Montreal Canadiens	1902–03	Ottawa Silver Seven
1914–15	Vancouver Millionaires	1901–02	Montreal AAA
1913–14	Toronto Blueshirts	1900–01	Winnipeg Victorias
1912–13**	Quebec Bulldogs	1899–1900	Montreal Shamrocks
1911–12	Quebec Bulldogs	1898–99	Montreal Shamrocks
1910–11	Ottawa Senators	1897–98	Montreal Victorias
1909–10	Montreal Wanderers	1896–97	Montreal Victorias
1908–09	Ottawa Senators	1895–96	Montreal Victorias
1907–08	Montreal Wanderers		(December, 1896)
1906–07	Montreal Wanderers (March)	1895–96	Winnipeg Victorias (February)
1906–07	Kenora Thistles (January)	1894–95	Montreal Victorias
1905–06	Montreal Wanderers	1893–94	Montreal AAA
1904–05	Ottawa Silver Seven	1892–93	Montreal AAA

**Victoria defeated Quebec in challenge series.

NATIONAL HOCKEY LEAGUE INDIVIDUAL AWARD WINNERS

ART ROSS TROPHY WINNERS (SCORING LEADER)

1990	Wayne Gretzky	Los Angeles
1989	Mario Lemieux	Pittsburgh
1988	Mario Lemieux	Pittsburgh
1987	Wayne Gretzky	Edmonton
1986	Wayne Gretzky	Edmonton
1985	Wayne Gretzky	Edmonton
1984	Wayne Gretzky	Edmonton
1983	Wayne Gretzky	Edmonton
1982	Wayne Gretzky	Edmonton
1981	Wayne Gretzky	Edmonton
1980	Marcel Dionne	Los Angeles
1979	Bryan Trottier	NY Islanders
1978	Guy Lafleur	Montreal

1977	Guy Lafleur	Montreal
1976	Guy Lafleur	Montreal
1975	Bobby Orr	Boston
1974	Phil Esposito	Boston
1973	Phil Esposito	Boston
1972	Phil Esposito	Boston
1971	Phil Esposito	Boston
1970	Bobby Orr	Boston
1969	Phil Esposito	Boston
1968	Stan Mikita	Chicago
1967	Stan Mikita	Chicago
1966	Bobby Hull	Chicago
1965	Stan Mikita	Chicago
1964	Stan Mikita	Chicago
1963	Gordie Howe	Detroit
1962	Bobby Hull	Chicago
1961	Bernie Geoffrion	Montreal
1960	Bobby Hull	Chicago
1959	Dickie Moore	Montreal
1958	Dickie Moore	Montreal
1957	Gordie Howe	Detroit
1956	Jean Béliveau	Montreal
1955	Bernie Geoffrion	Montreal
1954	Gordie Howe	Detroit
1953	Gordie Howe	Detroit
1952	Gordie Howe	Detroit
1951	Gordie Howe	Detroit
1950	Ted Lindsay	Detroit
1949	Roy Conacher	Chicago
1948	Elmer Lach	Montreal
1947*	Max Bentley	Chicago
1946	Max Bentley	Chicago
1945	Elmer Lach	Montreal
1944	Herbie Cain	Boston
1943	Doug Bentley	Chicago
1942	Bryan Hextall	NY Rangers
1941	Bill Cowley	Boston
1940	Milt Schmidt	Boston
1939	Toe Blake	Montreal
1938	Gordie Drillon	Toronto
1937	Dave Schriner	NY Americans
1936	Dave Schriner	NY Americans
1935	Charlie Conacher	Toronto
1934	Charlie Conacher	Toronto
1933	Bill Cook	NY Rangers
1932	Harvey Jackson	Toronto
1931	Howie Morenz	Montreal
1930	Cooney Weiland	Boston
1929	Ace Bailey	Toronto
1928	Howie Morenz	Montreal
1927	Bill Cook	NY Rangers
1926	Nels Stewart	Montreal Maroons
1925	Babe Dye	Toronto
1924	Cy Denneny	Ottawa
1923	Babe Dye	Toronto
1922	Punch Broadbent	Ottawa

1921	Newsy Lalonde	Montreal
1920	Joe Malone	Quebec
1919	Newsy Lalonde	Montreal
1918	Joe Malone	Montreal

*Scoring leader prior to 1947–48

HART TROPHY WINNERS (MVP)

1990	Mark Messier	Edmonton
1989	Wayne Gretzky	Los Angeles
1988	Mario Lemieux	Pittsburgh
1987	Wayne Gretzky	Edmonton
1986	Wayne Gretzky	Edmonton
1985	Wayne Gretzky	Edmonton
1984	Wayne Gretzky	Edmonton
1983	Wayne Gretzky	Edmonton
1982	Wayne Gretzky	Edmonton
1981	Wayne Gretzky	Edmonton
1980	Wayne Gretzky	Edmonton
1979	Bryan Trottier	NY Islanders
1978	Guy Lafleur	Montreal
1977	Guy Lafleur	Montreal
1976	Bobby Clarke	Philadelphia
1975	Bobby Clarke	Philadelphia
1974	Phil Esposito	Boston
1973	Bobby Clarke	Philadelphia
1972	Bobby Orr	Boston
1971	Bobby Orr	Boston
1970	Bobby Orr	Boston
1969	Phil Esposito	Boston
1968	Stan Mikita	Chicago
1967	Stan Mikita	Chicago
1966	Bobby Hull	Chicago
1965	Bobby Hull	Chicago
1964	Jean Béliveau	Montreal
1963	Gordie Howe	Detroit
1962	Jacques Plante	Montreal
1961	Bernie Geoffrion	Montreal
1960	Gordie Howe	Detroit
1959	Andy Bathgate	NY Rangers
1958	Gordie Howe	Detroit
1957	Gordie Howe	Detroit
1956	Jean Béliveau	Montreal
1955	Ted Kennedy	Toronto
1954	Al Rollins	Chicago
1953	Gordie Howe	Detroit
1952	Gordie Howe	Detroit
1951	Milt Schmidt	Boston
1950	Charlie Rayner	NY Rangers
1949	Sid Abel	Detroit
1948	Buddy O'Connor	NY Rangers
1947	Maurice Richard	Montreal
1946	Max Bentley	Chicago
1945	Elmer Lach	Montreal
1944	Babe Pratt	Toronto

1943	Bill Cowley	Boston
1942	Tom Anderson	NY Americans
1941	Bill Cowley	Boston
1940	Ebbie Goodfellow	Detroit
1939	Toe Blake	Montreal
1938	Eddie Shore	Boston
1937	Babe Siebert	Montreal
1936	Eddie Shore	Boston
1935	Eddie Shore	Boston
1934	Aurel Joliat	Montreal
1933	Eddie Shore	Boston
1932	Howie Morenz	Montreal
1931	Howie Morenz	Montreal
1930	Nels Stewart	Montreal Maroons
1929	Roy Worters	NY Americans
1928	Howie Morenz	Montreal
1927	Herb Gardiner	Montreal
1926	Nels Stewart	Montreal Maroons
1925	Billy Burch	Hamilton
1924	Frank Nighbor	Ottawa

LADY BYNG TROPHY WINNERS (SPORTSMANSHIP)

1990	Brett Hull	St. Louis
1989	Joe Mullen	Calgary
1988	Mats Naslund	Montreal
1987	Joe Mullen	Calgary
1986	Mike Bossy	NY Islanders
1985	Jari Kurri	Edmonton
1984	Mike Bossy	NY Islanders
1983	Mike Bossy	NY Islanders
1982	Rick Middleton	Boston
1981	Rick Kehoe	Pittsburgh
1980	Wayne Gretzky	Edmonton
1979	Bob MacMillan	Atlanta
1978	Butch Goring	Los Angeles
1977	Marcel Dionne	Los Angeles
1976	Jean Ratelle	NY Rangers-Boston
1975	Marcel Dionne	Detroit
1974	John Bucyk	Boston
1973	Gilbert Perreault	Buffalo
1972	Jean Ratelle	NY Rangers
1971	John Bucyk	Boston
1970	Phil Goyette	St. Louis
1969	Alex Delvecchio	Detroit
1968	Stan Mikita	Chicago
1967	Stan Mikita	Chicago
1966	Alex Delvecchio	Detroit
1965	Bobby Hull	Chicago
1964	Ken Wharram	Chicago
1963	Dave Keon	Toronto
1962	Dave Keon	Toronto
1961	Red Kelly	Toronto
1960	Don McKenney	Boston
1959	Alex Delvecchio	Detroit
1958	Camille Henry	NY Rangers

291

1957	Andy Hebenton	NY Rangers
1956	Earl Reibel	Detroit
1955	Sid Smith	Toronto
1954	Red Kelly	Detroit
1953	Red Kelly	Detroit
1952	Sid Smith	Toronto
1951	Red Kelly	Detroit
1950	Edgar Laprade	NY Rangers
1949	Bill Quackenbush	Detroit
1948	Buddy O'Connor	NY Rangers
1947	Bobby Bauer	Boston
1946	Toe Blake	Montreal
1945	Bill Mosienko	Chicago
1944	Clint Smith	Chicago
1943	Max Bentley	Chicago
1942	Syl Apps	Toronto
1941	Bobby Bauer	Boston
1940	Bobby Bauer	Boston
1939	Clint Smith	NY Rangers
1938	Gordie Drillon	Toronto
1937	Marty Barry	Detroit
1936	Doc Romnes	Chicago
1935	Frank Boucher	NY Rangers
1934	Frank Boucher	NY Rangers
1933	Frank Boucher	NY Rangers
1932	Joe Primeau	Toronto
1931	Frank Boucher	NY Rangers
1930	Frank Boucher	NY Rangers
1929	Frank Boucher	NY Rangers
1928	Frank Boucher	NY Rangers
1927	Billy Burch	NY Americans
1926	Frank Nighbor	Ottawa
1925	Frank Nighbor	Ottawa

VEZINA TROPHY WINNERS (BEST GOALIE)

1990	Patrick Roy	Montreal
1989	Patrick Roy	Montreal
1988	Grant Fuhr	Edmonton
1987	Ron Hextall	Philadelphia
1986	John Vanbiesbrouck	NY Rangers
1985	Pelle Lindbergh	Philadelphia
1984	Tom Barrasso	Buffalo
1983	Pete Peeters	Boston
1982	Bill Smith	NY Islanders
1981	Richard Sevigny	Montreal
	Denis Herron	
	Michel Larocque	
1980	Bob Sauvé	Buffalo
	Don Edwards	
1979	Ken Dryden	Montreal
	Michel Larocque	
1978	Ken Dryden	Montreal
	Michel Larocque	
1977	Ken Dryden	Montreal
	Michel Larocque	

1976	Ken Dryden	Montreal
1975	Bernie Parent	Philadelphia
1974	Bernie Parent	Philadelphia
	Tony Esposito	Chicago
1973	Ken Dryden	Montreal
1972	Tony Esposito	Chicago
	Gary Smith	
1971	Ed Giacomin	NY Rangers
	Gilles Villemure	
1970	Tony Esposito	Chicago
1969	Jacques Plante	St. Louis
	Glenn Hall	
1968	Lorne Worsley	Montreal
	Rogie Vachon	
1967	Glenn Hall, Denis Dejordy	Chicago
1966	Lorne Worsley	Montreal
	Charlie Hodge	
1965	Terry Sawchuk	Toronto
	Johnny Bower	
1964	Charlie Hodge	Montreal
1963	Glenn Hall	Chicago
1962	Jacques Plante	Montreal
1961	Johnny Bower	Toronto
1960	Jacques Plante	Montreal
1959	Jacques Plante	Montreal
1958	Jacques Plante	Montreal
1957	Jacques Plante	Montreal
1956	Jacques Plante	Montreal
1955	Terry Sawchuk	Detroit
1954	Harry Lumley	Toronto
1953	Terry Sawchuk	Detroit
1952	Terry Sawchuk	Detroit
1951	Al Rollins	Toronto
1950	Bull Durnan	Montreal
1949	Bill Durnan	Montreal
1948	Turk Broda	Toronto
1947	Bill Durnan	Montreal
1946	Bill Durnan	Montreal
1945	Bill Durnan	Montreal
1944	Bill Durnan	Montreal
1943	Johnny Mowers	Detroit
1942	Frank Brimsek	Boston
1941	Turk Broda	Toronto
1940	Dave Kerr	NY Rangers
1939	Frank Brimsek	Boston
1938	Tiny Thompson	Boston
1937	Normie Smith	Detroit
1936	Tiny Thompson	Boston
1935	Lorne Chabot	Chicago
1934	Charlie Gardiner	Chicago
1933	Tiny Thompson	Boston
1932	Charlie Gardiner	Chicago
1931	Roy Worters	NY Americans
1930	Tiny Thompson	Boston
1929	George Hainsworth	Montreal
1928	George Hainsworth	Montreal
1927	George Hainsworth	Montreal

JAMES NORRIS TROPHY WINNERS (BEST DEFENSEMAN)

1990	Ray Bourque	Boston
1989	Chris Chelios	Montreal
1988	Ray Bourque	Boston
1987	Ray Bourque	Boston
1986	Paul Coffey	Edmonton
1985	Paul Coffey	Edmonton
1984	Rod Langway	Washington
1983	Rod Langway	Washington
1982	Doug Wilson	Chicago
1981	Randy Carlyle	Pittsburgh
1980	Larry Robinson	Montreal
1979	Denis Potvin	NY Islanders
1978	Denis Potvin	NY Islanders
1977	Larry Robinson	Montreal
1976	Denis Potvin	NY Islanders
1975	Bobby Orr	Boston
1974	Bobby Orr	Boston
1973	Bobby Orr	Boston
1972	Bobby Orr	Boston
1971	Bobby Orr	Boston
1970	Bobby Orr	Boston
1969	Bobby Orr	Boston
1968	Bobby Orr	Boston
1967	Harry Howell	NY Rangers
1966	Jacques Laperrière	Montreal
1965	Pierre Pilote	Chicago
1964	Pierre Pilote	Chicago
1963	Pierre Pilote	Chicago
1962	Doug Harvey	NY Rangers
1961	Doug Harvey	Montreal
1960	Doug Harvey	Montreal
1959	Tom Johnson	Montreal
1958	Doug Harvey	Montreal
1957	Doug Harvey	Montreal
1956	Doug Harvey	Montreal
1955	Doug Harvey	Montreal
1954	Red Kelly	Detroit

LESTER PATRICK TROPHY WINNERS
(OUTSTANDING CONTRIBUTION TO HOCKEY IN THE U.S.)

1990	Len Ceglarski
1989	Lou Nanne
	Bud Poile
	*Dan Kelly
	*Lynn Patrick
1988	Keith Allen
	Fred Cusick
	Bob Johnson
1987	*Hobey Bakey
	Frank Mathers
1986	John MacInnes
	Jack Riley
1985	Jack Butterfield
	Arthur M. Wirtz
1984	John A. Ziegler, Jr.

	*Arthur Howie Ross
1983	Bill Torrey
1982	Emile P. Francis
1981	Charles M. Schulz
1980	Bobby Clarke
	Edward M. Snider
	Frederick A. Shero
	1980 U.S. Olympic Hockey Team
1979	Bobby Orr
1978	Philip A. Esposito
	Tom Fitzgerald
	William T. Tutt
	William W. Wirtz
1977	John P. Bucyk
	Murray A. Armstrong
	John Mariucci
1976	Stanley Mikita
	George A. Leader
	Bruce A. Norris
1975	Donald M. Clark
	William L. Chadwick
	Thomas N. Ivan
1974	Alex Delvecchio
	Murray Murdoch
	*Weston W. Adams, Sr.
	*Charles L. Crovat
1973	Walter L. Bush, Jr.
1972	Clarence S. Campbell
	John Kelly
	Ralph "Cooney" Weiland
	*James D. Norris
1971	William M. Jennings
	*John B. Sollenberger
	*Terrance G. Sawchuk
1970	Edward W. Shore
	*James C. V. Hendy
1969	Robert M. Hull
	*Edward J. Jeremiah
1968	Thomas F. Lockhart
	*Walter A. Brown
	*Gen. John R. Kilpatrick
1967	Gordon Howe
	*Charles F. Adams
	*James Norris, Sr.
1966	J. J. "Jack" Adams

*awarded posthumously

CALDER MEMORIAL TROPHY WINNERS (ROOKIE OF THE YEAR)

1990	Sergei Makarov	Calgary
1989	Brian Leetch	NY Rangers
1988	Joe Nieuwendyk	Calgary
1987	Luc Robitaille	Los Angeles
1986	Gary Suter	Calgary
1985	Mario Lemieux	Pittsburgh
1984	Tom Barrasso	Buffalo

295

1983	Steve Larmer	Chicago
1982	Dale Hawerchuk	Winnipeg
1981	Peter Stastny	Quebec
1980	Raymond Bourque	Boston
1979	Bobby Smith	Minnesota
1978	Mike Bossy	NY Islanders
1977	Willi Plett	Atlanta
1976	Bryan Trottier	NY Islanders
1975	Eric Vail	Atlanta
1974	Denis Potvin	NY Islanders
1973	Steve Vickers	NY Rangers
1972	Ken Dryden	Montreal
1971	Gilbert Perreault	Buffalo
1970	Tony Esposito	Chicago
1969	Danny Grant	Minnesota
1968	Derek Sanderson	Boston
1967	Bobby Orr	Boston
1966	Brit Selby	Toronto
1965	Roger Crozier	Detroit
1964	Jacques Laperrière	Montreal
1963	Kent Douglas	Toronto
1962	Bobby Rousseau	Montreal
1961	Dave Keon	Toronto
1960	Bill Hay	Chicago
1959	Ralph Backstrom	Montreal
1958	Frank Mahovlich	Toronto
1957	Larry Regan	Boston
1956	Glenn Hall	Detroit
1955	Ed Litzenberger	Chicago
1954	Camille Henry	NY Rangers
1953	Lorne Worsley	NY Rangers
1952	Bernie Geoffrion	Montreal
1951	Terry Sawchuk	Detroit
1950	Jack Gelineau	Boston
1949	Pentti Lund	NY Rangers
1948	Jim McFadden	Detroit
1947	Howie Meeker	Toronto
1946	Edgar Laprade	NY Rangers
1945	Frank McCool	Toronto
1944	Gus Bodnar	Toronto
1943	Gaye Stewart	Toronto
1942	Grant Warwick	NY Rangers
1941	Johnny Quilty	Montreal
1940	Kilby MacDonald	NY Rangers
1939	Frank Brimsek	Boston
1938	Cully Dahlstrom	Chicago
1937	Syl Apps	Toronto
1936	Mike Karakas	Chicago
1935	Dave Schriner	NY Americans
1934	Russ Blinko	Montreal Maroons
1933	Carl Voss	Detroit

FRANK J. SELKE TROPHY WINNERS (BEST DEFENSIVE FORWARD)

1990	Rick Meagher	St. Louis
1989	Guy Carbonneau	Montreal
1988	Guy Carbonneau	Montreal
1987	Dave Poulin	Philadelphia
1986	Troy Murray	Chicago
1985	Craig Ramsay	Buffalo
1984	Doug Jarvis	Washington
1983	Bobby Clarke	Philadelphia
1982	Steve Kasper	Boston
1981	Bob Gainey	Montreal
1980	Bob Gainey	Montreal
1979	Bob Gainey	Montreal
1978	Bob Gainey	Montreal

CONN SMYTHE TROPHY WINNERS (PLAYOFF MVP)

1990	Bill Ranford	Edmonton
1989	Al MacInnis	Calgary
1988	Wayne Gretzky	Edmonton
1987	Ron Hextall	Philadelphia
1986	Patrick Roy	Montreal
1985	Wayne Gretzky	Edmonton
1984	Mark Messier	Edmonton
1983	Bill Smith	NY Islanders
1982	Mike Bossy	NY Islanders
1981	Butch Goring	NY Islanders
1980	Bryan Trottier	NY Islanders
1979	Bob Gainey	Montreal
1978	Larry Robinson	Montreal
1977	Guy Lafleur	Montreal
1976	Reggie Leach	Philadelphia
1975	Bernie Parent	Philadelphia
1974	Bernie Parent	Philadelphia
1973	Yvan Cournoyer	Montreal
1972	Bobby Orr	Boston
1971	Ken Dryden	Montreal
1970	Bobby Orr	Boston
1969	Serge Savard	Montreal
1968	Glenn Hall	St. Louis
1967	Dave Keon	Toronto
1966	Roger Crozier	Detroit
1965	Jean Béliveau	Montreal

JACK ADAMS AWARD WINNERS (COACH OF THE YEAR)

1990	Bob Murdoch	Winnipeg
1989	Pat Burns	Montreal
1988	Jacques Demers	Detroit
1987	Jacques Demers	Detroit
1986	Glen Sather	Edmonton
1985	Mike Keenan	Philadelphia
1984	Bryan Murray	Washington
1983	Orval Tessier	Chicago

1982	Tom Watt	Winnipeg
1981	Gordon "Red" Berenson	St. Louis
1980	Pat Quinn	Philadelphia
1979	Al Arbour	NY Islanders
1978	Bobby Kromm	Detroit
1977	Scott Bowman	Montreal
1976	Don Cherry	Boston
1975	Bob Pulford	Los Angeles
1974	Fred Shero	Philadelphia

KING CLANCY MEMORIAL TROPHY WINNERS
(LEADERSHIP ON AND OFF THE ICE)

1990	Kevin Lowe	Edmonton
1989	Bryan Trottier	NY Islanders
1988	Lanny McDonald	Calgary

BILL MASTERTON TROPHY WINNERS
(SPORTSMANSHIP, HARD WORK, PERSEVERANCE AND DEDICATION TO THE GAME)

1990	Gord Kluzak	Boston
1989	Tim Kerr	Philadelphia
1988	Bob Bourne	Los Angeles
1987	Doug Jarvis	Hartford
1986	Charlie Simmer	Boston
1985	Anders Hedberg	NY Rangers
1984	Brad Park	Detroit
1983	Lanny McDonald	Calgary
1982	Glenn Resch	Colorado
1981	Blake Dunlop	St. Louis
1980	Al MacAdam	Minnesota
1979	Serge Savard	Montreal
1978	Butch Goring	Los Angeles
1977	Ed Westfall	NY Islanders
1976	Rod Gilbert	NY Rangers
1975	Don Luce	Buffalo
1974	Henri Richard	Montreal
1973	Lowell MacDonald	Pittsburgh
1972	Bobby Clarke	Philadelphia
1971	Jean Ratelle	NY Rangers
1970	Pit Martin	Chicago
1969	Ted Hampson	Oakland
1968	Claude Provost	Montreal

WORLD HOCKEY ASSOCIATION
AVCO CUP WINNERS AND FINALISTS

SEASON	CHAMPION	FINALIST	GP IN FINAL
1978–79	Winnipeg Jets	Edmonton Oilers	6
1977–78	Winnipeg Jets	New England Whalers	4
1976–77	Quebec Nordiques	Winnipeg Jets	7
1975–76	Winnipeg Jets	Houston Aeros	4
1974–75	Houston Aeros	Quebec Nordiques	4
1973–74	Houston Aeros	Chicago Cougars	4
1972–73	New England Whalers	Winnipeg Jets	5

THE HOCKEY HALL OF FAME

Any person who is, or has been distinguished in hockey as a player, executive or referee/linesman shall be eligible for election to the Hockey Hall of Fame. Player and referee/linesman candidates will normally have completed their active participating careers three years prior to election, but in exceptional cases this period may be shortened by the Hockey Hall of Fame board of directors. Veteran player candidates must have concluded their careers as active players in the sport of hockey for at least 25 years. Candidates for election as executives and referees/linesmen shall be nominated only by the board of directors and upon election shall be known as builders or referees/linesmen. Candidates for election as players shall be chosen on the basis of "playing ability, integrity, character and their contribution to their team and the game of hockey in general."

PLAYERS

Year of election to the Hall is indicated in brackets after the members' names.

Abel, Sidney Gerald (1969)
*Adams, John James "Jack" (1959)
Apps, Charles Joseph Sylvanus "Syl" (1961)
Armstrong, George Edward (1975)
Bailey, Irvine Wallace "Ace" (1975)
*Bain, Donald H. "Dan" (1945)
*Baker, Hobart "Hobey" (1945)
Barber, Bill (1990)
*Barry, Martin J. "Marty" (1965)
Bathgate, Andrew James "Andy" (1978)
Beliveau, Jean Arthur (1972)
*Benedict, Clinton S. (1965)
*Bentley, Douglas Wagner (1964)
*Bentley, Maxwell H. L. (1966)

Blake, Hector "Toe" (1966)
Boivin, Leo Joseph (1986)
*Boon, Richard R. "Dickie" (1952)
Bouchard, Emile Joseph "Butch" (1966)
*Boucher, Frank (1958)
*Boucher, George "Buck" (1960)
Bower, John Willam (1976)
*Bowie, Russell (1945)
Brimsek, Francis Charles (1966)
*Broadbent, Harry L. "Punch" (1962)
*Broda, Walter Edward "Turk" (1967)
Bucyk, John Paul (1981)
*Burch, Billy (1974)
*Cameron, Harold Hugh "Harry" (1962)
Cheevers, Gerald Michael "Gerry" (1985)
*Clancy, Francis Michael "King" (1958)
*Clapper, Aubrey "Dit" (1945)
Clarke, Robert "Bobby" (1987)
*Cleghorn, Sprague (1958)
Colville, Neil MacNeil (1967)
*Conacher, Charles W. (1961)
*Connell, Alex (1958)
*Cook, William Osser (1952)
Coulter, Arthur Edmund (1974)
Cournoyer, Yvan Serge (1982)
Cowley, William Mailes (1968)
*Crawford, Samuel Russell "Rusty" (1962)
*Darragh, John Proctor "Jack" (1962)
*Davidson, Allan M. "Scotty" (1950)
Day, Clarence Henry "Hap" (1961)
Delvecchio, Alex (1977)
*Denneny, Cyril "Cy" (1959)
*Drillon, Gordon Arthur (1975)
*Drinkwater, Charles Graham (1950)
Dryden, Kenneth Wayne (1983)
*Dunderdale, Thomas (1974)
*Durnan, William Ronald (1964)
*Dutton, Mervyn A. "Red" (1958)
*Dye, Cecil Henry "Babe" (1970)
Esposito, Anthony James "Tony" (1988)
Esposito, Philip Anthony (1984)
*Farrell, Arthur F. (1965)
Flaman, Fern (1990)
*Foyston, Frank (1958)
*Frederickson, Frank (1958)
Gadsby, William Alexander (1970)
*Gardiner, Charles Robert "Chuck" (1945)
*Gardiner, Herbert Martin "Herb" (1958)
*Gardner, James Henry "Jimmy" (1962)
Geoffrion, Jos. A. Bernard "Boom Boom" (1972)
*Gerard, Eddie (1945)
Giacomin, Edward "Eddie" (1987)
Gilbert, Rodrigue Gabriel "Rod" (1982)
*Gilmour, Hamilton Livingstone "Billy" (1962)
*Goheen, Frank Xavier "Moose" (1952)
*Goodfellow, Ebenezer R. "Ebbie" (1963)
*Grant, Michael "Mike" (1950)

*Green, Wilfred "Shorty" (1962)
*Griffis, Silas Seth "Si" (1950)
*Hainsworth, George (1961)
 Hall, Glenn Henry (1975)
*Hall, Joseph Henry (1961)
 Harvey, Douglas Norman (1973)
*Hay, George (1958)
*Hern, William Milton "Riley" (1962)
*Hextall, Bryan Aldwyn (1969)
*Holmes, Harry "Hap" (1972)
*Hooper, Charles Thomas "Tom" (1962)
 Horner, George Reginald "Red" (1965)
*Horton, Miles Gilbert "Tim" (1977)
 Howe, Gordon (1972)
*Howe, Sydney Harris (1965)
 Howell, Henry Vernon "Harry" (1979)
 Hull, Robert Marvin (1983)
*Hutton, John Bower "Bouse" (1962)
*Hyland, Harry M. (1962)
*Irvin, James Dickenson "Dick" (1958)
*Jackson, Harvey "Busher" (1971)
*Johnson, Ernest "Moose" (1952)
*Johnson, Ivan "Ching" (1958)
 Johnson, Thomas Christian (1970)
*Joliat, Aurel (1947)
*Keats, Gordon "Duke" (1958)
 Kelly, Leonard Patrick "Red" (1969)
 Kennedy, Theodore Samuel "Teeder" (1966)
 Keon, David Michael (1986)
 Lach, Elmer James (1966)
 Lafleur, Guy Damien (1988)
*Lalonde, Edouard Charles "Newsy" (1950)
 Laperriere, Jacques (1987)
*Laviolette, Jean Baptiste "Jack" (1962)
*Lehman, Hugh (1958)
 Lemaire, Jacques Gerard (1984)
*LeSueur, Percy (1961)
 Lewis, Herbert (1989)
 Lindsay, Robert Blake Theodore "Ted" (1966)
 Lumley, Harry (1980)
*MacKay, Duncan "Mickey" (1952)
 Mahovlich, Frank William (1981)
*Malone, Joseph "Joe" (1950)
*Mantha, Sylvio (1960)
*Marshall, John "Jack" (1965)
*Maxwell, Fred G. "Steamer" (1962)
*McGee, Frank (1945)
*McGimsie, William George "Billy" (1962)
*McNamara, George (1958)
 Mikita, Stanley (1983)
 Moore, Richard Winston (1974)
*Moran, Patrick Joseph "Paddy" (1958)
*Morenz, Howie (1945)
*Mosienko, William "Billy" (1965)
*Nighbor, Frank (1945)
*Noble, Edward Reginald "Reg" (1962)

*O'Connor, Herbert William "Buddy" (1988)
*Oliver, Harry (1967)
 Olmstead, Murray Bert "Bert" (1985)
 Orr, Robert Gordon (1979)
 Parent, Bernard Marcel (1984)
 Park, Douglas Bradford "Brad" (1988)
*Patrick, Joseph Lynn (1980)
*Patrick, Lester (1945)
 Perreault, Gilbert (1990)
*Phillips, Tommy (1945)
 Pilote, Joseph Albert Pierre Paul (1975)
*Pitre, Didier "Pit" (1962)
*Plante, Joseph Jacques Omer (1978)
 Poile, Norman (Bud) (1990)
 Pratt, Walter "Babe" (1966)
 Primeau, A. Joseph (1963)
 Pronovost, Joseph René Marcel (1978)
*Pulford, Harvey (1945)
 Quackenbush, Hubert George "Bill" (1976)
*Rankin, Frank (1961)
 Ratelle, Joseph Gilbert Yvan Jean "Jean" (1985)
 Rayner, Claude Earl "Chuck" (1973)
 Reardon, Kenneth Joseph (1966)
 Richard, Joseph Henri (1979)
 Richard, Joseph Henri Maurice "Rocket" (1961)
*Richardson, George Taylor (1950)
*Roberts, Gordon (1971)
*Ross, Arthur Howie (1945)
*Russell, Blair (1965)
*Russell, Ernest (1965)
*Ruttan, J.D. "Jack" (1962)
 Savard, Serge A. (1986)
*Sawchuk, Terrance Gordon "Terry" (1971)
*Scanlan, Fred (1965)
 Schmidt, Milton Conrad "Milt" (1961)
 Schriner, David "Sweeney" (1962)
 Seibert, Earl Walter (1963)
*Seibert, Oliver Levi (1961)
*Shore, Edward W. "Eddie" (1945)
*Siebert, Albert C. "Babe" (1964)
 Simpson, Harold Edward "Bullet Joe" (1962)
 Sittler, Darryl (1989)
*Smith, Alfred E. (1962)
*Smith, Reginald "Hooley" (1972)
*Smith, Thomas James (1973)
 Stanley, Allan Herbert (1981)
*Stanley, Russell "Barney" (1962)
*Stewart, John Sherratt "Black Jack" (1964)
*Stewart, Nelson "Nels" (1962)
*Stuart, Bruce (1961)
*Stuart, Hod (1945)
*Taylor, Frederic "Cyclone" (O.B.E.) (1945)
*Thompson, Cecil R. "Tiny" (1959)
 Tretiak, Vladislav (1989)
*Trihey, Col. Harry J. (1950)
 Ullman, Norman Victor Alexander "Norm" (1982)

*Vezina, Georges (1945)
*Walker, John Phillip "Jack" (1960)
*Walsh, Martin "Marty" (1962)
*Watson, Harry E. (1962)
*Weiland, Ralph "Cooney" (1971)
*Westwick, Harry (1962)
*Whitcroft, Fred (1962)
*Wilson, Gordon Alan "Phat" (1962)
  Worsley, Lorne John "Gump" (1980)
*Worters, Roy (1969)

BUILDERS

*Adams, Charles Francis (1960)
*Adams, Weston W. (1972)
*Aheam, Thomas Franklin "Frank" (1962)
*Ahearne, John Francis "Bunny" (1977)
*Allan, Sir Montague (C.V.O.) (1945)
  Ballard, Harold Edwin (1977)
  Bauer, Father David (1989)
*Bickell, John Paris (1978)
*Brown, George V. (1961)
*Brown, Walter A. (1962)
  Buckland, Frank (1975)
  Butterfield, Jack Arlington (1980)
*Calder, Frank (1945)
*Campbell, Angus D. (1964)
*Campbell, Clarence Sutherland (1966)
*Cattarinich, Joseph (1977)
*Dandurand, Joseph Viateur "Leo" (1963)
  Dilio, Francis Paul (1964)
*Dudley, George S. (1958)
*Dunn, James A. (1968)
  Eagleson, R. Alan (1989)
  Francis, Emile (1982)
*Gibson, Dr. John L. "Jack" (1976)
*Gorman, Thomas Patrick "Tommy" (1963)
  Hanley, William (1986)
*Hay, Charles (1974)
*Hendy, James C. (1968)
*Hewitt, Foster (1965)
*Hewitt, Willam Abraham (1945)
*Hume, Fred J. (1962)
*Imlach, George "Punch" (1984)
  Ivan, Thomas N. (1974)
*Jennings, William M. (1975)
  Juckes, Gordon W. (1979)
*Kilpatrick, Gen. John Reed (1960)
*Leader, George Alfred (1969)
  LeBel, Robert (1970)
*Lockhart, Thomas F. (1965)
*Loicq, Paul (1961)
*Mariucci, John (1985)
*McLaughlin, Major Frederic (1963)
*Milford, John "Jake" (1984)
  Molson, Hon. Hartland de Montarville (1973)
*Nelson, Francis (1945)

*Norris, Bruce A. (1969)
*Norris, James, Sr. (1958)
*Norris, James Dougan (1962)
*Northey, William M. (1945)
*O'Brien, John Ambrose (1962)
*Patrick, Frank (1958)
*Pickard, Allan W. (1958)
 Pilous, Rudy (1985)
 Pollock, Samuel Patterson Smyth (1978)
*Raymond, Sen. Donat (1958)
*Robertson, John Ross (1945)
*Robinson, Claude C. (1945)
*Ross, Philip D. (1976)
*Selke, Frank J. (1960)
 Sinden, Harry James (1983)
*Smith, Frank D. (1962)
*Smythe, Conn (1958)
 Snider, Edward M. (1988)
*Stanley of Preston, Lord (G.C.B.) (1945)
*Sutherland, Cap. James T. (1945)
 Tarasov, Anatoli V. (1974)
*Turner, Lloyd (1958)
 Tutt, William Thayer (1978)
 Voss, Carl Potter (1974)
*Waghorn, Fred C. (1961)
*Wirtz, Arthur Michael (1971)
 Wirtz, William W. "Bill" (1976)
 Ziegler, John A., Jr. (1987)

REFEREES/LINESMEN

 Ashley, John George (1981)
 Chadwick, William L. (1964)
*Elliott, Chaucer (1961)
*Hayes, George William (1988)
*Hewitson, Robert W. (1963)
*Ion, Fred J. "Mickey" (1961)
 Pavelich, Matt (1987)
*Rodden, Michael J. "Mike" (1962)
*Smeaton, J. Cooper (1961)
 Storey, Roy Alvin "Red" (1967)
 Udvari, Frank Joseph (1973)

*Deceased